SAMS
Teach Yourself

Mac OS X

John Ray
Robyn Ness

in **24** Hours

SECOND EDITION

SAMS *201 West 103rd St., Indianapolis, Indiana, 46290 USA*

Sams Teach Yourself Mac OS X in 24 Hours, Second Edition

Copyright © 2003 by Sams Publishing

International Standard Book Number: 0-672-32474-1

Library of Congress Catalog Card Number: 200210475

Printed in the United States of America

First Printing: November 2002

05   04   03   02   4   3   2   1

Trademarks

Warning and Disclaimer

ACQUISITIONS EDITOR
Betsy Brown

DEVELOPMENT EDITOR
Damon Jordan

MANAGING EDITOR
Charlotte Clapp

PROJECT EDITOR
Matthew Purcell

COPY EDITOR
Mike Henry

INDEXER
Chris Barrick

PROOFREADER
Mike Henry

TECHNICAL EDITOR
Kate Binder

TEAM COORDINATOR
Amy Patton

MULTIMEDIA DEVELOPER
Dan Scherf

INTERIOR DESIGNER
Gary Adair

COVER DESIGNER
Alan Clements

PAGE LAYOUT
Michelle Mitchell

GRAPHICS
Steve Adams
Tammy Graham
Oliver Jackson
Laura Robbins

Contents at a Glance

Table of Contents

Part V Advanced Mac OS X Features

About the Authors

John Ray is an award-winning developer and security consultant with more than 16 years of programming and administration experience. He has worked on projects for the FCC, the National Regulatory Research Institute, The Ohio State University, Xerox, and the State of Florida, as well as serving as IT Director for Blue Cosmos Design, Inc. He has written or contributed to more than 10 titles currently in print, including *Mac OS X Unleashed*, *Special Edition Using TCP/IP*, *Sams Teach Yourself Dreamweaver MX Application Development in 21 Days*, and *Maximum Linux Security*. He bought his first Macintosh in 1984 and remains a strong proponent for the computer and operating system that revolutionized the industry.

Robyn Ness holds a master's degree in psychology with a specialization in judgment and decision making. She currently works as a Web developer for the Section of Communications and Technology at The Ohio State University, focusing on issues of usability and content design.

Dedication

I dedicate this book to you. Yes, you. Or maybe the person behind you. I haven't quite decided yet.
—John Ray

I dedicate this book to my co-author, John Ray, who made me a switcher even before Apple made switching into an ad campaign.
—Robyn Ness

Acknowledgments

We would like to acknowledge the many helpful people at Sams Publishing who worked to make this book possible. Betsy Brown, Damon Jordan, Matt Purcell, and Michael Henry were instrumental in helping us bring *Sams Teach Yourself Mac OS X in 24 Hours* to press. Through the work of this dedicated team, we're able to bring you, the reader, this up-to-date guide to Mac OS X 10.2.

We Want to Hear from You!

As the reader of this book, *you* are our most important critic and commentator. We value your opinion and want to know what we're doing right, what we could do better, what areas you'd like to see us publish in, and any other words of wisdom you're willing to pass our way.

You can email or write me directly to let me know what you did or didn't like about this book—as well as what we can do to make our books stronger.

Please note that I cannot help you with technical problems related to the topic of this book, and that due to the high volume of mail I receive, I might not be able to reply to every message.

When you write, please be sure to include this book's title and author as well as your name and phone or email address. I will carefully review your comments and share them with the author and editors who worked on the book.

Email: consumer@samspublishing.com

Mail: Mark Taber
          Associate Publisher
          Sams Publishing
          201 West 103rd Street
          Indianapolis, IN 46290 USA

Reader Services

For more information about this book or others from Sams Publishing, visit our Web site at www.samspublishing.com. Type the ISBN (excluding hyphens) or the title of the book in the Search box to find the book you're looking for.

Introduction

When the Macintosh was introduced in 1984, it came with the most revolutionary operating system anyone had seen. Built on the desktop metaphor, the Macintosh quickly became known as the most advanced and easy-to-use personal computer available. Over the years, the Macintosh continued to do well, but Apple fell into the same line of thinking that many of us do: "If it isn't broken, don't fix it." The Mac OS *worked*, but it had a number of problems that prevented it from advancing at the same rate as other operating systems. Apple continued to add features to the OS, but didn't address the underlying deficiencies. By 1994, Apple had been running for 10 years on the same base operating system with only minor core changes.

With the release of Windows 95, Microsoft began to push ahead of the Mac OS with features such as preemptive multitasking and memory protection. Apple finally realized it was in a bind and needed to produce a version of the Mac OS that would again revolutionize the desktop operating system industry. Unfortunately, its problems were just beginning.

What happened next kicked off a nightmarish sequence of events that would change the "face" of the Macintosh forever.

Apple announced that it would be creating a new system for the Macintosh called Copland. Copland (originally known as Mac OS 8) was to turn the Macintosh into a fully modern operating system with multiple users and true multitasking capabilities. Mac users rejoiced at the news and began what they assumed would be a relatively short wait for the long-overdue upgrade.

Months passed. Then a year.

Finally, in 1996, just weeks after the yearly Apple developer conference, Apple announced that the Copland project was officially cancelled. The Macintosh had become a platform without a future. During this time, Microsoft released Windows NT, using the same interface as Windows 95. The NT operating system provided many of the same features as Copland, but was available immediately—on the PC platform.

As the desperation of its situation sank in, Apple looked for another solution to its problem. Two companies sprang to the forefront of Apple's attention: Be Inc. and NeXT Computer, both run by ex-Apple employees. Although BeOS was attractive and already ran on the Macintosh, Apple decided to go with a time-tested solution: NeXT's OpenStep operating system. In December 1996, as a last-ditch effort to save the Macintosh, Apple purchased NeXT Computer for 400 million dollars.

Unfortunately, the problems didn't end there. The OpenStep operating system was extremely mature, but it didn't run on the Macintosh platform. At the 1997 developer conference, Apple announced Rhapsody as the future for the Mac OS, yet it would be another year before the first product based on Rhapsody would start shipping.

To make matters worse, Apple also announced that developers would need to completely rewrite their software for it to work on Rhapsody. This infuriated programmers, who threatened to drop support for the Macintosh platform unless they could use their existing source code with Rhapsody.

Apple set its engineering teams to work on a solution that would make everyone happy. Finally, another year later, at the 1998 developer conference, Apple announced Mac OS X. Based on the original foundation in Rhapsody, Mac OS X promised to enable developers to easily port their existing software to the new operating system. Things were finally looking up.

Three years later, in September 2001, the Mac OS X project was fully realized. Mac OS X 10.1 delivered everything that Apple originally set out to create. It provided a powerful modern core and a revolutionary user interface that was easy to use.

Mac OS X 10.2 picks up where the original Mac OS X left off, with attention to both the technical and usability requirements of its users. Jaguar, as it's affectionately known, includes improved versions of old favorites as well as entirely new and exciting components, including built-in capacity for handwriting recognition and messaging.

The future for the Macintosh has never been better.

About This Book

Sams Teach Yourself Mac OS X in 24 Hours aims to give you the information you need to successfully use the advanced features of Mac OS X. Our goal in creating this book was to give you, the reader, the most information possible about the operating system in as friendly and straightforward a manner as possible. You'll find step-by-step instructions for everything from setting up your system to playing DVDs and exploring the hidden Mac OS X command line.

As you read through this book, keep in mind that the easiest way to learn is by doing. Even though Mac OS X might present a bit of a culture shock to longtime Mac owners and converted PC users, after spending a few hours playing with the system, you'll wonder how you ever survived without it!

If you have any questions or comments, please feel free to e-mail us.

Thanks for reading!

Robyn Ness (robynness@mac.com)

John Ray (johnray@mac.com)

PART I
Introduction to Mac OS X

Hour

Hour **1**

A Tour of Mac OS X

The release of Mac OS X in 2001 represented a revolutionary departure from the traditional Mac OS, with greater system stability and flexibility wrapped in a luxurious user interface. Mac OS X Version 10.2 Jaguar, the second major release, builds on the original Mac OS X.

We begin this hour with a quick look at the initial set up of Mac OS X and at the components that give Mac OS X its power. We then examine System Preferences, basic desktop controls, and some of the applications included with 10.2, which are examined in depth in later hours.

In this hour, you explore

- Mac OS X Setup Assistant
- Mac OS X system architecture
- System Preferences
- Desktop basics

Setting Up Mac OS X

The first time Mac OS X starts, it runs Setup Assistant, which helps you set up the basic features of the operating system. During the setup procedure, your network settings are configured and your registration details are sent back to Apple.

Apple began shipping Mac OS X on its computers in the fall of 2001. According to Apple, Mac OS X runs on all original G4 computers, all iBooks and iMacs (including the Bondi 233), all PowerBooks (except the original Powerbook G3), and all beige desktop G3s. However, keep in mind that the computers in that list with slower processors or little memory might run Mac OS X less than optimally.

For help installing Mac OS X from scratch, consult Appendix A, "Installing Mac OS X."

Creating Your Account

Mac OS X is a multiuser operating system that requires you to set up the account for at least one user. As part of the setup process, you must configure your first user account. That account is used to control access to the system and to prevent unauthorized changes from being made to your software. The Create Your Account dialog box is shown in Figure 1.1.

If more than one person uses your computer and you want to keep your work separate, you can create multiple user accounts. Each user has a private password to access the operating system. This provides a measure of security and keeps different programs from interfering with each other. On the other hand, if you're the only user and don't want to log in each time, you can configure your system to start without a login. Both of these issues are covered in Hour 15, "Sharing Your System: Multiple Users."

The account setup fields are explained here:

Name—Enter your full name.

Short Name—The short name is the name of your account. It should be composed of eight or fewer lowercase letters or numbers. Spaces and punctuation aren't allowed.

Password—The Password field is used to enter a secret word or string of characters that Mac OS X uses to verify that you are who you say you are.

Figure 1.1
Create the account you use to access your Mac OS X system.

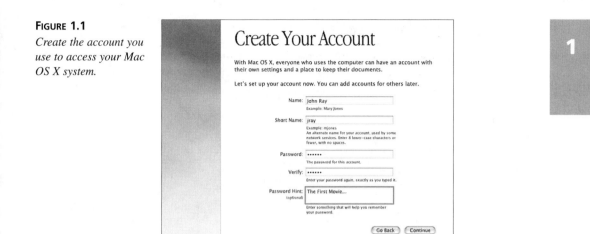

Verify—The Verify field requires you to type the same string you entered in the Password field. This step ensures that the password you typed is actually what you intended.

Password Hint—Type a phrase or question that reminds you of your password. If you attempt to log in to your system three times without success, the hint is displayed.

After you fill in this user information, click Continue to proceed.

Additional Settings

After you create a user account, you can set up your Internet connection. If you already have Internet access, but don't have all the information required to connect to your network or dial in to your ISP, skip this step for now. We cover specifics about Internet access in Hour 9, "Setting Up Mac OS X Networking," and .Mac accounts in Hour 10, "Web Browsing and .Mac Membership."

The next step is to specify the time zone for your computer. After you choose the appropriate zone and set the date and time, click Continue.

Congratulations! You've reached the last step of the configuration process. When prompted, click the Done button, and Mac OS X will take you to the desktop. Now let's briefly explore the structure of Mac OS X.

Understanding Mac OS X Architecture

Mac OS X consists of 11 separate pieces that work together and complement each other (as represented in Figure 1.2). Let's take a brief look at the components that make up Mac OS X. As we do so, we'll also examine how they influence the its features.

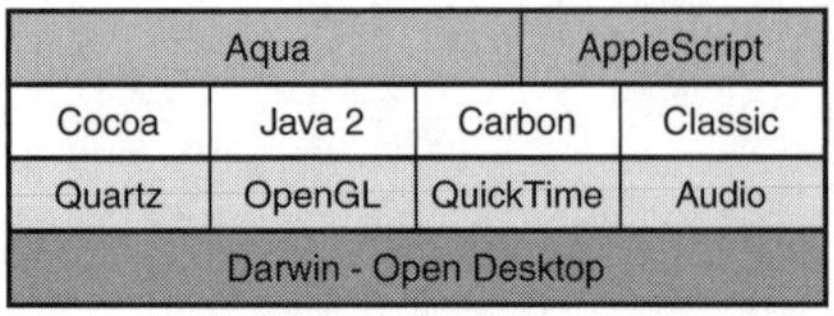

FIGURE **1.2**

This layered model represents the complex architecture of Mac OS X.

Aqua			AppleScript
Cocoa	Java 2	Carbon	Classic
Quartz	OpenGL	QuickTime	Audio
Darwin - Open Desktop			

Mac OS X is made up of several components that work together to run applications, generate images, and provide a cutting-edge user experience:

- **Aqua**—Aqua provides a graphical user interface (GUI) that controls the appearance of windows, buttons, and other onscreen controls.

- **AppleScript**—The AppleScript language enables users to write scripts that interact with other software on the computer.

- **Cocoa**—Cocoa is a programming environment that enables applications for Mac OS X to be built from scratch quickly.

- **Java 2**—Mac OS X supports the development and deployment of Java-based programs.

- **Carbon**—Carbon is an interface for developing programs that run on Mac OS 8/9 as well as Mac OS X.

- **Classic**—The Classic environment enables existing Mac OS applications to run under Mac OS X.

- **Quartz**—Quartz is Apple's new 2D imaging framework and window server, which is based on the Portable Document Format (PDF).

- **OpenGL**—OpenGL is the industry standard for 3D graphics.

- **QuickTime**—Apple's award-winning multimedia technologies are built into the graphics foundation of Mac OS X. Jaguar's QuickTime 6.0 includes the new MPEG-4 standard for Internet viewing.

- **Audio**—Mac OS X continues Apple's tradition of providing world-class audio support for musicians and audiophiles.

- **Darwin**—The UNIX-based core operating system.

Let's start at the bottom with Darwin and work our way up.

Darwin

Darwin is a UNIX-based system with all the power and stability of other forms of UNIX. If Mac OS X were a building, Darwin would be the rock-solid foundation on which the other elements stand.

NEW TERM   *UNIX* (pronounced *YOU-nix*) is an operating system developed at Bell Labs during the 1970s. UNIX was created to be a stable and powerful development platform for programmers. However, it has traditionally been run in the form of text commands, which can be a bit intimidating for casual computer users. Mac OS X preserves the power of UNIX while adding the usability of a Mac interface.

Darwin itself is composed of two parts: the Mach kernel and the BSD subsystem. A *kernel* is a small piece of controlling code that serves as a gatekeeper for all other processes and programs. In Mac OS X, only the Mach kernel can directly access hardware, such as the keyboard, the monitor, and even the memory. By allowing only a single piece of software to perform these critical activities, individual applications can no longer crash or corrupt the system. (As any user familiar with Mac OS 9 and earlier knows, this is not how the Macintosh operating system worked in the past.)

Above the Mach kernel is the Berkeley Software Distribution (BSD) subsystem, which is a collection of software that makes up a UNIX operating system. In many respects, Mac OS X is a composite of two operating systems. The BSD system is a completely functional environment in its own right that can be accessed through text commands. Mac OS X, however, is known for its user-friendly graphical environment. Together they form a system that's suitable for use by people with a broad range of computer experience.

Although this might seem complex, the good news is that Mac OS X shields all these technical details from your view—unless you choose to know more. Although software developers can create new modules that operate at the kernel level, the rest of us need do nothing more than sit back and reap the benefits. Those who want to access the BSD subsystem can learn more about it in Hour 20, "UNIX Command Line Tour."

The Imaging Layer

The second layer of the Mac OS X foundation is the imaging layer. It comprises the tools that your applications call on to create images.

The first of these tools is the QuickTime Application Programming Interface (API). For many people, QuickTime is nothing more than a media player that's used to listen to music or watch video clips, but it's far more than that. QuickTime forms the heart of all multimedia operations in Mac OS X. Using QuickTime, applications can support reading and writing dozens of image file formats. It also enables you to preview some supported file formats through the Get Info panel of the Finder, as shown in Figure 1.3. We discuss this further in Hour 2, "Using the Finder and the Dock."

FIGURE 1.3

Getting file information now includes a preview of QuickTime-supported content.

	spiderman_tlr1_mm480.mo
▼ General:	
	spiderman_tlr1_mm480.mov
Kind:	QuickTime Movie
Size:	21.1 MB on disk (22,152,670 bytes)
Where:	Desktop:
Created:	Tue, Jul 30, 2002, 9:31 PM
Modified:	Tue, Jul 30, 2002, 9:31 PM
☐ Stationery Pad	
☐ Locked	
▶ Name & Extension:	
▶ Open with:	
▼ Preview:	
Duration: 02'29	
Dimensions: 480 x 260	
▶ Ownership & Permissions:	
▶ Comments:	

Working with QuickTime is Apple's new audio system. Capable of handling large numbers of input and output sources, it can be used to create and work with complex sounds and external audio equipment.

Three-dimensional imaging is performed by another component: OpenGL. Used to create realistic special effects in games and productivity applications, OpenGL produces effects ranging from texture mapping to motion blur.

Mac OS X, with the help of OpenGL, performs a variety of eye-catching visual effects, such as seamlessly fading between screensaver images and scaling icons. However, some computers that can handle the other demands of Mac OS X have a graphics card that isn't capable of producing these effects. If you find that transitions between images are jerky, your graphics card might be to blame. However, rest assured that the other less-cosmetic aspects of Mac OS X are unaffected.

The final piece of Apple's imaging framework is Quartz, which is based on a standard developed by Adobe called PDF, the Portable Document Format.

> You might recognize PDF as a common file type for forms and documents available on the Internet. PDFs are especially useful for distributing forms because they reproduce the page layout regardless of the type of computer receiving the information. If your Internet browser has called for you to downloaded Adobe's Acrobat Reader, you've already encountered PDFs.

Quartz, like all PDFs, renders images precisely and makes them immensely scalable. These qualities allow Mac OS X to display dramatic desktop visuals. Open any window and then double-click on its title bar. You'll see that the window you viewed in full-size has shrunk into a tiny version of itself to fit in the *Dock* (which is the name for the row of icons along the bottom of the screen).

New to Mac OS X 10.2 is a variation on Quartz called Quartz Extreme. Quartz Extreme pairs the image manipulation capabilities of Quartz with the powerful graphic transformation features of OpenGL. (Although powerful for 3D rendering, OpenGL can also manipulate 2D images with ease.) Video cards, such as the Radeon and GeForce, perform the work of OpenGL rendering using the card's dedicated graphics processing unit (GPU), virtually eliminating the burden of Quartz from your computer's processor.

Application Programming Layer

The next layer of Mac OS X consists of APIs under which applications are created.

The first of these APIs is called Classic. It was created because Apple knew it would take time before applications compatible with Mac OS X started to appear. Using Classic, almost any application that's functional in Mac OS 9 can run inside Mac OS X, as long as a fairly recent version of Mac OS 9 is also installed. (This is truly astounding because Mac OS X's foundation is in no way similar to the traditional Mac operating system.)

If you want to see the difference between a native Mac OS X application and a Classic application, here's an example:

1. Make sure that "Finder" appears in the upper-left corner of your screen and press Command+F to open the Find window.
2. In the text field, type `Sherlock 2` and click Search.
3. From the files displayed in the lower portion of the screen, double-click the item whose Kind setting is Classic Application. Choosing that application boots Mac OS 9 and opens Sherlock 2 in the Mac OS X desktop. (If this is the first time that a Classic application has run under Mac OS X, you're asked to okay some minor changes to your computer's settings.)

After Mac OS 9 boots, you'll notice subtle changes in the desktop—including a return of the multicolored Apple icon at the upper left! For more detail about using applications in the Classic environment, see Appendix B, "Running Classic Applications."

In addition to Classic, there are three other development platforms for creating software that will run under Mac OS X: Carbon, Cocoa, and Java 2.

Carbon is a rewrite of the traditional Macintosh development toolbox to take advantage of the new technologies in Mac OS X. When an application is written in Carbon, it can run on both Mac OS X and Mac OS 8/9.

Cocoa provides a compelling development environment for Mac OS X. Compared to traditional programming methods, Cocoa offers the ability for a single programmer to create full-scale applications in a fraction of the time required for other approaches.

The final programming environment included in Mac OS X is Java 2. Java applications can be developed easily to run on a variety of operating systems, broadening the range of applications available for use under OS X.

Aqua and AppleScript

The final layer, composed of Aqua and AppleScript, provides a GUI to the Mac OS X operating system and a scripting language to control it. With translucent colors, transparent windows, and graphics that morph in and out of position, Aqua does for computer desktops what the iMac did for the aesthetics of computer design.

In Aqua, all the standard Mac OS user interface elements have been replaced. Scrollbars, buttons, window shapes, and every other control are now represented with the translucent theme. The only true way to understand Aqua is to use it. You have plenty of opportunity to do just that later in this hour.

AppleScript provides a way for a user to control all the layers underneath it by writing simple scripts or programs. You learn about AppleScript's capabilities in Hour 19, "Automating Tasks with AppleScript."

Now that you have an idea of what Mac OS X is made of, let's take a look around.

Applications Included with Mac OS X

As you've already learned, Mac OS X was built to allow the continued functioning of many applications written to operate under Mac OS 9. However, in the time since Mac OS X was unveiled, many fun and helpful programs have been ported to it from other operating systems or created especially for use with Mac OS X.

Here are just a few of the applications that come bundled with Mac OS X:

- **iTunes** stores music as MP3 files and helps you burn custom CDs as well as listen to Internet radio stations. Figure 1.4 shows iTunes' Visualizer, which displays colors and patterns in time with the music. You learn more about iTunes in Hour 5.

FIGURE 1.4

Here's a glimpse of iTunes.

- **iPhoto** helps you import and organize digital photographs as well as adjust photo quality and share your work. You find out more of the details in Hour 6.
- **iMovie** enables you to edit digital video. It also includes features that let you add titles and visual effects to your movies. You learn more about it in Hour 7.
- **Internet Explorer**, a Mac OS X–native version of the popular Web browser, comes bundled with Mac OS X. In Hour 10, you find out about accessing the Web and some special features available to Mac users.
- **Mail** sends and receives e-mail, including text and image attachments. It's also integrated with a built-in address book. Hour 12 explores e-mail and related settings.

If your favorite applications weren't mentioned, remember that many other applications are included with Mac OS X and still more are available for purchase or download. We discuss additional software that you might want to add in Hour 4, "Installing New Applications."

System Preferences

Mac OS X enables you to control many aspects of your system, from desktop appearance to user access. Conveniently, you can tailor these settings to your own needs from one centralized place, System Preferences, as shown in Figure 1.5.

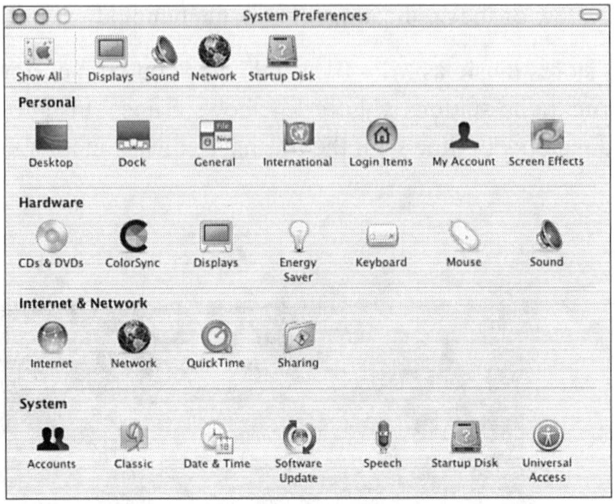

FIGURE 1.5

Many system settings are accessible through System Preferences.

To access System Preferences, simply click the Dock icon that resembles a light switch; it should be located in the row of icons at the bottom of your screen - or choose System Preferences from the Apple menu. As you can see in Figure 1.5, the elements of System Preferences are organized by function. You'll learn more details about System Preferences throughout this book as we discuss different topics.

Now let's move on to exploring the desktop!

The Mac OS X Desktop

One of the best features of the Macintosh operating system has always been its interface filled with pictorial icons and easy-to-access menus. The Mac OS X desktop, shown in Figure 1.6, continues that tradition.

Let's take a look at several elements of the Mac OS X environment and their basic use. We continue our exploration with discussion of the Finder and the Dock in Hour 2.

The Apple Menu

The Apple menu provides access to small applications and system controls. You open the Apple menu by clicking the Apple icon in the menu bar. It remains accessible and its options are unchanged regardless of which program is in use. This menu is shown in Figure 1.7.

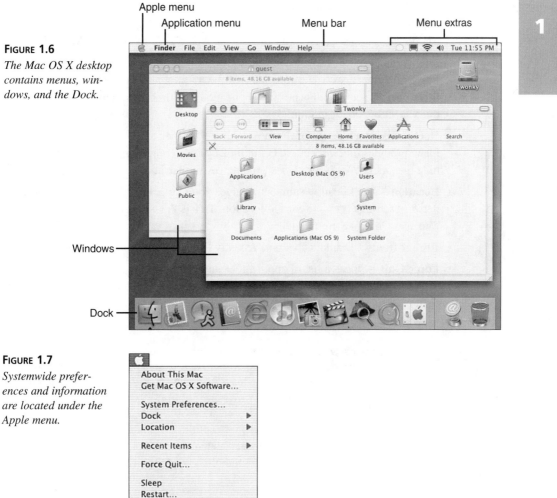

1

FIGURE 1.6
The Mac OS X desktop contains menus, windows, and the Dock.

Apple menu
Application menu
Menu bar
Menu extras
Windows
Dock

FIGURE 1.7
Systemwide preferences and information are located under the Apple menu.

About This Mac
Get Mac OS X Software...
System Preferences...
Dock ▶
Location ▶
Recent Items ▶
Force Quit...
Sleep
Restart...
Shut Down...
Log Out...   ⇧⌘Q

These options are available in the Apple menu:

- **About This Mac**—Displays information about the computer, such as the current version of the operating system, the amount of available memory, and the type of processor that the system is using.

- **Get Mac OS X Software**—Launches the user's preferred Web browser and loads the URL `http://www.apple.com/downloads/macosx/`. At that Web page, you can download third-party applications from Apple's list of available Mac OS X software.

- **System Preferences**—The equivalent of the traditional control panels, the System Preferences selection launches the application used to control almost all aspects of the Mac OS X configuration.

- **Dock**—The Dock is one of the most visible additions to Mac OS X. The Apple menu provides quick access to common Dock preferences, such as the ability to hide the Dock. We discuss Dock preferences further in Hour 2.

- **Location**—The Location submenu enables you to quickly adjust the Mac OS X network settings for your current location. This is the equivalent of the Location Manager Control Strip module.

- **Recent Items**—Displays the most recently launched applications and documents.

- **Force Quit**—Opens a list of applications and allows you to select which to quit. This is equivalent to pressing Command+Option+Esc to exit an application that has frozen.

> Traditional Mac users know that Command+Option+Esc is an example of a *key command*, which is a kind of shortcut activated by holding down a set of keys. For those new to the Mac, the Command key shows outlines of an apple and a cloverleaf.

- **Sleep**—Places your computer in a sleep state that requires very little power and can be restarted in a matter of seconds without the need for a full reboot.

> Although the Sleep option is convenient for momentarily powering down and allowing a quick start, PowerBook/iBook users might want to prevent battery drain by shutting down their computers completely rather than putting them to sleep for long periods.

- **Restart**—Quits all applications, prompts the user to save open files, and gracefully reboots the computer.

- **Shut Down**—Quits all applications, prompts the user to save open files, and shuts down the computer.

- **Log Out**—Quits all applications, prompts the user to save open files, and then returns to the Mac OS X login screen.

The Application Menu

Immediately to the right of the Apple menu is the application menu, which provides functions specific to the application currently in use. When an application launches in Mac OS X, a menu based on its own name appears to the right of the Apple icon. For example, if you start an application named TextEdit, the TextEdit application menu is the first menu item after the Apple icon.

The application menu contains items that act on the entire application rather than on its files. Figure 1.8 displays the application menu for Mail—an application included with Mac OS X.

FIGURE 1.8

Application menus contain functions that act on an entire application.

Mail	
About Mail	
Preferences...	⌥⌘;
Junk Mail	▶
Services	▶
Hide Mail	⌘H
Hide Others	
Show All	
Quit Mail	⌘Q

Seven default items make up an application menu:

- **About**—The About command reveals information about the running program.
- **Preferences**—An application menu provides a standardized location for application preferences.
- **Services**—Services are an interesting feature of Mac OS X. When a service is installed by an application, it can act on a selected item on the system. For example, if you want to e-mail some text from a Web page, you could select the text in your Web browser's window, and then choose Mail Text from the Mail submenu under Services. This would automatically launch the Mail application and create a new message containing your text.
- **Hide**—This hides all windows of the active application.
- **Hide Others**—Hides the windows of all applications other than the frontmost application. This effectively clears the screen except for the program you're currently using.

- **Show All**—Shows all hidden applications.
- **Quit**—Quits the current application. Command+Q is the universal Quit shortcut.

Windows

One of the most obvious places in which you interact with the Mac OS X interface is through onscreen windows, as illustrated in Figure 1.9. Let's take a look at the controls for a Mail window.

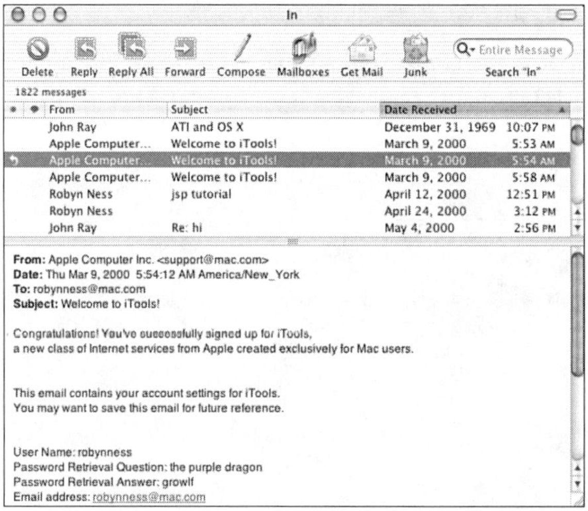

FIGURE 1.9

Mac OS X windows are familiar, but the position of common elements has changed and a few new elements have been added.

Close/Minimize/Zoom

In the upper-left corner of each window are the Close (red ×), Minimize (yellow –), and Zoom (green +) buttons. Differentiated only by color and position, the corresponding symbol appears in each button when the mouse cursor nears.

Clicking the Close button closes the open window. The Mac OS X Minimize button shrinks the window into an icon view and places it in the Dock. This icon is a miniature of the original window—down to the items it contains. In some cases, the icon even updates its appearance when the parent application generates new output. Clicking the icon in the Dock restores the window to its original position and size on the screen.

Double-clicking the title bar of a window has the same effect as clicking the Minimize button. The window shrinks to fit in the Dock.

The Zoom button (usually) opens the window to the size necessary to display the available information. Most Windows PC users expect the maximized window to fill the entire screen. However, if there are only three icons to be shown, Mac OS X doesn't waste space by filling up your window with blank space.

> Holding down Option while clicking the Minimize or Close button results in all the windows in the current application being minimized or closed.

Hide/Show Toolbar

In the upper-right corner of some windows (including the Finder and Mail windows) is an elongated button, called Hide/Show Toolbar, that can be used to quickly show or hide special toolbars in the top of the application window. The result of hiding the toolbar in the Mail application is shown in Figure 1.10.

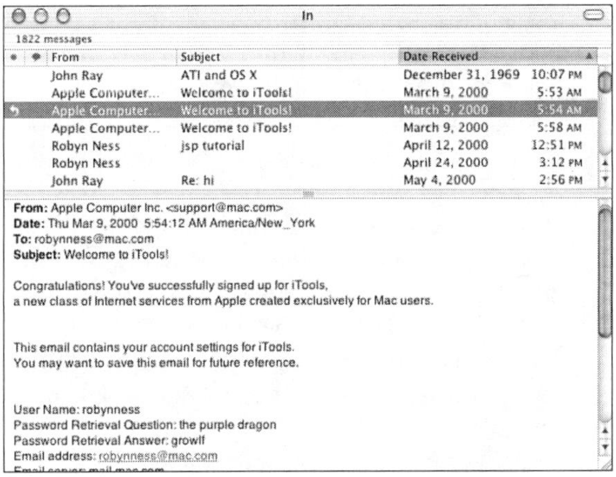

FIGURE 1.10

With the task toolbar hidden, the window occupies less screen space.

Apple advocates toolbars in applications to increase usability and efficiency. However, because individual developers must write their programs to support the toolbar button, you shouldn't expect all applications with toolbars to have the Hide/Show Toolbar button.

Window Moving and Resizing

Another characteristic of Mac OS X windows is the borderless content area. As shown in Figure 1.11, the display in most Mac OS X application windows stretches to the edge of the content window. In contrast, some operating systems such as Mac OS 9 and Windows offer window borders for dragging.

FIGURE 1.11

The content in a window goes right to the edge.

To drag a window, you must grab it by its title bar.

To resize a window, click and drag the resize icon in the lower-right corner of each window. Many applications in Mac OS X take advantage of live resizing; that is, as you resize the window, its contents adjust in real-time (such as Web pages in Internet Explorer). However, unless you have a fast computer, live resizing can be slow.

There are a few new tricks you can use when working with Mac OS X windows. If you hold down the Command key, you can drag inactive windows located behind other windows. If fact, holding down Command enables you to click buttons and move scrollbars in many background applications.

Another fun trick is holding down the Option key while clicking on an inactive application's window. This hides the frontmost application and brings the clicked application to the front.

Finally, rather than switching to another window to close, minimize, or maximize it, positioning your cursor over the appropriate window controls highlights them—enabling you to get rid of obtrusive windows without leaving your current workspace.

Sheet Windows and Window Trays

Two other unique interface elements in Mac OS X are sheets and window trays. Sheets are used in place of traditional dialog boxes. Normally, when a computer wants to get your attention, it displays a dialog box containing a question such as, "Do you want to save this document?". If you have 10 open documents on your system, how do you know which one needs to be saved?

Sheets connect directly to the title bar of an open window. As shown in Figure 1.12, these messages appear inside the window they're associated with.

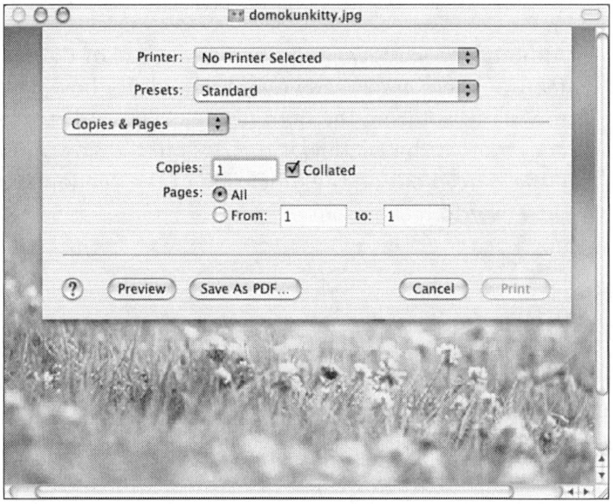

FIGURE 1.12

The sheet appears to drop from an open window's title bar.

Sheets are used just like regular dialog boxes, except that they're attached to a document. Unlike many dialog boxes, which keep you from interacting with the rest of the system until you interact with them, sheets limit access only to the window in which they appear.

A window tray is an interface element that can be used by developers in new and retooled applications. A tray is used to store commonly used settings and options that might need to be accessed while a program is running. Figure 1.13 shows the Mac OS X Mail application's window tray holding a list of active mailboxes.

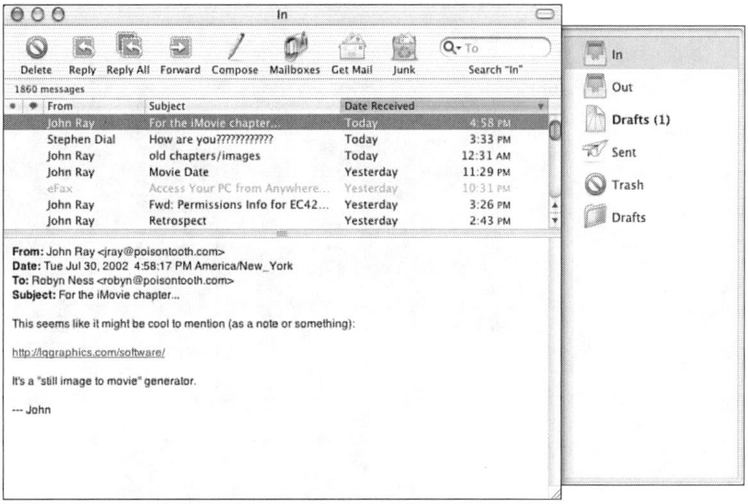

FIGURE 1.13

Window trays hold options that are needed often during a program's execution.

To use active trays in applications that support their use, you typically click a button in the toolbar. After a tray is open, you can drag its edge to change the tray's size.

Although only a few applications make use of the Mac OS X window tray feature, there are already two standards for how it operates. By default, the tray slides out from the right of the main window after you click a button to activate it. If the window is too close to the side of the screen, the tray is either forced out on the other side of the window or pushes the main window over to make room.

Window Widgets

Other functions of the interface are activated by controls collectively called *window widgets*. Samples of many of the Mac OS X Aqua interface elements are shown in Figure 1.14.

FIGURE 1.14
These are the Mac OS X window widgets.

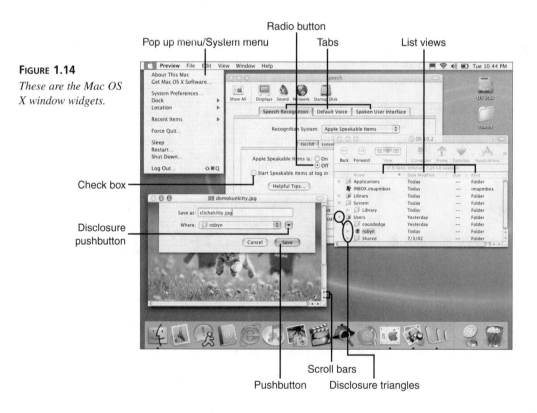

Aqua interface elements include the following:

- **Pushbuttons**—Pushbuttons are rendered as translucent white or aqua ovals with appropriate label text. They're typically used to activate a choice or to respond to a question posed by the operating system or application. The default choice, which is activated by pressing the Enter key, pulses for easy visual confirmation.

- **Check boxes/radio buttons**—Check boxes are used to choose multiple attributes (AND), whereas radio buttons are used to choose between attributes (OR).

- **List views**—Clicking a category, such as the Date Modified heading shown in Figure 1.14, sorts by that selection. Clicking the category again reverses the direction of the sort (ascending to descending or vice versa). To resize category headings, click the edge of the heading and drag in the direction you want to shrink or expand the column.

- **Pop-up menus/system menus**—Single-clicking a menu drops down the menu until you make a selection. The menu can stay down indefinitely. With Mac OS X's multitasking system, other applications can continue to work in the background while the menu is down.

- **Disclosure triangles**—Disclosure triangles continue to work as they always have. Click the triangle to reveal addition information about an object.

- **Disclosure pushbuttons**—Like disclosure triangles, these pushbuttons are used to reveal all possible options (a full, complex view) or to reduce a window to a simplified representation. They are used in the new File Save sheets.

- **Scrollbars**—Scrollbars visually represent the amount of data in the current document by changing the size of the scrollbar slider in relation to the data to display. The larger the slider, the less data there is to scroll through. The smaller the slider, the more information there is to display.

- **Tabs**—Tabs separate settings within a single window into categories by their functions, and you can see different options in each tab. By breaking up long lists in this way, windows with many options are less overwhelming, but you might have to click between tabs to find the control options you're looking for.

Menu Extras

Mac OS X offers a feature that gives users quick access to common system settings: Menu Extras. They appear as icons at the upper right of the menu bar. A number of Menu Extras are shown in Figure 1.15.

FIGURE 1.15

Menu Extras provide quick access to system settings.

Each Extra is added to the menu bar through individual Preferences panels that correspond to an item's function. You can activate or deactivate an Extra by clicking the Show *<option>* in Menu Bar check box for the corresponding option. For example, under Displays in the Hardware group, you can turn on the Displays Menu Extra.

A few of the Menu Extras available under Mac OS X include

- **Date & Time**—Displays the time and date graphically as a miniature clock or by using the standard text format.
- **Displays**—Adjusts the resolution and color depth of the display from the menu bar.
- **Volume**—Changes the sound volume.
- **Battery**—For PowerBook and iBook users, this option tracks battery usage and recharge time.
- **AirPort**—Monitors AirPort signal strength and quickly adjusts network settings. (The AirPort is a device that enables computers to be connected to the Internet without wires. It's discussed further in Hour 10.)

Clicking a Menu Extra opens a pop-up menu that displays additional information and settings. Items such as Battery and Date & Time can be modified to show textual information rather than a simple icon status representation, as shown in Figure 1.16.

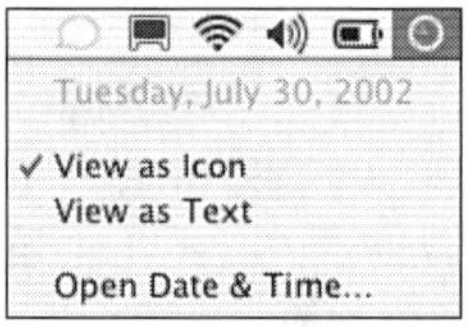

FIGURE 1.16

Set the time or switch between icon view and text view.

Tuesday, July 30, 2002

✓ View as Icon
View as Text

Open Date & Time...

Users can alter the order of Menu Extras by holding down the Command key and dragging an icon to a different position.

Summary

A lot of care went into making Mac OS X the versatile, powerful, and attractive system that's available today. In this hour, you learned a bit about the structure of Mac OS X as

1

well as some basic features to help you find your way around the Mac OS X desktop. The focus was on elements such as the Apple and application menus and window controls. We also briefly discussed some of the applications bundled with Mac OS X and System Preferences, which are covered in more detail in later hours. In the next hour, "Using the Finder and the Dock," you explore the Mac OS X file system and some useful shortcuts to your favorite applications.

Q&A

Q I'm converting to Mac OS X from Mac OS 9, and I can't find some of the features that used to be in the old Apple menu, including the Chooser. Where did they go?

A The Apple menu underwent a transformation between Mac OS 9 and Mac OS X. Previously, the menu contained control panel applications that configured systemwide functionality. It also acted as a simple folder in which a user could place applications or folders for easy access. Over time, as more items were added, the Apple menu became increasingly complex and cluttered. Under Mac OS X, items in the Apple menu have been limited to systemwide tasks.

Here are some common items that used to be in the Apple menu, and where they've gone:

- **Chooser**—Mac OS X moves the functionality of mounting network volumes directly into the Finder, under the Go menu. Printer selection is handled by the Print Center application (located in the Utilities folder within the Applications folder). Network connections are covered at length in Hour 13, "Using Network Sharing," and Print Center is documented in Hour 16, "Setting Up Printers and Fonts."

- **Key Caps**—This function has long assisted users in locating alternative characters. A Mac OS X Key Caps program is located in the Utilities folder within the Applications folder.

- **Sherlock**—Sherlock, which now manages only Internet searches, can be found in the Dock by default and can always be launched from the Applications folder. The system search functions of Sherlock are available in the Finder's Find command, which is launched from the File menu or by pressing Command+F.

- **Stickies and Calculator**—The Stickies application and Calculator are found in the Applications folder.

Q I've been using a program that runs in Mac OS X, but there's no Preferences item under the application menu as you described. Why is that?

A The formats for several features, including options in the application menu, are recommended practices. Individual programmers have the choice not to follow those guidelines.

Workshop

The workshop contains quiz questions and activities to help you solidify your understanding of the material covered. Try to answer all questions before looking at the "Answers" section.

Quiz

1. What's the operating system underlying Darwin?
2. What's a Classic application?
3. What kind of functions can be found under the Apple menu?
4. Where must you click in a window to move it?

Answers

1. UNIX
2. An application that was written to operate under Mac OS 9
3. Those that relate to systemwide controls
4. The title bar

Activities

1. Click the various icons on the screen. When windows appear, test the different kinds of window widgets.
2. Turn on several of the Menu Extras. (Hint: This requires you to click through the items in the System Preferences application.) After you've added several Menu Extras, view their available options by clicking their icons. Finally, decide which ones you want to keep and remove the others from the menu bar.

HOUR 2

Using the Finder and the Dock

You're now ready to take an inside look at Mac OS X and its operation as we focus on the Finder and the Dock. Even though they're technically separate applications, each plays an important role in user interaction with the operating system.

In this hour, you look at how these two features operate and how to customize the Finder's tools to suit your tastes. In this hour, you

- Navigate Finder windows
- Learn the Mac OS X file structure
- Burn a disc
- Set your desktop and Finder preferences

The first part of this hour takes a detailed look at the Finder and its features. The Finder is the application that Mac OS X uses to launch and manipulate files and applications. Unlike other tools and utilities, the Finder starts immediately after you log in to the system and is always active. In addition to helping you locate your files, the Finder handles all common tasks, such as creating, deleting, moving, and copying files and folders. If you'd like a refresher course in these functions, Appendix C, "Working with Files, Folders, and Applications," provides a quick reference to the Finder's standard file and application operations.

You can interact with the Finder in several different ways. There's a menu bar for the Finder, but there's also the Finder window, which has several different modes and view options. The Finder window is perhaps the easiest way to move through the Mac OS X file system, so let's look at it first.

The Finder Window

To help users manage their files, the Finder includes a specialized window, which is accessed by double-clicking the icon for the Mac OS X hard drive on the desktop.

Mac OS X introduces two modes of operation in the Finder window. The first of the two, single-window mode, is the toolbar version of the Finder, as shown in Figure 2.1. When the toolbar is present, double-clicking a folder opens the item you just clicked in the current window, replacing the previous contents.

FIGURE 2.1

The toolbar version of the Finder window enables you to navigate between recently opened folders.

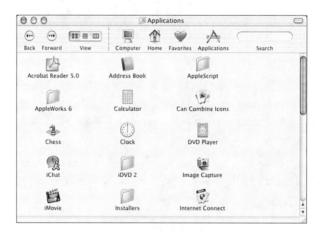

The second mode, a toolbar-less version of the Finder window, can be entered by clicking the toolbar button in the upper-right corner of the Finder window. In this mode, you can double-click folders to open additional windows.

Finder Toolbar

The toolbar version of the Finder window provides several useful controls for viewing and navigating your files.

In the upper-left corner of the toolbar is the Back arrow—click it to return to the previous folder. Using this technique, you can dig many levels deep into the file system, and then quickly back out by using this button. The Forward arrow enables you to follow the same path back to inner levels.

By default, there are several other elements in the toolbar, as shown in Figure 2.1. From left to right, you see the View selector, buttons to Computer, Home, Favorites, and Applications, and the Search text entry field. We talk more about using the Finder to find files later on in this hour.

> Separate from the Finder toolbar is the status bar, which shows the number of items in a folder and the amount of space available on the drive. The status bar can be toggled on and off by using the Show/Hide Status Bar command in the Finder's View menu. The status bar can also contain one of two icons in the left corner of the bar: a grid pattern that indicates use of the snap-to-grid function, and a pencil with a slash through it that indicates a folder is read-only.

You can customize your Finder toolbar by adding other predefined Mac OS X shortcuts or by removing the default items in this way:

1. Choose Customize Toolbar from the View menu.
2. From the window containing all the available shortcuts (shown in Figure 2.2), locate the item you want to add.

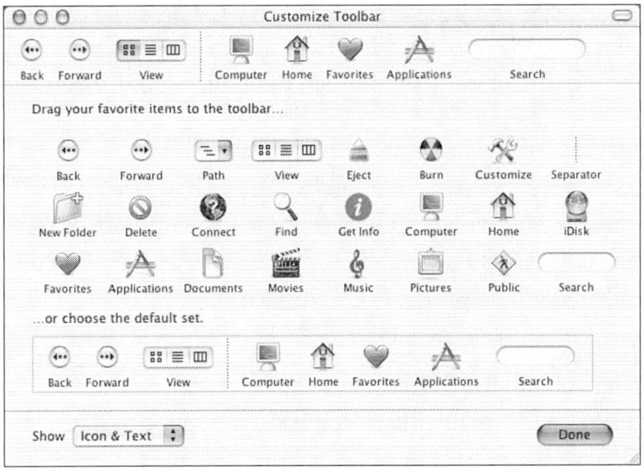

FIGURE 2.2

Finder shortcuts give you single-click access to applications, folders, and special features.

3. Add a shortcut by dragging it from the window to wherever you want it to appear on the toolbar.

In addition to these predefined options, users can define their own shortcuts. To do this, simply drag common applications, documents, and folders to any place on the toolbar.

> When you modify your toolbar, it's modified for all Finder windows in your workspace, not just the currently open folder. However, the changes that you make to your toolbar don't affect other user accounts on the same computer.

When folders and applications are added to the toolbar, a single click on the icon opens or launches the selected item. Users can also drag documents onto an application icon or folder icon in the toolbar to open the file by using the application or to move the file into a folder.

Finder Window View Options

In addition to choices that enable you to show and remove the Finder window toolbar, there are additional view options from which to choose. Three buttons in the View selector enable you control the way information is displayed in the Finder window.

Icon View

The first time you log in, the Finder is in toolbar mode and using Icon view. If you've already been using the Finder and are no longer in Icon view, you can quickly switch to Icon view by choosing As Icons from the View menu or by clicking the first button in the View selector of the toolbar. Figure 2.1 shows the Finder window in Icon view. In Icon view mode, you can navigate through the folders on your drive by double-clicking them.

List View

The next view to explore is the Finder's List view. You can switch to List view by clicking the middle button in the Finder's View selector or, if the toolbar isn't present, by choosing As List from the Finder's View menu. Demonstrated in Figure 2.3, the List view is a straightforward means of displaying all available information about a file or folder in tabular form.

The columns in the List view represent the attributes for each file. Clicking a column highlights it and sorts the file listing based on that column's values. For example, if you want to locate the most recent files in a folder, you can view the folder contents in List view and click the Date Modified header. By default, the column values are listed in descending order. Clicking a column header again reverses the sorting order. An arrow pointing up or down at the right of each column indicates the current sort order.

FIGURE 2.3

List view packs a lot of information into a small amount of space.

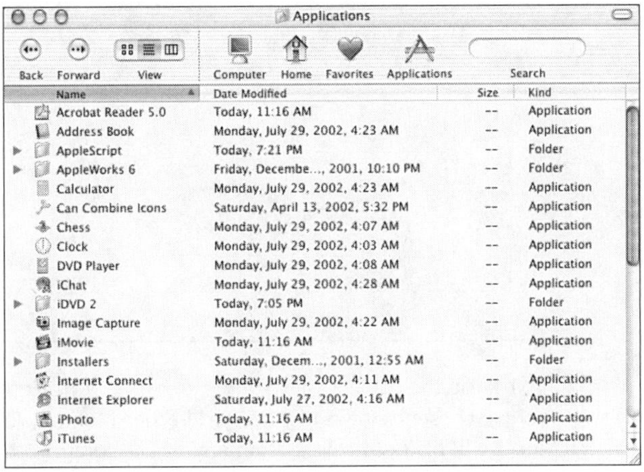

You can change the width of the columns by placing the mouse cursor at the edge of the column and click-dragging to the left or right. You can reposition the columns by clicking and dragging them into the order you want. However, the first column, Name, cannot be repositioned.

When a folder appears in the file listing, a small disclosure triangle precedes its name. Clicking the triangle reveals the file hierarchy within that folder. As with Icon view, double-clicking a folder anywhere in this view either opens a new window (if you're in toolbar-less mode) or refreshes the contents of the existing window with the new location.

Column View

Unlike other views, which can either overwhelm you with information or require multiple windows to move easily from point to point, the Column view is designed with one thing in mind: ease of navigation.

The concept is very simple: Click an item in the first column and its contents are shown in the next column. Click a folder in this new column and its contents are shown in the next column, and so on. Figure 2.4 shows a multicolumn display that reaches down two levels.

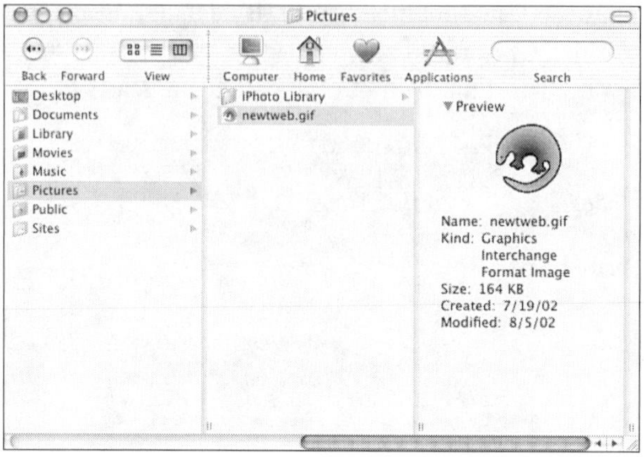

FIGURE 2.4

Using the Column view, you can easily navigate through the folders on your hard drive.

If you use the horizontal scrollbar to move back along a path, the folders you've chosen remain highlighted in the columns. You can, at any time, choose a different folder from any of the columns. This refreshes the column to the right of your choice. There's no need to start from the beginning every time you want to change your location.

One *big* bonus of using Column view is the ability to instantly see the contents of a file without opening it. If you choose a file or application, a preview or description of the selected item appears in the column to the right. For an example, take a look at the far right column in Figure 2.4, where a representation of an image file is displayed. When you choose an application or a file that cannot be previewed, only information about the file is displayed, such as the creation/modification dates, size, and version.

Show View Options

For each of the three Finder window views, there are additional settings that you can customize by choosing Show View Options from the View menu. You can also choose whether your changes apply to the current window only or to all Finder windows.

For Icon view, you can scale icons from the smallest to largest size by dragging the Icon Size slider from the left to the right. You can choose how the icon is labeled, including the font size and label placement. You can set how the icons are arranged and what color the window background is.

List view enables you to choose small or larger icons, text size, and which columns of information to display with the filenames.

Column view gives you options for text size and whether to include icons or the preview column. There are no global settings for this view.

Now that you understand how to navigate within the Finder window and alter your view options, let's move on to exploring the file system and some ready-made shortcuts.

The Desktop

The desktop is, for all intents and purposes, a global Finder window that sits behind all the other windows on the system. You can copy files to the desktop, create aliases on the desktop, and so on. The primary difference is that the desktop is always in Icon view mode.

As with other Finder windows, the desktop layout is controlled by the View Options in the View menu. Use the Icon Size slider, text, and arrangement settings exactly as you would adjust any other window in Icon view mode.

 You can change the background image of your desktop in the Desktop preferences pane of System Preferences. There you'll find many background images from which to choose, and you can also add your own images.

Finder Preferences

The Finder Preferences can be used to adjust settings that control how you interact with your desktop and icons. Open these settings by choosing Preferences from the Finder application menu. The available options are shown in Figure 2.5.

FIGURE 2.5

Finder Preferences control file extensions, Trash warnings, and more.

```
Finder Preferences

Show these items on the Desktop:
  ☑ Hard disks
  ☑ Removable media (such as CDs)
  ☑ Connected servers

New Finder Window shows:
  ○ Home
  ⦿ Computer

  ☐ Always open folders in a new window
  ☐ Open new windows in Column View

  ☑ Spring-loaded folders and windows
  Delay: ━━━━━━━━◉━━━━━━━
         Short    Medium    Long
  Press the Space bar to open immediately.

  ☑ Show warning before emptying the Trash
  ☐ Always show file extensions

Languages for searching file contents:
  ( Select... )
```

Among the preference settings are whether to display icons for the hard drive, removable media, or connected servers on the desktop and the default content displayed by new Finder windows. You can also adjust the delay for spring-loaded folders. *Spring-loading* is the desktop behavior that occurs when you drag a file or folder on top of another folder, and it springs open to move inside.

Close the Finder Preferences pane when you're satisfied with your settings.

The File System

Now, let's explore the Finder's file system.

After you double-click the icon for your Mac OS X drive, you see a collection of permanent folders. These folders contain preinstalled applications, utilities, and configuration files for your system, known collectively as *system folders*. You cannot modify these system-level directories or move them from their default locations. Don't worry too much about that because you can create folders and files *within* these locations, if necessary.

The following list describes the folders at this level, which are the starting point for accessing most of your system's functions:

- **Applications**—The Applications folder contains all the preinstalled Mac OS X applications, such as TextEdit, Mail, QuickTime Player, and many others. Within the Applications folder is the Utilities folder, which contains the tools necessary to set up your printers, calibrate your display, and other important tasks.

> Unlike most other system-critical folders, the Utilities folder *can* be modified by a Mac OS X user. You can move, rename, or delete the folder if you like, but such changes should be made only with great caution because the performance of some applications could be disrupted.

- **Library**—Although it doesn't have a strict definition, Library serves as a storage location for systemwide application preferences, application libraries, and information that should be accessible to any user application. Some of the folders in Library are used by applications to store data such as preferences, whereas others hold printer drivers or other system additions made by the user.
- **System**—Next on the list is the Mac OS X System folder. By default, the System folder contains only a folder called Library—a more specific version of the other Library folder. Within the System's Library folder are the components that make up

the core of the Mac OS X experience. These files and folders shouldn't be changed unless you're aware that any modifications you make could result in your computer becoming unbootable.

- **Users**—As mentioned in Hour 1, "A Tour of Mac OS X," Mac OS X is a true multiuser operating system in which each user has a private account and password to access the operating system. The Users folder contains the home directories of all the users on the machine.

Figure 2.6 shows the Users folder in List view for a system with three users: robyn, jray, and guest. Your home folder can be considered your workplace. It's yours alone because most of the files and folders stored there are protected from other users. Even though you can see the folders for every user, you can access only the Public and Sites folders in another user's home folder. Other folders are displayed with a red minus symbol in their lower-right corner to indicate that no access is available to that location. Hour 15, "Sharing Your System: Multiple Users," further discusses setting up additional user accounts.

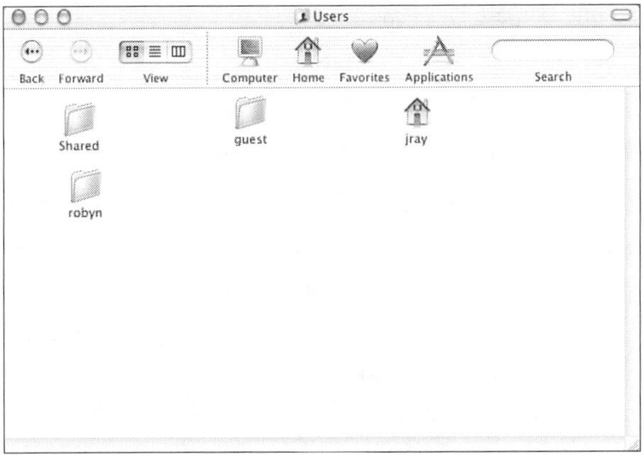

FIGURE 2.6

All users have their own home folder, but they cannot access the contents of each other's home folder.

- **System Folder (Mac OS 9)**, **Applications (Mac OS 9)**, **Desktop (Mac OS 9)**, and **Documents**—If you have a version of Mac OS 9 installed along with Mac OS X, you might see folders for Classic system files and applications as well as documents created under Classic mode. (For more information about using Classic applications, see Appendix B.)

Now that you understand how the Finder window operates, let's take a look at the default shortcuts in the toolbar: Computer, Home, Favorites, and Applications.

The "Computer Level" of the File System

Although you can see your computer's hard drives on the desktop, they are also visible in the Computer view of your Finder window. This is one of several default shortcuts available in the Finder toolbar. To see the Computer view, click the Computer icon. You can also access this window when you don't have the Finder window open by choosing Computer from the Go menu in the Finder menu bar.

 Any additional FireWire or USB drives (and other types of removable media) that are plugged into the system appear as icons in the Computer view of the Finder window in addition to being displayed on the desktop.

The Home Directory

Another default shortcut is to the home directory. As mentioned previously, your home directory is the start of your personal area on Mac OS X. There, you can save your own files and no one can alter or read them.

Your home directory is named with the short name you chose when you created your Mac OS X user account. Several default folders are created inside your home directory. Those folders and their purposes are as follows:

- **Desktop**—The Desktop folder contains everything that shows up on your desktop.
- **Documents, Movies, Music,** and **Pictures**—These four folders are generic store-all locations for files of these kinds. You don't have to use these folders; they're merely recommended storage locations to help you organize your files.
- **Library**—The Library folder is the same as the top-level Library folder and the Library folder in the System folder. Within the subfolders in this folder, you can store fonts, screensavers, and many other extensions to the operating system.
- **Public**—The Public folder provides a way for you to share files with other users on your computer without granting total access. Also, if you plan to share your files over a network, you can do so by placing them in the Public folder and activating file sharing in the Sharing System Preferences panel. This is discussed in Hour 13, "Using Network Sharing."
- **Sites**—If you want to run a personal Web site, it must be stored in the Sites folder. To share your site with the outside world, you also have to enable Personal Web Sharing, which we discuss in Hour 13.

Although folders for different file types exist by default, you can do nearly anything you like with your home folder. The only folders that should not be modified are the Desktop and Library folders. They are critical to system operation and must remain as they are.

Favorites and Applications

The remaining toolbar options, Favorites and Applications, are shortcuts to programs and files that make those programs and files accessible from anywhere in the Finder.

You determine the contents of Favorites. Favorites enable you specify the folders that you want to access quickly. To add an item, simply select the folder you want to be a favorite and drag it to the Favorites icon on the Finder window toolbar, or choose Add to Favorites from the File menu (Command+T).

Clicking the Applications icon jumps you to the system Applications folder.

2

Performing File and Content Searches

In addition to organizing your files, the Finder enables you to find applications by filename, and documents by filename or by content. But the best part is that the search results are interactive. You can launch located programs and applications by double-clicking their icons in the results window. Also, dragging a file or folder to the desktop or a Finder window moves that object to a new location. This is a quick way to clean up when you accidentally save a file to the wrong folder.

An easy way to search for a file by name only is through the Finder window. To do this, open a Finder window by double-clicking the folder or drive containing the file you want to find. Then type your search term in the Search box in the toolbar. Remember, if the toolbar isn't visible, you can show it by clicking the oblong button at the upper right of the window's title bar. If the search box isn't visible, you might have to enlarge your window by dragging from the diagonal lines in the bottom-right corner.

If you'd like to do a search of file contents or search more than a defined folder, choose Find (Command+F) from the File menu. The File dialog box is shown in Figure 2.7.

When the screen in Figure 2.7 appears, follow these steps:

1. Choose what to search. Your options are
    - **Everywhere**—Examines all drives and user accounts.
    - **Local Disks**—Examines only the current drive, but all user accounts.
    - **Home**—Examines only the home directory of the person currently logged in.
    - **Specific Places**—Displays a list of available drives for you to choose from. You can also click the Add/Remove button to insert or remove specific folders.

2. Pick whether to search for filenames, contents, or both. Enter your search text into the appropriate field(s). If you want to add additional search terms in these categories, click the + button for each option.

FIGURE 2.7

Use the Find dialog box to locate files by name or content.

● ○ ○	Find
Search in: Everywhere	
Search for items whose:	
file name contains ⟂ chapter	⊖ ⊕
content includes	⊖
Add criteria... ⟂	Search

3. If you want to refine your search further, click the Add Criteria pop-up menu for setting options, including Date Modified, Date Created, Kind, and Extension. The additional search parameters appear below the filename and content search boxes followed by - and + buttons to remove them or add additional variations.

4. Click the Search button to start the search.

In a few moments, the search results are displayed. For each result, Find lists the filename, the date it was modified, its size, and the kind of file it is. After an item is highlighted, its path is shown in the details pane at the bottom of the window. Double-clicking the path opens the file, folder, or application.

> Searching for file contents requires that the directory containing the file be indexed or cataloged. You can index a folder, or check for the last date of last indexing, using the Get Info command, which is discussed shortly.

The Finder Menu Bar

We've talked about the Finder window, but there's also a Finder menu bar, which provides access to a range of features. Some of those features are standard and shouldn't require much description. The standard features include options in the Edit menu to Undo/Redo, Copy, Paste, and Select All and an option in the Window menu to access all open Finder windows. You might want to click through the menus to familiarize yourself with their contents.

Some menu bar options offer other ways to perform actions that we've already discussed. For example, several of the View options duplicate settings in the Finder window toolbar. The options covered in the following sections are unique.

Getting File Information with the File Menu

The Info window can display detailed information, such as graphical previews and user permissions, about your files and folders. The default view of the Info window can be displayed by selecting the file you want to examine in the Finder, and then choosing Get Info (Command+I) from the File menu. As shown in Figure 2.8, the General section supplies basic facts about the selected resource.

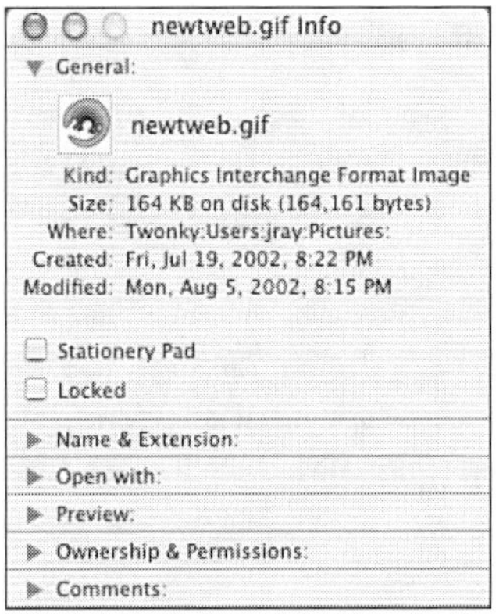

FIGURE 2.8

General information includes basic size, location, and type information about a file.

If the file you're viewing is an alias file (an *alias* is a shortcut to the place where the real file is stored), the General section shows the location of the original file along with a Select New Original button that enables you to pick a new file to which the alias should be attached.

Name & Extension

When you name your documents, you may include a *file extension*—a period followed by several letters at the end of a name that indicates what kind of file it is. Common examples of file extensions are .doc for Microsoft Word documents and .html for Web pages. The Name & Extension section enables you to choose whether to view the filename with or without its extension. For folders and applications, the Name & Extension section simply shows the name of the item. Many other operating systems rely on file extensions to identify file types. If you plan to exchange files with other systems (Windows), you might want to verify that your files include them before sending them through e-mail and so on.

Open with Application

If you select a document icon (not an application or a folder), you should be able to access the Open With section in the Info window. If you download a file from a non–Mac OS X system, your computer might not realize what it needs to do to open the file. The Open With section enables you to configure how the system reacts.

To use this feature, click the disclosure triangle next to Open With. The default application name is shown as the current choice in a pop-up menu containing alternative application choices. Use the pop-up menu to display options and make a selection. If the application you want to use isn't shown, choose Other, and then use the standard Mac OS X File dialog box to browse to the application you want to use.

If you have a group of files that you want to open with a given application, you can select the entire group and follow the same procedure, or use the Change All button at the bottom of the window to update all files on your system simultaneously.

Content Index

When you view the Info panel for a folder, the Content Index option enables you to index the folder's contents or check the last time it was indexed. Indexing allows searches on a folder to be performed on the text within files, not just on the filenames.

Preview

If you select a QuickTime-recognized document, another Get Info option is available: Preview. Preview enables you to quickly examine the contents of a wide variety of media files, including MP3s, CD audio tracks (AIFFs), JPEGs, GIFs, TIFFs, PDFs, and many more.

If you're previewing a video or audio track, the QuickTime Player control appears and enables you to play the file's contents. Figure 2.9 shows a movie trailer being played within the Preview section.

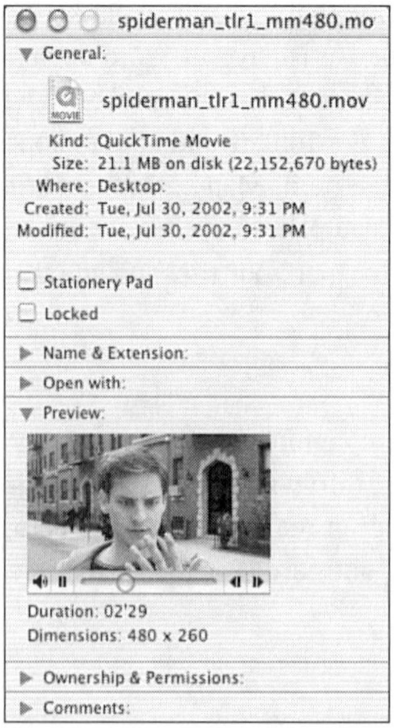

FIGURE 2.9

Play movie files using the Finder's Get Info Preview feature.

If you select a folder or an application, the Preview section displays its icon.

Languages

For an application, the Info panel includes a section called Languages that enables you to see which languages the application recognizes. If you uncheck the currently active language, the application's menus are presented in another available language the next time you open it.

Ownership & Permissions

Mac OS X is a multiuser system, and by default all the files and folders on your system identify themselves with the user who created them. That means only the owner can move or modify them. Applications have different permissions depending whether they are shared or stored in a personal account. The Ownership & Permissions section enables you to change who owns a file, what other groups of users can access it, and what actions can be performed on it. You learn more about working with multiple user accounts and administrative access in Hour 15.

Comments

The Comments section enables you to create notes attached to specific files, folders, and applications.

The Go Menu

If you want to navigate quickly from any view, you can use the folder shortcuts in the Go menu. This menu enables you to jump to one of several predefined locations. These options are the same ones that can be set in the Finder window's toolbar.

The Go menu also enables you to manually enter the name of a directory to browse. This quick-navigation option is the Go to Folder dialog box (Shift+Command+G). Here, you can tell the Finder where you want to be, based on the pathname you enter. Figure 2.10 shows the Go To Folder dialog box.

You can type any folder pathname in the Go to the Folder field. Folder names are separated by the / character (think of a pathname as being similar to a Web URL). For example, if you want to open the Documents folder in your home directory, you would type the following:

```
/users/[your Home directory name]/Documents
```

This pathname notation, with slashes between folders, is used throughout this book as an efficient way to guide to you to specific subfolders.

FIGURE 2.10

The Go To Folder dialog box lets you enter your destination by hand!

Task: Burn a Disc

One unexpected feature of the Finder is the Burn Disc option, an essential feature for those with CD-RW drives.

Mac OS X Finder makes writing a CD very similar to moving files to any other storage device. To make the process as simple as possible, Mac OS X stores applications, files, and folders in a special folder until you tell the system to burn the CD. Files are actually transferred to the CD media only after the burn starts.

To choose Burn Disc from the File menu, the active Finder window must be the CD's window. If the CD is not the active window, the menu item will be disabled.

These are the steps to write your own data CD using the Finder:

1. Insert a blank CD into the CD writer. The Mac OS X Finder prompts you to prepare the CD. This doesn't actually write anything to the CD yet, but it tells the computer what your intentions are for the disc in order to ensure that you use the appropriate kind of CD.

2. Choose the Open Finder option from the Action pop-up menu. (We talk about burning from iTunes and Disk Copy in later hours.)

3. Enter a name for the CD you're writing. The disc appears with this name on the desktop.

4. Click the OK button to start using the CD on your system. An icon representing the CD appears on your desktop. At this point, you can interact with this virtual volume as you would any other under Mac OS X. You can copy files to it, delete files, and so on.

5. When you create the CD layout you like, you can start the burn process by choosing Burn Disc from the File menu or by clicking the Burn toolbar shortcut. In addition, dragging the CD to the Trash also prompts burning to begin. This process takes a few minutes, and is tracked by the Finder much like a normal Copy operation.

If you decide against writing the CD, you can click the Eject button in the CD burning dialog box to remove the media and erase the CD layout you created. If you want to insert a CD in the drive but don't want to prepare it (for use in another CD-burning application), click Ignore rather than OK in the window that appears when you first insert a CD.

The Dock

The Dock, shown in its default state in Figure 2.11, has several functions. Among its functions are displaying icons for open applications, providing access to the System Preferences panel, and providing a resting place for the Trash.

FIGURE 2.11
The Dock is a useful tool for organizing your desktop.

The Dock can also be customized to hold files, folders, and applications that you want to keep close at hand. It can also be changed from a horizontal row to a vertical column on either the left or right edge of the screen. As you add more items to the Dock, it grows until it reaches the edge of the screen. But don't worry about space—the Dock automatically shrinks the icons to fit the available space.

The Dock has two parts, separated by a vertical divider line. On one side are static documents, folders, and application windows that are in use. On the other side are application files.

Docked Windows, Files, and Folders

Let's talk about the document side of the Dock. You can drag commonly used documents to the right side (or bottom, if the Dock is in vertical orientation), and a link to them is stored for later use. You can also drag commonly used folders to this area of the Dock for easy access. Click-holding (or right-clicking) a docked folder displays a list of its contents and the contents of the subfolders in that folder.

Moving an icon to the Dock doesn't change the location of the original file or folder. The Dock icon is merely a shortcut to the real file. Unfortunately, the Dock icon is not the same as an alias. If a docked application has been moved, the Dock can no longer launch that application.

Minimized windows labeled by the icon for their associated application are also placed in this portion of the Dock. In addition to easy window recognition, these window miniatures can serve another useful purpose. Depending on the application, minimized windows might continue to update as their associated applications attempt to display new information. QuickTime Player, for example, continues to play movies.

You can also drag URLs into the document side of the Dock. A single click launches your default Web browser and opens it to the saved address.

Trash Can

Located on the far-right side of the Dock (or very bottom, in vertical orientation) is the Trash. You can drag files and folders to this icon to place them in the Trash. To empty the Trash, use the Finder application menu and choose Empty Trash (Shift+Command+Enter), or click-and-hold (or Ctrl-click) the Trash icon and choose Empty Trash from the pop-up menu.

The Trash is also used for ejecting disks and CDs. To avoid user fears that this might hurt the contents of the disk, Mac OS X now conveniently changes the Trash icon into the Eject symbol when you drag a disk icon to it.

You don't have to use the Trash when ejecting disks. Ctrl-clicking a mounted volume opens a contextual menu with an Eject option. Alternatively, you can highlight the disk to remove and choose Eject (Command+E) from the Finder's File menu or press the Eject key on some models of the Apple USB keyboard.

2

Docked Applications

The other side of the Dock contains all docked and currently running applications. You can add applications to the left side (or the top in vertical orientation) of the Dock to create a quick launching point, no matter where the software is located on your hard drive. Dragging an application icon to the Dock adds it to that location in the Dock.

To make an active application a permanent member of the Dock, simply do the following:

1. Make sure that the application is running and that its icon appears in the Dock.

2. Click and hold on the icon to pop up a menu.

3. Choose the option Keep in Dock. (If the application already has a place in the Dock, you won't be given this option.)

After you've placed an application on the Dock, you can launch it by single-clicking the icon. To switch between active applications, just click the icon in the Dock that you want to become the active application.

You can also switch between open applications by holding down Command+Tab. This moves you through active applications in the Dock in the order in which they appear. When you reach the item you want to bring to the front, release the keys to select it.

Dropping is a shortcut for opening documents. To open a document in a specific application, you can drag and drop the document icon on top of the application icon. In Mac OS X, you can use the application's Dock icon instead of having to locate the real application file on your hard drive. Also, to force a docked application to accept a dropped document that it doesn't recognize, hold down Command+Option when holding the document over the application icon. The icon is immediately highlighted, enabling you to perform your drag-and-drop action.

To remove an item from the Dock, make sure that the item isn't in use and drag it out of the Dock. It disappears in a puff of smoke (literally—try it and see).

In addition to providing easy access to commonly used applications, the Dock icons also give you feedback about the functions of their applications. While an application is loading, its icon begins to bounce (unless configured not to) and continues bouncing until the software is ready. Also, if an open application needs to get your attention, its icon bounces intermittently until you interact with it. The Dock also signals which applications are running by displaying a small triangle in those application icons. Some applications even customize the Dock's icons to display useful information, such as Mail's ability to show the number of new messages in its Dock icon.

Customizing the Dock

After you get used to the idea of the Dock, you probably want to customize it to better suit your needs.

If you have a small monitor, you might want to resize the Dock icons to cover less area. The easiest and fastest way to resize the Dock is to click and hold on the separator bar that divides the Dock areas. As you click and hold on the separator bar, drag up and down or left and right (if your Dock is placed vertically). The Dock dynamically resizes as you move your mouse. Let go of the mouse button when the Dock has reached the size you want.

> After playing with different Dock sizes, you might notice that some sizes look better than others. That's because Mac OS X icons come in several native icon sizes, and points between those sizes are scaled images. To choose only native icon sizes, hold down the Option key while using the separator bar to resize.

For more fine-tuning of the Dock, turn to the System Preferences panel. The Dock has a settings panel in System Preferences for adjusting its size and icon magnification and for making it disappear when not in use.

When you've made your selections, choose Quit (Command+Q) from the System Preferences application menu.

2

Summary

The Mac OS X Finder and Dock are powerful tools for managing your files and folders. Each offers a high degree of customization to help you work efficiently. The Finder also provides some special functions, including CD burning, that make it more than just a filing system.

Q&A

Q I want to customize the look of my computer. Are there ways to do that in Mac OS X?

A Yes, you can customize the appearance of your desktop in several ways.

One way is by changing your desktop background. To do this, go to the Desktop Preferences panel of System Preferences, and drag the icon from any image file into the image well in the panel. If you don't have any images of your own, you can browse the options in the Collection pop-up menu.

You can also replace Mac OS X icons with other images. Simply click the object's icon in the General Information section of the Get Info panel, and then use the Copy and Paste commands in the Edit menu to paste in other icons or images. If you're looking for replacement images, two excellent sources for high-quality Mac OS X icons are Iconfactory at `http://www.iconfactory.com` and Xicons, located at `http://www.xicons.com`.

Q I've been saving my files where I want them, but sometimes when I look for them, they aren't where I put them. Why?

A This could be the result of two things. First, Mac OS X has a more structured file system than previous Mac operating systems. If you're trying to save or move your files to restricted folders, the system won't allow it. Restricted folders include folders with a designated purpose (such as those folders in the top level of the Mac OS X hard drive) and other users' folders (with a couple of exceptions). Also, sometimes Mac OS X defaults to folders in your user account rather than placing your files on the desktop.

Or, the problem might simply be that the file has been saved, but its icon doesn't appear right away. Sometimes you need to click out of a window and click back to see newly placed files.

Workshop

The workshop contains quiz questions and activities to help you solidify your understanding of the material covered. Try to answer all questions before looking at the "Answers" section that follows.

Quiz

1. What are the three View options for the Finder window?

2. How do you view the contents of a docked folder?

3. What is the major difference between the Finder window with a toolbar and without a toolbar?

Answers

1. Icon, List, and Column.

2. A list of the files in a docked folder appears if you click and hold (or Ctrl-click) on the folder icon.

3. Double-clicking a folder icon in windows without a toolbar opens the contents into a new window, but double-clicking a folder icon in windows with a toolbar refreshes the same window to show the folder's contents.

Activities

1. Go to Customize Toolbar under the View menu of the Finder and add or remove items. If you don't like the result, return to that menu and reset the default items by dragging the default set (located at the bottom of the customization window) to the toolbar.

2. Add any folders or applications you use regularly to the Dock. If you change your mind, drag them back out and watch them disappear.

Hour 3

Basic Applications for Productivity and Recreation

Mac OS X includes a number of utilities and applications that enable you to start working as soon as your Mac is up and running. The included software ranges from games to simple desk accessories. This hour looks at many of those applications. Because they require no installation or additional setup, we recommend giving each of the following applications a try as a way to familiarize yourself with the Mac OS X desktop. In this hour, you look at

- Calculator, Clock, and Stickies
- Preview and TextEdit
- Ink
- Chess

Desk Accessories

Desk accessories used to be a special type of application located under the Apple menu. In Mac OS X, a number of included applications, such as Calculator, Clock, and Stickies, fill the roles previously played by the now-extinct desk accessories.

Calculator

The Mac's system Calculator, shown in Figure 3.1, is located in the Applications folder (path: /Applications/Calculator). You can toggle between basic mode and advanced mode, which supports trigonometry functions and exponents.

FIGURE 3.1

The Calculator in default mode offers basic arithmetic functions.

You can operate the Calculator by clicking the buttons in the window or by using your numeric keypad. The number keys on your keypad map directly to their Calculator counterparts, and the Enter key is equivalent to clicking the equal button. The Paper Tape button opens and closes a tray to display inputs. You can print the tape by choosing Print Tape from the File menu.

Another useful, if unexpected, feature is the Calculator's Conversion function. It enables you to easily perform conversions of currency, temperature, weight, and a variety of other measurement units. Simply enter a value in the Calculator, and then choose the desired conversion type from the Convert menu. In the sheet that appears from the top of the Calculator, choose the units to convert from and those to convert to and click OK. A currency conversion is depicted in Figure 3.2.

Clock

The Clock (path: /Applications/Clock) is a digital/analog timepiece designed to fit into the Mac OS X Dock or float on the desktop as a *windoid* (a floating, non-editable window). By default, starting the Clock application places a clock face in the Dock.

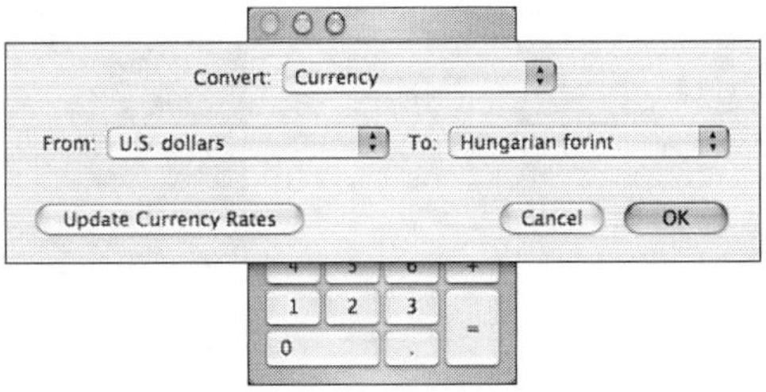

FIGURE 3.2

You can update currency rates when choosing monetary units in the currency conversion sheet.

To configure the Clock application's time display, choose Preferences from the application menu. The Clock Preferences dialog box is displayed in Figure 3.3.

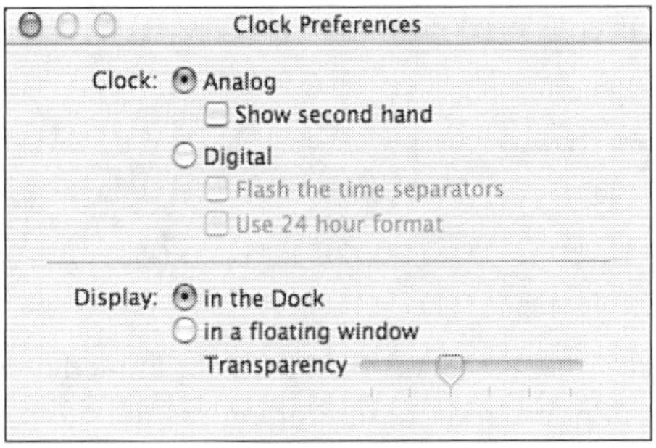

FIGURE 3.3

Configure the Clock application's display.

Choose your Clock settings based on a combination of analog, digital, and window types:

- **Analog**—The default view of the Clock is the analog wall-clock style. If you like, click the Show Second Hand check box to display the Clock's second hand in addition to the minute and hour hands.

- **Digital**—The digital Clock display resembles a tear-off calendar page. Both the date and time can be seen in this view. The digital display offers the options of flashing the time separators (:) each second and displaying the time in 24-hour mode.

- **Display**—Finally, the Clock can be shown as an icon contained in the Dock (its default mode) or in a windoid with variable transparency, as shown in Figure 3.4. If you choose the floating window option, drag the transparency slider from left to right to change the window's transparency.

FIGURE 3.4

When on the desktop, the Clock floats on top of everything else.

After you make your choices, the changes take effect immediately. To automatically launch the Clock at startup, use the Login Preferences dialog (see Chapter 18 for details).

Stickies

Stickies (path: /Applications/Stickies) is a digital version of a Post-it notepad. You can store quick notes, graphics, or anything you might want to access later. Stickies offer several formatting features, such as multiple fonts, colors, and embedded images. The screen displayed in Figure 3.5 is covered with sticky notes.

Stickies does not use the standard Mac OS X window. Instead, each window appears as a colored, borderless rectangle when it isn't selected. When a window is active, three controls appear:

- **Close box**—The close box in the upper-left corner of the sticky note closes the active note. Closing a note erases it.
- **Maximize/Minimize**—In the upper-right corner is a second box that changes the shape of the current note to best fit the text. Clicking the box toggles between two sizes for the current note.
- **Grow box**—Dragging the grow box, located in the lower-right corner, dynamically shrinks or expands the window.

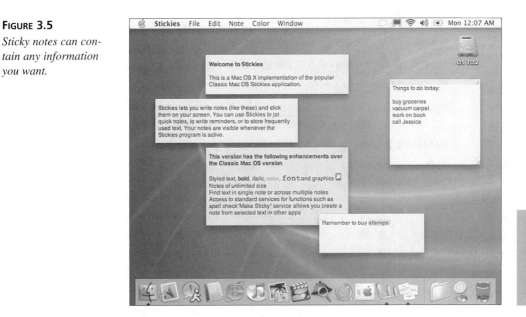

FIGURE 3.5

Sticky notes can contain any information you want.

In addition to the three visible controls, Mac OS X Stickies also supports windowshading. Double-clicking the title bar of an active window shrinks it to the size of the title bar. Double-clicking the title bar a second time returns the window to its previous size. When in windowshaded mode, the sticky note displays the top line of text from its contents in the title bar of the collapsed window.

Strangely enough, you cannot minimize Stickies into the Dock. Choosing Miniaturize Window from the Window menu will windowshade the active note.

The Stickies application has very few configuration options—using the Preferences located under the application menu, you can enable or disable confirmation of window closing. The rest of the menus enable you to customize the sticky notes that you currently have open.

Sticky notes are not, as you might think, individual documents. All the notes are contained in a single file that's written to your Library folder. The File menu in Stickies enables you to create new notes, export individual notes to text files, and print the contents of notes:

- **New Note** (Command+N)—Creates a new blank note.
- **Close** (Command+W)—Closes the active sticky note.
- **Save All** (Command+S)—Saves changes to all notes.
- **Import Classic Stickies**—Imports note files from Mac OS 8/9.
- **Import Text**—Imports a text file into a new note. Text can be in plain text or rich text format (RTF). Font style information is retained if you use rich text format.
- **Export Text**—Exports the active note to a text file.
- **Page Setup**—Configures printer page setup.
- **Print Active Note** (Command+P)—Prints the active note.
- **Print All Notes**—Prints all notes.

In addition to the normal Edit menu items are two components you might not expect in a simple Post-it application: Find and Spell Checking.

 Stickies also installs a service that's accessible from the Stickies application menu's Services item (Shift+Command+Y). Using the Stickies service, you can quickly store selected text from any application in a sticky note.

The Note menu offers control over the text formatting in each note, including font and text formatting and colors. Copy Font is an unusual selection that copies the font style from the current text selection (size, font face, color, and so on) so that you can easily apply it elsewhere by using the Paste Font command. Floating Window enables you to set the chosen note to float in front of all other windows, even when other applications are active. Translucent Window makes the selected note transparent so that whatever is behind it will show through. The Use as Default option enables you to apply the current color, location, and font setting as the default for new notes. Use the Note Info option to display the creation and modification dates for the active note.

What would a sticky note be without a bright-colored background? The Color menu contains the common Post-it colors for your enjoyment (yellow, blue, green, pink, purple, and gray).

Preview

For viewing PDF files and images of all sorts, Mac OS X comes with the Preview application (/Applications/Preview).

> The standard graphic file format in Mac OS X 10.2 is PDF. One nifty result is that you can make a PDF of nearly any document on your system. Simply choose Print from the File menu and click the Save As PDF button, or use the Print Preview command to open your file in the Preview application and save from there.

Preview can be launched in a number of ways. First, you can double-click the application file. Doing so starts Preview, but doesn't open any windows. You must then choose Open from the File menu to select a file to view.

Second, you can open Preview by dragging the image or PDF files onto the Preview icon in the Finder or Dock.

Third, Preview is integrated into the Mac OS X printing system, so clicking Preview in any Print dialog box starts it.

> If you want to view a series of images in one Preview window, select them all and drag the set on top of the Preview icon in the Applications folder or in the Dock.

When you open an image or PDF document in Preview, it shows up in a window with a toolbar across the top, as shown in Figure 3.6. The following options are located in the toolbar:

- **Thumbnails**—Opens and closes a tray window, shown in Figure 3.6, which displays small representations of the pages or files open in the current Preview window. Clicking a thumbnail will show it the main viewing area.

- **Zoom In** and **Zoom Out**—These two options enable you to view a larger or smaller version of the selected image or PDF. If the image is larger than the Preview window, scrollbars will appear.

- **Rotate Left** and **Rotate Right**—Enable you to turn the viewed file counter-clockwise or clockwise by 90 degrees at a time.

- **Backward** and **Forward**—If you have more than one image open in the current Preview window, you can move through the set using the Backward and Forward arrows.

- **Page Number**—When you're viewing a multipage TIFF or PDF file, Page Number enables you to enter a page number to jump directly to that page.

FIGURE 3.6

The Preview window includes a toolbar where you can easily alter the viewing style of your files or move between pages.

Just as you can for Finder windows, you can hide the Preview toolbar by using the oblong button at the upper right of the window's title bar.

In addition to viewing files, you can use Preview to convert a file to one of several common file types and export it to a new location. To do this, choose Export from the File menu and enter a filename. Then choose a location to save in and a file format. The Options button reveals additional settings for color depth and filter options.

Overall, Preview is fine tool for viewing PDFs and images of different formats. However, if you have a file that won't open in Preview or needs additional editing, download and register GraphicConverter from `http://www.lemkesoft.com/us_index.html`. GraphicConverter handles dozens of image formats and provides basic editing utilities.

TextEdit

Mac OS X automatically installs the text editor TextEdit (path: /Applications/TextEdit). TextEdit can save files in plain text or the RTF format and uses many built-in Mac OS X features to give you advanced control over text and fonts. Its RTF files can be opened in popular word processing programs, such as Microsoft Word, and display all formatting attributes.

What Is Unicode?

TextEdit also handles Unicode editing. *Unicode* is a character-encoding format that uses 16 bits (as opposed to the traditional 8) for storing each character. This allows more than 65,000 characters to be represented, which is necessary for some languages such as Japanese and Greek. Unicode is expected to entirely replace ASCII encoding (which can represent a total of only 255 characters) eventually.

When you start it, TextEdit opens a new `Untitled.rtf` document for you to begin working. If you want to open an existing document, choose Open (Command+O) from the File menu.

TextEdit's Open dialog box enables you to select any type of file, including binary files such as images. To read a file, however, it must be a supported document type, such as plain text, Hypertext Markup Language (HTML), or RTF. By default, TextEdit opens HTML documents and displays the styled information similar to the way a Web browser would display it. Figure 3.7 demonstrates TextEdit's rich text editing capabilities. To open an HTML file and edit the source code, you must adjust the preferences—the rendered view of a Web page cannot be edited.

FIGURE 3.7

TextEdit can edit styled text documents stored in RTF.

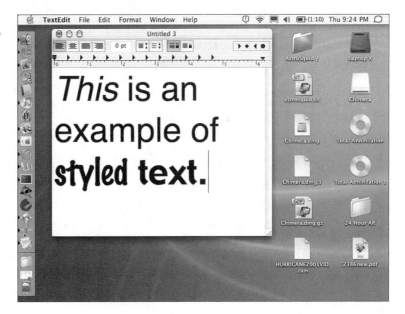

For the most part, you should be able to open TextEdit and start creating and editing text documents. However, you can use a number of preferences and features to customize its appearance and functionality.

Preferences

The TextEdit Preferences dialog, shown in Figure 3.8, controls the default application preferences. Most of these options can be chosen from the menu bar and stored on a per-document basis as well as for the entire application.

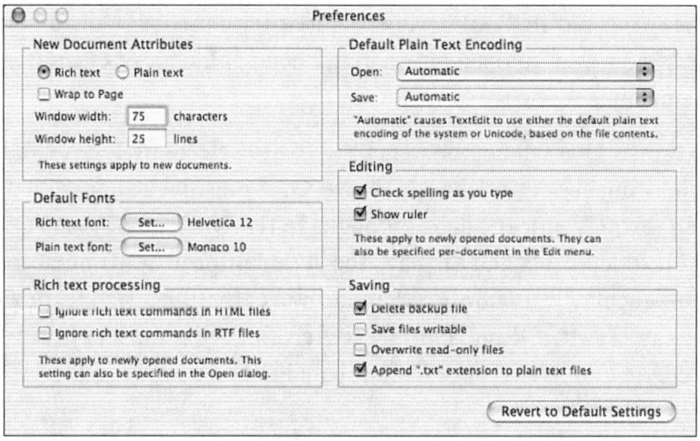

FIGURE 3.8

The TextEdit Preferences dialog enables you to control a range of features.

Use the Set buttons in the Default Fonts section to choose new default fonts for rich text and plain text documents. The default fonts are Helvetica 12 and Monaco 10, respectively.

The New Document Attributes section of the dialog includes an option for Rich Text or Plain Text. It enables you to select the Wrap to Page check box so that lines will fit the page width.

The Window Width setting lets you to specify the width of new windows in characters. Similarly, the Window Height setting enables you to set the height of new windows in lines.

To have TextEdit automatically check your spelling as you type, select the Check Spelling as You Type check box in the Editing section. Misspelled words will be underlined in red. Ctrl-click the misspelled word to open a contextual menu that enables you to choose from a list of corrections, ignore the word, or add it (the Learn option) to the Mac OS X dictionary.

The options in the Saving section include

- **Delete Backup File**—Removes the TextEdit backup file after a document is successfully saved.
- **Save Files Writable**—Saves files with write permissions turned on; that is, they can be edited later.
- **Overwrite Read-only Files**—Overwrites files, even if their permissions are set to read-only.
- **Append ".txt" Extension to Plain Text Files**—Adds a .txt extension to the end of plain text files for cross-platform compatibility and ease of recognition.

By default, TextEdit attempts to read style information in whatever file it opens. Allowing automatic detection enables TextEdit to open files created on other operating systems, such as Windows, and transparently translate end-of-line characters.

When opening or saving a document, TextEdit gives you the opportunity to override automatic detection of the appropriate file encoding type to use. To choose an alternative encoding, such as Unicode, use the pop-up menus in the Default Plain Text Encoding section.

To disable rich text commands in HTML and RTF files, click the corresponding check box in the Rich Text Processing section. Ignoring the style information opens the document as a plain text file, showing all the control codes and tags used to embed the original styles. This is required for editing HTML tags within a Web page.

To save your settings, close the TextEdit Preferences panel. To revert to the original configuration, click the Revert to Default Settings button.

Menus

The TextEdit menus provide control over fonts and other document-specific information. Most of the application preferences can be overridden on a per-document basis from the main menus.

You can open, save, and print documents by using the File menu.

The Edit menu contains the basic copy and paste functions, along with the find, replace, and spell-checking features introduced in Stickies.

The Format menu enables you to control your font settings and text alignment. In addition, you can toggle wrapping modes, rich text and plain text, and hyphenation.

Rulers

During the discussion of Stickies, you learned that find/replace and spell checking are common features in Mac OS X applications. The Ruler, accessed from the Text option of the Format menu in TextEdit, is another common component. Using the Ruler, you can visually adjust tabs and other layout features of the active document. You can also use it to easily and visually change formatting and placement of text.

Ink

Mac OS X 10.2 includes a handwriting recognition feature called Ink, which enables you to write input to any application including word processing programs, e-mail clients, and even Web browsers. Built on Apple's Recognition Engine, Ink requires no special alphabet, although people with messy handwriting might require practice to understand how Ink interprets characters. Figure 3.9 shows Ink being used with Mail, Mac OS X's built-in e-mail program.

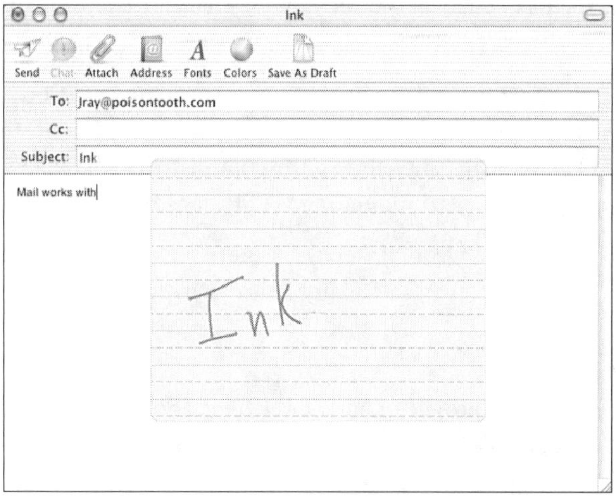

FIGURE 3.9

Ink enables you to set your keyboard and mouse aside.

To run Ink, you must have a Wacom graphics tablet with a USB connector. You must also install the Wacom tablet driver for Mac OS X, available for download from http://www.wacom.com/. A wizard guides you through the installation steps. A Tablet Preferences window, in which you can set such things as pressure sensitivity and click rate, appears when installation is complete. (If you need more information about downloads or software installation, read Hour 4, "Installing New Applications.") By the time you read this, additional tablet drivers might be available.

When a graphics tablet is plugged into one of your computer's USB ports, an Ink icon shows up under the Hardware section of System Preferences. The Ink Preferences panel gives you options to turn handwriting recognition on or off and to change several settings.

Turning on handwriting recognition will launch the InkBar, a toolbar that floats on top of all other application windows. From the InkBar, you can toggle between handwriting recognition mode and pointer mode, select common menu command and keyboard shortcut characters, and open InkPad, as shown in Figure 3.10. With InkPad open, you can switch between the writing and drawing modes using the buttons at the lower left.

FIGURE 3.10

InkPad appears below the InkBar to provide a space for you to write or draw.

The text or drawings you create in InkPad can be inserted into other documents. Simply create the content of your choice in the workspace, and click the Send button to add it to the active document at the current insertion point. For instance, when you finish composing the text of an e-mail message, you could sign your name in the drawing view of InkPad and insert your signature at the bottom of your message. Note, however, that you cannot insert pictures into applications that don't support image display.

Although InkPad enables you to compose your additions before you add them to a document, you can also write directly into a program, as shown in Figure 3.9. To do add text directly to an application, touch the stylus to the tablet to open a writing space with guiding lines in which to form characters and begin writing words. If a writing space doesn't appear, try touching the stylus to the graphics tablet in a different place. Because your stylus can also act as a mouse, some areas of the screen, such as window controls or menus, activate commands other than opening a writing space.

Although Ink doesn't require you to learn special letter forms, you must write linearly—as if you were using paper—rather than writing letters on top of one another as you would on a personal digital assistant (PDA). When you pause, your markings are converted to text at the top of the writing space. To correct a mistake, draw a long horizontal line from right to left and pause to see the last character disappear. If you have larger sections to delete, switch to pointer mode in the InkBar, select the part you want to redo, and switch back to writing mode to try again.

Some applications that don't use standard Mac OS X text controls behave unpredictably with Ink's text recognition. If you're using an application in which spaces don't appear between words as needed, try writing your content in InkPad and using Send to insert it in the other application.

Ink Preferences

Now that you know a little about what Ink is and how it works, let's take a look at the Ink Preferences tabs. The following adjustments can be made under the Settings tab:

- **Allow me to write**—Choose whether you can write to all programs or only InkPad.

- **My handwriting style is**—Move the slider to describe your handwriting as closely spaced, widely spaced, or somewhere in between.

- **InkPad font**—Set a font for InkPad. For greatest accuracy, Apple recommends keeping the font set to Apple Casual, which contains letter shapes that are the most similar to those recognized by Ink, so that you can model your writing after it.

- **Play sound while writing**—Check this box to activate the sound of pen scratching against paper while you write.

Clicking the Options button opens a sheet with additional handwriting recognition options, including the amount of delay before writing is converted to type, how much the stylus must move before a stroke is recorded, how long the pen must be held still to act as a mouse, and several other options. If you change your mind about configuration you've made in either the Settings tab or the Options sheet, choose Restore Defaults to revert to the originals.

The Gestures tab displays shapes that have special meaning in Ink, such as vertical or horizontal spaces, tab, and delete. Click on an item to see both a demonstration of drawing the shape and a written description of it. You can also activate or deactivate Gesture actions using the check box in front of each item. Apple recommends that you provide extra space in front of a Gesture shape and exaggerate the ending stroke so that the system does not confuse it with a letter.

The Word List tab enables you to add uncommon words that you use frequently. Ink uses a list of common words to help decipher people's input. If you come across a word that Ink doesn't know, click the Add button and type the new word in the text box.

Chess

The only game application bundled with Mac OS X is Chess (path: /Applications/Chess), a full-featured chess game that includes support for speech recognition. The Chess interface, shown in Figure 3.11, is simply beautiful.

 In all honesty, the underlying chess engine isn't Apple's, but that of GNUChess, a free chess application available for the UNIX platform since the mid-1980s.

FIGURE 3.11
Chess is a GUI front end to GNUChess.

When Chess starts, it displays a new board ready for play. Move a piece by dragging it from its original position to the location you want. If a move is invalid, Mac OS X plays the system beep, refuses the move, and displays a message in the window's title bar.

Preferences

To control the game's difficulty or to change to a computer-computer or human-human game, open the Chess Preferences dialog box. Use Chess's preferences to control how difficult the game will be, who is playing, and whether speech recognition should be used.

> If you're using speech recognition, be aware that Chess recognizes only a few patterns to control your pieces:
>
> `<Piece> <Square> to/takes <Square>`
>
> `Castle kingside`
>
> `Castle queenside`
>
> `Take back move`
>
> For example, `pawn b2 to b4` is a valid opening move.

Finally, if you've selected the Computer vs. Computer option in the Chess Preferences dialog box, the game won't start until you click the Start Computer Vs. Computer Game button in the Controls dialog box, which is accessed via the Game menu.

Menus

You can access a few additional preferences by choosing the Controls option from the Game menu. In the Controls dialog box, each player is represented by a chess piece, as shown in Figure 3.12. Beneath each player's settings is a white progress bar. When the computer is thinking about a move, the bar fills in from left to right to indicate how close the computer is to making a move. To force the computer to move before it has finished thinking, click the Force Computer To Move button.

Clicking the color well to the right of the player name launches the system Colors panel where you can choose a new color for each player's pieces. The color is not applied until you click the Set Piece Colors button. Keep in mind, however, that the game still makes references to the pieces using their original colors.

The Move menu is used to ask for a hint and to replay or take back the last move. In a sense, the Move menu lets you cheat.

Use the View menu to toggle between a grayscale two-dimensional representation of the board (Shift+Command+A) and the default 3D board (Shift+Command+B).

FIGURE 3.12
Use the Controls dialog box to set some additional game preferences.

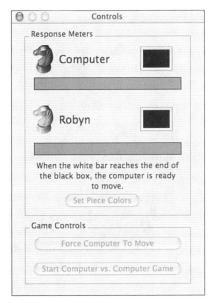

Summary

Mac OS X includes a wealth of applications and utilities, ranging from the simple (but not so simple!) Stickies to a full-featured, voice-controlled Chess application. The experience of using one application applies to the next, and so on. This is especially true for Stickies and TextEdit, which use the Mac OS X system-level spell-checking and font controls, as do many other applications.

Q&A

Q I changed my TextEdit preferences, but they don't seem to be changed. Did I do something wrong?

A Results are inconsistent when changes are applied in TextEdit. When making changes, try exiting TextEdit and relaunching it to ensure that your settings become active.

Q Can speech recognition be used with applications other than Chess?

A Speech recognition is built to work throughout the operating system. We talk about using Speakable Items in Hour 18, "Accessibility Features and Additional System Preferences."

Q Can I get other games for Mac OS X?

A Yes. You can find many games for Mac OS X at
`http://www.versiontracker.com/macosx/` by searching for *game*. We talk about
how to download and set up additional software in the next hour, "Installing New
Applications."

Workshop

The workshop contains quiz questions and activities to help you solidify your understanding of the material covered. Try to answer all questions before looking at the
"Answers" section that follows.

Quiz

1. In which folder are Calculator, Clock, Stickies, TextEdit, and Chess found?
2. Where do you set preferences for these applications?

Answers

1. The system Applications folder
2. Under Preferences in their self-titled application menus located in the menu bar,
   except for Calculator, which has no preferences

Activities

Give Calculator, Clock, Stickies, TextEdit, and Chess a try. Bonus: Using Services (under
the application menu of TextEdit), make a sticky note from a text passage.

Hour **4**

Installing New Applications

Although Mac OS X comes with many programs and tools offering a wide range of features, at some point you'll probably want to add additional software to your system. In this hour, we talk about how to install additional software in Mac OS X. Even though software installation is not difficult, Mac OS X support several different methods of doing so.

We also look at software sources and several standout applications that are available for download. Over the next hour, you'll

- Learn common installation methods
- Delve into software issues for multiuser systems
- Discover interesting applications available for your system

Software Sources

When it comes to expanding your collection of software, your first question might be "What are my options?" You'll be pleased to hear that, despite being a relatively new operating system, Mac OS X already has many available applications. The only tricky part is knowing where to find them.

Fortunately, a number of good online libraries feature Mac OS X software. (If you need to learn more about how to get online or how use a Web browser, those topics are discussed in Hours 9, "Setting Up Mac OS X Networking," and 10, "Web Browsing and .Mac. Membership.")

The following sites present the latest and greatest Mac OS X programs that are available for download or on CD-ROM (by purchase):

- **VersionTracker**—www.versiontracker.com/vt_mac_osx.shtml —Updated continually, VersionTracker's Web site is often the first to carry new Mac OS X software. As a nearly comprehensive catalog, it also works as a handy reference guide. To find what you need, just type the name or a keyword for a product into the search field.
- **Mac OS X Apps**—www.macosxapps.com/—This site features in-depth discussions about new software and uses.
- **Apple's Mac OS X Downloads**—www.apple.com/downloads/macosx/—Although less up-to-the-minute than the previous two sites, Apple's software compendium is well documented and easily navigated.

Later in this hour, we recommend several interesting applications on these sites that you might want to try.

Task: Downloading and Installing Software

Although there's no single installation technique for all software that's available for the Mac OS X, you'll see in this hour that there are two common methods. Obviously, you should read the documentation that comes with your software if you want to be certain of the results, but for those who are anxious to double-click, this section offers a basic description of what to expect.

If you would rather purchase your software from a mail-order or in-store vendor, just make sure to read the product information to ensure compatibility with Mac OS X, or with Mac OS 9 if you need to run the application in Classic mode, as discussed in Appendix B, "Running Classic Applications." The installation process for disc images (explained later in the hour) still applies.

After you locate a piece of software you want to try, you're ready to begin:

1. On the software download page, determine which version your system requires and click that link. Be sure to choose a version that's made for Mac OS X.

2. If you're using Internet Explorer, your system begins downloading your selection, and a Download Manager window, similar to that shown in Figure 4.1, appears on your screen.

FIGURE 4.1

You can monitor the status of an item as it downloads.

File	Status	Time	Transferred
Virex_7.1.dmg	Complete	About one minute	3.5 MB
V7020718.dmg	Complete	< 1 minute	2.9 MB
RealOnePlayerOSX...	Complete	< 1 minute	4.7 MB
neko_saver.0_91a...	Complete	< 1 minute	33 KB
PixelNhance.dmg		< 1 minute	1.1 MB of 3.9 MB, 159 KB/sec

3. When the download is finished, several icons appear on your desktop, similar to Figure 4.2. The icon with the extension .gz represents a special file that has been encoded for easy storage and download. We'll talk more about this in the "Opening Compressed Files with StuffIt Expander" section of this hour. Another common type of download file ends with a .sit extension and contains the same files, but in an unencoded and compressed form.

4. The final installation step could differ, depending on the application you're working with. Here are the three major variations:

   If a folder icon appears on your desktop, you must open it to reach the application file. The folder also usually contains a ReadMe file that explains what to do next. This kind of install exists only for very small programs.

   If a file icon with the extension .pkg or .mpkg appears, double-clicking will start the Apple Installer, which provides a simple step-by-step guide to installation.

Finally, if a disk image icon appears, as with the Chimera disk icon shown second from the bottom in Figure 4.2, double-clicking it mounts the disk, which you can then double click to open a Finder window that contains instructions. Disk images have the .dmg file extension.

For example, when installing the Chimera Web browser, opening the disk icon results in the screen shown in 4.3, which contains an icon for you to drag to the Applications folder on your hard drive.

FIGURE 4.2

When you download software, several new icons appear on the desktop.

FIGURE 4.3

To install Chimera, simply drag the image to a folder in a Finder window.

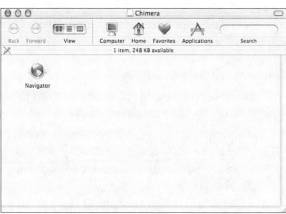

When you've placed the file or folder where you want it, your application is ready for use. You can drag all the files that appeared on your desktop during download and installation to the Trash.

Opening Compressed Files with StuffIt Expander

You might have noticed that the downloaded files launch another application whose icon appears briefly in the Dock, as shown in Figure 4.4. That application is StuffIt Expander.

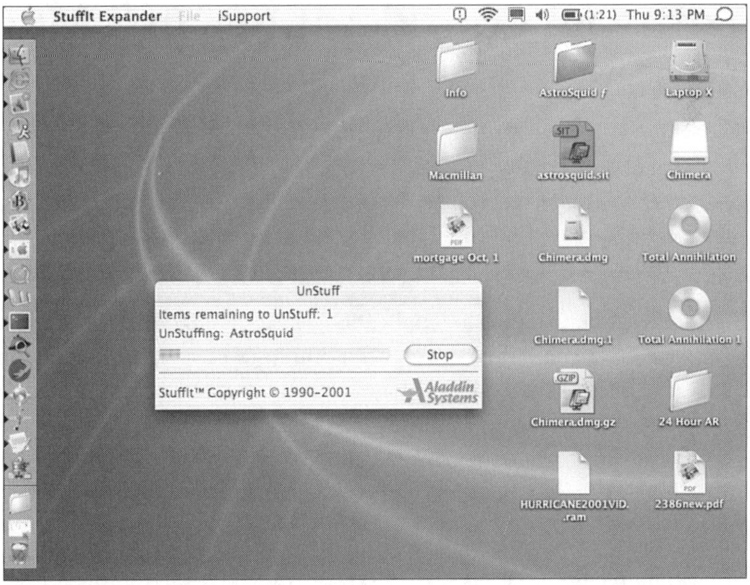

FIGURE 4.4

When the download is finished, StuffIt Expander goes to work.

You need StuffIt for use with compressed files. Because applications tend to be very large files, they come in a compressed form that takes up less space and makes downloading them faster and easier. These compressed files are also referred to as *archive files* because they're compact and easily stored.

Compression can be done in several different ways. Mac OS X supports the same methods used on the Macintosh system for the past decade, including .sit (StuffIt) files. In addition, it supports UNIX standards, such as .tar and .gz files.

To install applications that come as archive files, you must return them to their original state. Recovering a full-sized file from its archive file is known as *extraction*. That's where StuffIt Expander, a tool included with Mac OS X, comes into play.

StuffIt Expander uncompresses most common archive types, and makes it simple for anyone to start downloading software. Most of the time, StuffIt Expander opens automatically when it's needed and leaves uncompressed folders on the desktop along with the original archive file. An example of this was shown in Figure 4.2 (the icon with the .gz text below it).

StuffIt Expander is located on your system at Applications/Utilities/StuffIt Expander. You might never need to start it manually, but you can use a number of settings in its Preferences dialog box to control actions, such as how StuffIt deals with files after extraction.

Software Considerations in a Multiuser System

Mac OS X is a multiuser system. When it comes to installing software, this seemingly small detail really matters. For one thing, not all users might have the same privileges on the system. When you set up user accounts, as will be explained in Hour 15, "Sharing Your System: Multiple Users," you have the option to prevent others from modifying the system in any way. That includes installing additional software.

Also, when you install applications, keep in mind that other users don't necessarily have access to your home directory. If you install a large application in your home directory, you might be the only person who can use it, which could lead to other users installing copies of this same application on the same machine. To best utilize disk space and resource sharing, major applications should be installed in the system's Applications folder or in a subdirectory of Applications, rather than inside your home directory.

One other issue: Be sure to read your software license agreements regarding operation by multiple users. If an application is licensed for only a single user (rather than a single computer), it should not be placed in the Applications folder where any Mac OS X user can have access.

Some Software Suggestions

For the rest of the hour, we look at some applications currently available for Mac OS X. These programs have been selected based on their unique features and immediate availability (either in full or demo form) over the Internet.

Although we recommend the following software, keep in mind that many other fine programs are available and that number grows daily. The following should serve only as a starting point for exploring the possibilities.

Useful Applications

Even before Mac OS X was released, developers were looking forward to exploiting its advanced networking, multitasking, and graphics capabilities. The following sections describe a few interesting applications. Some you might have heard of, whereas others are entirely new to the Mac platform.

Mozilla

Mozilla (www.mozilla.org) is a Web browser related to Netscape Communicator—in fact, it's the open source project from which recent versions of Netscape were developed. The Mozilla software developers emphasize standards compliance and stability, and their product includes many new features before they appear in Netscape. (Chimera, a version of Mozilla built especially for Mac OS X, is also available.)

OmniWeb

OmniWeb, by the Omni Group (www.omnigroup.com/), is an alternative Web browser with some amazing features. For example, if you've been annoyed by Web sites that spontaneously open lots of new browser windows that fill your screen, you can limit JavaScript's capability to open new windows. In addition, OmniWeb has a top-notch rendering engine that produces crisp pages and is an excellent choice for online presentations.

Games

As you learned in the previous hour, the only game packaged with Mac OS X is Chess, but that doesn't mean you can't download other favorites. If you're looking for recreation, try one of these:

- **Burning Monkey Solitaire** (www.freeverse.com/flash/bms.mgi) offers several versions of the Solitaire card game, including Klondike, Freecell, and 52 Card Pick-up, delivered in an interface filled with taunting monkeys, as shown in Figure 4.5.
- **Battle Cocoa** (eng.osxdev.org/battlecocoa/), which was written especially for Mac OS X using Cocoa, is a smooth-playing Tetris clone with network play capacity.

Screensavers

Mac OS X comes with several attractive screensavers, but many people delight in finding new and interesting ones. Spice up your system by downloading one of these excellent replacements:

4

- **Mac OS X Screensavers 3.0** (`www.epicware.com/macosxsavers.html`) is a collection of popular screensavers that have been transplanted from another platform. Although several years old, this set is still pleasing to the eye.

- **Neko.saver**
  (`homepage.mac.com/takashi_hamada/Acti/MacOSX/Neko/index.html`) turns one or more animated cats loose on your desktop to play, sleep, and scamper across your screen.

FIGURE 4.5

Burning Monkey Solitaire offers traditional Solitaire in an untraditional setting.

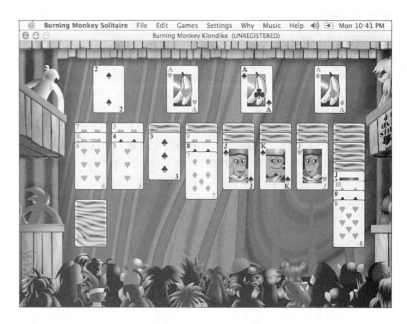

To install a screensaver, simply place its application file in the system folder Library/Screen Savers or in your own ~/Library/Screen Savers folder, depending on whether you want public or private access. Remember that after you've installed a new screensaver, you still must choose it in the your ScreenEffects Preferences to activate it.

Summary

In this hour, we discussed the basics of adding new software—from finding what you need to downloading and installing it. Although we focused on easy-to-obtain, downloadable software, the issues we discussed also apply to purchased software discs. Remember that, in Mac OS X, it matters where you place new applications on your system.

Q&A

Q Now that I've learned how to install software, how do I uninstall it?

A To uninstall most software, simply locate the application file or folder and drag it to the Trash. Under Mac OS X, you should find most application folders in the systemwide Applications folder.

One thing to note: There are programs that install invisible files elsewhere in your system. Hour 23, "Security Considerations," tells you how to find such files.

Q I tried to drag a disk image to the Trash, but I get an error message saying the item is in use. What's going on?

A To eject a disk image from your computer, you can't be running the software contained on that disk.

What has most likely occurred is that you didn't copy the contents of the disk image to your hard drive and are instead working off the disk image. To fix the problem, close the file, and then copy the disk image to the Mac OS X drive. Now the disk image should eject.

Workshop

4

The workshop contains quiz questions and activities to help you solidify your understanding of the material covered. Try to answer all questions before looking at the "Answers" section that follows.

Quiz

1. Where in your system should you install software that you don't want to share with other users of the computer?

2. Which application that comes with Mac OS X uncompresses archive files?

Answers

1. In your home folder

2. StuffIt Expander

Activities

Go to one of the Web sites listed at the beginning of the hour and find an application you want to try. Download and install it, making sure to place the application in the correct place on the hard drive.

PART II
Graphics and Multimedia

Hour

HOUR 5

iTunes

Steve Jobs has spent a lot of time recently talking about making the Mac OS the center of your digital lifestyle. Mac OS X 10.2 carries this vision forward with the inclusion of iTunes 3. This application gives you access to audio media in a straightforward and entertaining manner, and features such as Smart Playlist and user ratings make organization a snap. In this hour, you learn how to

- Create and manage a digital music collection
- Visualize your music with amazing graphics
- Burn customized CDs with ease

iTunes

If you like music, iTunes can serve as your CD player, MP3 ripper, song organizer, jukebox, eye candy, and CD burner. Amazingly, iTunes is simple enough to use that even if you've never burned a CD, ripped an MP3, or listened to Internet radio, you can be doing all three within five minutes—tops.

First Run Setup

The first time you launch iTunes, it runs through a setup assistant to locate MP3s and configure Internet playback. At any time during the setup procedure, click Next to go to the next step, or click Previous to return to the preceding step. Clicking Cancel exits the setup utility and starts iTunes.

The first step of the setup process, displayed in Figure 5.1, enables you to set Internet access options.

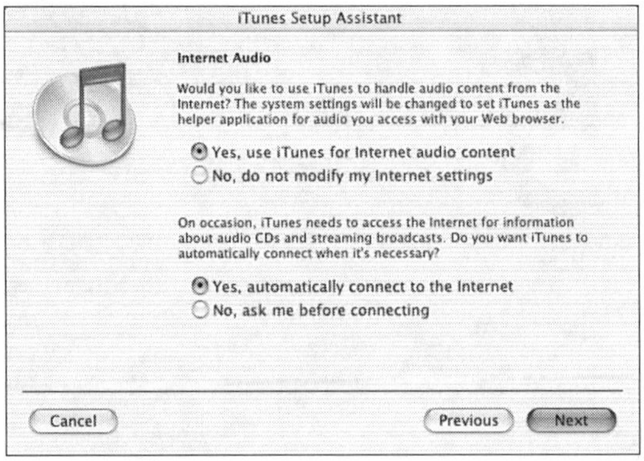

FIGURE 5.1

Choose how iTunes works with your Internet applications.

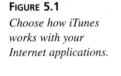

iTunes is perfectly suited for handling streaming MP3s. If you've never listened to Internet radio before, you'll appreciate how quickly and easily iTunes enables you to find the type of music you want to hear and start listening. If you already have a streaming music player, tell iTunes not to modify your Internet settings.

iTunes also interacts with the Internet to look up information about your CDs, such as the artist and song title. The Yes, Automatically Connect to the Internet radio button, selected by default, enables this feature. To force iTunes to prompt you before connecting to the Internet, click No, Ask Me Before Connecting. Click Next when you're satisfied with your responses.

During the final step of the configuration, you're prompted to decide how iTunes will find MP3s: By default, iTunes locates all the MP3 files on your drive. To disable this feature, click No, I'll Add Them Myself Later. The process of searching the drive for MP3 files can take a while, so I prefer to add MP3s when I want to.

Click Done to begin using iTunes.

The iTunes Interface

Everything you need to do anything in iTunes is found in the main window, pictured in Figure 5.2. The main control areas are listed here.

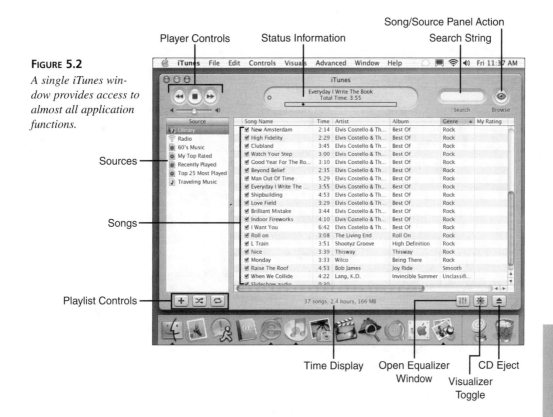

FIGURE 5.2

A single iTunes window provides access to almost all application functions.

Player Controls—The player controls move between different songs, play, pause, and adjust the output volume of the currently playing track. Clicking directly on the sound slider moves the volume adjustment immediately to that level.

Status Information—Displays information about the currently playing song. The top line displays the artist, the name of the song, and the name of the album. Clicking each of the status lines toggles between different types of information. Likewise, the Elapsed Time line can be toggled to display remaining time and total time.

The progress bar shows how far the playback of the current song has progressed. Dragging the progress bar handle moves the playback back or forward in the audio track.

Finally, a stereo frequency monitor can be displayed by clicking the arrow on the right of the status display.

Search String—Typing a few letters into the iTunes Search field immediately displays all audio tracks in the current playlist or library that match the string in any way (artist, song, album).

Song/Source Panel Action—The action button performs a different function depending on what source is currently being viewed. As you work in different areas of the program, this button changes to an appropriate action for that area:

- **Library**—When viewing the main song library, the action button toggles between two different browse modes. The first mode, shown in Figure 5.2, is similar to the Finder's List view. Each audio track is listed on its own line. The second mode uses a layout similar to the Column Finder view: The first column lists the artist and the second column shows the albums for that artist. Finally, a lower pane shows a list of the song tracks for that artist and album.

- **Radio Tuner**—The Radio Tuner's action button is Refresh, which reloads all available stations from the iTunes Internet radio station browser.

- **Playlist**—A *playlist* is your own personal list of music that you've compiled from the main library. Playlists are the starting point for creating a CD. When viewing a playlist, the action button is Burn CD.

- **CD**—When a CD is inserted, iTunes prepares to import the tracks to MP3 files. The action button is Import when a CD is selected as the source.

- **Visual Effects**—No matter what source is selected, iTunes can always be toggled to Visualizer mode to display dazzling onscreen graphics. When the visual effects are active, the action button becomes Options for controlling the visual effects.

Source—The Source pane lists the available MP3 sources. Attached MP3 players, CDs, playlists, the central music Library, and Radio Tuner make up the available sources.

 Double-clicking a source icon opens a new window with only the contents of that source. This is a nice way to create a cleaner view of your audio files.

Songs—A list of the songs in the currently selected source. When in the main Library view, you can click the action button to toggle between a simple list and a column-based browser. Double-clicking a song in the list starts playback of the selected list beginning at that song. To change the visible fields in the list, choose View Options from the Edit menu. Among the available pieces of information for each song are Name, Time, Artist, Album, Genre, Play Count, and the time it was Last Played.

Playlist Controls—Three playlist controls are available: Create Playlist, Shuffle Order, and Loop. As their names suggest, these buttons can be used to create new playlists and control the order in which the audio tracks are played back.

Time Display—At the bottom of the iTunes window is information about the contents, playing time, and total file size of the currently selected source. The default mode displays approximate time—clicking the text toggles to precise playing time.

Open Equalizer Window—The Equalizer, shown in Figure 5.3, enables you to choose preset frequency levels by musical genre or to set them manually by dragging the sliders. The mode defaults to Flat, which means all the controls are set in the middle of their range.

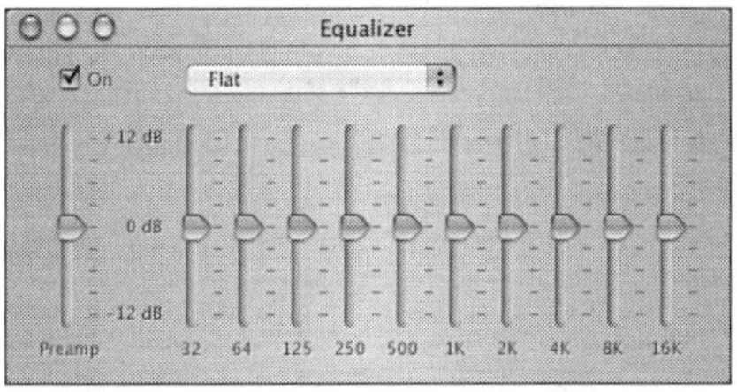

FIGURE 5.3

Choose how iTunes plays your music using iTunes' built-in equalizer.

Visualizer Toggle—Turns the visualization effects ("music for the eyes") on and off.

CD Eject—Ejects the currently inserted CD.

So, now that you know what the controls are for, let's take a look at putting iTunes through its paces.

Adding MP3s

Encoding, or ripping, CDs enables you to take the tracks from a CD and save them in the MP3 (MPEG Layer 3) format. MP3 is a highly compressed audio format that has become very popular in recent years—much to the dismay of the recording industry.

Those with .Mac memberships have access to free music through their iDisk under Software/Extras/FreePlay Music. Categories include Pop, Techno, Country, and TV Themes. You learn more about other features of .Mac membership in Hour 10, "Web Browsing and .Mac Membership."

To encode your own MP3 files from a CD, find the CD you want to use and then follow these steps:

1. Insert the CD into your Macintosh.

2. iTunes queries an Internet CD database to get the names of all the tracks on your disk. During iTunes setup, if you chose to not have this happen automatically, select Get CD Track Names from the Advanced menu and press the Stop button.

3. Click the CD name in the Source pane to display all the available tracks.

4. Select the tracks you want to encode. If no tracks are selected, the entire CD is imported.

5. Click the Import action button to encode the selected tracks. As the tracks are importing, the CD plays and a small graphic appears to show whether it has been imported or is currently being imported.

The CDDB Internet database contains information on hundreds of thousands of CDs. In the unlikely event that your CD isn't located, it is listed as Untitled.

After you add songs to your Music Library, iTunes enables you to easily assign ratings to them. Simply locate the My Rating column in the song listings and click on the placeholder dots to add from 1 to 5 stars for each song. To sort by rating, simply click the My Rating header.

By default, the encoded MP3s are stored in Music/iTunes/iTunes Music found in your home directory. An entire CD can take from 5–74 minutes to process, depending on the speed of your CD-ROM drive. To pass the time, you can continue to use iTunes while the tracks are imported. When the import finishes, your computer chimes and the MP3s are available under the Library source listing.

If iTunes couldn't find your song information, or you aren't connected to the Internet, you can edit each MP3 file's stored artist/title information by hand by selecting the file and choosing Get Info (Command+I) from the File menu.

You can even submit your updated information back to the Internet CD database by choosing Submit CD Track Names from the Advanced menu.

If you're working with an existing library of MP3s rather than a CD, you can easily add them to your MP3 Library. Use the Add To Library option from the File menu to choose a folder that contains MP3s. Alternatively, you can simply drag a folder of MP3s from the Finder into the Library song list.

The process of importing MP3s takes time. Each MP3 is examined for ID3 tags (which identify information such as artist and title about a song) and is cataloged in the iTunes database. If you're adding MP3s to iTunes from a network drive, be prepared to take a quick lunch break.

Task: Creating and Working with Playlists

The key to many of the remaining iTunes features lies in creating a playlist. As we mentioned earlier, a playlist is nothing more than a list of songs from your Library.

1. To create a new playlist, click the Create Playlist button in the lower-left corner of the iTunes window, or choose New Playlist (Command+N) from the File menu.

2. The new playlist ("untitled playlist") is added to the Source pane. Select the playlist, and then press the Enter key to rename it. The next step is to add songs to the playlist.

3. Select Library in the Source pane.

4. Verify that the song you want is in the main MP3 Library. If it isn't, you must first add the song to the Library.

5. Select one or more songs in the Songs pane.

6. Drag your selection to the playlist in the Source pane.

Using the Smart Playlist option, you can automatically create playlists based on criteria such as genre or your personal song ratings. Simply choose New Smart Playlist from the File menu, set your criteria, and name your playlist. As an added bonus, Smart Playlists can also be set to update themselves with the Live Updating option as new material is added to your Music Library.

The selected songs are added to your playlist. Click the playlist to display the songs. You can drag the tracks within the song pane to choose their order.

Burning CDs and Exporting to MP3 Players

After a playlist has been built, you can drag its name from the Source pane to any listed MP3 player source. The files are automatically copied to the connected player. If the player does not have enough available space, you must remove files from your playlist or select the external player and remove tracks from its memory.

If you have a Mac with a supported CD burner, you can use a playlist to burn an audio CD laid out exactly like the playlist. Click the Burn CD action button in the upper-right corner of the iTunes window, and then follow the onscreen instructions, inserting a recordable CD when prompted. You'll find that the process is very similar to burning CDs from the Finder, which you learned about in Hour 2, "Using the Finder and Dock."

Listening to Internet Radio

Depending on your connection speed, Internet radio could be your ticket to high-quality commercial-free music. Unfortunately, most dial-in modems have poor sound quality, but DSL and cable modem users can listen to much higher quality streams. To see what's available and start listening requires only a few clicks:

1. To display a list of available streaming stations, click Radio in the Source pane. After a few seconds querying a station server, a list of available music genres is displayed.

2. Each genre can be expanded to show the stations in that group by clicking its disclosure triangle. Stations are listed with a Stream (station) name, Bit Rate, and Comment (description). The bit rate determines the quality of the streamed audio— the higher the bit rate, the higher the quality—*and* the higher the bandwidth requirements.

3. Double-click a station to begin playing, or select the station and then click the Play button. iTunes buffers a few seconds of audio, and then starts playing the streaming audio. If iTunes stutters while playing, look for a similar station that uses a lower bit rate.

Conversely to what seems logical, you can drag stations from the Radio Tuner source and play them in a playlist. The playlist plays as it normally would, but starts playing streaming audio when it gets to the added Internet radio station.

You cannot burn a radio station to a CD or store it on an external MP3 device.

Playing Audio

As I'm sure you've discovered by now, the iTunes player controls work on whatever source you currently have selected. After a song plays, iTunes moves to the next song. You can also control the playing via keyboard or from the Controls menu:

- **Play/Stop**—Spacebar
- **Next Song**—Command+right-arrow key
- **Previous Song**—Command+left-arrow key
- **Volume Up**—Command+up-arrow key
- **Volume Down**—Command+down-arrow key
- **Mute**—Option+Command+down-arrow key

Some of these functions are also available from the iTunes Dock icon. Click and hold the Dock icon to display a pop-up menu for moving between the tracks in the current audio source.

To randomize the play order for the selected source, click the Shuffle button (second from the left) in the lower left of the iTunes window. If you want to repeat the tracks, use the Loop button (third from the left) in the lower-left corner to toggle between Repeat Off, Repeat Once, and Repeat All.

The iTunes window is a bit large to conveniently leave onscreen during play-back. Luckily, there are two other window modes that take up far less space. Quite illogically, you access these smaller modes by clicking the window's Maximize button.

After clicking Maximize, the window is reduced to the player controls and status window. Even this window is a bit large for some monitors, though. To collapse it even more, use the resize handle in the lower-right corner of the window.

To restore iTunes to its original state, click the Maximize button again.

Visualizer

The iTunes Visualizer creates a graphical visualization of your music as it plays. While playing a song, click the Visualizer button (second from the right) in the lower-right corner of the iTunes window, or select the Turn Visualizer On (Command+T) option from the Visuals menu to activate the display. Figure 5.4 shows the Visualizer in action.

FIGURE 5.4

The Visualizer displays images to match your music.

The Visuals menu can control the size of the generated graphics as well as toggle between full-screen (Command+F) and window modes. To exit full-screen mode, press Esc or click the mouse button.

While the windowed Visualizer display is active, the Options action button in the upper-right corner of the window is active. Click this button to fine-tune your Visualizer settings.

Summary

This hour introduced you to iTunes, which can be used to turn your Macintosh into the centerpiece of your entertainment system. The iTunes software can quickly convert your CDs into a library of MP3s or vice versa, and give you access to thousands of radio stations that play the kind of music you want to hear, 24 hours a day. If you're a music enthusiast, Mac OS X is the operating system for you.

Q&A

Q Is it wrong to download MP3s and burn them to CDs?

A It depends on the MP3 you've downloaded. There are thousands of freely available songs on the Internet.

Q How can I control the quality of the MP3s I'm encoding?

A The iTunes application preferences give you access to a variety of MP3 quality settings and even enable you to encode WAV files.

Workshop

The workshop contains quiz questions and activities to help you solidify your understanding of the material covered. Try to answer all questions before looking at the "Answers" section that follows.

Quiz

1. Can anyone use Internet radio stations?
2. Where is the master listing of iTunes songs found?
3. What do you need to set up before you can burn a CD?

Answers

1. Anyone with an Internet connection can use the radio stations, but only the fastest connections will have exceptional quality.
2. The listing of all MP3 files is found by clicking the Library item in the Source pane.
3. To create a CD, you must first set up a playlist containing the songs you want to record.

Activities

Use iTunes to rip a few MP3s from your favorite CDs. After creating your library, make a playlist with the best songs from each CD, and then burn a new CD from the playlist (if possible).

5

HOUR 6

iPhoto

Have a digital camera? If so, you've probably struggled to keep track of image files with names such as 200214057. With Mac OS X, there's an easy way to store, organize, edit, and even share your photographs. It's called iPhoto. iPhoto connects directly to many cameras, so you can skip loading special software. In this hour, you learn how to

- Import photos from your camera
- Organize your image collection with keywords and albums
- Edit and share your work

Using iPhoto

Apple's iPhoto brings all the functions you need for working with digital photographs together in one interface, shown in Figure 6.1, with different modes for Import, Organize, Edit, Book, and Share. You move between modes by clicking the row of buttons under the viewing area.

Many recent digital cameras with USB connections are compatible with iPhoto. You can find out whether yours is one of them at `http://www.apple.com/iphoto/compatibility/`.

Those without digital cameras can still use iPhoto to organize digital images sent from other people and to store scanned images. We talk more about importing files from your hard drive later in this chapter.

The iPhoto interface contains several distinct areas, some of which change depending on the current mode. The bottom pane contains mode-specific functions, and the viewing area at upper right takes on different appearances to support the mode you're in. You can resize the contents of the viewing area using the slider to the right of the mode buttons.

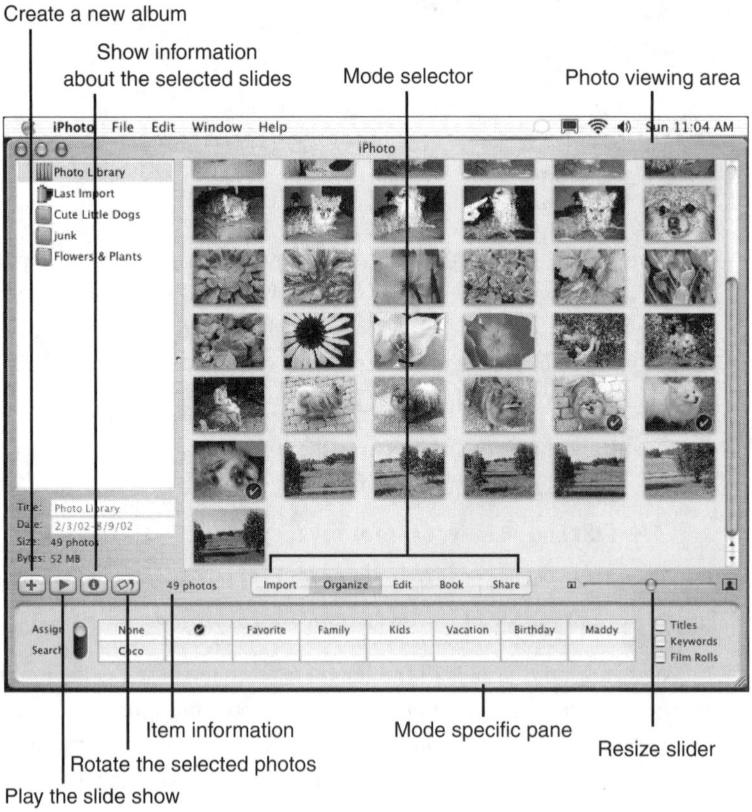

FIGURE 6.1

The iPhoto window contains all the settings you need to import, organize, edit, and share your photos.

The elements along the left side are available regardless of iPhoto's mode. Let's take a look at them now.

The Photo Library contains all the images imported by iPhoto. Last Import is a special unit containing the most recent pictures. Below Last Import are albums, the special sets of pictures you put together. Selecting one of these items fills the viewing area with thumbnail images of its contents.

Below the Photo Library and albums is a section containing information about the selected item. For example, in Figure 6.1, Photo Library is selected, so the information section displays the name of the selection, the date range it contains, and the total file size of its contents. If a specific thumbnail image were selected, the given information would be the image title, date imported, size of image, and file size. You can change the title or the date by typing in those fields.

> Additional details about a selected image can be accessed from the Show Info command in the File menu. This launches a window containing information about the image, file, and originating camera. If your camera supports it, the window also contains technical details such as shutter speed, aperture, and use of flash for the photograph.

There are also four buttons just above the mode-specific pane:

- **Create a new album**—Enables you create a special group of chosen photos that you can arrange in any way or export as a unit. We'll talk more about albums later.

- **Play the slide show**—Plays a full-screen slide show, complete with music, of all the photos currently displayed in the viewing area. You can alter the slide show settings in the iPhoto preference panel, including the length of time each slide plays and the song to accompany the slide show—you can even choose a song from your iTunes folder.

- **Show information about the selected photos**—Toggles the information area through its different configurations, including one containing a field to add comments about the selected photo.

- **Rotate the selected photos**—Rotates the selected items. You can set the rotation direction to clockwise or counterclockwise in the iPhoto application preference dialog.

Importing Image Files

The first time youconnect a supported camera to your computer and set the camera to its playback or transfer mode, iPhoto opens automatically. If it doesn't, you can manually launch iPhoto either from the Dock or the Applications folder. The iPhoto window will be in Import mode.

Mac OS X includes the Image Capture application that downloads images and media files from supported cameras and card readers. It also works with TWAIN-compliant flatbed scanners (given an appropriate driver) to scan images.

The Import pane, shown in Figure 6.2, displays the camera status, Import button, and an option to delete images from the camera after they're stored in iPhoto.

To import the photos on your camera, click the Import button. If the box for Erase Camera Contents After Transfer is checked, the Confirm Move sheet appears and asks you to approve deletion of the original photo files from the camera. Thumbnails of the transferring images appear in the image well of the Import pane. When the import is complete, the new images show up in the photo viewing area.

FIGURE 6.2

The Import mode enables you to follow the progress of your files as they're transferred from the camera to your computer.

 By default, new *rolls* (groups of pictures imported at one time) are added to the bottom of the viewing area, but you can change that to order with most recent at top inside the application preference panel.

To import images already stored on your hard drive or other media, simply select them and drag them onto the Photo Library. Thumbnails appear as if the images were another roll of film.

Organizing Images

After you've imported some image files into iPhoto, switch to the Organize mode to view them conveniently. The iPhoto window in Organize mode, shown in Figure 6.1, looks very similar to the Import mode except for the controls in the bottom pane. Here you can choose whether to show the images in your Photo Library with additional information, including their titles, keywords, and film rolls, using the check boxes at the lower right.

Checking the box for Titles displays the title of each image beneath its thumbnail image. The default titles of images imported by iPhoto are in the form Roll [*number*] – [*image number*], which isn't very helpful. You can give them more meaningful titles as explained earlier.

The Keywords option shows any keywords you've attached to an image file to the right of its thumbnail image. We'll look further at applying keywords in just a moment.

Displaying by Film Rolls divides the photos in the viewing area into sections labeled with roll number, date of import, and number of photos imported.

> You can tell iPhoto whether to order the images by film roll number or date by selecting the appropriate option in the Arrange Photos submenu of the Edit menu.

You can select an image in the viewing area by single-clicking it. You can select a group of consecutive pictures by clicking just outside the edge of the first photo and dragging to create a box connecting all the photos that you want to select, or select a group of non-consecutive pictures by holding down the Command key as you click the desired images.

If you want to delete a photo or several photos that are visible in the viewing area, highlight the photos you don't want to keep and then press the Delete key on your keyboard. You'll see an alert message asking you to confirm permanent deletion of the selected item or items.

> Deletion in iPhoto does not move the items to the Trash—it's permanent. Always check to make sure that the number of selected photos in the alert message matches the number of items you planned to delete and that the highlighted items are really those you intended to select.

6

You can also drag selected photos to your desktop to make additional copies or into a new album, which we'll discuss later in this hour.

Applying Keywords

A good way to organize your photo collection is with keywords. When applied, keywords appear next to the image thumbnails in the viewing area whenever you check the box for Keywords.

You can use the default keywords included in iPhoto or create your own custom keywords. To write your own, choose Edit Keywords from the Edit menu. Then click to highlight a blank keyword button, or click on the existing keyword you want to change, and type a word. When you change an existing keyword, keep in mind that the change is passed along to any photos that were assigned the previous keyword.

To apply keywords to a photo, select its thumbnail in the viewing area and click the buttons for any keywords you want to apply to the photo. The buttons for keywords you've added are highlighted. To remove a keyword, click its highlighted button.

> Included with the keywords is a check mark symbol, which is slightly different than the others. Whereas other keywords are visible only when the Keywords box is checked, the check mark is visible in Organize mode at all times, superimposed in the lower-right corner of the thumbnails it has been applied to. Also, the check box cannot be edited as the other keywords can.

After you've applied keywords, you can search your image collection for photos labeled with a given keyword or combination of keywords. Simply drag the Assign/Search slider to Search and click the desired keywords. The selected keyword buttons are highlighted, and only those pictures that match your search appear in the viewing area. Clicking a highlighted keyword button removes it from the search set. Use the Show All button to return to the full photo listing. Drag the Assign/Search slider back to Assign to leave the Search mode.

> Only 14 editable spaces are available for keywords, including the default keywords. When those spaces are filled, you cannot add additional keywords unless you alter an old one. However, in the Preferences panel launched from the iPhoto application menu, you can set Assign/Search to look in the Comments fields of your images (and prevent it from looking at the keywords altogether). Within a Comments field, you can type any description you want. To reveal a Comments field, click the button for Show Information About Select Photo once or twice to toggle between views.

Task: Creating an Album

You can't arrange the individual images in your Photo Library in just any old way. To choose the sequence of a set of images, you must create an album and add the photos you want to work with. Albums are an especially useful way to organize your photographs into collections, especially if you have a large number of photos. Albums are also a basic unit in iPhoto that's used when creating books, slide shows, and Web pages, which we'll discuss later on.

The option to make a new album is available from any mode in iPhoto. To create a new album, perform the following steps:

1. Click the button showing a + sign near the left edge of the iPhoto window, or choose New Album from the File menu.

2. A dialog box appears, into which you can type a name for your album. (If you change your mind later, you can double-click the name of the album in the album list to type a new one.)

3. When you've named your album, click OK.

The album you created appears at the bottom of the album list at the upper left of the iPhoto interface. If you want to change the order of your albums, select the one you want to move and drag it to a new position. A black bar indicates where the album will be inserted. If you want to remove an album, select it and press the Delete key on your keyboard. Unless the album is empty, you will see an alert asking you to confirm deletion.

To add images to your album, make sure that you're in Organize (or Import) mode and select the images you want from the viewing area. You can select them one at a time or in groups. Drag your selection to your album name until a black border appears around it. As you drag, a faded version of one of the selected images appears behind your cursor, along with a red seal showing how many items you're dragging.

The images within albums are something like aliases on your desktop—you can delete a photo from an album without affecting the original file. However, when you delete an image from the Photo Library, it also disappears from any albums to which it has been added.

After you've created an album and added images, you can open the album and drag the contents into any order you want. You can also remove images from the album by selecting them and pressing the Delete key on your keyboard.

Editing Photos

iPhoto's Edit mode enables you to improve your existing photos by resizing them and adjusting their coloration. To edit a photo, select it in Organize mode and click the Edit button. You'll see a screen similar to that shown in Figure 6.3. While in Edit mode, you can use the Previous and Next buttons at bottom right to move through a group of images without going back into Organize mode.

6

When editing a photo that's been added to an album, bear in mind that any changes appear in both the Photo Library and the album.

FIGURE 6.3

In Edit mode, you can crop your images or change their color properties.

A major function available in Edit mode is *cropping* or trimming away the unimportant edges around a subject. iPhoto enables you to constrain the size of your cropped images to fit the common photos sizes 4×6, 5×7, and 8×10, as well as ratios such as square, 4×3, and a size to fit the resolution of your monitor.

Depending on the resolution of the images produced by your digital camera, you might not be able to crop to a small section of a photo without the resulting image becoming grainy or fuzzy. This is especially a problem if you plan to order prints from your photos because the images might look okay onscreen, but could be unsuitable for printing. When ordering prints or books, watch out for the low-resolution warning symbol, which appears when creating a book or ordering prints if iPhoto determines that an image's resolution is not sufficient for the requested size of the finished image.

To crop an image, open it in Edit mode and follow these steps:

1. Set a Constrain option if you want to maintain a specific image ratio.

2. In the viewing area, place your mouse pointer at one corner of the object or scene you want to select. Click and drag to form a selection box around it, as shown earlier in Figure 6.3. To reposition the selection box, move your mouse pointer to the center of the selected area until it changes to a hand and then drag the box where you want it.

3. Click the Crop button to apply your change and see the result in the viewing area.

If you find that you don't like the look of the cropped image as well as the original, you can undo your most recent edit by choosing Undo from the Edit menu.

> After you make changes to images in iPhoto, you can always revert to the image as it was first imported by choosing Revert to Original from the File menu. This enables you to make changes freely without fear of losing your original. However, if you achieve an effect you like, you might want to duplicate the photo in that state before trying additional edits. To do so, select the desired photo and choose Duplicate from the File menu. That way, choosing Revert to Original after further editing returns you to that state instead of the original form of the image.

In addition to cropping, you can edit your images with the Brightness and Contrast sliders. Brightness makes a photo brighter or darker overall—it can fix minor problems from underexposure or overexposure. Contrast increases the difference between light and dark elements by making lighter areas lighter and darker areas darker. Contrast also increases the saturation of colors. Although these settings are good for small corrections, keep in mind that they can't save a photograph shot in really poor light conditions.

The Red-Eye and Black & White features enable you to change the coloration of entire photos or the area within a selection box. The Red-Eye option is most useful for reducing red tint from the eyes of people and pets, but it also removes the red tones from any selected area. To correct red eye, mark a crop selection box as tightly around the red eyes as possible and then click the Red-Eye button. Use the Black & White option to convert an entire image to black-and-white or create interesting effects by selecting portions to convert.

Designing a Photo Book

Book mode, shown in Figure 6.4, is a specialized option that's used to arrange an album's photos into a book format, including supporting text. You can then order copies of your book in the Share mode, as we'll discuss later.

In the Book options pane, the Theme pop-up menu enables you to choose a basic style, including Story Book, Picture Book, and Catalog. The options differ in their picture layouts and built-in text areas. When you choose a theme, the photos in the selected album are placed in a basic template in the order they appear in the album. The individual pages appear in a row at the bottom of the photo viewing area.

It's best to choose the look you want for your book carefully before you start customizing it. If you change from one theme to another, you lose any text or special page formatting you've made.

FIGURE 6.4

Book mode enables you to lay out the photos in an album as a book.

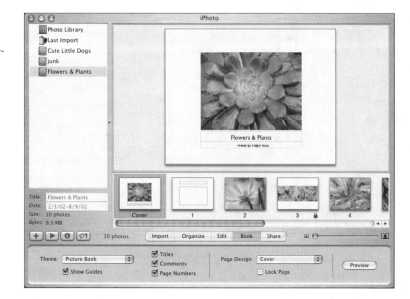

Check boxes in the Book options pane also enable you to choose whether to show image Titles, Comments, and book Page Numbers on the pages, if the theme you've chosen includes space for them.

You can also choose whether to show guides for the text boxes. You should check the Show Guides box if you want to edit the text. To edit text within a text area, select a page and type inside the space. If you want to check your spelling for a given page or change the font of an entire book, you can do so by choosing Check Spelling from the Spelling submenu of the Edit menu.

When you choose a theme, photos in the selected album are inserted into a basic page template in the order in which they appear in your album. For example, the first image in the album is the default cover shot. The Page Design pop-up menu enables you to adjust the templates to show more or fewer images on a selected page. If you like the composition of some of the pages and don't want them to be shifted when you apply new templates to other pages, you must select the pages and check the Lock Page box. You can alter the layout of any page except the cover.

 You can change the order of whole pages by dragging them to a new position. However, to change the cover photo, you must go into Organize mode and rearrange the images in your album to place another photo first. Any changes made to page order in your book are reflected in the order of images in the album.

To get a better feel for the chosen layout, use the Preview button to page through your book in a separate window.

Sharing Your Photos

The Share mode, shown in Figure 6.5, offers a variety of ways for you to share your photos with others, both in print and onscreen.

FIGURE 6.5
The options for sharing your photos range from printing to creating Web pages.

| Print | Slide Show | Mail | Order Prints | Order Book | HomePage | Desktop | Screen Saver | Export |

Sharing Printed Photos

For those who want to share their photos the traditional way, iPhoto offers three button choices at the bottom of the window: Print, Order Prints, or Order Book.

Clicking the Print button enables you make print settings for the selected item, including page size, margin width, and number of copies. If you select the Photo Library but not a specific photo, you can print the entire group.

The Order Prints and Order Book buttons connect you to remote Web sites where you can choose what to order and supply your billing information. You can order prints of your pictures just as you would with pictures captured on film, or you can order a bound book of an album as you designed it using the book mode. If you order a book, keep in mind that the base size is 10 pages. If your book has fewer than 10 pages, several pages at the end are left blank. Also, additional charges are made on a page-by-page basis for books of more than 10 pages.

Sharing Photos Digitally

To share your photos digitally with others, use the Mail, HomePage, or Export features.

6

The Mail option enables you to easily email a photo stored in iPhoto. Clicking the Mail button brings up a dialog box in which you can choose the size of the image and whether to include the image title and comments. Click the Compose button to open a mail window containing the selected photograph and then add the email address of the recipient.

If you are a .Mac member, clicking the HomePage button enables you to select up to 48 images from your Photo Library or a specific album to insert into a basic Web page layout to be stored in your .Mac account. You can view a sample page at `homepage.mac.com/robynness/PhotoAlbum2.html`. You'll learn more about .Mac services in Hour 10, "Web Browsing and .Mac Membership."

Clicking the Export button provides three easy methods to take your images outside of iPhoto. File Export enables you to generate photograph files in JPEG, TIFF, or PNG format. You can also choose an image size and where to save the new file. The Web Page option is similar to the HomePage option discussed earlier, except that a basic Web page and supporting files are saved to your computer so that you can edit and place them on any Web server you would normally use. The QuickTime tab enables you to create an exportable slide show from selected images, an album, or your entire Photo Library. You'll learn more about QuickTime as a media format in Hour 7, "QuickTime and iMovie."

Viewing Your Own Digital Photos

In addition to sharing your photos with others, you can also enjoy them at your own computer with the iPhoto Slide Show and the Desktop and Screen Saver options.

The Slide Show option brings up a dialog box in which you can set the duration each image stays onscreen, whether the slides repeat, and which music accompanies the show. These are the same slide show options that are available in the application Preferences dialog box, and adjusting them in either place has the same effect. When you've made your settings, clicking OK starts the iPhoto slide show.

The Desktop option enables you to choose a single photo from your collection for use as a desktop background. To set a desktop, simply select the image you want and click Desktop. Your desktop background is immediately replaced with the selected image. To change your background back to a non-iPhoto background, open the Desktop panel of System Preferences and choose a new image.

With Screen Saver, you can set an entire album for use as your desktop screen saver. After clicking the Screen Saver icon to set an album, you must open the Screen Effect system preferences panel and choose the Pictures folder to activate your screen saver.

Summary

This hour covered the different modes of iPhoto: Import, Organize, Edit, Book, and Share. You learned how to make albums and lay out your own photo book. You also looked at the various ways in which iPhoto helps your share your images both through print and onscreen.

Q&A

Q I have a digital camera, but it's not compatible with iPhoto. What should I do?

A If your digital camera isn't compatible with iPhoto, Apple recommends using a peripheral device to read the camera's memory card directly. The type of storage media used by your camera dictates whether you need a PCMCIA Flash Card reader or some other kind.

Q Can I use another photo-editing program on the images I've imported to iPhoto?

A Yes. To open an iPhoto image file in another program, click and drag an image thumbnail from the Organize view onto the icon for the photo-editing program. If you plan to edit with an outside program frequently, you can go into the iPhoto Preferences and set images to open automatically in the outside program when double-clicked.

Keep in mind that changes saved to an original image from an outside program replace the original file in iPhoto's files, so you cannot revert to the original image as you normally would. It might be best to make a duplicate before you begin editing.

If you choose to further edit an image that has already been altered from within iPhoto, the image is already a copy, so you can revert to the original version. To check whether a file is an original or a copy before you begin editing, look at the File menu to see whether Revert to Original is an available option.

6

Workshop

The workshop contains quiz questions and activities to help you solidify your understanding of the material covered. Try to answer all questions before looking at the "Answers" section that follows.

Quiz

1. What's the difference between HomePage and the Web Page option under Export in iPhoto's Share mode?

2. What must you do to arrange your photos in any order you choose?

3. If a photo has been edited within iPhoto, how do you return to the original state of the image?

Answers

1. HomePage transfers the Web page created in iPhoto to the user's home directory on the .Mac server maintained by Apple. The Export as Web Page option saves the Web page and associated files on the user's computer.

2. Because the Photo Library can be sorted only by roll or by date, you must create an album and add the photographs you want to arrange. Within the album, you can drag them into any order.

3. Choose Revert to Original from the File menu.

Activities

1. If you have a supported digital camera, take some photos and import them to iPhoto. If you don't have a digital camera or yours is not supported within iPhoto, add any photos you've received in email (or save a few of the images from my .Mac sample page to your desktop). You can drag images on your computer into the Photo Library to create a collection of found images.

2. Create an album, add a keyword, and try editing the best photos to make them better. Then set one of your favorites as a desktop background. (Remember, to remove an iPhoto background, you must open the Desktop panel of System Preferences and choose another background.)

HOUR 7

QuickTime and iMovie

In the last hour, you learned to use iPhoto. In this hour, our focus shifts to two additional media-related applications included with Mac OS X: QuickTime and iMovie. A versatile media player, QuickTime is often used to view video clips, whereas iMovie enables you to easily edit your own digital video and prepare it for sharing with others.

In this hour, you'll learn how to

- Set up QuickTime
- Use the QuickTime controls
- Use iMovie

QuickTime

You learned in Hour 1, "A Tour of Mac OS X," that QuickTime is one of Mac OS X's imaging components. By using its technology, system applications can support reading or writing many different image formats. You might know that QuickTime is used to play digital media, both from within a Web browser and as an application on your desktop. In the first half of this hour, we look at using QuickTime 6.

> QuickTime supports most common digital media formats, including those for movies, MP3 files, WAV files, images, and interactive applications. QuickTime 6 also supports MPEG-4, the global standard for multimedia, which is designed to deliver high-quality video using smaller file sizes.
>
> You can learn more about the supported formats by visiting Apple's QuickTime specification page at http://www.apple.com/quicktime/products/qt/specifications.html.

Watching QuickTime movies play in your Web browser window is probably the most common place you view streaming media, so let's take a look at the controls of the QuickTime browser plug-in. Figure 7.1 shows a QuickTime movie playing in the Internet Explorer browser.

FIGURE 7.1

Many users experience QuickTime through their browsers.

The movie controls are located across the bottom of the video. If you've used a VCR or other media player, you've certainly seen these before. However, there are a few shortcuts you might want to know.

For example, clicking the speaker icon on the far left can instantly mute the volume. You can also control the volume level using the up-arrow and down-arrow keys on the keyboard.

> To increase the volume beyond its normal limit, hold down the Shift key while dragging the volume control.

Playback controls also can be activated from the keyboard, saving the need to mouse around on your screen. To toggle between playing and pausing, press the Spacebar. To rewind or fast forward, use the left-arrow and right-arrow keys, respectively.

At the far right of the control bar is the QuickTime menu (indicated by the down arrow), which gives you easy access to QuickTime settings.

If the movie being played is streaming from a remote server, some of these controls might not be available. For example, on-demand streaming video can't be fast-forwarded or rewound, but static files can be. The available controls depend entirely on the movie you're viewing.

The QuickTime Player

The QuickTime Player application provides another means of viewing movies and streams. In fact, many users might be surprised to find that they can use the QuickTime Player application to tune in to a variety of interesting streams—ranging from news to entertainment—without the need for a separate Web browser. Apple has been working with entertainment and news outlets for the past few years to develop QuickTime TV. The stations available in QuickTime TV provide streaming media 24 hours a day. Don't have a good source for National Public Radio (NPR) in your neighborhood? Use QuickTime TV to play a high-quality NPR stream anytime, anywhere.

> Minimizing a QuickTime Player movie *while* it is playing adds a live icon to the Dock. The movie (with sound) continues to play in the minimized Dock icon. Even if you don't have a use for this feature, give it a try—it's extremely cool!

To use QuickTime Player, open it from its default home in the Dock or from the Applications folder. After the default QuickTime window opens, click the QuickTime icon button at the lower right to launch the Apple QuickTime view, as shown Figure 7.2.

7

Figure 7.2

The Apple QuickTime view enables you to choose from several categories of content.

The left side of this view lists several categories from which you can choose what to view or listen to. Clicking a category launches your default Web browser and brings up a page listing the available content Selecting a listed item launches a new Apple QuickTime window in your desktop to play the item.

When QuickTime starts to load a streaming video clip, it goes through four steps before displaying the video:

- **Connecting**—Makes a connection to the streaming server.
- **Requested Data**—Waits for acknowledgement from remote server.
- **Getting Info**—Retrieves information about the QuickTime movie.
- **Buffering**—QuickTime buffers several seconds of video to eliminate stuttering from the playback.

If the player stalls during any of these steps, there might be a problem with the remote server or your transport setting (how your computer talks on the Internet). Try another streaming source, and if it still fails, use the QuickTime System Preferences panel to select an alternative transport.

You can use QuickTime Player to play information from other sources in addition to QuickTime TV. QuickTime refers to every media type as a movie. For example, you can open and play CD audio tracks and MP3s by selecting the Open Movie command from the File menu. Even though there aren't any visuals, these media types are referred to as *movies* in QuickTime's vocabulary.

You can :open local movie files by choosing Open Movie from the File menu (Command+O) or by dragging a movie file onto the QuickTime Dock icon. If you have a streaming server URL, you can select Open URL (Command+U) from the File menu to directly open the stream.

QuickTime Preferences

The Preferences submenu, found in the QuickTime Player application menu in your menu bar contains three different choices: Player Preferences, QuickTime Preferences, and Registration.

The Player Preferences settings are preferences for the QuickTime Player application itself, whereas the QuickTime Preferences settings refer to the QuickTime System Preferences panel. If you're interested in registering QuickTime (which we highly suggest), the Registration option provides an input area for entering your registration code.

The Player Preferences dialog box is shown in Figure 7.3.

FIGURE 7.3

Choose how QuickTime Player reacts to opening and playing movies.

Use the following options in the Player Preferences dialog box to control how the application handles multiple movies and playback

- **Open Movies in New Players**—By default, QuickTime Player reuses existing windows when opening new movies. To open new movies in new windows, select this check box.

- **Automatically Play Movies When Opened**—Does what it says! When checked, QuickTime Player starts playing a movie immediately after it's opened.

- **Play Sound in Frontmost Player Only**—By default, sound is played only in the active player window. To hear sound from all playing movies simultaneously, uncheck this option.

- **Play Sound When Application Is in Background**—If this option is checked, sound continues to play even when QuickTime Player isn't the active application.

- **Show Hot Picks Movie Automatically**—Automatically fetches and plays Apple's Hot Pick movie when QuickTime Player is started.

7

Click OK to save the application preferences.

The QuickTime System Preferences panel (located in the Internet & Network section of System Preferences) enables you to change QuickTime's settings for better quality playback and to make other modifications. Let's discuss some of the more useful settings.

The first tab controls QuickTime's plug-ins, shown in Figure 7.4. Plug-ins are used when movies are viewed in a Web browser.

FIGURE 7.4

Use QuickTime's System Preferences to optimize display for your system.

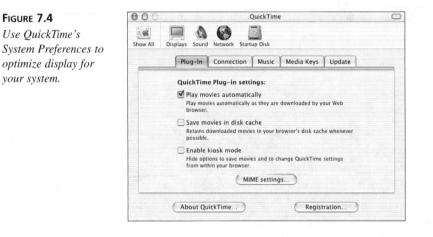

The Play Movies Automatically option directs QuickTime to start playing a movie after enough of it has been buffered. This option applies to movies that aren't streamed. Select the Save Movies in Disk Cache option to temporarily store a clip to speed up repeated viewings. The Enable Kiosk Mode option makes it possible for movies to run continuously unattended for demonstrations and presentations.

Click the MIME Settings button to open a list of all the MIME types that QuickTime can handle and everything it's currently configured to display. MIME stands for Multipurpose Internet Mail Extension and defines a set of document types, such as text, HTML, and so on.

Some items (such as Flash) are intentionally disabled because they're better handled by other browser plug-ins.

The Connection tab, shown in Figure 7.5, configures the type of network access QuickTime can expect your computer to have. This information helps QuickTime choose the appropriate type of media to display, depending on how fast it can be received.

FIGURE 7.5

Choose your connection speed and transport type for best movie quality.

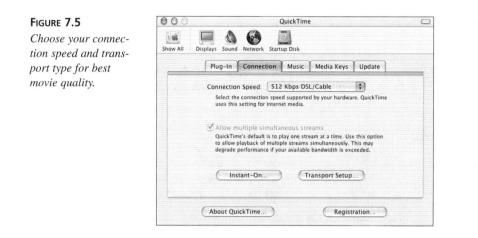

The Transport Setup button is used to choose the protocol used for streaming. By default, QuickTime attempts to choose the best transport based on your network type. It's best not to change these settings unless you're having difficulty viewing media.

By default, QuickTime allows only a single media stream. If your bandwidth enables you to do so, click the Allow Multiple Simultaneous Streams option to stream many sources at once. This option is automatically selected when you specify a high-speed connection method.

The Music and Media Keys panes enable you to change QuickTime's default MIDI music synthesizer and to enter access keys for secured media files, respectively. Most users won't need to use these panes. The final tab, Update, contains settings for updating your version of QuickTime, either manually or automatically

As you work with QuickTime, you quickly discover the thousands of high-quality video streams available on the Internet. For starters, be sure to check out Apple's http://www.apple.com/quicktime/ site for the best movie-trailers anywhere. To sample some real-time streaming video of a nature site, point your browser to http://www.racerocks.com/—an interactive and very live nature preserve.

Of course, playing movies is only part of the fun of using your Mac. Another piece of software, iMovie, enables you to create your own motion pictures and streaming sensations.

7

iMovie

In this half hour, we examine another piece of software bundled with Mac OS X: iMovie, a digital video editor. Although it's amazingly simple to use, iMovie enables you to combine video clips, add sound effects and voiceovers, create title text, and export your final work into formats others can view.

The Supporting Technology

Until researching this hour's lesson, I had never tried iMovie. Frankly, I expected it to be difficult to use and—considering the amount of data required for video images—very, very slow. Watching television commercials proclaiming the effortlessness of iMovie didn't convince me otherwise. However, within minutes of using iMovie myself, I learned that it is neither difficult nor slow. And it's as much fun as Apple's marketing campaign would have us believe.

A large part of what makes iMovie work so well is FireWire. Developed by Apple, FireWire is a peripheral transmission standard used to convey data between computers and attached devices. However, it is much faster than the other popular standard, USB. For that reason, FireWire is ideal for working with information-rich content, such as audio and video. In fact, it works so well that Apple won a Primetime Emmy Award in 2001 for its contributions to the television industry.

FireWire is great for video transfer because it enables you to feed digital data straight to your computer, and that's the form you need it in to edit it. However, this does mean you'll need a computer with a FireWire port and a digital video camera that supports FireWire. The Web site `http://www.apple.com/imovie/compatibility.html` lists compatible video cameras. It also provides references for those who hope to adapt a camera that shoots 8mm, Hi8, VHS, or SVHS format for use with iMovie.

 Not all compatible cameras refer to this technology as FireWire. Depending on the manufacturer, it might also be known as IEEE 1394 or i.LINK, but they work just the same.

Using iMovie

To open iMovie, double-click on its icon in the Applications folder or in the Dock. The first time it's opened, an animated window offers you the option to create a new project, open a project, or cancel. Here, you can give your project a working title and choose where to save it. The next time you use it, iMovie opens automatically to the last project you worked on. To create a new project or open another project, you can select those options from the File menu.

> Don't worry too much about the title you give your project. This title basically labels a folder in which to store your project elements. You're given the chance to name your finished movie anything you like when you export it for viewing.

Before you start using the application, let's take a look at the interface. It's composed of three main parts that encompass the entire screen, as shown in Figure 7.6. At upper left is the Preview pane, where clips, other elements, and the project in progress can be viewed. A pane containing clips and effects controls is in the upper right. Each of the tabbed options in this pane (including Clips, Transitions, Titles, Effects, and Audio) is referred to as a *shelf*. Along the bottom of the screen is the Project View pane representing video and sounds of the project in progress, which can be viewed by element or in a timeline. To add an item to your movie, just click an item on a shelf and drag it to this pane. The standard application menu bar also runs across the top of the screen. Note that when you're using iMovie, the Dock is hidden so as to avoid obstructing the screen.

FIGURE 7.6

The iMovie interface shows previews on the left, the element shelves on the right, and a project view along the bottom.

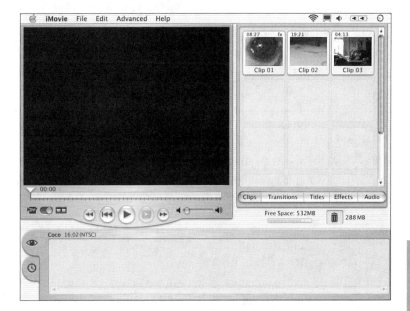

7

Transferring Video Clips

To begin your movie, you must have some video clips to work with. To transfer existing footage from your video camera, here's what you need to do. The exact terms your camera uses might be different from what's presented here, but the process should be almost identical:

1. Insert the tape containing the footage you want to edit into a camcorder.

2. Connect the camcorder to the computer via the FireWire port, using the FireWire cable that came with the camera. Turn the camera on and set it to playback mode.

3. In the Preview pane of the iMovie interface, slide the switch toward the DV camera icon.

4. Set the camera to play. As the tape runs, recorded images appear in the iMovie Preview pane, and the accompanying sound track comes through your system speakers. If your camera supports it, you might want to play back in slow motion to better judge where you want to start importing video.

5. When you reach the approximate section that you want to use in your movie, click the button labeled Import at the bottom of the iMovie Preview pane (not shown here). Click Import again to stop gathering the clip. (Remember that you can edit clips after they're saved in iMovie, but that means you should leave a little bit of extra space at the beginning and ending of your chosen clips.)

Repeat this process to import more clips until you have enough to begin the editing process. As you add clips, the spaces in the Clips shelf show them as numbered items, as shown in Figure 7.6. If you want to give a text label to a slide, click the bottom of the slide until the title area turns gray, and then change the label.

Video clips take up a lot of hard drive space. Keep an eye on the Free Space status bar just below the shelf panel as you add clips so that you don't run out of drive space.

Also, even with FireWire, transferring video is a resource-intensive process. Shut off other system processes (such as e-mail checking) to avoid dropping frames, which creates apparent skips in the picture.

Cropping Video Clips

After you've imported clips, you can begin making your movie. The first thing you want to do is refine the cropping you performed when transferring clips from the camera. The most important control in cropping is the scrubber bar—the blue bar that appears below the Preview pane to represent the duration of the clip.

To crop a clip, follow these steps:

1. Select a clip from the Clips shelf. Your chosen clip is highlighted in yellow and appears in the Preview pane.

2. In the Preview pane, click the Play button to review your clip. When you find the point at which you want your finished clip to start or end, drag the white arrow above the scrubber bar to that exact point.

3. To choose your segment, hold down the Shift key and drag the white arrow in whichever direction you want the clip to cover. This produces a yellow bar representing your cropped clip, as shown in Figure 7.7.

FIGURE 7.7
To crop footage, drag the arrows to the appropriate start and end points.

4. When you're happy with your clip, choose Crop from the Edit menu to trim the parts you didn't select from that item on the Clip shelf.

Repeat this cropping procedure for all your clips, saving the good parts and leaving out the rest.

If you want to use multiple segments from a single clip, you must first copy it. To do so, select the clip and choose Copy and then Paste from the Edit menu. A duplicate appears in the Clips shelf, enabling you to preserve the original in its entirety.

Assembling Your Movie

After you've cropped your clips, you can begin assembling your movie. Simply drag the clips from the Clips shelf into the Clip Viewer tab (it's represented by an icon that looks

like an eye) of the Project pane, shown in Figure 7.8, along the bottom of the window. Here, you can rearrange by dragging items to the order you want them. You can preview your work at any time by clicking the Play button in the Preview pane. However, if you want to preview the entire project, be sure that no clip is selected in the Project View pane, or only the selected clip will play.

FIGURE 7.8

Drag chosen clips to the Clip Viewer tab.

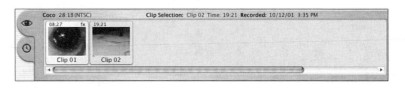

The Project View pane can also be used in Timeline view by clicking the tab with the clock icon. The length of each element is displayed, as shown in Figure 7.9.

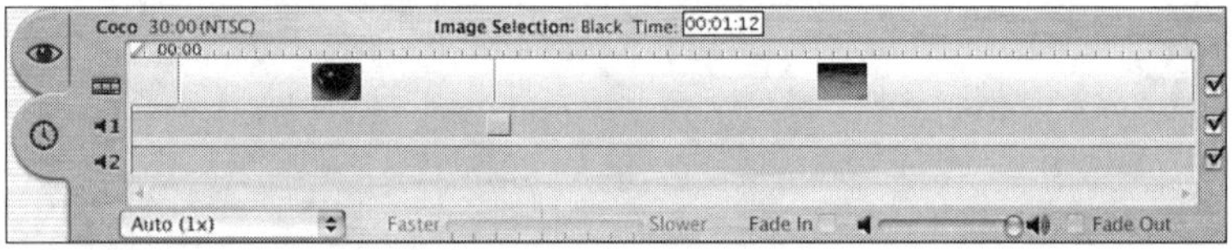

FIGURE 7.9

The Timeline view shows the video and audio elements as well as their duration.

Adding Extras

When you're happy with the order of clips, you can choose other elements to complete your movie. These elements can be accessed through the tabs in the pane at the right and, for the most part, can be added by dragging them to the appropriate point in the Project View pane.

- **Transitions** are visual effects placed between scenes to soften the cut between clips. Figure 7.10 shows the Transitions shelf. Notice that the icon next to each option tells you whether a given transition acts on the clip preceding the transition (like Fade Out), the clip following the transition (like Fade In), or both (like Cross Dissolve).

- **Titles** are text elements, such as film credits or the dialog cards used in silent films. iMovie comes with several title styles, which can be customized with font and, for animated titles, direction options that determine which way the titles move.

- **Effects** enable you to change the appearance of the video images, such as converting a clip to black-and-white or adjusting its color contrast. Rendering these effects is a resource-intensive process that does not happen instantly. While rendering is in progress, an orange status bar appears in the icon for an inserted item.

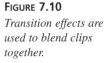

FIGURE 7.10
Transition effects are used to blend clips together.

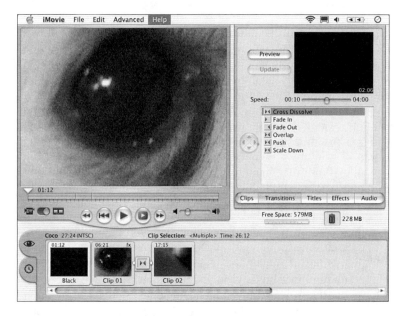

- **Audio** lets you introduce two additional soundtracks to your movie in addition to the audio recorded by the video camera. You can add music from CDs, use prerecorded sound effects, or record your own audio track. To add additional audio, drag items to the appropriate location in the audio tracks of the Timeline view that was shown in Figure 7.9.

> If you want to remove the audio track that accompanies a video clip, you can choose Extract Audio from the Advanced menu. This separates the audio portion of the recording and places it in one of the separate audio tracks, where you can select and delete it. You could also use this option to obtain audio clips by deleting the video clip and retaining the sound.

When you're satisfied with your movie, you can prepare it for view in one of many different formats by choosing Export Movie from the File menu. In addition to exporting it to your camera, you can choose among several QuickTime formats or iDVD. Choosing QuickTime opens the dialog box shown in Figure 7.11. We discuss more about differences in QuickTime formats in the questions at the end of this hour.

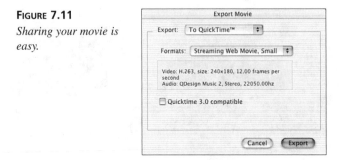

FIGURE 7.11

Sharing your movie is easy.

When exporting your movie to QuickTime or iDVD, you're asked for a title and the folder to which the file should be saved

Summary

This hour focused on viewing and editing digital video. You looked at QuickTime's uses as well as its controls and preferences. Then you moved on to iMovie, Apple's user-friendly video editor, which enables virtually anyone to splice together scenes and add effects.

Q&A

Q **Every time I use QuickTime Player, I'm asked if I want to upgrade to QuickTime Pro. Should I?**

A That depends entirely on your needs. QuickTime Pro gives you access to a number of video-editing functions, such as copying and pasting portions of video tracks, applying effects filters, and altering video codecs. Users can also extract and convert audio and video tracks—even export video tracks as image sequences. Basic playback features are also improved. Users can present a movie on the entire screen, rather than just in a window, as well as control contrast, tint, and brightness on a per-movie basis. If you're the type to use such features, QuickTime Pro is worth the price.

Q **What are the differences among iMovie's export options?**

A First, by using the To Camera option, you can return your movie to the camera that shot the footage and then record it to videotape.

You can also use QuickTime to distribute your movie. Here you have several options. You can make a free-standing QuickTime movie by choosing Email Movie, Small. You can also choose between two different Web formats: Web

Movie, Small and Streaming Web Movie, Small for longer movies. Note, however, that creating a movie with Streaming Web Movie, Small requires additional software support.

If you're lucky enough to have access to iDVD and a DVD-R drive, you can burn your movie as a DVD using the For iDVD option.

Q Where can I see finished movies made with iMovie?

A Apple has devoted a section of its Web site (`http://www.apple.com/imovie/gallery/`) to films made with iMovie. You can even submit your own project for possible display on the site.

Workshop

The workshop contains quiz questions and activities to help you solidify your understanding of the material covered. Try to answer all questions before looking at the "Answers" section that follows.

Quiz

1. What should you do to maximize QuickTime's performance for your connection speed?

2. By what other names is IEEE 1394 called?

Answers

1. Adjust the settings in the Connection tab of QuickTime's System Preferences panel

2. FireWire and i.LINK

Activities

Adjust your QuickTime System Preferences to optimize play for your system, and then test your settings by watching some movie trailers at `http://www.apple.com/trailers/`.

7

HOUR 8

DVD Player and iDVD

DVDs are growing more common by the day. With Mac OS X, not only can you watch DVDs, you can make your own. DVD Player provides a simple way to view DVDs on Macintosh computers with DVD-ROM drives or SuperDrives. For those with SuperDrives who want to make their own DVDs, iDVD is flexible authoring tool that enables you to create projects easily. This hour explores

- Using DVD Player
- Creating DVDs with movies, slide shows, and files
- Customizing iDVD themes

DVD Player

Included with Mac OS X is DVD Player, an application for displaying DVD content on computers equipped with internal DVD drives. To start DVD Player, simply insert a video DVD into your system, or double-click the application icon (path: /Applications/DVD Player). By default, Mac OS X launches DVD Player automatically when it detects a DVD in the drive. At startup, a video window and playback controller appear onscreen. The playback controller is shown in Figure 8.1.

FIGURE 8.1

DVD Player's controller window keeps all the needed controls in one convenient place.

Use the controller window as you would a standard DVD remote. Basic playback buttons are provided, along with a selection control and a volume slider directly under the primary playback controls.

Six additional advanced controls are accessible by clicking the three dots right of the controller window. This opens a window tray containing Slow, Step, Return, Subtitle, Audio, and Angle buttons. In Figure 8.1, the controller window is shown with the window tray extended. If you prefer a horizontally oriented player control, choose Controller Type, Horizontal (Shift+Command+H) from the Controls menu. You can switch back to the vertical layout at any time by choosing the Vertical (Shift+Command+V) option from the same menu.

To navigate onscreen selections without the use of the controller, you can simply point-and-click at a DVD menu item to select it. To navigate with the keyboard, use the arrow keys and press Return.

Although the onscreen controller can be used for most everything, DVD Player also provides keyboard commands for controlling playback. The following options are available under the Controls menu:

- **Controller Type**—Choose Horizontal (Shift+Command+H) or Vertical (Shift+Command+V) orientation.
- **Play/**Pause—(Spacebar) Play or pause the video
- **Stop**—(Command+.) Stop the current video from playing
- **Fast Forward**—(Command+right arrow) Speed through the video playback
- **Rewind**—(Command+left arrow) Move backward through the video playback
- **Previous Chapter**—(right arrow) Skip to the previous chapter on the DVD
- **Next Chapter**—(left arrow) Skip to the next chapter on the DVD

- **DVD Menu**—(Command+`) Stop playback and load the menu for the active DVD
- **Volume Up**—(Command+up arrow) Increase the volume
- **Volume Down**—(Command+down arrow) Decrease the volume
- **Mute**—(Command+K) Mute the sound
- **Eject**—(Command+E) Eject the current DVD

> When fast-forwarding or rewinding, the view is displayed at an accelerated rate. Use the Scan Rate option under the Controls menu to set the speed to two, four, or eight times faster than normal.

DVD Player Preferences

The preferences for DVD Player are split across three tabs. The Player tab, shown in Figure 8.2, enables you to set how DVD Player reacts upon system startup and insertion of a DVD. You can also choose the viewer size.

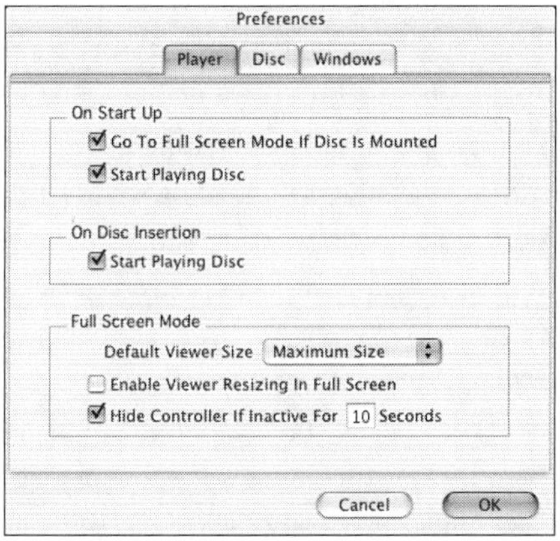

FIGURE 8.2

Change how DVD Player is activated and the size of the viewing window.

The Disc tab contains settings for default language and the option to enable DVD@ccess, which allows DVD Player to recognize and react to embedded hot spots that link to Internet Web sites.

The Windows tab controls turns on and off controller help tags and window status messages, which appear while a movie is playing.

iDVD Basics

High-end DVD authoring systems, such as Apple's DVD Studio Pro, can add program-matic logic within DVD menus and adjust video stream encoding ad infinitum. For per-sonal users, however, iDVD takes a more simplified approach to DVD creation that seems immediately familiar to anyone who has created Web pages, used the old Apple HyperCard program, or even just filed documents in the Finder. There are four potential components to an iDVD-authored DVD:

- **Folders (Menu)**—An iDVD folder (or *menu* in traditional DVD lingo) holds the different components that a user can access visually through her DVD player. If you have four different movies of your puppy chasing butterflies, you can create a folder with four buttons for each of the movies. You can also create additional folder items that lead to another video clips and even other folders. Much like fold-ers can be used to categorize documents on your computer, they can also be used to organize the movies and images on your DVD.

- **Movies**—Most DVDs contain video, and presumably yours does too. iDVD can use almost any QuickTime movie on a DVD, except those in the MPEG1 format or QuickTime VR and Flash animations. For the best results, however, you should use DV format video from a digital video camera. DV-encoded files are produced by iMovie 2, so any iMovie 2 production is immediately iDVD ready.

- **Slideshows**—iDVD contains a unique slide show feature that enables users to add still images to their finished product. Slide shows can be driven automatically or manually, and can include an accompanying soundtrack.

- **DVD-ROM files**—Although not part of what most of us think of when we hear *DVD*, DVD-ROM files can be included as a value-added feature of any iDVD pro-duction. DVD-ROM files are simply files that you can use on your computer, rather than watch on a DVD player. For example, you can include the actual images that make up an iDVD slide show so that someone watching the DVD could pop it into his computer and copy the images files directly off for use as desktop backgrounds, and so on.

Using these four iDVD components, you can create a homegrown DVD that rivals those that you can buy shrink-wrapped from your local video store.

Collecting Your Resources

To get starting using iDVD, you first need a compatible Macintosh. At the time of this writing, *compatible Macintosh* means a SuperDrive-equipped iMac or G4. It's expected that the SuperDrive will be introduced in Apple's portables at some time in the near future. Next, you need iDVD source material. This includes any images you want to use for slideshows, your DV movie files, and any files that you want to include on your DVD-ROM.

> As you'll learn shortly, iDVD enables you to change the backgrounds (and background sounds) of the different folders (menus) and buttons on your DVD. If you have additional movie, image, or sound files that you want to use to customize your iDVD project, you should collect them before starting.

It's best to organize the files you're going to use in a folder that can remain onscreen while you're using iDVD because you'll be dragging and dropping files from the Finder into the iDVD window.

Using iDVD

After you've found the components that you want to use to build your DVD (and you have a SuperDrive-equipped Mac), open the iDVD application (Path: /Applications/iDVD 2/iDVD). If this is the first time you've opened the application, it immediately prompts you to open an existing project, create a new project, or open the tutorial, as shown in Figure 8.3. If you have an existing project (including the tutorial) in progress, iDVD automatically opens that project. You must choose New Project (Command+N) from the File menu to save the current project and start fresh.

FIGURE 8.3
iDVD prompts you to open a project or tutorial, or create a new project.

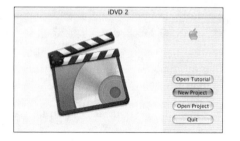

Click the New Project button, choose a name and a location for your iDVD project, and finally, click Create. This remains the active iDVD project (even if you exit the application) until you manually start a new project.

The project name is used as the default label for the DVD that you create. Even though it might seem appropriate to name the project file "My stupid client's DVD," keep in mind that unless you manually change the DVD label, the name might bite you later. The DVD's disc name can be changed at ant time by choosing Project Info from the Project menu.

When your new project is started, the iDVD workplace appears, as shown in Figure 8.4. This window provides a view of what will appear on your television screen when the DVD plays. If it doesn't look right here, it won't look right on the finished product.

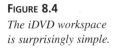

FIGURE 8.4
The iDVD workspace is surprisingly simple.

Along the bottom of the window are the six primary controls that you'll use while creating your DVD:

- **Theme**—A DVD is more than just a collection of video clips—it's also an artistic medium for presenting those clips. Your DVD can have animated backgrounds that appear on the menu screens, animated buttons to play your video clips, and even a sound track that plays while the person viewing the CD navigates the menu options. Apple calls the collection of backgrounds, sounds, and buttons that you can use to customize your DVD a *theme*. The Theme button opens a window tray containing the tools for selecting one of more than a dozen Apple-supplied themes or creating your own. The default theme, Chalkboard, is shown in Figure 8.4.

- **Folder**—Creates a new folder (or menu) on the DVD. After a folder is added, double-clicking it in the DVD workspace window takes you inside that folder, where you can add other folders, video clips, slide shows, and so on.

- **Slideshow**—Adds a slide show of your favorite image files to the current DVD folder (menu).

- **Motion**—Many themes contain motion, such as animated folder backgrounds or animated buttons. Displaying all these animated items at once can slow down your computer. Click the Motion button to toggle motion on and off within the iDVD workspace or choose Motion (Command+M) from the Advanced menu.

- **Preview**—View the current DVD project as it will appear on your DVD player. The Preview button even opens a small DVD remote for controlling the DVD.

- **Burn**—Finalizes your iDVD project by burning it to a DVD-R. This is the last step you take when creating your DVD.

Adding to the iDVD Workspace

Your DVD project starts with a blank workspace. This is the top-level folder (menu) of your DVD—what the people viewing your DVD see when they first put the disc into their player. Let's see what you can do to customize the workspace and how you can add your media elements to it.

Screen (Menu) Titles

Each folder has a title that's displayed as part of the screen background. The default title is set by the theme that you currently have selected. In Figure 8.4, the Chalkboard theme is shown and the default title is Chalkboard. To change the title, simply click the default text to select it, and then start typing. Figure 8.5 shows the title editor in action.

At this point you might be thinking, "Hey, I don't want a chalkboard as my background. Why bother editing the title if I don't like this theme?" Don't worry, the title is an element of the current folder (menu), no matter what theme you choose, it is still there. It changes its size and appearance, but is always present (unless you remove all the title text). Our goal is to explore the elements that make up a DVD, and then delve into how they can be customized.

FIGURE 8.5
*Click the title to select
and edit it.*

Movies

To add a movie to the current iDVD folder, drag its icon from your Finder window into the iDVD workspace. iDVD adds a new movie button to your current folder (menu). When viewing your DVD, this is the button you click to watch your movie clip. The button is labeled with the same name as the movie file stored on your computer. To change the label, click the text in the workspace and then start typing.

In addition to changing a button's label, you can change the background image of the button. By default, any movie button that's added automatically plays the movie itself within the button! (You must have the Motion button enabled to see this effect.)

If you find this distracting, you can change the background to any still frame within the movie or to a shorter sequence of the video. To do this, click the button in the workspace to highlight it. This displays a button control above the selected button, as shown in Figure 8.6.

Drag the slider handle from left to right to choose the start point for where the button motion begins within the video clip. If you want to remove the motion altogether, uncheck the Movie check box. The video freezes, and you can use the slider to control the frame that's displayed in the button background.

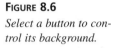

Figure 8.6

Select a button to control its background.

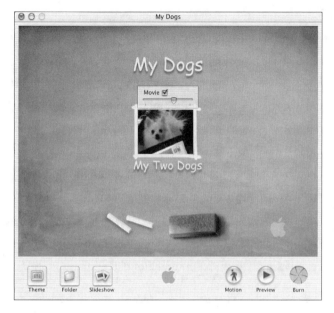

You can add up to six buttons to a given folder including the default parent folder. If you want to add more, you must create folders (menus) to hold them.

Folders

Additional folders can be added to a DVD by clicking the Folder button at the bottom of the workspace, or by choosing Add Folder (Command+K) from the Project menu. A new folder button labeled My Folder is added to the current workspace folder. Edit the folder button's label using the same technique as you used to edit a movie button. Figure 8.7 shows the iDVD workspace with two folders added—Coco and Maddy—and a movie button labeled My Two Dogs.

You can immediately open a new folder by double-clicking its icon in the workspace. Inside a new folder, your screen shows a new empty workspace. You can edit the screen title of your new folder, drag new movie files into the workspace, or add more folders or slide shows. You'll also notice a small return arrow in the lower-left corner of the workspace. This arrow, shown in Figure 8.8, is an automatically added control that, when clicked either by you (in the workspace) or by your viewers (watching the DVD on their television), takes you or your viewers to the previous folder. Think of it as providing the same function as the back arrow within the Finder window toolbars.

FIGURE 8.7
Folder buttons add new levels to your DVD.

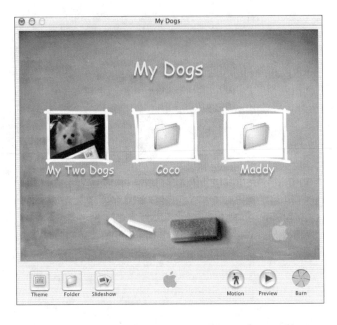

FIGURE 8.8
Additional folder levels contain a back arrow to move to the previously visited folder (menu).

Back button

As with movie buttons, folder buttons can be customized. Clicking a folder button image selects the button and displays a control similar to the movie button, but without the movie check box. Dragging the slider switches the button's background among the first frame of all the movies that it contains.

Slide Shows

One final element that you can add to the iDVD workspace is a slide show. Slide shows are exactly what they sound like: groups of still images that can be either manually or automatically viewed. To add a slide show, click the Slideshow button at the bottom of the workspace window or choose Add Slideshow (Command+L) from the Project menu. A new slide show button named My Slideshow appears. You can customize the name of the slide show button in the same manner as you did with the folder and movie buttons.

To create the actual contents of the slide show, double-click its button. The slide show creation screen, shown in Figure 8.9 appears.

FIGURE 8.9

The slide show features its own editor.

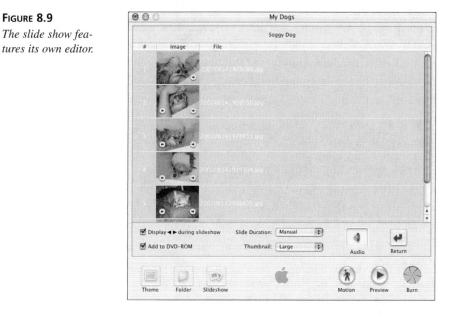

Add images to the slide show by selecting and dragging them to the slide show editor window. You can rearrange their ordering by dragging the entries within the list.

Images are scaled to fit the resolution. For best results, make sure that your images are sized to 640×480 pixels before you add them to the slide show.

Near the bottom of the slide show editor are a few options that you can use to customize how the slideshow runs and controls the editor:

- **Display <> during slideshow**—If selected, iDVD adds arrow controls to move forward and backward during the slide show. The arrows are superimposed over each of the slide show icons in the editor window.

- **Audio**—To add background music to the slide show, drag a sound file, such as an MP3 or AIFF file, to the Audio well. If you want to use the audio from a movie, you can also drag movie files to the well and iDVD will use the first audio track from the movie as its soundtrack.

- **Slide Duration**—The length of time the slide is displayed on the screen. If set to manual, the person viewing the slides must manually page from one slide to the next. If you're accompanying your slide show with music, choose the Fit To Audio option to time the slide show to end with the soundtrack.

- **Thumbnail**—Choose the size of the image thumbnails that appear in the slide show list.

- **Add to DVD-ROM**—Add all of the images in the slide show automatically to the DVD-ROM contents.

After customizing your slide show, click the Return button to return to the main iDVD workspace view. As a final step, you might want to change your Slideshow button background. Like the other buttons we've looked at, just select the Slideshow button, and then use the slider to change the background to one of the images within the slide show.

You've seen three types of iDVD buttons and three unique ways they can be customized, but iDVD's button background customization doesn't stop there. You can also add a static image as a button background by dragging an image from the Finder onto the button in the Workspace mode. Or, if you prefer, you can use a video clip as your button's background by dragging the movie file onto the button. This works for all three types of buttons, and doesn't change what the button does when it's clicked. That is, if an existing movie button is playing its own video clip, dragging a new video clip to the button does *not* change what happens when the button is clicked—it changes only what background the button displays.

Button Arrangement

By default, the iDVD buttons arrange themselves (you can customize this with themes, which you learn about in a few minutes). To change the position of a button, drag it on the screen. It snaps to one of the theme's predetermined locations. To remove an existing button, highlight it and press your Delete key. The remaining buttons automatically rearrange to fill the empty space.

If you find that you've built a portion of your DVD (a folder containing movies, a movie, a slide show, and so on) and you want to move it somewhere else on your DVD (perhaps into another folder), just use the Edit menu to cut the button from the existing location and paste it wherever you want it to be. Cutting and pasting a folder moves the contents of that folder along with it.

Previewing

To preview how a DVD will look when it is finished, click the Preview button in the lower-right corner of the workspace. The workspace locks and doesn't allow further changes until the Preview button is clicked again. At the same time, a DVD controller appears, as shown in Figure 8.10.

FIGURE 8.10
Use the iDVD controller to interact with the DVD.

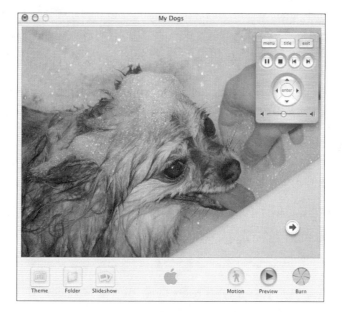

The controller can be used just like a real DVD controller. Use the Play, Pause, and Stop buttons to control video, and the forward and back arrows to page through your slide shows.

Click the Menu button while playing a video clip to return to the current iDVD folder, and the Title button to move to the top folder.

The circular control in the button of the iDVD controller can be used to highlight and select buttons on the DVD, just like on a real DVD controller. Finally, the volume slider sets the sound level for the preview.

> If you don't like using the controller, you can simply click the buttons within the iDVD window itself to accomplish the same thing.

Click the Exit button on the controller or the Preview button in the iDVD window to exit Preview mode.

Burning

The final step of creating a DVD is burning. To burn a DVD, click the Burn button and insert a DVD when prompted to do so. Be sure to enable motion prior to clicking the Burn button. If motion isn't enabled in iDVD, it won't enabled in your final DVD product.

In some cases, you might notice that your DVD cannot be burned immediately. All video tracks on a DVD must first be encoded in the MPEG2 format. This is an extremely processor-intensive activity that's likely to take awhile. iDVD automatically starts encoding your movies as soon as they're added to the project, but if you're a fast worker, you might finish your project before it finishes encoding. If this happens to be the case, just wait, and it will quickly catch up.

> You can check on the encoding status of any video track by using the Status tab of the Theme tray. We take a look at this feature shortly.

After burning, your DVD is ready to use in your Macintosh or a consumer DVD player. Almost all current DVD players support DVD-R playback, but if you're purchasing a new DVD player, you might want to check to be sure.

Advanced Features

The iDVD application is so easy to use that even it's advanced features are a breeze to master. There are a few more options that we'll take a look at now—most notably themes. If you don't like your DVD's interface, this is where you can learn how to change it.

Themes

Themes are what can make a generic DVD into something that looks like it came out of a professional development studio. Each folder within a DVD can contain its own theme. Apple ships iDVD with a number of predesigned themes that you can use out of the box or customize with your own graphics, fonts, and sounds. All the screen shots up to this point have used the default Chalkboard theme. To switch to a new theme, click the Theme button at the bottom the iDVD workspace. A window tray appears with all of the customization options. Click the Themes tab to display the prebuilt themes, as shown in Figure 8.11.

FIGURE 8.11

Choose from one of Apple's predesigned themes.

Use the menu at the top of the theme list to choose between displaying all themes, or those with motion, just a picture, picture with audio, or any favorite customized themes you've created. Motion themes are set off in the theme list by a little person (motion)

icon in the lower-right corner of the theme thumbnail. Clicking a theme thumbnail applies that theme to the current folder that you're viewing in the iDVD workspace—it doesn't change the themes of other folders. To change all the themes within folders under the current folder, choose Apply Theme To Folders from the Advanced menu. To apply a theme to the entire project, choose Apply Theme To Project from the Advanced menu.

Customize

If you don't like any of Apple's built-in themes, you can easily create one of your own. First, choose the theme that you like most from the theme list, and then click the Customize tab. Your screen refreshes and displays the theme customization settings, as demonstrated in Figure 8.12. Here you can change almost all the attributes of a given theme.

FIGURE 8.12

Use the Customize option to change a theme to your liking.

Change any of the following settings to customize the appearance of the theme:

- **Motion Duration**—If you're using a theme with a motion background or animated (video clip) buttons, the motion duration setting controls how long the motion lasts (from 0 to 30 seconds) before it starts repeating. If your clips are longer than 30 seconds, they're truncated to this setting. This affects all onscreen motion, both background and buttons—they cannot be set separately.

- **Background**—Use the Background Image/Movie and Audio wells to customize the theme background. Drag a new movie to the well to create a new motion background, or drag an image to set a still background. Drag any audio file (including a movie with an audio track) to the Audio well to set the background soundtrack.

- **Title**—Control the positioning, font, color, and size of the theme's title text. The font, color, and size attributes work as you would expect. The position setting provides several aesthetically pleasing presets, and a Custom option, which enables you to drag the title text anywhere you want within the screen.

- **Button**—The button settings change the appearance (border, labels, and so on) of the onscreen folder, slide show, and movie buttons. By default, the large rectangular button selector (at the top left of the button controls) is set to From Theme, which uses the button style from the theme you're customizing. Click the button selector to choose from several other button shapes and sizes. Use the Snap to Grid and Free Position settings to choose how the buttons are positioned on the screen. Finally, use the Position, Font, Color, and Size settings to control how the button labels are drawn on the screen.

If you want a text-only or no-text button, those options are available from the Position settings within the button customization controls.

When you've created a theme that you want to save, click the Save In Favorites button. iDVD prompts you for a theme name, and gives you the option of sharing your theme with all iDVD users.

To apply the theme to your project, use the Apply options under the Advanced menu.

Status

The Status display, although found in the window tray along with the Themes and Customize tabs, has nothing to do with themes. Instead, it provides control over your DVD-ROM contents and enables you to view how your movie encoding is progressing. At the top of the Status tab is a display of how much time or space you have left on your DVD. As you add more files and movies to the DVD, the DVD icon fills to show your usage.

By default, iDVD provides 60 minutes of recordable space per DVD. If you exceed this amount, it automatically switches to a lower quality (lower bitrate) recording to fit up to 90 minutes of video.

The default status view is Encoder Status, which is set using the pop-up menu at the top of the display. The Encoder Status view shows how far along each video clip is in MPEG2 encoding. A DVD cannot be burned until all video tracks are successfully encoded. The Encoder Status view is seen in Figure 8.13.

FIGURE 8.13

Check the encoding status of your video clips.

The second status display, DVD-ROM Contents, (shown in Figure 8.14) is a display of all the files that will be added as DVD-ROM material to your finished DVD. You can drag-and-drop files and folders to the list to add them to the DVD-ROM. If you created a slide show and used the Add to DVD-ROM option, it automatically appears in this pane.

To remove existing files, highlight them in the list and then press your Delete key, or drag them to the Mac OS X Trash. New folders can be created using the New Folder button at the bottom of the display. Folders can be renamed by double-clicking their name in the list; filenames cannot be changed after the files are added.

When finished with the window tray, click the Theme button in the iDVD workspace window and the tray slides shut.

FIGURE 8.14

Add or remove DVD-ROM contents in the status area.

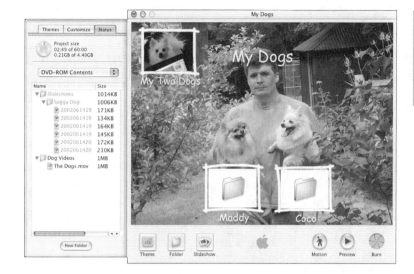

Project Info

If you move files around, iDVD might lose track of them. The Project Info window, accessed by choosing Project Info from the Project menu (Command+I), displays a complete list of the files that are in use by your project, their paths, and a file status indicating whether there were any problems reading the file (which might occur if you've moved or deleted the source movies). In addition, the Project Info window provides the only place where you can change your DVD disc's label. Be aware that no spaces are allowed in DVD volume names—any space that you enter is automatically converted to the underscore (_) character by iDVD.

TV Safe Area

Not all TVs are created equal. Many conventional (nondigital) televisions suffer from overscan, in which portions of the image are lost off the edges of the screen. iDVD can provide a visual representation of what might be lost from your DVD by turning on the Show TV Safe Area (Command+T) in the Advanced menu. This drags a border around the workspace that should be considered unsafe for important content. If, for example, you've customized a theme and your buttons and title fall within the bordered area, you might want to reconsider the positioning.

Apple has been very liberal with its TV Safe Area—it should be considered a worst-case display of your DVD. Most modern televisions don't suffer from the same overscan issues as older sets and provide controls for positioning onscreen images.

Preferences

The final controls for iDVD are its Preferences (shown in Figure 8.15), found under the iDVD application menu. Use the project settings to control whether the MPEG2-encoded (*rendered*) files are deleted after a project is closed, and whether the Apple watermark (in the lower-right corner of your iDVD workspace) is displayed.

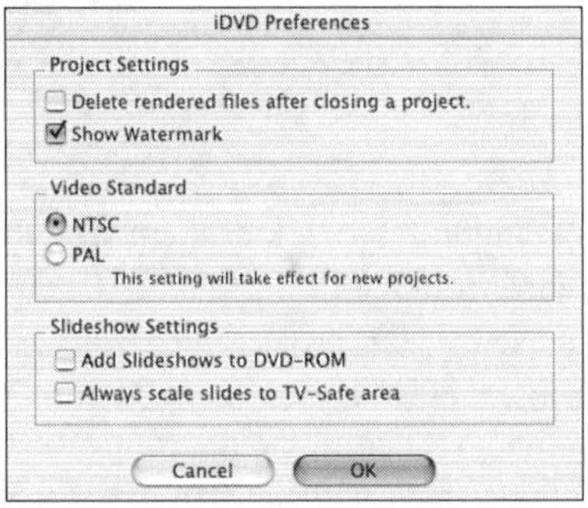

FIGURE 8.15

A few final settings for iDVD can be found in iDVD Preferences.

iDVD Preferences

Project Settings
☐ Delete rendered files after closing a project.
☑ Show Watermark

Video Standard
◉ NTSC
○ PAL
    This setting will take effect for new projects.

Slideshow Settings
☐ Add Slideshows to DVD–ROM
☐ Always scale slides to TV–Safe area

[Cancel]   [OK]

The Video Standard setting can be used to choose NTSC or PAL output for the final DVD. You must choose between NTSC or PAL before starting a project—you cannot convert your project on-the-fly. The default setting should be correct for your country.

Finally, the Slideshow settings provide global control over whether slide shows are always added to the DVD-ROM (remember, you can choose this on a per slide show basis when setting up your show) and whether slides should be scaled to the TV Safe Area.

Click OK to save and apply your preferences.

Summary

In this hour, you learned about the DVD capabilities of Mac OS X. DVD Player is an application for viewing content on DVDs. iDVD enables you to design and burn your own DVDs containing movies, slide shows, and data files. It includes template-like themes that help you create professional-looking menus. Both are easy-to-use complements to your digital lifestyle.

Q&A

Q Can I play any region DVD in the DVD Player application?

A For copyright purposes, DVDs are encoded with region codes that restrict which players can display them. When you first insert a DVD, or when you insert a disc for another region, you're prompted to choose a region for your player. Apple gives you the option of resetting the region code on your DVD drive a limited number of times. After the limit is exceeded, you're stuck with the last region you used, and reinstalling the operating system won't change that.

Q Can I use an external DVD burner with iDVD?

A The answer, unfortunately, is no. You must have a Macintosh computer equipped with a SuperDrive to use iDVD.

Workshop

The workshop contains quiz questions and activities to help you solidify your understanding of the material covered. Try to answer all questions before looking at the "Answers" section that follows.

Quiz

1. How do you launch DVD Player?
2. How do you customize a theme in iDVD?
3. Where do you turn on the TV Safe Area setting?

Answers

1. By default, DVD Player starts when a DVD is inserted. You can also launch it from the Applications folder.
2. Open the Themes tray window and click to the Customize tab.
3. Under the Advanced menu.

Activities

1. If your computer is equipped with a DVD-ROM drive or a SuperDrive, put a DVD in the drive and practice using the DVD Player controls.

2. Those with SuperDrives can launch iDVD and start a project or work through the tutorial.

PART III

Network and Internet

Hour

HOUR 9

Setting Up Mac OS X Networking

Mac OS X is extremely easy to configure for dial-in, ethernet, AirPort, cable modem, and DSL service. If you have a connection to the Internet, this hour helps you set up your Mac to access it. Specifically, in this hour, you learn

- What tools exist for setting up your network
- Where to configure your connection settings
- How to manage multiple locations with different settings

Creating an Internet Connection

The first step in connecting to any network (including the Internet) is determining what, exactly, is being connected. Mac OS X supports a number of technologies out of the box, such as standard wired (ethernet) networks, wireless AirPort networks, and, of course, broadband and dial-in ISPs. For each different type of network, you must collect connection information before continuing. Your network administrator or ISP should be able to provide you with the details of your network access, including

- **IP address**—An Internet Protocol address that's used to uniquely identify your computer on the Internet.
- **Subnet mask**—A filter that helps your computer differentiate between which machines are on the local network and which are on the Internet.
- **Router**—A device address used to send and receive information to and from the Internet.
- **Domain name server**—A computer that translates the name you see in your Web browser, such as www.poisontooth.com, into the corresponding IP address.
- **ISP phone number**—A number used when creating a dial-in connection.
- **Account name**—A username for your ISP Internet account.
- **Password**—A password for your ISP Internet account.
- **Proxy**—A computer that your Macintosh must interact with to reach the Internet.

If you're using a dial-in connection, chances are good that all you need are a phone number, an account name, and a password. You should be absolutely positive that you have all the necessary information before you continue; otherwise, your computer could behave strangely when attempting to connect with incomplete or inaccurate information.

> Under no circumstances should you *ever* attempt to guess an IP address for your computer. Entering invalid information could potentially disrupt your entire network or cause intermittent (and difficult to diagnose) problems for other users.

With connection information in hand, open System Preferences, and click the Network button in the Internet & Network section. You should now be looking at the control center for all your network connections. Near the top of the panel is a Show pop-up menu. Use this menu to choose between the different types of connections that your computer uses, such as Internal Modem, Built-in Ethernet, AirPort, and Internet Sharing (Ethernet). Let's look at each one and how it can be set up for your ISP.

> If you use different types of connections (for example, a modem at home and AirPort at work), don't worry. A bit later, you'll see how several different connection types can get along without any conflicts.

Internal Modem

If you use a modem to connect to the Internet, choose the appropriate Modem option in the Show pop-up menu. The lower portion of your screen changes slightly to reflect the type of connection you're configuring. You see four tabs that lead to four individual setting panes:

- **TCP/IP**—TCP/IP settings are rarely needed for dial-in connections. Unless you know otherwise, I recommend not touching anything found here.

- **PPP**—The most important pane, shown in Figure 9.1, the PPP settings enable you to set your username, password, and ISP phone number.

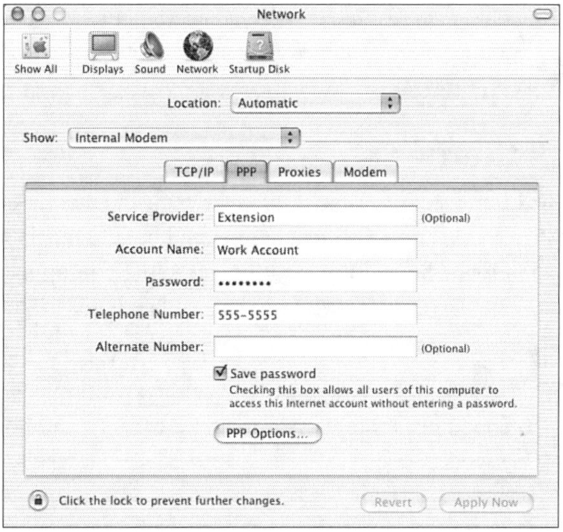

9

FIGURE 9.1

The PPP options are usually the only thing you need to make a connection.

- **Proxies**—If your ISP has provided proxy servers for your use, you might want to enter them here. A *proxy* manages requests to Internet resources on behalf of your computer to either increase speed or security.

- **Modem**—Settings specific to your computer's modem. If you don't like hearing the annoying connection sound, you can shut off the speaker here. Most important, you can activate the option to Show Modem Status in Menu Bar, which provides a Menu Extra that enables you to easily connect and disconnect from the Internet.

In the PPP tab, enter the username and password you were given for your ISP, along with the phone number for the ISP's servers. If you'd like to keep your password stored with the machine, click the Save Password check box.

There are a number of settings you might want to look at by clicking the PPP Options button. You can configure settings in a sheet to give you the ability to redial a busy connection, automatically connect when starting TCP/IP applications, and automatically disconnect if you choose Log Out from the Apple menu.

Click Apply Now to save the settings. If you chose the PPP option to connect automatically when needed, you should be able to start Internet Explorer and begin surfing the Web.

> If you didn't choose to connect automatically, you can use the modem Menu Extra (go to the Modem tab to activate it) to add a quick-control icon to your menu bar. Alternatively, the Internet Connect application can start and stop a dial-in setting. We talk more about that later.

Built-in Ethernet

The next type of connection we look at is the built-in ethernet connection. If you have a wired 10BASE-T LAN or a DSL/cable modem hookup, this is where you'll need to focus your attention. Choose Built-in Ethernet in the pop-up menu. Again, the onscreen tabs change to enable you to fine-tune several related areas. The tabs for the Ethernet settings are

* **TCP/IP**—Unlike the modem TCP/IP settings you saw earlier, the Ethernet TCP/IP pane, displayed in Figure 9.2, offers more configuration options than are typical of a wired network.

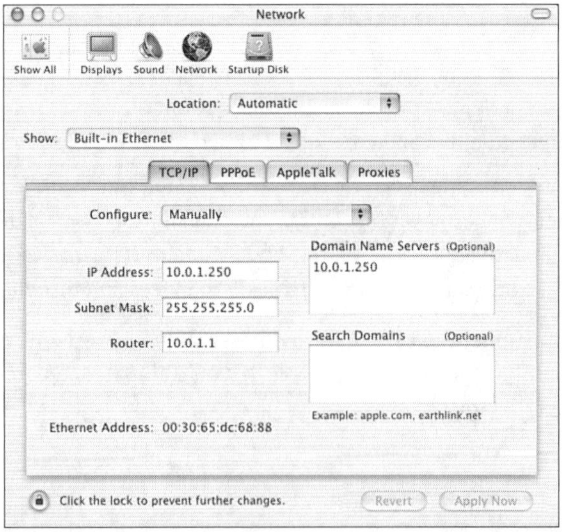

FIGURE 9.2

TCP/IP settings are important for Ethernet-based connections.

- **PPPoE**—PPP over ethernet is a common way for DSL-based services to connect. They generally require a username and password as a modem-based PPP connection does, but operate over a much faster ethernet wire.

- **AppleTalk**—The AppleTalk tab is used to control whether you become part of a local AppleTalk network. AppleTalk is Apple's traditional file-sharing protocol and is discussed further in Hour 13, "Using Network Sharing."

- **Proxies**—If your ISP has provided proxy servers for your use, you might want to enter them here.

9

As you can see in Figure 9.2, you definitely need a few items before you can successfully operate an ethernet connection. Fill in the information that you collected from your network administrator or ISP now. If you're lucky, at least a portion of these settings can be configured automatically by a BOOTP (boot protocol) or DHCP Dynamic Host Configuration Protocol) server on your network.

BOOTP and DHCP often provide automatic network setup on corporate and cable modem networks. If your network supports one of these services, you can use the Configure pop-up menu in the TCP/IP tab to select the appropriate protocol for your connection. Again, it's important that you do not *guess* what you need to connect—using invalid settings could disrupt your entire network.

If you're required to use PPPoE, click the PPPoE tab. In this pane, you can supply a username and password for your connection and enter optional identifying data for the ISP.

Near the bottom of the pane is a check box that enables you to view your PPPoE status in the menu bar. Clicking this check box adds a new Menu Extra that displays activity on your connection and gives you quick control over your settings.

Click the Apply Now button when you're satisfied with your ethernet setup. You should be able to immediately use the network software on your computer, such as Mail and Internet Explorer.

AirPort

The next connection method, AirPort, is available only if you've added an AirPort card to your system and are within range of a wireless base station. AirPort is Apple's 802.11b-based wireless networking device that enables you to connect to the Internet without the burden of running network wires or phone lines.

To configure your AirPort connection, choose AirPort in the Show pop-up menu. AirPort setup, surprisingly, is identical to ethernet. The same TCP/IP, AppleTalk, and Proxies tabs apply. There is, however, one additional tab that's essential to configure properly: the AirPort tab, shown in Figure 9.3.

FIGURE 9.3

Choose the AirPort network you want to connect to or set criteria so that your system can choose.

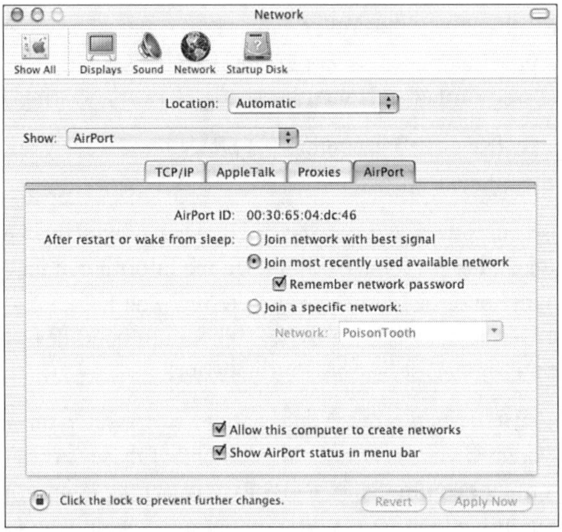

In the AirPort tab, you can direct your computer to Join the Network with Best Signal, Join the Most Recently Used Available Network, or Join a Specific Network.

AirPort networks are identified by a network name. When the Join a Specific Network radio button is selected, you can use the Network pop-up menu to choose one of the detected AirPort (or AirPort-compatible) networks, or manually type the name into the Preferred Network text field.

Finally, as with the modem and PPPoE settings, you can activate yet another Menu Extra—the AirPort signal strength—by clicking Show AirPort Status in Menu Bar. This Menu Extra also gives you the ability to instantly switch between the different available wireless networks and even shut down AirPort service if you like.

Click Apply Now to start using your wireless network.

Internet Sharing (Ethernet)

The final Networking option is a bit different than the ones previously discussed. Internet Sharing allows computers with multiple network cards to be connected to the Internet in a traditional way (using modem, ethernet, or AirPort) and to share their connection with another computer using either ethernet or AirPort. Although it's an interesting feature, it should be used with great care because this configuration can interfere with established networks.

Click the Start button to start sharing your active Internet connection.

Other computers should be configured to obtain their settings automatically (DHCP) and should be connected to the same network interface that's being shared.

For example, let's imagine that you have a computer connected via Ethernet and you want to share the connection via its AirPort card. First, start Internet Sharing, and then configure your other AirPort-capable computers to connect to the wireless network you just created. The client computers that have their AirPort TCP/IP settings configured to DHCP are immediately able to connect to the Internet.

Internet Sharing uses your computer to create a miniature local TCP/IP network that it manages. It controls all the settings on the client computers and ensures that requests to (and from) the Internet move back and forth as they should.

Setting Network Port Priorities and Locations

That wasn't so bad, was it? Everything that you need to get yourself connected to the Internet is all located in one System Preferences panel. Unfortunately, not all users' network setups are so easy. Many of us use our PowerBooks at home to dial in to the network, and then go to work and connect via ethernet, and, finally, stop by a coffee shop on the way home to relax and browse the Web via AirPort.

In Mac OS X, all your different network connections can be active simultaneously! This means that if it is possible for your computer to find a way to connect to a network, it will! Obviously, you don't want it trying to dial the phone if it has already found a connection, and, true to form, Mac OS X is smart enough to understand that if it *is* connected, it doesn't need to try any of the other connection methods. In fact, you can alter the order in which it tries to connect to the network by choosing Network Port Configurations in the Network Preferences panel's Show pop-up menu. This configuration pane is shown in Figure 9.4.

Here you can see that there are four port configurations: one modem, two ethernet, and one AirPort. I can drag these different configuration settings up and down in the list to determine the order in which Mac OS X attempts to use them. If you prefer that the computer *doesn't* attempt to connect using one of these configurations, deselect the check box in front of that item.

FIGURE 9.4

Adjust which connection settings take precedence over the others.

Network

Show All   Displays   Sound   Network   Startup Disk

Location: Automatic

Show: Network Port Configurations

Check a configuration to make it active. Drag configurations into the
order you want to try them when connecting to a network.

On	Port Configurations
☑	Internal Modem
☑	Built-in Ethernet
☑	AirPort
☑	Internet Sharing (Ethernet)

New...

Duplicate

Delete...

To change the name of a port configuration, double-click it.

🔒 Click the lock to prevent further changes.   Revert   Apply Now

Using the New, Duplicate, and Delete buttons on the right side of the pane, you can create alternative configurations for each of your built-in connection methods. These new configurations appear in the Show pop-up menu and are set up just as you set up the modem, ethernet, and AirPort connections earlier.

Locations

Mac OS X creates collections of port settings called *locations* that you can easily switch between. So far you've been dealing with a location called Automatic, shown in the Location pop-up menu of the Network Preferences panel.

To create a new location, choose New Location from the Location pop-up menu. After you create a new location, you can edit the port configurations and priorities just as you have under the default Automatic location. To manage the locations that you've set up, choose Edit Locations in the Location pop-up menu.

Switching from one location to another is simply a matter of choosing its name in the Location pop-up menu or the Location submenu under the systemwide Apple menu.

Choosing a new location immediately makes the new network settings available and could disrupt any connections currently taking place.

Using Internet Connect

The Internet Connect application is the final stop in your tour of Mac OS X network utilities (/Applications/Internet Connect). This is a rather strange application that offers a shortcut to the same features found in the Network Preferences panel. It can be used for both modem and AirPort connections to quickly log in to different configurations in your current location.

The Modem side of the Internet Connect application is displayed in Figure 9.5.

FIGURE 9.5

The Internet Connect application enables you to easily log in to your ISP.

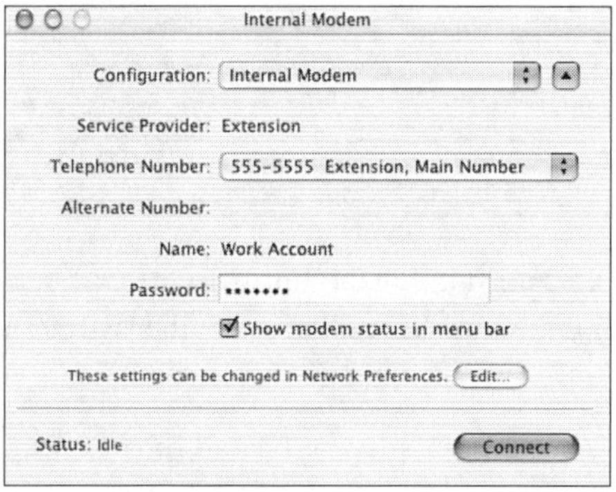

Internal Modem
Configuration: Internal Modem
Service Provider: Extension
Telephone Number: 555-5555 Extension, Main Number
Alternate Number:
Name: Work Account
Password: ••••••
☑ Show modem status in menu bar
These settings can be changed in Network Preferences. Edit...
Status: Idle   Connect

If your window appears much smaller than this, you might need to click the disclosure pushbutton at the far right of the window.

To log in to your ISP via modem, follow these steps:

1. Choose the modem configuration you created earlier in the Configuration pop-up menu at the top of the window.
2. Enter the phone number for your ISP or choose from in the pop-up menu.
3. The login name should already be set as configured in the Network Preferences panel. If you didn't save your password in the panel, you must enter it here.
4. Click the Show Modem Status in Menu Bar check box to add the modem Menu Extra to your screen.
5. Click Connect to start using your dial-in connection.

After you've connected to your ISP, the Connect button changes to Disconnect, giving you a quick way to break the modem connection.

AirPort users also stand to benefit from the Internet Connect application. Along with modem configurations, AirPort settings are also shown in the Configuration pop-up menu. Choosing an AirPort-based configuration displays the status of the connection and signal strength, as shown in Figure 9.6.

FIGURE 9.6

Internet Connect can also control your AirPort settings.

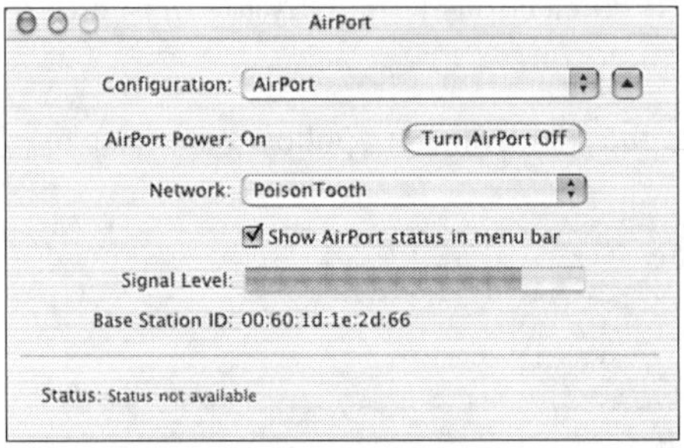

Use the Turn AirPort Off (and subsequent Turn AirPort On) button to disable or enable the AirPort card in your computer. To switch to another wireless network, use the Network pop-up menu.

Finally, to see a readout of the signal strength at all times, check the Show AirPort Status in Menu Bar check box.

As you can see, many of the features of the Internet Connect application are already accessible through the Network Preferences panel. Regardless, the Internet Connect application offers a quick means of viewing your connection status and changing common settings.

Summary

In this hour, you learned how to set up your Mac OS X computer for network access through traditional wired networks, wireless AirPort connections, and, of course, dial-up ISPs. Mac OS X networking has a number of advantages, including the ability to automatically configure itself to whatever type of network is currently available. This feature, combined with a simplified Location Manager, makes it easy to adapt your computer to any sort of network environment.

Q&A

Q **What if I don't have the information for my connection? What should I do?**

A Call your ISP or network administrator! You must use very specific values when setting up your network, and if you use the wrong ones, you could cause problems for a large number of people.

Q **What are search domains? I see them listed in the TCP/IP settings.**

A A *search domain* is the domain that is "searched" for a given computer if you don't enter a complete hostname. You can use it to save yourself typing. For sites such as apple.com that have valid addresses in the form info.apple.com and developer.apple.com, you could enter **apple.com** in the search domain text box and then only type **info** or **developer** into your browser to go to those sections.

Q **I have an ISDN connection. What do I do?**

A You likely need to get special software for your USB ISDN adapter. Contact your ISP for more information.

Q **Can I use the Mac OS X Location Manager for setting sounds or other system attributes?**

A No. In Mac OS X, only the network settings are affected when choosing a location.

Q **I have an AirPort base station. How can I set it up?**

A There are two AirPort utilities—AirPort Admin Utility and AirPort Setup Assistant—in your Utilities folder. Use these utilities along with the instructions that came with your base station to set up your hardware.

Workshop

The workshop contains quiz questions and activities to help you solidify your understanding of the material covered. Try to answer all questions before looking at the "Answers" section that follows.

Quiz

1. What are DHCP and BOOTP?
2. What network-related Menu Extras are available?
3. True or False: You must create a different location for each network configuration you want to use.
4. What types of connections can you control through the Internet Connect application?

Answers

1. DHCP and BOOTP are two protocols that often are used to automatically provide network settings to your computer.

2. PPPoE, AirPort, and modem settings can be accessed directly through their corresponding Menu Extras.

3. False. A single location can contain multiple network configurations.

4. The Internet Connect application can be used to monitor and start modem and AirPort-based connections.

Activities

Configure your system's network settings. If you use your computer in multiple environments, set up each of the connections and test them.

HOUR **10**

Web Browsing and .Mac Membership

Many people today purchase computers just to access the Internet. As you saw in the last hour, a Mac is easy to connect to the Internet. In this hour, you look at how to use Internet Explorer as your Web browser for surfing the World Wide Web, and what you can gain from membership to .Mac. In this hour, you'll

- Use Internet Explorer to browse the Internet
- Customize your Web browser preferences
- Discover the features available through .Mac

The Internet Explorer Interface

Mac OS X makes Web browsing easy with Internet Explorer (IE), a Web browser that enables you to open pages on the World Wide Web by typing in an address (better known as a URL or Uniform Resource Locator) or by clicking on hyperlinks.

To open Internet Explorer, simply click on the large blue lowercase letter e icon in the Dock. You can also find Internet Explorer in the Applications folder on your hard drive if it's been moved.

When launched, the IE window, shown in Figure 10.1, opens and connects to a default home page.

FIGURE 10.1
The default home page.

When you open IE, it's possible for five bars to be visible around the display window. If you want to hide or show any of them, you can do so by using the View menu.

- **Button bar**—Contains buttons of commonly used commands such as Back, Home, and Stop.
- **Address bar**—Where you type in an Internet address.
- **Favorites bar**—An area where you can place button shortcuts to several of your favorite sites for easy access.
- **Status bar**—The bar at the bottom of the window that gives you information, such as the name of the link your mouse pointer is currently hovering over. It also shows you whether the site you're visiting is secure.

- **Explorer bar**—A column of tabs on the left side of the screen for quickly opening commonly used lists in IE, such as your list of favorites, your history, and search sites.

Now that you know where all the bars are and their general purposes, let's take a look at some of IE's basic features.

Task: Using the Address Bar and the Button Bar

First, let's look at navigating the Web in general:

1. Click in the text box in the address bar, and type in **www.yahoo.com**. Press the Return key to bring up the Yahoo! home page. Notice that you didn't need to type the `http://`; it simply appears after you press Return.

2. Move your cursor over one of the blue underlined words on the page, and look in the lower-left corner of the window at the status bar to see the address to which this hyperlink will take you. Click on the link to go to that page.

3. If you decide you want to go back to the main Yahoo! page, just click the Back button in the button bar.

4. Click the Forward button to return to the page you just left.

5. To return to the default home page, click the Home button. If you want to know how to change your home page, see the "Setting Preferences" section later in this hour.

Two other buttons on the button bar are very important. The first is the Stop button. When you're visiting some Web sites, you might notice an error when connecting to the server or the page loading slowly. When this happens, click the Stop button to stop connecting to that page.

If you desperately need to reach that page, or if only part of the page is showing in the browser window, try clicking the Refresh button. The Refresh button reconnects to the server where that page is housed and tries to display it again.

Three other buttons appear on the button bar by default: AutoFill, Print, and Mail. These buttons are not used nearly as much as the five we've already discussed, but here's a brief description of what each one does:

- **AutoFill**—Click this button to have information you set in your preferences automatically entered in Web forms. If you're sick of repeatedly typing your name and address, the AutoFill button might become your favorite new toy.

10

- **Print**—This button does exactly what you would think: It opens a Print dialog box in which you can send the current Web page to the printer. We talk about setting up printers in Hour 16, "Setting Up Printers and Fonts."
- **Mail**—This button launches the mail program of your choice and opens an empty email message.

Now that you have an idea of what the button bar and address bar do, let's take a look at the favorites bar and the explorer bar. These two bars are used for marking places you like on the Internet or for retracing your steps to find a page you liked.

Favorites

First, let's look at Favorites in the explorer bar. Favorites, often called *bookmarks*, are the sites you have visited and want to visit again. The Favorites list can get incredibly long, so the makers of IE have given you a way to organize your favorites into folders. There are several default Favorites folders in IE. If you need to, you can create other folders or delete folders to better organize your favorites.

Task: Using and Adding Favorites in the Explorer Bar

Let's examine some of the default favorites and make a few of your own:

1. Click the Favorites tab in the explorer bar on the left side of the window. When you do, a new pane appears, as shown in Figure 10.2. This pane contains the same list and functions as the Favorites menu in the menu bar.

FIGURE 10.2

The Favorites pane on the left side of the window displays your list of favorites.

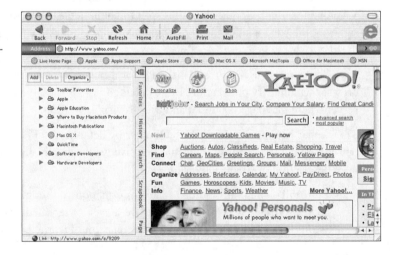

2. Click a folder to expand it so that you can see all the favorite sites in it. Notice that a favorite has an @ icon to its left and a folder has an icon of a folder.

3. Click one of the listed favorites. The main pane on the right changes to show the page you've chosen.

You might be thinking, "Gee, that was easy, but what about the pages I really want to visit? I'm sure Apple didn't think of all of them." Of course not, so your next task is to add your own favorites to this list and make folders to organize them.

1. Click in the address bar, type **www.yahoo.com**, and press Return. If you worked through the previous example and entered www.yahoo.com, the address begins to fill in for you as you start typing. This is part of the AutoComplete feature used in many Microsoft products. When you see the address appear, simply press Return.

2. To add Yahoo! to your Favorites list, point to the @ symbol to the left of the address in the address bar and drag it to the bottom of the Favorites list in the Favorites pane. Next, you'll make a folder to store favorites for all your search sites.

> Alternatively, you might want to simply click the Add button in the Favorites pane. This enables you to add the favorite and place it into any folder you want without using the drag-and-drop technique.

3. Click the Organize button in the Favorites pane and select New Folder. You should see a new folder appear in the list; simply type a name for the folder, such as **My Search Sites**, and press Return when you are finished.

4. Drag the Yahoo! favorite to the My Search Sites folder and drop it. You have your first search favorite!

> You can drag a site straight from the address bar into the folder of your choice—simply drag the @ at the left of the address into the Favorites pane and onto the folder of your choice.

Changing favorites is very much like changing files. If you want to rename a favorite, Ctrl+click on the name of the favorite to open a pop-up menu. From here you can choose to edit the name of the favorite or the address the favorite points to, or you can simply delete a favorite.

You might also want to organize your favorites in their own window. To do this, click on the Organize button and select Open Favorites Window. This opens the Favorites window, shown in Figure 10.3, where you can click on the name of a favorite to rename it, or select a favorite and press Delete to remove it from the Favorites list.

FIGURE 10.3

The Favorites window enables you to add and delete favorites from your list as well as rename and move them.

Name	Address
▼ 🗁 Toolbar Favorites	
Live Home Page	http://livepage.apple.com/
Apple	http://www.apple.com/
Apple Support	http://www.apple.com/support/
Apple Store	http://www.apple.com/store/
.Mac	http://www.mac.com/
Mac OS X	http://www.apple.com/macosx/
Microsoft MacTopia	http://www.microsoft.com/mac/
Office for Macintosh	http://www.microsoft.com/macoffice/
MSN	http://www.msn.com/
▼ 🗁 Apple	
Apple	http://www.apple.com/
Apple Product Information	http://www.apple.com/products/
Apple Customer Support	http://www.apple.com/support/
Apple Software Updates	http://www.apple.com/swupdates/
Apple Hot News	http://www.apple.com/hotnews/
.Mac	http://www.mac.com/
Mac.com Email	http://webmail.mac.com/
iCards	http://icards.mac.com/WebObjects/iCards
Contacting Apple	http://www.apple.com/about/phonenumbers.html
MacDirectory	http://www.macdirectory.com/

If you have trouble organizing your favorites with only folders, you might want to add a divider line. To do so, click on the Organize button and choose New Divider. A divider that you can move anywhere in the list appears at the bottom of the Favorites list.

For a few sites you visit on a regular basis, you might want to add them to the favorites bar, located directly below the address bar. If you want to add a favorite to the favorites bar, simply go to that page and drag the @ symbol next to the address in the address bar down to the place in the toolbar where you want it to appear. When your mouse pointer turns into a bar, drop the favorite and it becomes part of the toolbar.

Many pages have such long titles that they take up almost one-third of the Favorites toolbar. If a page you've added has a long title on the button, simply Ctrl+click on the button and choose Edit Name. This displays the Toolbar favorites in an Organize View with that favorite ready to have its name edited.

History

In addition to showing Favorites, another function of the explorer bar is to show you a history of the sites you've visited (see Figure 10.4). This enables you to return to pages you've visited recently. If you want to change the number of pages the History pane records, you can do so in the Preferences, which you'll look at later in this hour.

FIGURE 10.4

By default, the History pane shows the last 300 pages you've visited.

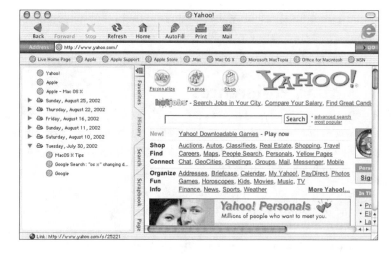

Downloading

To update your software or get new software, you might need to download a file from the Internet as discussed in Hour 4, "Installing New Applications." IE makes this task easy with the Download Manager (shown in Figure 10.5), which opens when you're downloading a file to show you the file's status (such as how far it has progressed) and to enable you to stop the download if you change your mind. The Download Manager also shows you the last 10 files you downloaded—a handy feature if you have a memory like mine, when you can't remember what you have done and what you haven't.

When you're downloading files, you should be aware that you're transferring someone else's files to your hard drive and those files could carry a virus. A *virus* is a malicious program meant to harm your hard drive or network. When downloading, use a reputable site and never download a file if you don't know what that file does. You might also want to have antivirus software on your computer to scan for viruses. See Hour 24, "Maintenance and Troubleshooting," for more information.

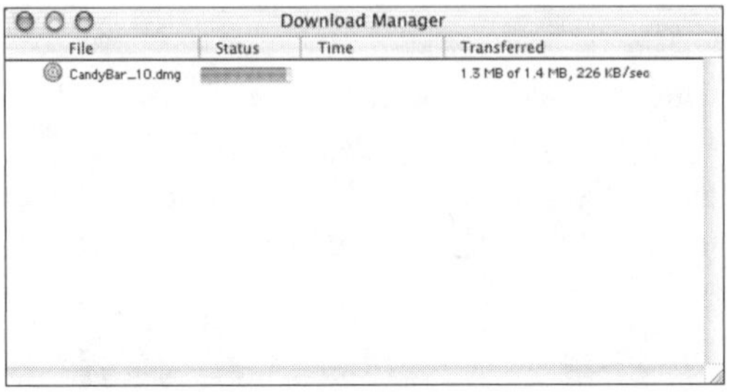

FIGURE 10.5

The Download Manager is a separate window in Internet Explorer.

⊜ ◯ ⊜		Download Manager		
File	Status	Time	Transferred	
⊙ CandyBar_10.dmg	▓▓▓▓▓▓		1.3 MB of 1.4 MB, 226 KB/sec	

Refer to Hour 4 for examples of downloading and installing programs.

Setting Preferences

So far you've learned how to use a Web browser to visit different sites on the Internet. You're now going to take a look at all the aspects of IE that can be customized and altered to fit your needs. To do this, you use the Preferences dialog box found in the Explorer application menu.

Click on Explorer in the menu bar and select Preferences, or simply press Command+;. The first time it's opened, the dialog box shows preferences from the Browser Display category on the left. After that, it remembers the last thing you chose. If it isn't already open, click Browser Display in the Preferences dialog box. Here you can change your default home page. In the Home Page section in the middle of the Browser Display panel, select the URL (Web address) in the Address field, and type `http://www.yahoo.com`. This makes Yahoo! your home page, so it appears whenever you open Internet Explorer. Click on OK. Close IE by choosing File, Quit from the menu bar, or by using Command+Q. Open IE again by clicking the icon in the Dock or in your Applications folder. Notice that the page that opens first is Yahoo!. You can set any page on the Web or on your hard drive to be your home page.

Whenever you want to view this home page, click the Home button in the button bar.

Although there are far too many categories of preferences to cover in this hour, there are a few you should be aware of. One is the Toolbar Settings in the Browser Display category. By default, the toolbar (also known as the button bar) displays both icons and text. If you're running low on screen space, you might want to have these buttons display only icons or text to reduce the height of the toolbar.

If you select the Web Content category in the list in Internet Explorer Preferences, you can choose several options that speed up the time it takes to load a page in your browser. The most useful thing you can do if you're using a slow connection is to uncheck the Show Pictures check box. If this box isn't checked, the large picture files that slow down many pages aren't displayed.

Many sites today rely heavily on pictures to create their menu structure and convey the general message of the Web site. Although a good Web designer should have alternative tags that display text instead of the picture, many designers don't take the time to code them into their pages, rendering the text tags useless if you don't display the pictures.

In the Advanced panel of the Preferences dialog box, as shown in Figure 10.6, you find some of the settings referred to earlier in this hour. One setting is the number of pages you visited that your browser stores in its history. The history stores 300 pages by default, but this number can vary from 0 to 1,000. Another thing to notice in the History section is the big button labeled Clear History. Regardless of how many places you've told the browser to remember, when you click Clear History, all those places are no longer part of the browser's history. You might say they're history! Doing so prevents anyone else using your account from discovering where you've been.

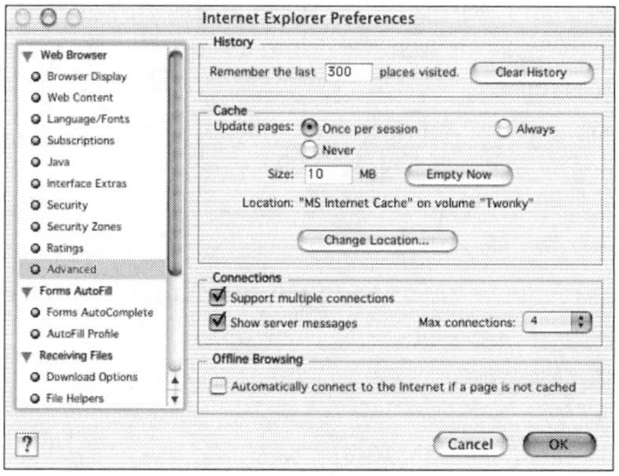

Figure 10.6

The Advanced panel in the Preferences dialog box is where you can go to clear the history.

.Mac

Now that you've mastered the basics of Web browser use, let's look at .Mac—a Web-based set of applications and services designed by Apple for Mac users (although some services are also available to PC users). You can purchase a year-long membership at www.mac.com to receive the following:

.Mac replaces a now-defunct free service from Apple called iTools. Some applications on your system, including iPhoto 1.1.1, might still refer to iTools rather than .Mac.

- **Email**—Accessible from anywhere you have a Web browser, mac.com email accounts include 15MB of storage space.

- **iDisk**—100MB of storage space, accessible from both Macs and PCs, for backing up or sharing your files across the Internet. You can connect to the iDisk from the Go menu of the Finder and choosing iDisk (Shift+Command+I).

- **HomePage**—As discussed in Hour 6, "iPhoto," Apple's HomePage application can generate a basic Web page and transfer it to the Apple server. You can further edit the created pages or substitute pages of your own design.

- **Backup**—Created by Apple, Backup helps transfer your files to iDisk or burn to CD or DVD using an internal CD-RW or SuperDrive. It also helps you schedule regular backups and, if the time comes, restore your files. See Hour 24 for more information.

Full access to .Mac benefits requires a paid subscription, but you can sample some .Mac features for free. A 60-day free trial of .Mac includes an email address and 5MB of space, 20MB of iDisk space, Backup software to help you store files in your iDisk, and use of HomePage to create and share your Web page.

Without either full or trial membership to .Mac, you can send iCards and access the public folders of .Mac members.

- **iCards**—Send iCards via email to your friends and family. Members of .Mac have the added ability to use photos of their own.

Another small application available through .Mac is the .Mac Slide Publisher, which enables you to upload a set of images to your iDisk for use as a screen saver by others running Mac OS X 10.2. Even though you can only have one slide show operational at a time, this is a fun way to share pictures with friends and family.

To set a .Mac slide show as your screen saver, go to the Screen Effects panel of System Preferences and choose .Mac in the Screen Effects list. Then click the Configure button to enter the .Mac membership name of the person whose slides you want to view—you're welcome to subscribe to my .Mac slide show by entering **robynness** in the text entry field. Click OK to set your selection. It takes a moment for the images to be downloaded from the Internet to your computer. You can test the slide show by clicking the Test button in the Screen Effects tab.

- **Anti-Virus**—Download McAfee's Virex software to protect yourself again harmful computer viruses. See Hour 24 for more information.

Setting .Mac Preferences in Mac OS X

The applications that make up .Mac are easily and seamlessly integrated into Mac OS X. If you sign up for a .Mac account, you'll find that the easiest way to make sure that your .Mac account works with your operating system is to set up your account in System Preferences for Mac OS X.

Click the System Preferences icon in the Dock or choose System Preferences from the Apple menu. In the System Preferences panel, click the Internet button under the Internet & Network category. Click the .Mac tab at the top of the panel, as shown in Figure 10.7. Enter your information in the .Mac Member Name and Password fields. By entering the .Mac member information, you're giving Mac OS X access to the information so that you don't have to enter it in multiple applications that interact with .Mac.

10

FIGURE 10.7

The Internet Preferences panel opened from System Preferences.

The iDisk tab of the Internet preference panel helps you monitor the amount of space your files use. Under the Public Folder Access section of this tab, you can set read/write permissions and even password protect your public folder.

Summary

In this hour, you learned how to use Internet Explorer to visit sites on the World Wide Web. You learned how to save and edit favorites, how to change the look of IE, and how to clear the history so that no one knows where you've been. You also learned about the services available through .Mac membership.

Q&A

Q What are some other browsers besides Internet Explorer?

A There are several other browsers besides Internet Explorer, including Netscape, OmniWeb, and Opera. If you want to try one, go to the Mac OS X page of `www.versiontracker.com` and search for Web browsers to download and install.

Also, if you install a new browser that you want to use as your system's default Web browser instead of Internet Explorer, you can change this setting in the Web tab of the Internet panel of System Preferences.

Q You said that files in the public folder of my iDisk are accessible to other users. How can someone else connect to my iDisk?

A From another computer running Mac OS X, choose Connect to Server from the Finder's Go menu and enter the address of the iDisk you want to access as `http://idisk.mac.com/[membername]/Public/`, filling in *[membername]* with the appropriate information. If the folder is password protected, you must enter `public` for the username and the proper password in the password field.

From a computer running Mac OS 9, open the Chooser from the Apple menu. Select AppleShare and click Server IP Address button. Type `idisk.mac.com` in the Server Address text box and click Connect. Type the member name of the person whose folder you want to access and enter either the proper password for the folder or, if there is no password, the word `public`. Select the iDisk and click OK.

PC users operating Windows 98, 2000, or XP can also access iDisk. However, each of those systems does so in a slightly different way. Visit `www.mac.com` for detailed instructions.

For those who need to connect to multiple iDisks, iDisk Utility can help. You can download this application from www.mac.com.

Workshop

The workshop contains quiz questions and activities to help you solidify your understanding of the material covered. Try to answer all questions before looking at the "Answers" section that follows.

Quiz

1. By default, how many different bars do you find around the Internet Explorer window?
2. Where can you change the destination of the Home button in the button bar?
3. Where can adjust your .Mac preferences?

Answers

1. Five: the button bar, the address bar, the favorites bar, the explorer bar, and the status bar.
2. In the Preferences dialog box under the application menu.
3. Under the .Mac and iDisk tabs of the Internet panel of System Preferences.

Activities

1. To sharpen your skills, visit some sites that you think you would visit often and make them favorites. After you have made 10 Favorites, categorize them by using folders.
2. Go to www.mac.com and click the icon for iCards. Follow the site instructions to send a card to someone you know.

10

HOUR 11

Sherlock

As its name implies, Sherlock is something of a detective, tracking down information from the clues you provide. Some people might find it hard to get excited about a search tool, but Sherlock is far from ordinary. With specialized search categories, including yellow pages and dictionary, Sherlock will quickly become your one-stop reference tool. In this hour, you use Sherlock to

- Search the Internet and eBay auctions
- Get stock quotes and flight information
- Search for movies and businesses based on your location
- Look up definitions and perform rough translations between languages

Sherlock Channels

Sherlock is a collection of Internet search functions, each packaged as its own channel. The default channels are listed in the Channels panel, as shown in Figure 11.1. They're also listed in the toolbar at the top of the window, along with any additional channels to which you subscribe.

Long-time Mac users might be confused by the recent incarnation of Sherlock, which doesn't include the option to search the local machine's files. That feature is now available directly from the Finder by selecting Find from the Finder's File menu or with the keyboard shortcut Command+F. Refer to Hour 2, "Using the Finder and the Dock," for further information.

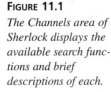

FIGURE 11.1

The Channels area of Sherlock displays the available search functions and brief descriptions of each.

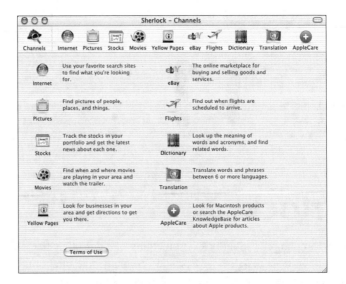

Each channel provides a specific kind of information, gathered from another source and displayed within the Sherlock interface. You'll notice that on the Channels page is a button labeled Terms of Use, which opens a sheet explaining that Apple doesn't produce most of the content displayed in Sherlock.

Let's take a look at each default channel's use and special features.

The Internet Channel

The Internet channel compiles search results from popular Internet search sites, such as Ask Jeeves and Lycos. As shown in Figure 11.2, each search result lists the title and address of a Web page, a relevance rating, and the search site or sites that provided the entry.

FIGURE 11.2

Searching the Internet from a variety of search engines is simplified by Sherlock.

Sherlock – Internet	
Channels Internet Pictures Stocks Movies Yellow Pages eBay Flights Dictionary Translation AppleCare	
Topic or Description	
iPhoto	

Web Sites	Relevance	Search Sites
iPhoto – Apple Computer http://www.apple.com/iphoto		Ask Jeeves, Best Site First, LookSma
Welcome to iPhoto! http://www.iphoto.ca/		Ask Jeeves, Lycos
No Title http://www.apple.co.jp/iphoto/		LookSmart, Lycos
CNET Shopper.com – Apple iPhoto http://www3.overture.com/d/		Overture
iPhoto http://www.iphoto.to/		LookSmart, Lycos
Iphoto download page at WebAttack.com, http://www.webattack.com/get/iphoto.shtml		Ask Jeeves
iPhoto Plus 4 Tutorial http://mustek.com/Imaging/support/tutorials/doc7206.htm		Ask Jeeves
Consumer DTP Profile – Joe http://desktoppub.about.com/library/profiles/consumer/		About.com

Visit www.apple.com for the latest news, the hottest products, and technical support resources from Apple Computer, Inc.

Content provided by About ???? ???? looksmart LYCOS overture Sprinks

To perform an Internet search, simply type your search terms into the text entry field at the top of the Internet channel panel and click the green Search button or press Return. When the results listing appears, you can select an entry with a single click to see a site description if one is available. Double-clicking launches your default Web browser and opens the page you requested.

The Pictures Channel

Similar to searches using the Internet channel, the Pictures channels queries photo databases for digital images based on your search terms. Thumbnail images of the results are displayed in the results pane, as shown in Figure 11.3. Double-click a thumbnail image in the results to open a Web page displaying the full-sized picture.

The photos displayed in the Pictures channel searches might not be free for commercial use. Read the terms of service from the originating site if you have any questions about what's allowed.

The Stocks Channel

The Stocks channel, shown in Figure 11.4, provides details about the market performance of publicly traded companies. The information shown includes the stock price at last trade, price change, price range over the course of the day, and the volume of shares traded. You can also view charts of a company's performance over the past year or week or for the current day.

11

FIGURE 11.3

Results appear as thumbnail images— double-click one to see the original.

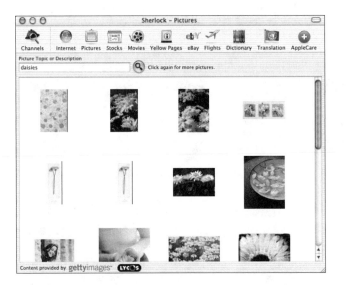

FIGURE 11.4

Enter a company's name or market symbol to see information about it, including recent news stories.

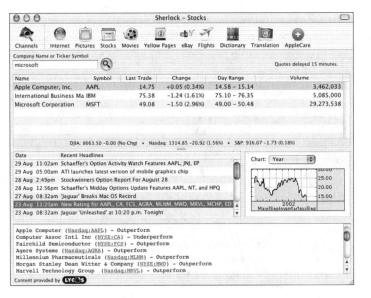

To find information about a company, enter its name or market symbol. Market symbols are unique identifiers, but many companies have similar names or several separate divisions. If you enter a name, you might see a sheet asking you to choose the company you're interested in. When the correct name or symbol appears in the text entry field, click the green Search button or press the Return key.

Market symbols and companies with similar names can make it difficult to ask for the listing you really want. If you don't enter the exact market symbol, some guesswork might be involved for Sherlock to return any results. Always check to make sure that the displayed information is for the company you thought you requested!

In addition to providing stock quotes, Sherlock also displays recent news articles pertaining to the selected company. To read a story, select its headline from the left of the chart and the bottom pane displays the full text.

The Movies Channel

Sherlock's Movies channel, shown in Figure 11.5, pulls together all the information you need to choose a movie and a theater in which to view it.

FIGURE 11.5

The Movies channel displays a QuickTime preview of the selected movie as well as theater addresses.

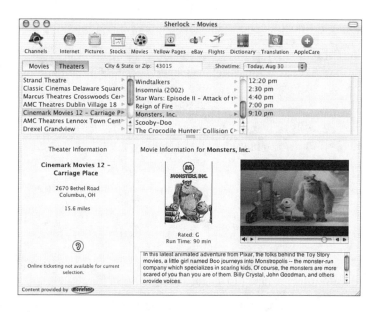

To use the Movies channel, you must enter either your city and state or your ZIP Code. Then you can choose to search either Movies or Theaters in your area. The Showtime pop-up menu enables you to choose the date of interest to you.

Choose one of the movie and theater listings at the top of the panel that's interest to you, and the bottom panes of the window fill with theater and movie information. In addition to a text summary of the movie, you can watch a preview for the selected option in QuickTime.

To play the QuickTime preview, you might be prompted to set your network connection information in QuickTime Preferences if you haven't already done so. Refer to Hour 7, "Quicktime and iMovie," for more details.

The Yellow Pages Channel

Use the Yellow Pages channel, shown in Figure 11.6, to obtain the phone number and address for a business and to view a map of its location. Simply enter the business name and either the city and state or the ZIP Code of the area to search, and click the green button. In the middle pane, choose from among the list of potential matches to see detailed information.

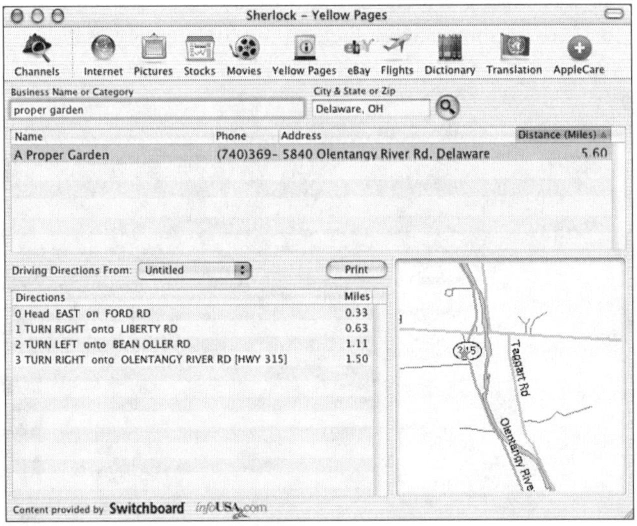

FIGURE **11.6**

Obtain contact information and personalized driving directions to businesses.

To receive driving directions, you must first enter an address in the Locations tab of the Sherlock Preferences. To do so, follow these steps:

1. Choose Preferences, shown in Figure 11.7, from the Sherlock menu.

2. Click the Add button to create an untitled entry under Locations.

3. To change the label of your new location, double-click on the word Untitled until only that word is highlighted and then type a new label. Keep in mind that you can have more than one location entered, so change it to something meaningful.

4. Fill in the information on the right side of the window.

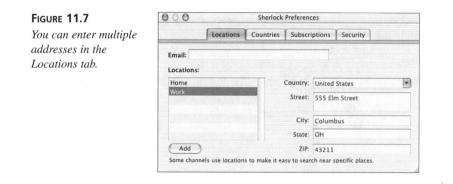

5. Close the Preferences window. Your entry is saved as you type. To delete an entry, simply select it from the Locations listing and press the Delete key on your keyboard.

When you return to the Yellow Pages channel, you can select the location you added in the Driving Directions From pop-up menu. The Directions pane fills with step-by-step instructions.

The eBay Channel

From the eBay channel, you can search active eBay auctions and track those of interest to you. To search, enter keywords in the Item Title text entry field and set your other parameters, such as product category, region, and price range, and then click the search button. When you choose a result from the search, its details fill the bottom panes of the screen, as shown in Figure 11.8.

To track as item, highlight it in the results listing and click the Track Auction button at lower right. Changing to Track mode using the button just below the search field reveals a list of only those items you're tracking. To remove an auction, select it and press the Delete key on your keyboard.

The Flights Channel

For information on current flights, go to the Flights channel. Here you can view flight status by route or by airline and flight number. Select a specific flight for details about the aircraft and flight. For some entries, you can also view a chart depicting the plane's position en route, as shown in the lower-right corner of Figure 11.9.

11

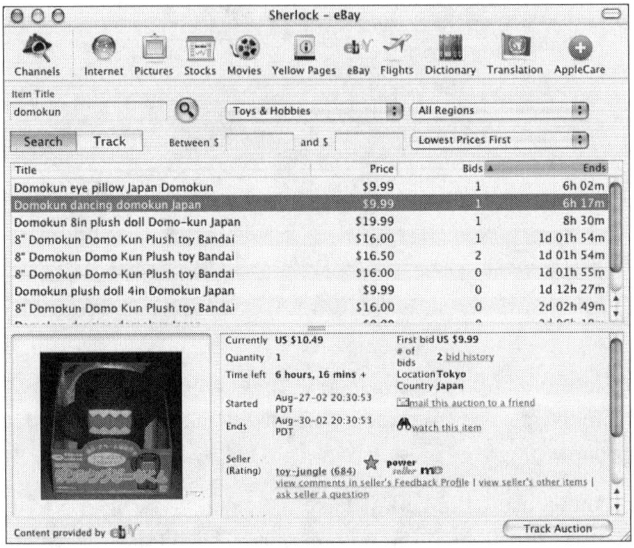

FIGURE **11.8**

If you enjoy online auctions, the eBay channel will delight you.

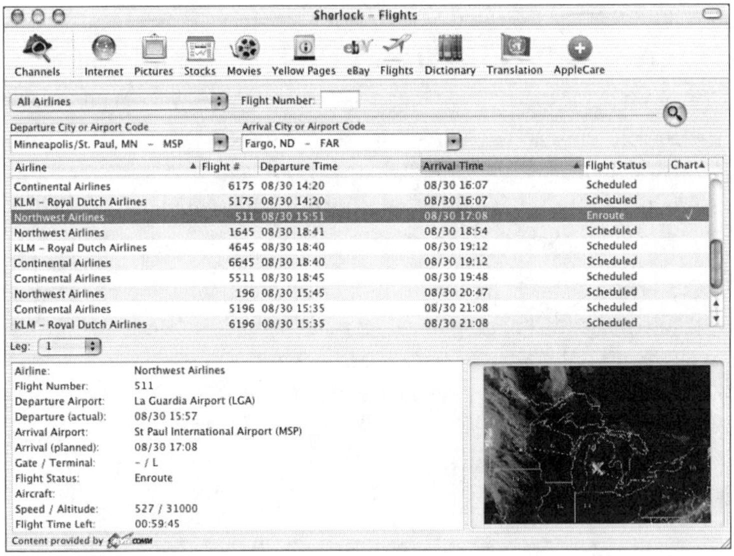

FIGURE **11.9**

View the status of specific flights, including a chart of the flight path.

The Dictionary Channel

As you might expect, you look up word definitions in the Dictionary channel. For some words, you also see a list of phrases containing that word from *Roget's II Thesaurus*.

The Translation Channel

The Translation channel performs rough translations between different languages. English speakers can translate into Simplified and Traditional Chinese, Dutch, French, German, Greek, Italian, Japanese, Korean, Portuguese, Russian, and Spanish, and then back to English. When using this service, keep in mind that computer-generated translations do not match the output of a skilled human translator.

The AppleCare Channel

If you have a specific technical question that Help Viewer can't resolve, the AppleCare channel enables you to search the AppleCare Knowledge Base for reports about Apple products and issues.

Now that we explored the channels, let's examine the features accessible in Sherlock's preferences.

Sherlock Preferences

Sherlock's preference dialog box, shown earlier in Figure 11.7, contains four tabs—Locations, Countries, Subscriptions, and Security—in which you can adjust Sherlock's settings. We discussed the Locations configurations earlier during our look at the Yellow Pages channel.

The Countries tab enables you to specify which countries' channels you want to receive. By default, only the country you selected during set up is turned on, but other countries in which the same language is spoken also appear. To see a list of all countries, check the Show All Countries box.

The Subscriptions tab enables you to add additional channels to Sherlock. Although the current version of Sherlock—version 3.5—is somewhat new, in the past it was common for Web site owners to write plug-ins for Sherlock that allowed it to include those sites in its searches. In the Subscriptions tab, you can add channels created by people outside of Apple.

The Security tab contains settings to enable channels from non-Apple sources. If you don't enable the Web sites of channels you've added in the Subscriptions tab, you are asked to approve each channel that's not part of Apple's basic set. The Security tab also contains settings to manage cookies that might be encountered by Sherlock as it searches the Internet on your behalf.

11

Cookies are small files sent to your computer from Web sites. Sites use cookies to keep track of you as a specific user as you interact with the site. (This is because the computer running the Web site doesn't have another way to recognize that you're the same person who looked at the preceding page.) Even though cookies are mostly harmless, some people don't like the idea of having others track their movements on the Internet, even if the information is most likely never seen by human eyes.

Summary

In this hour, you learned how to use Sherlock 3, your system's built-in Internet search tool. You saw the range of specialized search channels available, including movie listings, eBay auction tracking, and translation between languages. You also learned how to set a location in your application preferences so that Sherlock's Yellow Pages channel can provide driving directions.

Q&A

Q Can I use Sherlock when my computer is not connected to the Internet?

A No. Because Sherlock 3.5 is really just a convenient-to-read repackaging of information from online sources, you must be connected to the Internet to use any of the channels.

If you launch Sherlock without being connected to the Internet, you'll see a message asking if you would like to connect to the Internet. Clicking OK launches the Internet Connect program discussed in Hour 9, "Setting Up Mac OS X Networking."

Q You wrote that I can add other channels to Sherlock. Where can I find some?

A Sherlock 3.5 represents a major revision of previous versions of Sherlock, and plug-ins written for the previous versions don't work with it. It might take some time for additional channels to become available. Rest assured, however, that the loyal Apple community will rush to fill the Sherlock plug-in void.

Workshop

The workshop contains quiz questions and activities to help you solidify your understanding of the material covered. Try to answer all questions before looking at the "Answers" section that follows.

Quiz

1. Which channel enables you to obtain driving directions from your location to a selected business?

2. Where in Sherlock can you search the files on your local hard drive?

3. Where do you choose how to Sherlock reacts to cookies?

Answers

1. Yellow Pages.

2. This is a trick question—this feature is no longer available within Sherlock. You must open the Finder's Find dialog box from the File menu, or with the keyboard shortcut Command+F, to search your computer.

3. In the Security tab of Sherlock Preferences.

Activities

1. If you're connected to the Internet, perform an Internet search and a picture search on the same term to see what different items you find.

2. Set a location under Sherlock Preferences, and then use the Yellow Pages to produce a map and driving directions for your favorite restaurant or business.

3. Test the accuracy of the Translation channel by translating a phrase to a different language, and then translating the phrase back to the original language.

11

Hour 12

Mail and iChat

In this hour, we discuss applications that come with Mac OS X 10.2 to help you keep in touch with everyone you know. One such application is Mail, the most beautiful messaging program you'll find on any platform, and the other is iChat, a built-in instant messaging client through which you can send text messages. We also look at Address Book, a companion application to Mail and iChat that stores contact data. With these applications, your friends and family are only a click away. In this hour, you learn to

- Set up Mail accounts
- Receive and send email
- Send instant messages with iChat
- Use the Address Book

Mail

The Mac OS X Mail application is Apple's email client for the Macintosh. For years, Mac users have been using other companies' software (Microsoft, Qualcomm, Claris, and so on) to check their email. In Mac OS X, Apple has finally given us an email client worthy of the Apple logo. Mail provides excellent support for IMAP and POP services, and includes a cutting-edge interface, junk-mail detection heuristics, and searching mechanisms that can make managing hordes (or even a trickle) of email messages fast and painless.

> If you have a third-party email application that you want to use instead of Mail, you can set it as your default email program in the Internet panel of System Preferences under the Email tab. This enables Mac OS X to launch your mail program automatically when clicking on a `mailto:` link.

If you've used an email program such as Eudora or Outlook Express, you'll be completely comfortable with Mail's interface. The toolbar at the top of the window holds commonly used functions for creating, responding to, and searching messages.

In the center of the window is a list of the active messages in each mailbox. The list columns (from left to right) display read/unread status, online buddy status for iChat, sender, subject, and day/time sent by the sender. As with most list views, the columns can be sorted by clicking their headings or reordered by dragging the heading to the desired position.

Figure 12.1 shows the Mail application, ready for action.

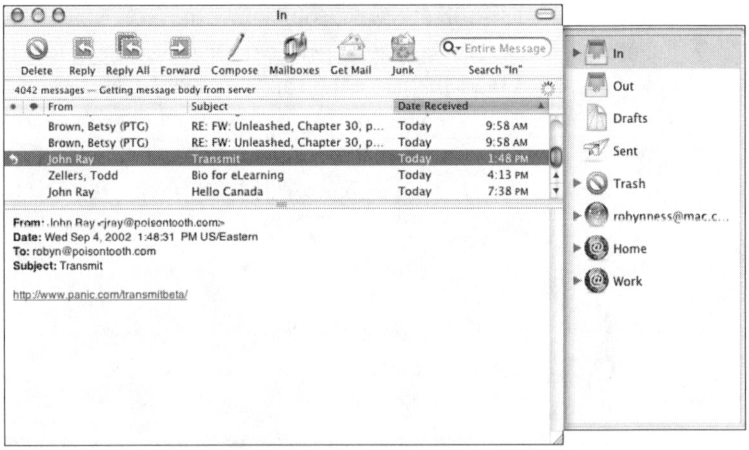

FIGURE 12.1

Mail uses Mac OS X interface elements to create an integrated user experience.

To display the accounts and mail folders that have been added to the system, click the Mailboxes toolbar button or choose Show Drawer (Shift+Command+M) from the View menu. The mailbox drawer slides out from the side of the Mail window. You can use the disclosure triangles to collapse and expand the hierarchy of mail folders that you create. The number of unread messages is displayed in parentheses to the right of each mailbox.

When Mail is open, its icon in the Dock displays the total number of unread messages in all Inbox folders.

Adding or Editing an Account

During the Mac OS X setup procedure, the Installer prompts for a default email account, which creates a single account for a single person. If you chose to skip that setup or want to add multiple accounts, you can add or edit email accounts in the Accounts pane of the Mail Preferences dialog box.

To open this dialog box, start Mail (path: /Applications/Mail) and then choose Preferences from the application menu and click the Accounts icon. Existing email accounts are listed on the left. The options available include

- **Add Account**—Add a new email account
- **Edit**—Edit the selected account
- **Remove**—Delete the selected account
- **Check for new mail**—Change how often *all* the email accounts are polled
- **New mail sound**—Select the sound that's played when a new message arrives on the server

To add a new account to the list, click the Add Account button. An account information sheet appears that's divided into three tabs: Account Information, Special Mailboxes, and Advanced. The general Account Information tab is shown in Figure 12.2.

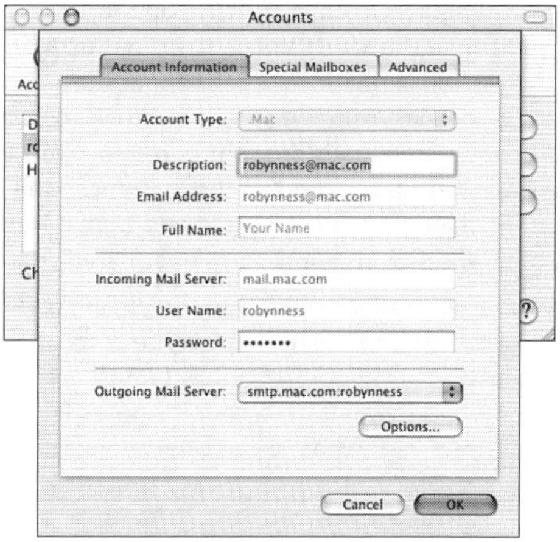

12

FIGURE 12.2

Enter the new email account information into this tab.

Accounts
Account Information   Special Mailboxes   Advanced
Account Type: Mac
Description: robynness@mac.com
Email Address: robynness@mac.com
Full Name: Your Name
Incoming Mail Server: mail.mac.com
User Name: robynness
Password: •••••••
Outgoing Mail Server: smtp.mac.com:robynness
Options...
Cancel   OK

Use the Account Type pop-up menu to set the account type. Instead of just IMAP or POP accounts, there are three options:

- **.Mac**—Configures a .Mac IMAP account with the appropriate Apple defaults. (See Hour 10, "Web Browsing and .Mac Membership," for more information about .Mac membership.)
- **POP**—Creates a basic POP3 account.
- **IMAP**—Creates a basic IMAP account.

POP3 Versus IMAP

If your email provider supports both POP3 and IMAP, you're in luck!

POP3, although extremely popular, is not practical for people with multiple computers. POP3 works much the way it sounds: Email is "popped" from a remote server. Incoming messages are stored on the remote server, which in turn waits for a connection from a POP3 client. The client connects only long enough to download all the messages and save them to the local hard drive.

In this process, the server stores email temporarily and handles short-lived connections, so the burden of long-term storage and filing rests squarely on the shoulders of the user. Unfortunately, after a message transfers from the server, it's gone. If you go to another computer to check your mail, it won't be there.

The more computers you use, the more fragmented your messages become. Some provisions exist for keeping messages on the server, but in reality it's a hassle and rarely works as planned. Although the same message can be downloaded to multiple machines, deleting it from one machine won't delete it from the others. The end result is, quite frankly, a mess!

IMAP takes a different approach. Instead of relying on the client for message storage, IMAP servers keep everything on the server. Messages and mail folders remain on the server unless the client explicitly deletes them. When new messages arrive, the IMAP client application downloads either the message body or header from the server, but the server contents remain the same. If multiple computers are configured to access the same email account, the email appears identical on all the machines—the same folders, messages, and message flags are maintained. In addition, IMAP supports shared folders among different user accounts and server-based content searches.

The drawback to IMAP lies mostly in the email provider—supporting IMAP's additional features and the added storage costs often aren't economical on a large scale. If your ISP doesn't support IMAP and you want to take advantage of it, sign up for an .Mac account. Apple's POP and IMAP services are fast, reliable, and—for what you get—economical.

After choosing your account type, you must fill in several other fields:

- **Description**—The description is a name you give the email account. It's for your use only and can be something simple, such as Work or Cable Modem.
- **Email Address**—Enter the full email address for the account you're adding.
- **Full Name**—This is the name that's transmitted with your email address. For example, I would fill it in with Anne Groves. You'll see the full name in the header of an email like this: "Anne Groves" <groves.54@osu.edu>.
- **Incoming Mail Server**—This could be something such as mail.mac.com.
- **User Name**—This is the name you use to log on to the server, such as agroves.
- **Password**—This is the password you need to log on to the server.
- **Outgoing Mail Server**—This is the server you use when sending mail.

Near the bottom of the Account Information tab is the Options button, which launches the SMTP Server Options window. *Authenticated SMTP* is used when the server you're sending mail through checks to make sure that you're authorized to send mail through it by requesting a username and password. To connect using authenticated SMTP, click the Use Authentication When Sending Mail check box, and then fill out the SMTP user and password fields. Consult your network administrator or ISP for this information.

> If you have multiple email accounts and want to be able to choose which address shows up in the From field of your outgoing messages, simply add your various accounts to Mail. The next time you send a message, a pop-up menu appears in the message composition window. From that menu, you can choose which account is listed as the sender. The default email address is the first one placed in the list of accounts. If you want to change this, drag the accounts listed in the Accounts pane of the Mail Preferences pane to the order you want.

12

After you've created an account, you can change additional settings in the Special Mailboxes and Advanced tabs.

Special Mailboxes Settings

By default, Mail includes special mailboxes for storing various kinds of messages, including drafts, sent messages, junk mail, and trash. The Special Mailboxes tab of the Accounts sheet enables you to activate features for these mailboxes.

The available options differ depending on whether the selected account is IMAP/.Mac or POP. For IMAP/.Mac accounts, you can configure the following settings:

- **Store Draft Messages on the Server**—Messages that you've started, but not sent, are called *draft messages*. Checking this option enables you to store a message on the server until you're ready to send it.

- **Store Sent Messages on the Server**—Opt to save sent messages on the server to be accessed from different computers. You can also choose intervals at which sent messages are deleted from the server.

- **Store Junk Messages on the Server**—Mail comes with a built-in junk mail filter. Choose to store messages deemed to be junk on the server to be accessed from different computers or to delete them quickly.

- **Move Deleted Messages to the Trash Mailbox**—Check this box if you want deleted messages to be stored in the Trash folder. Enable this setting if you want to be sure not to permanently delete messages you might need.

- **Store Deleted Messages on the Server**—Store deleted messages on the server to be accessed from different computers in case you still want to view them, even from other computers. You can also choose how long to wait before deleting them permanently.

For POP accounts, you can activate the following features:

- **Erase Copies of Sent Messages When**—Choose how long to store copies of the messages you send before they're erased.

- **Erase Messages in the Junk Mailbox When**—Choose how long to store messages deemed junk mail before they're erased.

- **Move Deleted Messages to a Separate Folder**—Check this box if you want deleted messages to be stored in a special folder. Enable this setting if you want to be sure not to permanently delete messages you might need. You can also choose how long the deleted messages remain in the folder before they're permanently erased.

Advanced Settings

Click the Advanced tab to further fine-tune your account settings. The available options change depending on the account type you've chosen. Figure 12.3 displays the Account Options tab for IMAP (or .Mac) accounts.

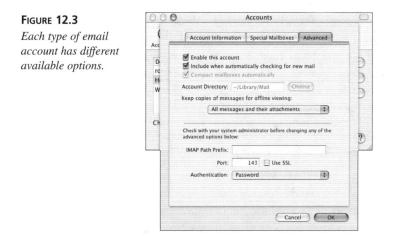

FIGURE 12.3
Each type of email account has different available options.

Choices available from the Advanced tab include

- **Enable This Account**—Includes the account in the listing under the Get New Mail In Account selection of the Mailbox menu. If not enabled, this account is ignored until you change the setting.

- **Include When Automatically Checking for New Mail**—If this option is selected, the account is polled for new messages at the interval set in the Preferences Account panel. If this option isn't selected, the account is polled only when the user manually checks the account.

- **Compact Mailboxes Automatically**—For IMAP/.Mac accounts, this option cleans up the local mailbox files when exiting Mail. The benefit of using this option is slight, and it can slow down the system when dealing with large mailbox files.

- **Remove Copy from Server after Retrieving a Message**— When this option is checked for POP accounts, messages are removed from the server at the interval selected in the pop-up window. Deselect this option to leave email on the server. The Remove Now button enables you to clean up your POP account on the server by deleting all messages that have already been downloaded to your local machine.

- **Prompt Me to Skip Messages over # KB**—For POP accounts, this option enables you to automatically skip messages larger than a set number of kilobytes. This is useful for keeping large attachments from downloading and bogging down your connection.

- **Account Directory**—The local directory where the Mail application stores your messages. It's best to leave this setting at its default of Library/Mail.

12

- **Keep copies of messages for offline viewing**—With IMAP/.Mac accounts, the local machine has the option of storing the text of all messages along with their attachments (All Messages and Their Attachments), storing only the text of all messages on the local machine (All Messages, but Omit Attachments), storing messages that have been read (Only Messages I've Read), or never storing messages on the local drive (Don't Keep Copies of Any Messages).

The remaining options are a bit more sensitive with regard to operating your mail. You shouldn't alter them without the help of your system administrator.

- **IMAP Path Prefix**—For IMAP/.Mac accounts, this specifies the IMAP prefix required to access your mailbox. Usually this field is left blank unless your mail server administrator specifies a value.

- **Port**—The default IMAP port is 143; the default POP server port is 110. If your server uses a different access port, enter it here. If you don't know what port you should use, contact your system administrator.

- **Authentication**—Some SMTP servers use authentication to prevent spamming and other unauthorized use. If your server requires authentication to *send* mail, use the authentication options to specify a username and password.

Composing Messages

To start a new email message, click the Compose button in the toolbar or choose New Message (Command+N) from the File menu. To reply to an existing message, select that message in the list view, and then click Reply in the toolbar to start a new message or choose Reply to Sender (Command+R) from the Message menu. If you want to reply to all recipients of the message, use the Reply All button.

The composition window appears, as shown in Figure 12.4.

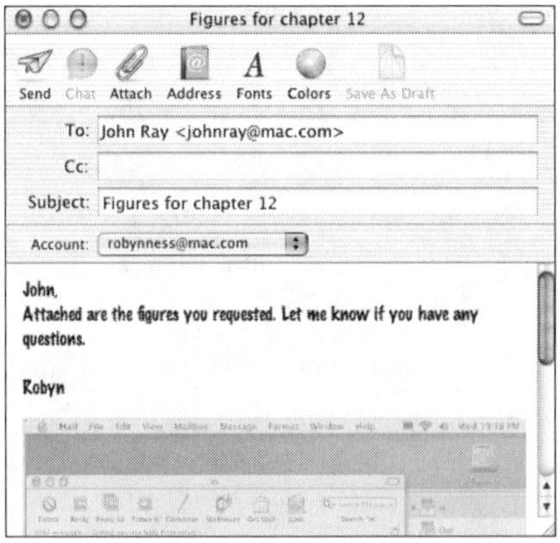

FIGURE 12.4

Mail supports styled messages and drag-and-drop attachments.

By default, three fields are provided for addressing the message. Fill in the To line with the address of the primary recipient. If you're sending the message to more than one person, separate multiple addresses with a comma. Use the Cc: line to add other recipients who aren't part of the main list. The primary recipients can see these addresses. The Subject line is used to show the subject, or title, of the email.

Additional fields are accessible from the Edit menu. Choose Add Bcc Header (Shift+Command+B) to add a Bcc: header, or Add Reply-To Header (Option+Command+R) to add an alternative reply address. A Bcc (blind carbon copy) header works like a normal carbon copy, but does not allow the recipients to view each other's email addresses or names. A Reply-To header is used to provide an alternative address for replying. For example, if I'm sending email from my `agroves@poisontooth.com` account but want replies to go to `agroves@mac.com` instead, I would enter the `mac.com` address in the Reply To field.

> If you would rather use your long-term memory for something other than email addresses, you can use the Address Book application to store your addresses. We discuss this later in the hour.

To create the message itself, type the text into the window's content area. You can use the toolbar to pick fonts and colors, and you can also drag images and files directly into the body of message to send them as attachments. Depending on the type of file, images and files are added to the message as an icon (application, archive, and so on) or shown within the message body (picture, movie).

12

> Be aware that to view email with special rich text formatting, the recipient must have a modern email program such as Outlook Express (or, better yet, Mail!). Rich text is the use of various fonts and formatting other than just plain old text. To create a message that anyone can view as you intend it, compose the content in Plain Text mode, which is selected in the Format menu.

To send the message, click Send in the toolbar or choose Send Message (Shift+Command+D) from the Message menu.

Receiving Mail

To read a message, click the message in the listing. Its contents appear in the bottom window pane along with an abbreviated header containing information about the message such as who sent it and when.

You can also double-click a message to open it in its own message window. When you're finished reading the message you opened, click the Close button in the upper-left corner of the window or press Command+W.

> You can organize your mailbox by creating additional folders in which to store specific categories of messages. To do this, select New Mailbox from the Mailbox menu and enter a name.
>
> To file a message, click and drag it from the list view of the In box to the folder in the mailbox drawer where you want it. If the mailbox drawer isn't already open, it automatically pops open as the mouse approaches the edge of the window. Alternatively, you can use the Transfer option from the Message menu.

The simplest way to delete a message is to use the Delete button in the toolbar. Pressing the Delete key or choosing Delete from the Message menu also removes the active message or selected group of messages from the listing. Deleted messages aren't immediately removed from the system; they're transferred to a Trash folder. What happens from there can be configured in the Special Mailboxes tab of the Accounts Preference pane, which was discussed earlier.

Additional Mail Preferences

We already looked at the Accounts portion of Mail Preferences, but the Mail Preferences dialog box also contains many of the program's hidden features—including signatures and mailbox filters. Open the Mail Preferences dialog box by choosing Preferences from the application menu.

Fonts & Colors

The Fonts & Colors pane controls the default fonts used in the message list and message bodies. Options in the Font & Colors pane include font and text color settings.

Using a fixed-width font such (as Courier or Monaco) is recommended for plain-text messages. Many plain-text messages are formatted using spaces for positioning elements, so using a proportional (non-fixed width) font results in a skewed or sometimes unreadable display.

Viewing

The Viewing Preferences pane controls the amount of header detail that should be displayed as well as several features related to the appearance of messages, including highlighting of message threads and display of HTML-rendered messages.

Composing

Choose formatting options for your message. The Composing pane includes a variety of settings, including Rich/Plain Text options, automatic spell checking, addressing options, and reply format.

Signatures

A *signature* is a block of text added to the end of an email to tell others who you are or how to contact you. I use mine to add my job title and address. Others use signatures to insert a favorite quote. The Mail application handles multiple different signatures with ease in the Signatures pane of Mail Preferences, shown in Figure 12.5. Signatures added by the account owner are listed on the left side of the pane.

FIGURE 12.5

Create multiple signatures in the Mail application.

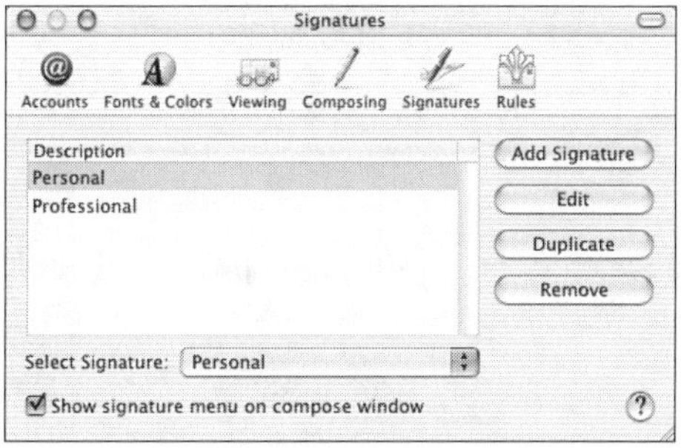

Options in the Signatures pane enable you to add, edit, duplicate, remove, and select signatures.

Rules

Using rules is like having your own personal assistant to tell you what messages are important and which ones are junk. Rules (also called *filters*) can perform actions on incoming messages, such as highlighting them in the message list, moving them to other folders, or playing special sounds.

Each rule in the list is evaluated once per incoming message (unless the Active box is unchecked). In fact, multiple rules can act on a single message. To change the order in which the rules are applied, drag rule entries in the list to the order you want.

Managing Junk Mail

With the increasing popularity of email has come an increase in annoying junk email. Mail attempts to help you avoid wading through unwanted mail with built-in junk mail filtering.

By default, the junk mail filter starts in training mode. When a message comes to you that Mail feels might be junk mail, the message is highlighted in brown. A button appears at the top of the message so that you can correct Mail if it has incorrectly identified the message as junk. If a junk mail message slips past Mail, you can select the message and choose Mark as Junk Mail from the Message menu or click the Junk icon in Mail's toolbar. Over time, Mail learns from your input.

When you feel that Mail is no longer misidentifying messages, you can switch to automatic mode. In automatic mode, Mail creates a Junk mailbox in which it automatically places suspected junk mail so you don't have to see it at all. However, it's suggested that you periodically review the contents of the Junk mailbox to make sure that nothing important was delivered there.

Remember, you can set the length of time mail stays in the Junk mailbox before it's deleted in the Special Mailboxes tab of the Accounts panel that appears when you create or edit an account.

There are four self-explanatory options for manipulating the rule list: Add Rule, Edit, Duplicate, and Remove.

Adding a rule is simple. Each rule is a single step that looks at portions of the incoming message to determine how to react. Figure 12.6 demonstrates the rule creation process.

Figure 12.6

Mail's rules are simple to create.

1. Click on the Add Rule button to make a new rule. The sheet shown in Figure 12.6 appears.

2. Enter a description; it's used to identify the rule in the listing.

3. Decide on the criteria that must match the incoming message. The search criteria are the header field to use in the comparison, what comparison to use (Contains, Begins With, and so on), and the text to look for. For example, to match a message from my editorsí accounts, I'd use From, contains, and samspuplishing. Clicking the + or - button adds or removes additional search criteria.

4. To finish the rule, set the action(s) that should run if the criteria match:

   - **Transfer Message**—Transfer the message into one of your system mail-boxes.

   - **Set Color of Message to**—Set the highlight color for the message.

   - **Play Sound**—Play a system (or custom AIFF) beep sound.

   - **Reply To/Forward/Redirect Message**—Send the message to another email address. Click the Set Message button to enter text that will be included with the message being sent.

   - **Delete Message**—Delete the message. Useful for automatically getting rid of common spam messages.

   - **Mark as Read**—Keeps the message, but doesn't display it as a new message.

   - **Mark as Flagged**—Marks the message with a flag in the status column of the message listing.

   Use the + and - buttons to apply and remove additional actions.

5. Click OK to set and activate the rule.

12

Address Book

Address Book is a contact information manager that integrates with Mail. The main window, shown in Figure 12.7, has two view modes: Card and Columns view and Card Only view. To toggle between them, use the View buttons at the upper left. You'll do most of your work with Address Book in Card and Columns view.

FIGURE 12.7

Address Book, shown here in Card and Columns view, keeps track of your contact information with a simple uncluttered interface.

⊖ ⊖ ⊖		Address Book	
			Search: ⬚
Group	**Name**		
All	Anne Groves		**Robyn Ness**
Directories	Robyn Ness		
OS X Book	John Ray		
		home robynness@mac.com	
		home page homepage.mac.com/robynness/	
		home robynness@mac.com (AIM)	
		Note:	
+	+	Edit	◀ ▶

Adding and Editing Cards

To add a card, select All from the Group column and then click the + button below the Name column. This opens a blank card in the far-right column where you can type what information you want to save.

There are fields for name, work and mobile phone, email address, homepage, AIM name, and address, as well as a space at the bottom for notes. You can tab between fields or click into the ones you want to insert. You can add as much or as little information as you like, but an e-ail address is required if you plan to use the card with Mail.

> If the label to the left of the field doesn't match the information you want to add, you can adjust it by clicking the up/down arrow icon. This opens a pop-up menu with several common labels, as well as an option to customize.

In the upper-right corner of the card column is the default card icon. If you want to add a custom picture, clicking the default icon opens a sheet from which you can navigate to any image stored on your computer or attached drive. A simple way to add icons for each of your contacts is to select an image from those stored in /Library/User Pictures or drag an image from the Finder into the image well.

When you're finished adding information, click outside the card pane.

To edit a card you've already created, select the name of the individual from the Name column and click the Edit button below the card column.

To delete a card, select it and press the Delete key on your keyboard. You are asked to confirm the action before it's carried out.

Adding Groups

You can organize your cards into your own custom groups, which can be used to send email to a common collection of people.

> If you have a large number of cards to work with but have no need for mailing to custom groups, you can enter keywords in the Notes section of the cards. You can then use the Search field, located at the upper right of the Card and Columns view, to see only those cards that contain your chosen keyword.

To create a group, click the + button under the Group column and type a name for it. Then select the All option in the Group column and drag contacts from the Name column to the group's name to populate your new group. You can hold down the Command key to select more than one addressee at a time.

> You might be wondering about the Directories item in the Group column. It represents a special feature of Address Book that connects to remote servers capable of sharing contact information using a technology called LDAP (Lightweight Directory Access Protocol). LDAP servers are commonly used to hold personnel account data for large companies. You can add an LDAP server to Address Book by selecting Directories and clicking the + button below the Group column, as long as you know the name or IP address of the server and the correct search base setting. If you don't know this information, it's best not to try to add a directory without help from your network administrator.

12

Using Address Book with Mail

Address Book integrates neatly into Mail. When you open a compose window, an Address icon appears in the toolbar. Clicking it opens a window, shown in Figure 12.8, that contains all the contacts and groups you've stored in Address Book. Simply double-click the names of everyone you want to send the message to, or select a previously created group, and the addresses appear in the To field. If you want to send a carbon copy, select the names and click the CC: button.

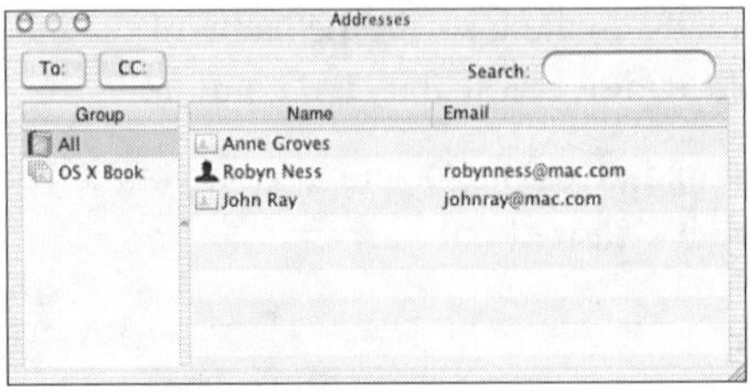

FIGURE 12.8

Mail's Addresses window display information stored in Address Book.

If you receive email and want to save the sender's address, you can add people to the Address Book from within Mail. Select the message and choose Add Sender To Address Book from the Message menu, or use the keyboard shortcut Command+Y. You must edit the card to add information in addition to the name and email address, but it's a start!

> Address Book uses the common vCard format (saved as a `.vcf` file) to store information. When using Mail, you can attach your own vCard to an email by dragging your listing from Address Book into the compose window. To add a vCard someone else has sent you to Address Book, simply drag the vCard attachment from the message window into Address Book.
>
> You can open an Address Book window at any time by choosing Address Book from the Window menu.

iChat

Apple's iChat (path: /Applications/iChat) is a program that enables you to send instant messages to other people while they're at their computers. These messages appear on the recipients' screens so that they can reply to you immediately. An example of a chat session in progress is shown in Figure 12.9.

FIGURE 12.9

Chatting with iChat is simple and fun.

iChat enables you to communicate in real-time with people who use Mac.com or have an AOL Instant Messenger (AIM) account. You also need one of those types of accounts yourself. If you want to purchase a Mac.com membership or sign up for a trial account (as discussed in Hour 10), visit www.mac.com. Alternatively, you can sign up for a free AOL Instant Messenger account at www.aim.com.

If there are other iChat users on your local network using iChat, you don't need to use an AIM or Mac.com account to chat with them. Apple has integrated a technology called Rendezvous into iChat that allows it to scan for other nearby users and add them to a special list for you to see and chat with. Also, if two or more people with AirPort wireless-capable computers are near each other, their computers can use Rendezvous to communicate without any Internet connection at all.

To set up iChat, choose Preferences from the iChat menu and click the Accounts button. Check the Enable AIM option, and then enter your AIM screen name or your full Mac.com email address, and then enter your password. You also have the option of activating or deactivating Rendezvous and adjusting how iChat is activated.

Adding Buddies

When you log in to AIM through iChat, a Buddy List window appears onscreen to show whether your friends are online and available to chat, as shown in Figure 12.10. If you're logged into Rendezvous as well, another window shows people on your local network.

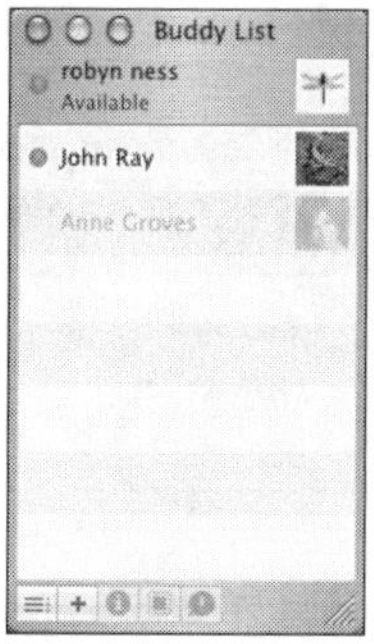

FIGURE 12.10
You can easily see who's available to chat with using the buddy list; the listings for people who aren't connected to the AIM server are dimmed.

12

Your buddy list is stored on the AOL Instant Message server, so you can log in to your account from any computer and see whether your buddies are online.

Let's see how to add buddies to the Buddy List:

1. If the Buddy List window is open, click the + button at the bottom of the iChat Buddy List window. (If the Buddy List window isn't open, make sure that you're logged in to AIM under the iChat menu, and then open the buddy list from the Window menu.)

2. A sheet containing your Address Book entries appears, as shown in Figure 12.11. If the person you want to add to your buddy list has an AIM or Mac.com listing, select the person and click Select Buddy.

   If the person doesn't show AIM or Mac.com information, click the Select Buddy button to add that information. If the person isn't currently in your Address Book, click the New Person button to create a new entry. Enter your friend's AIM or Mac.com screen name, as well as his real name and email address, in the window that appears. Click the Add button to save your new buddy.

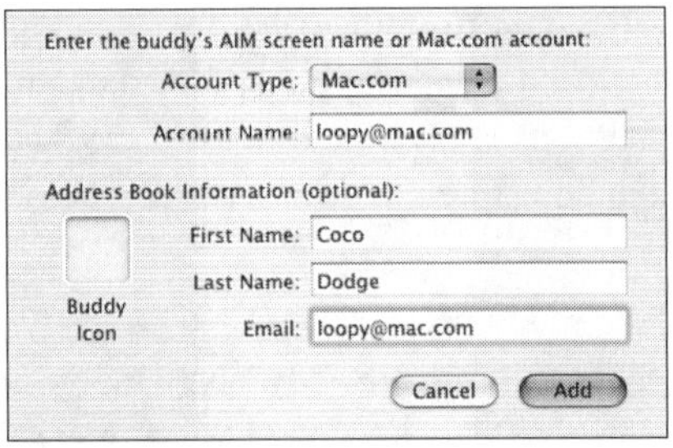

FIGURE 12.11

Choose a chat buddy from the list in your Address Book or add someone new.

Enter the buddy's AIM screen name or Mac.com account:

Account Type: Mac.com

Account Name: loopy@mac.com

Address Book Information (optional):

Buddy Icon

First Name: Coco

Last Name: Dodge

Email: loopy@mac.com

Cancel   Add

Address Book and iChat are integrated such that adding a new buddy to iChat automatically adds a new card in Address Book. However, because your buddy list is stored on the instant messenger server, you can't remove a buddy simply by deleting an Address Book card. Instead, you must select the buddy in the buddy list, and choose Delete from the Edit menu.

Also, keep in mind also that deleting a buddy from your buddy list does not remove that person's card from your Address Book.

Sending and Receiving Instant Messages

As you've learned, your buddy list shows who's available to chat at the very instant you're logged in. To start a chat session with someone who's online, just double-click that person's name in the buddy list, or select a person and click the Send Instant Message button at the bottom of the Buddy List window. This opens a chat window similar to the one shown in Figure 12.9. Type your message in the message area at the bottom of the window and press Return on your keyboard. In the upper portion of the window, you'll see your own message and whatever reply the other person sends.

> In addition to sending ordinary text messages, iChat enables you to send any kind of file. To send a file, drag its icon into the message area of a chat window and press Return on your keyboard. The recipient can then drag the file onto her desktop. If you send image files, they appear inside the chat window as part of the conversation. (For maximum compatibility with people using AIM programs other than iChat, it's recommended that you stick with JPEG and GIF image formats.)
>
> You can also send graphical emoticons to other users of iChat. The smiley button near the bottom of the chat window shows you what's available.

If you receive a message, your computer makes a sound and a message window pops up. When you click on the chat window, it expands to show the message area where you can type a response.

> Mail is linked to your buddy list, which shows whether the senders of messages in your In box are online when you check your mail. Also, if you've entered an email address for someone in your buddy list, you can select the entry and click the Compose Email button at the bottom of the Buddy List window to open a blank email message addressed to that person.

Group Chat Sessions

You can participate in chats with different people simultaneously, each contained in a separate window. You can also start a chat session with more than one other person in which all participants can see the messages from everyone else.

To start a group chat, perform the following steps:

1. Choose New Chat from the File menu.

2. Click the Add (+) button at the bottom of the participants list to choose the people you want to invite.

3. Type a message inviting the participants. When the invited buddies receive the chat request, they can choose to accept or decline. If they accept, they can send and receive messages as part of the group.

Additional Preferences and Application Settings

There are many ways to customize iChat, both in appearance and operation.

You can change the appearance of the chat windows under the Messages section of the iChat Preferences (shown in Figure 12.12), including changing your font, font color, and balloon color.

FIGURE 12.12

Change your Messages preferences to reflect your mood.

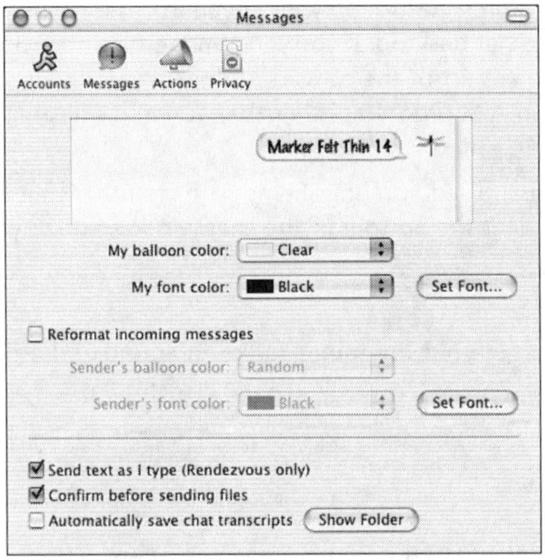

In addition to changing your font and balloon attributes, you can express your personality by replacing your buddy icon with an image of your choosing. Simply drag a new image into the image well at the top of the Buddy List window. A special editing window opens to enable you to position the image.

You can also replace the icons of people in your buddy list who haven't set their own. (Or, if someone has set an icon that you don't like, you can choose to display something you like better.) Open the Info window by clicking the Show Buddy Info button at the bottom of the Buddy List window, select a new image, and check the box for Only Use This Picture.

Under the Actions preferences, choose what iChat does when you or your buddies log in or out.

The Privacy preferences enable you to choose who in the AIM/Mac.com community can send you messages. Choose categories of users, such as those in your buddy list, or name individual users who can or cannot contact you.

If you're logged into iChat but don't want to be disturbed by requests to chat, you can change your status in the buddy list from Available to anything you choose. Simply choose Custom, and type a new message. It appears beneath your name in other people's buddy and Rendezvous lists.

Summary

In this hour, we covered Mail, Address Book, and iChat. You learned how to set up accounts in Mail and iChat as well as how to receive and send messages in each. You also saw how Address Book is integrated to store information about your contacts. This hour is by no means a comprehensive look at these programs; the best way to learn all the tricks of these applications is to roll up your sleeves and begin using them.

Q&A

Q I have a lot invested in my current mail program. Can I import the messages from that program into the Mac OS X Mail program?

A Yes, you can import from the following applications into Mail: Entourage, Outlook Express, Claris Emailer (2.0v3), Netscape (4.0+), and Eudora. There's also a setting for Standard Mbox format, which is often used in mail programs on Windows and Unix computers. The Import function is in the File menu and walks you through the steps you need to take.

Q My friends who use AIM can't seem to chat with me when I use iChat. What's wrong?

A People using older versions of AIM software might not be able to chat with iChat users. You might have to ask your friends to upgrade their software. Or, you could switch from iChat to another instant messaging client that's available for Mac OS X. One very nice program is Proteus, from Alien Technology at www.indigofield.com, which supports not only AIM, but also MSN, Yahoo!, and ICQ message formats.

12

Workshop

The workshop contains quiz questions and activities to help you solidify your understanding of the material covered. Try to answer all questions before looking at the "Answers" section that follows.

Quiz

1. What information do you need to set up an initial Mail account?

2. What feature can you use to filter out messages you want to set aside or delete?

3. What two types of standards does the Address Book application use?

4. How do you add a buddy to Rendezvous?

Answers

1. The seven pieces of information you're asked for when setting up your initial email account are Your Name, Email Address, Incoming Mail Server, Mail Server Type, User Account ID, Password, and Outgoing Mail Server.

2. The Rules pane has options for filtering messages as they arrive in your mailbox.

3. vCards and LDAP are the two standards used by Address Book.

4. Trick question—you can't add buddies to that list. Rendezvous looks for other users on your local network and adds them automatically.

Activities

1. Now that you have Mail and a great way to keep in touch with all your friends, open Address Book and enter all the information you would use to send electronic holiday cards.

2. If you don't already have one, sign up for a .Mac trial membership or an AIM account, and find a friend to send instant messages to. Then give iChat a try.

Hour 13

Using Network Sharing

The Macintosh has always made it simple to share files with other Macs on the same network and over the Internet. Mac OS X's strong UNIX roots bring even more sharing capabilities to the platform, including the capability to connect to Windows systems. At the same time, some limitations are placed on what you can share that might require changes in the way your Macintosh network is set up. Another feature of Mac OS X 10.2 is its capability to share your Internet connection itself with another computer. In this hour, you learn how to

- Set up and connect to shared files
- Work with Windows-based computers
- Host your own Web site with Personal Web Sharing
- Activate FTP and SSH-based sharing features
- Share your Internet connection

Sharing Services

A *service* is something that your computer provides to other computers on a network, such as running a Web server or sharing files. In Mac OS X 10.2, you can enable or disable all the standard information-sharing services from the Services tab of the Sharing panel in System Preferences, as shown in Figure 13.1.

> Be aware that turning on or off any service in the Sharing panel activates that service for everyone on the machine. If sharing is on for one user, it's on for everyone. If it's off, it's off for everyone!

FIGURE 13.1

The Services tab of Sharing Preferences enables you to choose which sharing services you want running on your computer.

You can enable or disable the following services:

- **Personal File Sharing**—Share your files with other Mac users across a local network. We'll discuss activating AppleTalk, if needed, in just a moment.

- **Windows File Sharing**—Share your files with Windows users on your local network.

- **Personal Web Sharing**—Serve Web pages from your own computer using the built-in Apache Web server. You'll learn more later in this hour.

- **Remote Login**—Allow Secure Shell (SSH) command-line access to your machine from remote machines. You'll learn more later in this hour.

- **FTP Access**—Allow access to your machine via FTP, (File Transfer Protocol). You'll learn more later in this hour.

- **Remote Apple Events**—Allow software running on other machines to send events to applications on your computer using the AppleScript scripting language. We don't delve into this option, but AppleScript is discussed in Hour 19, "Automating Tasks with AppleScript."

- **Printer Sharing**—Grant other computers access to the printers connected to your computer. With this service enabled, your printers appear in the Print Center's printer list for other users on your local network. General information about connecting to printers is covered in Hour 16, "Setting Up Printers and Fonts."

> The Firewall tab of the Sharing control pane contains a list of the same options as the Services tab. A *firewall* is something that sits between the outside network and network services on your computer to protect your computer from network-based attacks. The Firewall tab enables you to activate Mac OS X's built-in firewall software to prevent access to your computer through those services you don't want to run. We'll discuss this further in Hour 23, "Security Considerations."

Now, let's take at look at staring and using these services.

Activating Personal File Sharing and AppleTalk

Personal File Sharing is Apple's method of sharing files with other Mac users over a network, either via TCP/IP or AppleTalk. AppleTalk is a legacy protocol for browsing and accessing remote workstations that share files or services, such as printers. Apple is transitioning to using the TCP/IP-based Service Locator Protocol (SLP) and Rendezvous, as mentioned in Hour 12, "Mail and iChat," to provide this functionality on modern Mac networks. Unfortunately, until everyone is running Mac OS X, you might still need to enable AppleTalk to access older devices.

Follow these steps to share your files with another Mac user:

1. Determine whether you need to use AppleTalk to access computers and printers on your network. If all the other computers are Mac OS X machines and your printer is USB-based, you probably don't need AppleTalk support—skip ahead to step 8. If you're not sure, go to step 2.

2. Open the Network Preferences panel, found in the Internet & Network section of System Preferences.

3. Use the Show pop-up menu to choose the device you're using to access your network (such as AirPort or Ethernet).

13

4. Click the AppleTalk tab.

5. Check the box for Make AppleTalk Active, as shown in Figure 13.2. (To make the change, you might first have to click the small lock button at the bottom of the window and type an administrator's username and password.)

> If you don't understand the concept of administrative and nonadministrative users yet, don't worry. You learn more about this topic in Hour 15, "Sharing Your System: Multiple Users." For now, all you need to know is that the first-created user account is an administrative account. Other accounts may or may not be administrative, depending how they were set up.

FIGURE 13.2

Make sure that AppleTalk is active before trying share files on a mi XEd Mac OS network.

	Network
Show All Displays Sound Network Startup Disk	
Location: Automatic	
Show: AirPort	
TCP/IP AppleTalk Proxies AirPort	
☑ Make AppleTalk Active	
Computer Name: Robyn Ness' Computer (Can be changed in Sharing Preferences)	
AppleTalk Zone:	
Configure: Automatically	
🔒 Click the lock to prevent further changes. Revert Apply Now	

6. If necessary, choose an AppleTalk Zone to use. You might want to speak to your network administrator if you aren't sure what to choose.

7. Click Apply Now.

8. Open the Sharing Preferences pane, as shown in Figure 13.1, and check the box for Personal File Sharing, or highlight it and click the Start button.

9. Close the System Preferences window.

Your Mac OS X computer should now be able to share files with other Macs on your network. We'll talk about how to actually connect to other users' files later in this hour.

Task: Setting File and Folder Permissions

Inside your home directory is the folder named Public—this is where you must place any file or folder that you want others to have access to over the local network. Although people can read the files in this folder, you might need to adjust the access that people have to the resources within your Public folder by using the Finder's Get Info command.

For example, assume that you've placed a folder called Shared Images inside your Public folder and that you want to allow users to read and write files in this directory. Follow these steps to set the read and write permissions:

1. Select the folder (in this case, Shared Images) within your Public directory.

2. Choose Get Info (Command+I) from the File menu.

3. Expand the Ownership & Permissions section by clicking the disclosure arrow.

4. Use the permission pop-ups to set the appropriate access. In the case of a folder that everyone should be able to read or write, choose Read & Write from the Others pop-up menu, as shown in Figure 13.3. If you want to be more selective about who can write to a file, you can leave Others set to Read Only and adjust the ownership of Owner or Group and their level of access.

FIGURE 13.3

Set the permissions for the resource you're sharing.

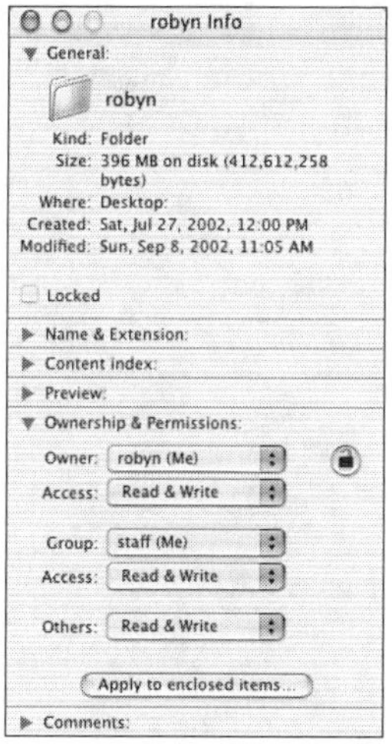

5. Click the Apply to All Enclosed Folders button to set the same permissions on any folders within the folder you're setting up. (Obviously, you don't have this option when working with files.)

6. Close the Info panel.

You might have noticed that a folder called Drop Box is already in your Public folder. This special folder is set to allow other users to write files, but not to read or even view them. The effect of these permissions is to create a folder that other users can drag files into, but after the files are added, they can't be erased or modified by anyone except the owner of the drop box.

Activating Windows Sharing (Samba)

Windows computers use a protocol called SMB (Simple Message Block) for file and print sharing. To share files with Windows computers, your Mac uses the same protocol through a piece of software called Samba.

> The latest version of SMB is known as CIFS (Common Internet File System), which is an open version of SMB with some Internet-specific modifications. For the sake of remaining reasonably sane, you can assume that CIFS and SMB are synonymous.

To turn on Windows Sharing (Samba), open the Sharing System Preferences panel to the Services tab, and then either click the check box in front of the Windows File Serving line, or highlight it and click the Start button. The Sharing panel updates and shows the path that can be used to map (mount) the drive of your Mac on a Windows-based computer, as demonstrated in Figure 13.4.

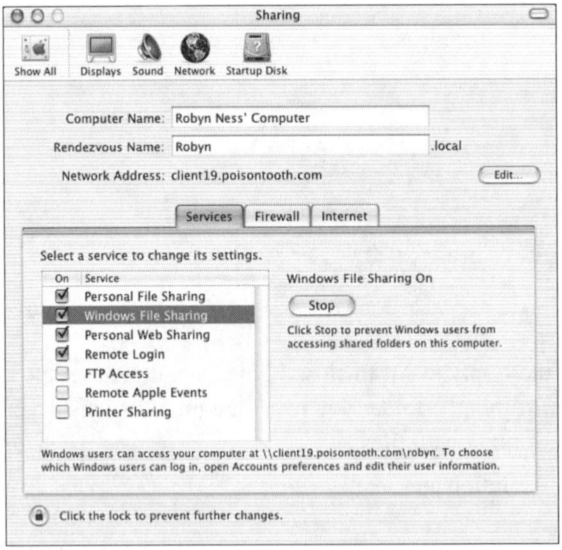

FIGURE 13.4

Activate Samba for file sharing with Windows computers by using the Sharing preference panel.

Like AppleShare file sharing in Mac OS X, the built-in Samba configuration is limited to sharing each user's home directory. By default, none of the user accounts are enabled for login. Enable login from Windows by opening the Accounts System Preferences panel, selecting the user to have Samba access, and then clicking the Edit User button. Your screen will look similar to Figure 13.5.

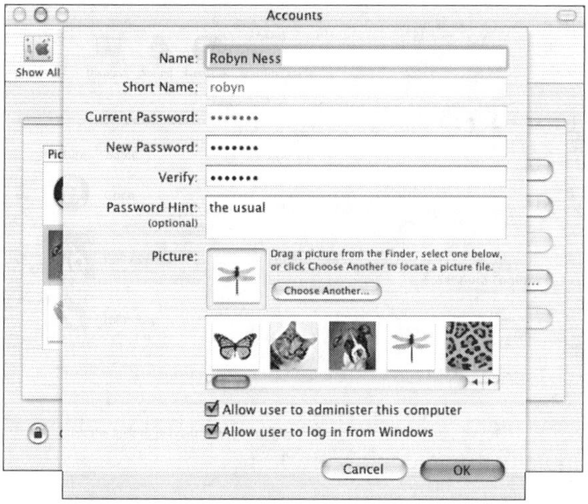

FIGURE 13.5

Edit the user accounts that should be able to access your computer from Windows.

If necessary, enter the current user password, press the Return key, and then click the Allow User to Log In from Windows check box. The home directory of the user can now be accessed through a path following the format:

```
\\<hostname or IP address>\<username>
```

Keep in mind that the person logging from Windows must be identified as the same user the Mac account recognizes, meaning it is necessary to log in to Windows using the username and password of the account on Mac OS X. Be sure to enter your username in all lowercase characters and the password just as you entered it in Mac OS X.

Activating Web Sharing

Mac OS X makes it easy to run a simple Web server using the popular open source Apache server. What makes this so astounding is that Apache is actually the server that powers most Internet Web sites. It's built to run extremely complex sites, including e-commerce and other interactive applications—and it's running on your desktop.

We'll discuss some of the advanced features of Apache a little later (in Hour 21, "UNIX Advantages: The Power of UNIX"). For now, let's just look at where it stores its files and how all the users on your computer can take advantage of it.

13

Mac OS X can share a personal Web site for each user on the computer. In addition, it can run a master Web site for the whole computer entirely independent of the personal Web sites.

To turn on Web sharing, open the Sharing System Preferences panel (shown in Figure 13.1), and check the box for Personal Web Sharing or highlight it and click the Start button. The Apache server starts running, making your Web site immediately available. Make a note of the URL shown at the bottom of the window, and then start Internet Explorer to verify that your personal site is online.

With Internet Explorer running, enter your personal Web site URL, which should look like the following:

http://<server ip or hostname>/~<username>

The tilde (~) is extremely critical. It tells the server that it should load the Web pages from the Sites folder located inside the user's home directory. Note that after you activate Web sharing for one user, it's active for all users, so be sure that all users are ready to have their Web sites shared with the rest of the world.

Assuming that you entered your URL correctly, you should see the default Mac OS X home page, as demonstrated in Figure 13.6.

FIGURE 13.6

Apple includes a default personal home page.

To edit your Web site, just look inside your Sites folder. The default page is generated from the file `index.html` and the Images folder.

Under Mac OS X's user interface, it isn't possible to change the filename of your home page. When you start creating files, be certain that the first page you want to be loaded is named index.html; otherwise, your site might not behave as you hope.

If you're the adventurous sort, you've probably tried typing in the URL of your machine without including the ~<username> portion. If you haven't, try it now. What you should see is that a different Web page loads. This is the system Web site and it can be used for anything you want, but you must do a bit of digging to reach the directory that holds it.

The system-level site is located in /Library/WebServer/Documents. Any administrator can make changes to this directory, so be sure that the other admin users on the system understand its purpose and that they don't assume that it's related to their personal Web sites.

For every person who visits a Web site that's located on your computer, the Apache Web server stores a hit in its logfiles. These hits can tell you who looked at your files, what they looked at, and where they came from. Keeping track of these logs helps you understand who the audience for your Web site is and what types of information they're seeking.

The logs for your server are located in the /var/log/httpd directory and are named access_log and error_log by default. You can open these files in a text editor, view them from the command line, or monitor them using the Console application by following these steps:

1. Open the Console application (path: /Applications/Utilities/Console).

2. Choose Open Log (Command+O) from the File menu.

3. In the Go To line of the File dialog box, type **/var/log/httpd/access_log** and press the Return key.

4. A window such as the one displayed in Figure 13.7 opens with the contents of the Apache log file.

FIGURE 13.7

The Console application can be used to monitor your logs.

```
access_log
127.0.0.1 - - [28/Aug/2002:23:15:44 -0400] "GET /~robyn/ HTTP/1.1" 200 6186
127.0.0.1 - - [28/Aug/2002:23:15:44 -0400] "GET /~robyn/images/macosxlogo.gif HTTP/1.1" 200 2829
127.0.0.1 - - [28/Aug/2002:23:15:46 -0400] "GET /~robyn/images/web_share.gif HTTP/1.1" 200 13370
127.0.0.1 - - [28/Aug/2002:23:15:46 -0400] "GET /~robyn/images/apache_pb.gif HTTP/1.1" 200 2326
10.0.1.119 - - [08/Sep/2002:11:16:25 -0400] "GET / HTTP/1.1" 200 1456
10.0.1.119 - - [08/Sep/2002:11:16:25 -0400] "GET /apache_pb.gif HTTP/1.1" 200 2326
10.0.1.119 - - [08/Sep/2002:11:16:37 -0400] "GET /~robyn HTTP/1.1" 404 292
10.0.1.119 - - [08/Sep/2002:11:16:41 -0400] "GET /~robyn HTTP/1.1" 301 336
10.0.1.119 - - [08/Sep/2002:11:16:42 -0400] "GET /~robyn/ HTTP/1.1" 200 6186
10.0.1.119 - - [08/Sep/2002:11:16:42 -0400] "GET /~robyn/images/macosxlogo.gif HTTP/1.1" 200 2829
10.0.1.119 - - [08/Sep/2002:11:16:42 -0400] "GET /~robyn/images/apache_pb.gif HTTP/1.1" 200 2326
10.0.1.119 - - [08/Sep/2002:11:16:42 -0400] "GET /~robyn/images/web_share.gif HTTP/1.1" 200 13370
```

13

5. As you and other users access the Web sites on your computer, Console displays information about each of the hits within the log window.

You can install a number of applications (both free and commercial) to help translate the raw Web logs into something a bit more meaningful. To help you get started, take a look at the following products and Web sites:

- **Analog**—http://www.summary.net/soft/analog.html
- **Summary**—http://www.summary.net/summary.html
- **Traffic Report**—http://www.seacloak.com/
- **Sawmill**—http://www.flowerfire.com/sawmill/

Activating Remote Login and FTP

Two additional methods of file sharing available in Mac OS X are FTP and SSH. File Transfer Protocol very simply provides cross-platform file-transfer services. The second type of sharing, SSH (secure shell), enables a remote user to access the command prompt of a Mac OS X computer from anywhere in the world.

As you might expect, both of these protocols can be turned on using the Sharing System Preferences panel. SSH is turned on through the Remote Login check box, shown in Figure 13.1. Activate FTP by simply clicking the Allow FTP Access check box. Alternatively, you can highlight the option you want to activate and click the Start button.

Now that you know how to turn these services on, let's see what they can do for you!

Remote Login (SSH)

SSH, or as Apple calls it in the Sharing panel: Remote Login, is an entirely new concept for most Mac users. If you've seen a Windows or a Linux computer before, you've probably occasionally seen someone open a command prompt and start typing. Contrary to the sentiment many Mac users have, the command line is not evil! In Mac OS X, it's a very powerful and entirely optional tool. As you start to explore the command line later in this book, you'll understand that it can be used to manage your files, monitor your system, and even control server processes.

SSH isn't the command line itself, but it provides a secure means of accessing the command line from a remote location. In an SSH connection, the entire session is encrypted. As such, administrators can log in to their systems using SSH and edit user accounts, change passwords, and so on, without the fear of giving away potentially damaging information.

For the most part, all you need to know about SSH is that from the Terminal application (/Applications/Utilities/Terminal), you can access your account on a remote system by typing **slogin *<ip address or hostname>***.

For example, I have an account on the machine www.ag.ohio-state.edu. To access that machine's command line through SSH, I simply type the following:

```
slogin www.ag.ohio-state.edu
```

The remote machine prompts me for a password and then gives me full control over my account and the resources I have access to. It's as if I launched the Terminal application on the remote system:

```
[vivian-dhcp-218:~] jray% slogin www.ag.ohio-state.edu
jray@www.ag.ohio-state.edu's password:
Last login: Wed Oct 17 15:47:42 2001 from primal.ag.ohio-
Welcome to Darwin!
[www:~] jray%
```

If you're not interested in the command line, don't worry—there's absolutely no reason why you have to use SSH. If you prefer a GUI solution to remote system administration, check out Timbuktu Pro from Netopia: http://www.netopia.com/software/products/tb2/mac/.

If you're planning to serve FTP and SSH only occasionally, shut off the services in the Sharing panel until you're ready to use them. This closes some potential points of attack on your computer. You can still use the Mac OS X clients and command line to access other SSH/FTP servers, but remote users can't connect to your machine.

FTP

With FTP enabled, a user can type into a remote Web browser a URL of the form:

```
ftp://<mac os username>:<mac os password>@<ip address or hostname>
```

This tells the Web browser to contact the Mac OS X computer running the FTP server, login with the given username and password, and display the files in that user's home directory.

A number of command-line tools in Mac OS X, such as ncftp and ftp, give you the capability to upload and download files from a Mac OS X computer. After learning about the command line in Hour 20, "UNIX Command Line Tour," feel free to play with these commands if you want to do so.

13

Most users are much happier accessing FTP servers using GUI tools. Thankfully, several FTP clients can be used to access remote FTP servers in a very Mac-like way:

- **Fetch**—`http://fetchsoftworks.com/`
- **Interarchy**—`http://www.interarchy.com/`
- **NetFinder**—
  `http://members.ozemail.com.au/~pli/netfinder/sw_and_updts.html`
- **Transmit**—`http://www.panic.com/transmit/download.html`

If you need to share files over the Internet, FTP is one of the best ways to do so. It's fast, effective, and a very efficient protocol. Unfortunately, it's also not easy to work with behind firewalls, and it transmits its passwords unencrypted. If you set up a nonadmin user account, perhaps called Transfers, for the sole purpose of moving files around, the password issue shouldn't be much of a problem. Firewalls, on the other hand, are something you might need to discuss with your network administrator before you activate FTP.

You learn how to use FTP from the Finder in the next section.

Connecting to Shared Folders

Your Mac OS X computer can connect to a number of types of network resources from the Finder, specifically:

- **Macintosh Systems**—Other Mac computers that are sharing files via AppleTalk or AppleShare IP.
- **Windows/Linux Computers**—If Windows or Linux computers are using SMB or CIFS file sharing (the standard for most Windows networks), your Mac can access the files easily.
- **WebDAV Shares**—WebDAV is a cross-platform file sharing solution that uses the standard Web protocols. Your iDisk uses WebDAV.
- **FTP Servers**—File Transfer Protocol servers are popular means of distributing software on the Internet. Your Mac OS X machine can connect (read-only) to FTP servers.
- **Linux/BSD NFS Servers**—NFS is the UNIX standard for file sharing. Your Mac (being UNIX!) can obviously talk to them as well!

Connecting to Macintosh and Windows servers is the easiest of the bunch. In Mac OS X, you use the Go menu in the Finder to choose Connect to Server (Command+K). This opens a new dialog box, shown in Figure 13.8, that enables you to connect to remote computers.

FIGURE 13.8

The Finder has the power to connect you to remote volumes directly.

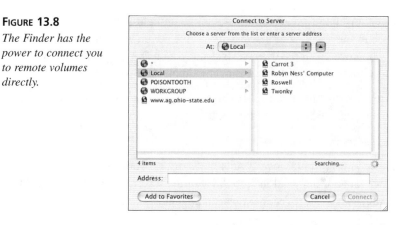

Depending on your network, you'll see several selections, including AppleTalk zones and Windows workgroups. Clicking the Network option displays servers and groups of servers located on your local network.

You can navigate through the AppleTalk zones or server groups the same way you navigate through the Finder in column mode. To make the connection, choose the server you want to use from the list and then click Connect. After a few seconds, you're prompted for a username and a password, as shown in Figure 13.9.

FIGURE 13.9

Enter your username and password, and then click Connect.

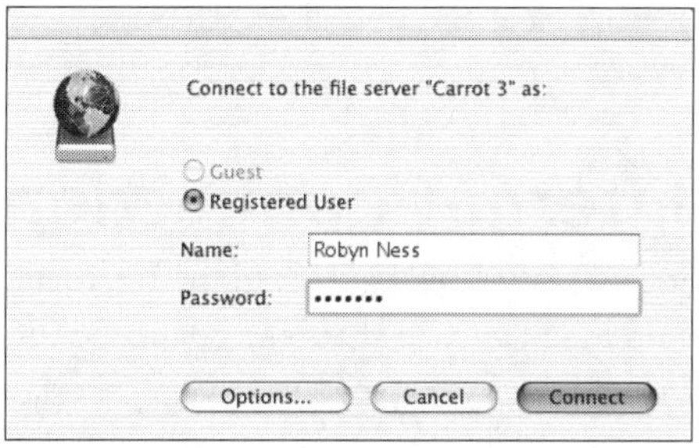

Click Connect, and after few seconds, the volume is mounted on your desktop.

13

> If you're connecting to another Mac OS X computer, you can use either your full name or your username to connect.

Connecting to WebDAV and NFS shared volumes is only slightly more difficult. You can't browse these resources on your network unless the administrator has registered them with a Service Locator Protocol server. Instead, you must type in a URL for the object you want to use into the Address field of the Connection window.

Your network administrator should be able to give you the exact information you need, but for the most part, the URLs follow a format like this:

FTP shares: `ftp://<server name>/<path>`

For example, I have an FTP server named Xanadu on my network (poisontooth.com) containing a folder called waternet at the root level of the server. To access it, I would type **ftp://xanadu.poisontooth.com/waternet** and then click Connect.

WebDAV is even simpler. WebDAV shares are actually just Web resources, so they use the same URLs that you would type into your Web browser. For example, to access the iDisk storage of your Mac.com account, you would type **http://idisk.mac.com/** **<your Mac.com username>**.

NFS follows the same pattern. If the remote server is configured to allow connections, an NFS connection URL looks like this `nfs://<server name>/<shared volume>`.

Windows (SMB) and Macintosh shares can also be mounted via the URLs prefixed with `SMB://` and `AFP://` respectively.

Sharing Your Internet Connection

If you have multiple computers that need access to the Internet but only one Internet connection, you can set up Mac OS X to share the connection it has with other computers on your network. If your primary connection is via AirPort, any machines connected to it via ethernet can connect to the Internet. If your primary connection is an ethernet connection, your machine becomes an AirPort base station, and shares its connection to others using AirPort (assuming it has an AirPort card, of course!). If your connection is a modem, your machine shares connections through both AirPort and ethernet.

Even though this sounds like a truly wonderful feature, it should be used with caution. Some network arrangements can be disrupted when their member computers start sharing Internet connections. Check with your network administrator, or any nearby network administrators of wireless networks, before you try this.

To share your Internet connection, open the Internet tab of the Sharing System Preferences pane, shown in Figure 13.10, and click the Start button.

FIGURE 13.10

Share your network connection with a friend.

Summary

The Macintosh has always made it simple to share file information between computers. Mac OS X keeps the process simple but imposes some limitations that users might not be prepared for. At the same time, it opens up compatibility with Windows and Linux computers by adding SMB/CIFS and WebDAV support. In addition to the standard file sharing services, Mac OS X can be configured to act as an FTP or SSH server, making it possible to access information and control your computer from anywhere on the Internet.

Q&A

Q I really need to share arbitrary folders on Mac OS X. How can I do this?

A If you aren't content to share only folders within your Public folder, install the shareware application SharePoints. It enables you to share any folder and is available for download at `http://www.hornware.com/sharepoints`.

Q Can I really serve a Web site from my desktop Mac?

A Yes, you can. However, depending on the speed of your Internet connection and whether you leave your computer on and connected at all times, it might not be practical for important sites or those with graphic-intensive pages.

13

Workshop

The workshop contains quiz questions and activities to help you solidify your understanding of the material covered. Try to answer all questions before looking at the "Answers" section that follows.

Quiz

1. What directory contains shared files?

2. Where should you put your personal Web site?

3. Starting and stopping a sharing service affects service only for the user clicking the control button—true or false?

4. Should you activate all sharing services on your computer?

Answers

1. The Public folder within each user's home directory is made accessible when file sharing is turned on.

2. Personal Web sites are placed within each user's Sites directory.

3. False. If a sharing service is on, it's on for everyone. Likewise, if it's off, it's off for everyone.

4. No! If you don't plan to use a service, shut it off. The more holes that are open on your computer, the greater the risk of network attack.

Activities

1. Explore the file-sharing services with as many platforms and shares as possible. Try connecting to Macs running Mac OS X, older Mac systems, Windows computers, and so on.

2. Turn on Web Sharing and create a systemwide Web page for your computer. You might want to include links from the systemwide site to the personal sites that are (or will be) created.

Keychain Access and Network Utility

Mac OS X is a system designed with networking in mind, and it comes with many great Internet applications. We've already explored several, including Internet Explorer, Sherlock, and Mail in Hours 10, 11, and 12. In this hour, we look at some more applications that are provided to assist you as you work online.

We focus our attention on the following:

- Storing and retrieving passwords with Keychain Access
- Functions available in the Network Utility application

Keychain Access

Keeping track of passwords for email servers, file servers, Web sites, and other private information can be difficult. That's why Apple has included a security application called Keychain to make managing your collection of passwords and PIN numbers much easier.

Think of Keychain as a database of your most sensitive information, all accessible through your Mac OS X account password. The Keychain Access software automatically stores passwords from Keychain-aware applications such as Mail and the .Mac Internet services. That means you don't have to enter your password every time you check your email.

Not all applications have been constructed to interact with Keychain. In those instances, you can manually add your own passwords or even store credit card information for convenient lookup when you need it.

Automated Access

If you open Keychain Access from the Utilities folder within the system Applications folder, you can see the contents of your default keychain. For an account that has set up email and ICQ messaging services, the Keychain Access window should look similar to the one shown in Figure 14.1.

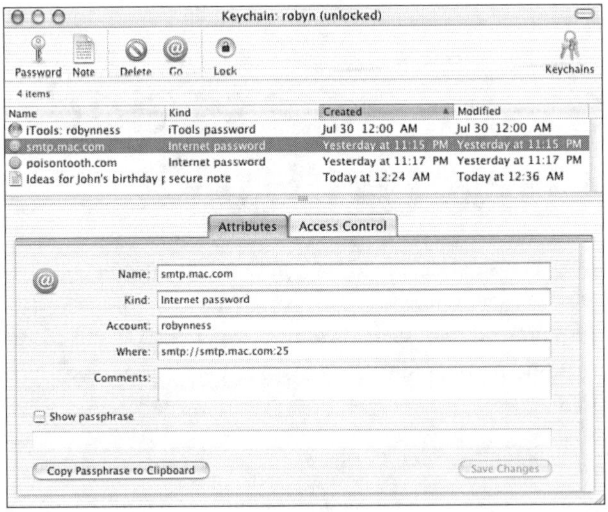

FIGURE **14.1**

The Keychain Access window displays a list of accounts with stored passwords.

The obvious question is, "How did these items get here?" They were added by Mac OS X applications. Typically, when an application wants to store something in Keychain, you're given the option of storing it. Choosing the Remember Name and Password option automatically adds the entered password to the default keychain. Over time, your keychain could become populated with items and you might not know it!

Manual Access

You can manually add new information to a keychain (or view what's already there) through the Keychain Access program. Each item listed in the Keychain window can be viewed by selecting it in the upper pane.

 If Keychain Access is something you want easy access to, you can add a menu extra to your menu bar by selecting Show Status in Menu Bar from the View menu in Keychain Access. A lock icon, open or locked, appears in the menu bar to show the status of your keychains, whether or not Keychain Access is running. Clicking it gives you options to lock or unlock all keychains and to launch the Keychain Access application.

Attributes

Two tabs of information for each Keychain entry are Attributes and Access Control. The Attributes tab provides basic information about the stored item, as shown in Figure 14.1. You can also add any additional comments about the item by typing them in the Comments field. Check the Show Passphrase button to display your password. To authorize revealing your saved password, you're prompted for your Keychain password.

 When authorizing Show Passphrase, you're asked for your password to access Keychain itself. At that time, you have the option to Allow Once, Always Allow, or Deny Permission. Because Keychain Access isn't listed as having unlimited access to stored items, it asks each time it needs to retrieve the information unless you choose the Always Allow option.

Access Control

When a Keychain-aware application wants to access information from your keychain, it must first make sure that the keychain is unlocked. Your default Mac OS X keychain is automatically unlocked when you're logged in, making its passwords accessible to the applications that stored them.

14

You can manually lock or unlock the entire keychain by clicking the Lock button in the toolbar of the Keychain Access window. After the keychain is locked, you're asked to enter a password—which, for the default keychain, is your account password—whenever an application attempts to access keychain information. Also, the details of keychain items within Keychain Access won't be shown until a password is entered. (However, the name of the items and when they were created are displayed.)

The Access Control tab, shown in Figure 14.2, enables the user to choose which applications can use information from Keychain. Click Always Allow Access to This Item to allow applications to transparently access the resource with no user interaction. If you prefer to monitor use of your passwords by programs, click the Confirm Before Allowing Access radio button to be prompted to decrypt each password when needed.

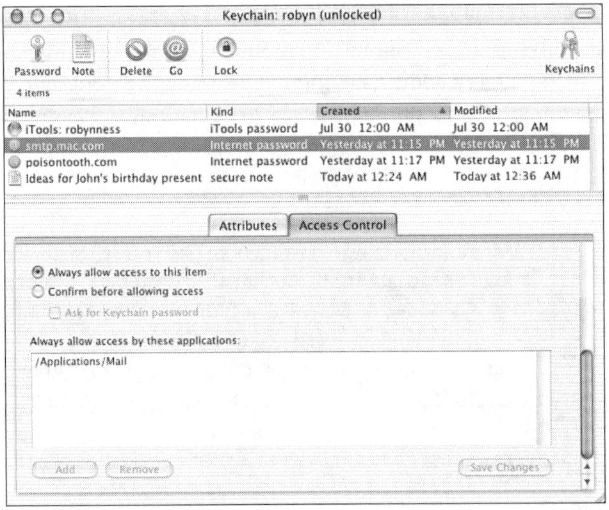

FIGURE 14.2

Access Control enables you to choose which applications can apply your passwords.

You can further specify how individual applications deal with passwords in the Always Allow Access by These Applications section. Use the Add and Remove buttons to add and remove applications from the list.

Adding New Entries to Keychain

New pieces of information can be added to Keychain by clicking the Password button in the toolbar in the Keychain window or choosing New Password Item from the New submenu of the File menu. This action opens a new window, shown in Figure 14.3, in which to enter the data to be stored.

FIGURE 14.3

New items can easily be added manually to an existing keychain.

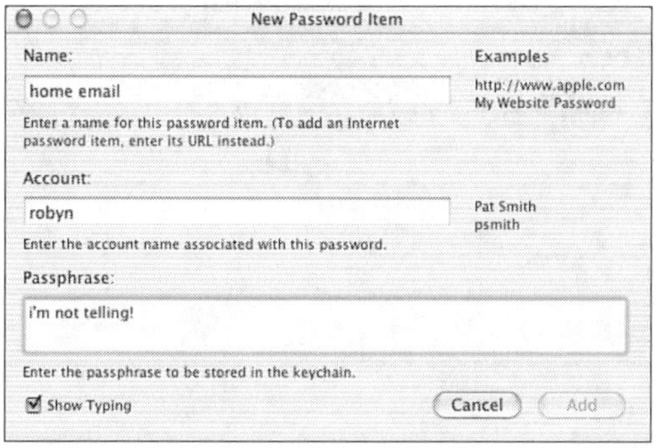

	New Password Item
Name:	Examples
home email	http://www.apple.com My Website Password
Enter a name for this password item. (To add an Internet password item, enter its URL instead.)	
Account:	
robyn	Pat Smith psmith
Enter the account name associated with this password.	
Passphrase:	
i'm not telling!	
Enter the passphrase to be stored in the keychain.	
☑ Show Typing	Cancel Add

To add a new item, follow these steps:

1. Enter the name (or for password-protected Web sites, the URL) of the new item into the Name field.
2. Enter the account name associated with the data into the Account field.
3. Enter the account password into the Password field. By default, the password is hidden as you type. To display the password as it's typed, click the Show Typing check box.
4. When you've completed these fields, click Add.

To remove any item from Keychain (either automatically or manually entered), select its name in the list and then click the Delete icon.

In addition to adding new passwords to your keychain, you can also create Secure Notes. To do this, click the Note icon in the toolbar or choose New Secure Note from the New submenu of the File menu. A new window opens in which to type your note. When you've typed the name and content of the note, click the Add button to save. The note is added to the list of items.

 When typing a note, keep in mind that pressing the Enter key saves the note rather than moving the cursor to a new line.

14

To view the contents of a secure note, check the box labeled Show Note and enter your password for authorization. You can then edit the note and save changes (see Figure 14.4).

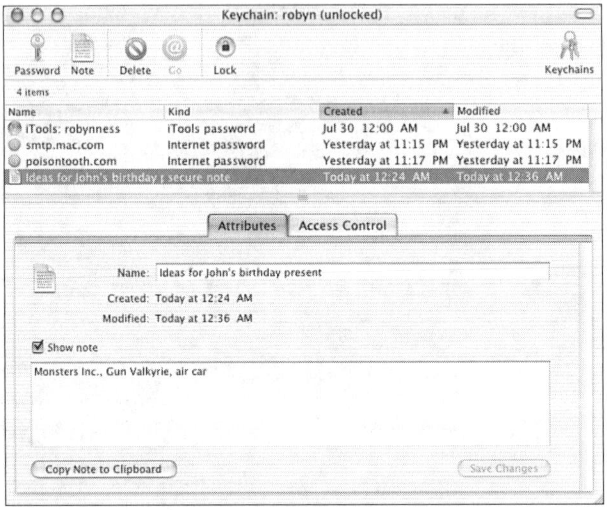

FIGURE **14.4**

*Private information
can be stored as a
secure note within
Keychain.*

Adding and Managing Keychains

Each user has a default keychain that's unlocked with the system password, but you can
have as many keychains as you would like. Extremely sensitive information can be
placed into a secondary keychain with a different password so that someone with your
account password won't have access to all your information.

To add a new keychain, do the following:

1. Choose New Keychain from the New submenu of the File menu.

2. You are prompted for a name and save location for the keychain. The default save
   location is ~/Library/Keychains in your home folder. When you've set these
   options, click Create.

3. A dialog box appears, prompting you to enter and verify the password that unlocks
   the new keychain. (It's best to choose something different from your account password to prevent people who might gain access to your account from seeing your
   most sensitive information.)

4. Click OK.

To switch between different keychains, click the Keychains icon in the toolbar to reveal a
tray containing the available options, as shown in Figure 14.5.

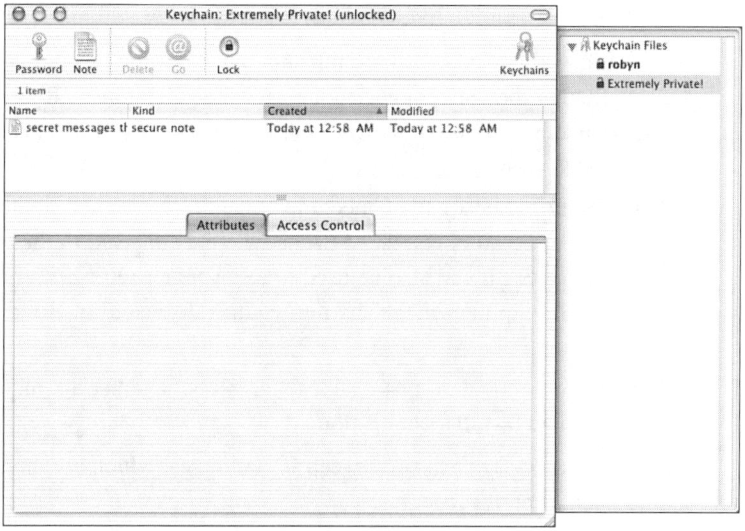

FIGURE 14.5

Choose a keychain from the tray—notice that a locked keychain shows nothing in the Attributes tab until its password is entered.

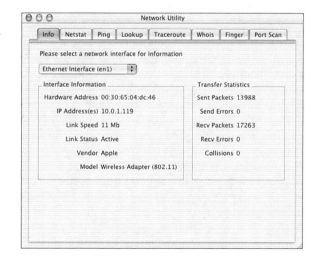

Network Utility: A Quick Overview

Also in the Utilities folder under Applications is something called Network Utility. This collection of functions, shown in Figure 14.6, is commonly used by people who manage networks. Most of these functions display information or are used to test network connections.

FIGURE 14.6

Network Utility brings together several network-administration tools under one roof.

14

The following is a brief description of the available options:

- **Info**—Enables you to see information about the installed network cards, including whether they are connected and to which IP address. It also lists any errors in transmission that have occurred. Figure 14.6 gives an example of the displayed data.

- **Netstat**—Shows all connections to and from your computer. It's of most use to server operators who need to see who is connected to the computer at a particular instant, but it can also be used to see whether remote users are connected to a personal computer via the sharing features discussed in Hour 13, "Using Network Sharing."

- **Ping**—A function that enables you to test whether a remote machine is responding and how fast that connection is.

- **Lookup**—Translates between IP addresses, which are numeric, and hostnames such as `apple.com`.

- **Traceroute**—Shows the path required to connect to a given IP address or hostname. If you've ever wondered how many computers are needed to connect you to your favorite Web site, Traceroute can give you some indication.

- **Whois**—Enables you to look up who owns and administers a domain name. Note that when using the default Whois server options, you might be directed to another host for more detailed information. This is useful if you need to contact a site administrator, check the expiration of your own domain names, or simply want to find a domain name that isn't already taken, as shown in Figure 14.7.

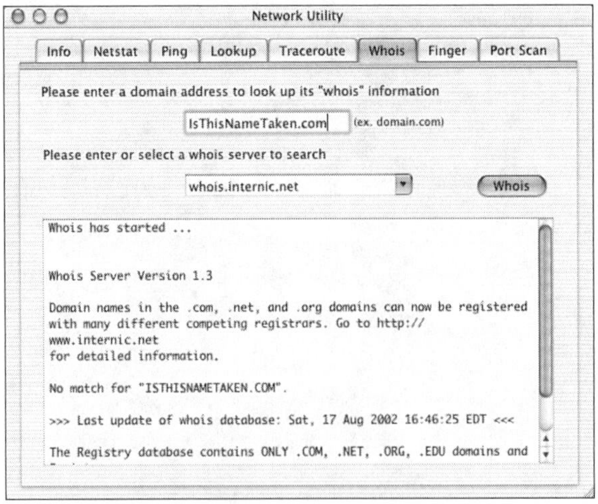

FIGURE 14.7

Whois lets you find information on domain names, including whether or not they are already taken.

- **Finger**—Enables you to look up information on a specific user on systems that have Finger enabled.

- **Port Scan**—Tests which services (such as FTP and file sharing) are running on a computer, but should not be used on any but your own machines. This feature is discussed further in Hour 23, "Security Considerations."

> Port Scan is nothing to play with. A system administrator I know was testing his own network when he mistakenly transposed two numbers in an IP address and scanned a completely different system. The administrator of the scanned system took offense at the possible security breach and sent a harshly worded letter of warning to my friend and his ISP.

For the most part, ordinary users don't need to use Network Utility. It's provided as a tool for network administrators to test computers that that might be having trouble on the network. For those interested in giving the application a test drive, you'll see a real-world example in Hour 23.

Summary

In this hour, we considered some of Mac OS X's network helpers. Keychain serves as a storage place for all the passwords and important data that a person needs close at hand. The functions located under Network Utility are less-commonly needed, but are equally easy to use. Several of the most important functions are discussed in upcoming sections.

Q&A

Q Are keychains really secure?

A The information stored for Keychain Access is encrypted, which makes it very difficult for someone to break into your computer and steal what's stored there. However, as one newsgroup contributor cautions, "As with all mathematical encryption, cracking is only really a matter of how hard you try to solve the equation." Also, if the passwords to access your keychains can be guessed, the rest of your passwords can be easily read.

Q You said I need my password to open my keychains, but I can't remember it.

A Hour 24, "Maintenance and Troubleshooting," tells you how to find out or reset your password.

14

Q I tried looking up people I know using the Finger feature of Network Utility, but I get the response "Connection refused." Am I doing something wrong?

A No, that message doesn't mean you've done something wrong. Many email systems do not support Finger as a function because they don't want to give out personal information about their users.

Workshop

The workshop contains quiz questions and activities to help you solidify your understanding of the material covered. Try to answer all questions before looking at the "Answers" section that follows.

Quiz

1. What is the default password of your default keychain?

2. How do you add a secure note to your keychain?

3. Which feature of Network Utility should you *never* user on a computer that you don't administer?

Answers

1. The system password you use to log in

2. Choose New Secure Note from the New submenu of the File menu

3. Port scan

Activities

1. Open your default keychain and add any passwords you have for Internet sites requiring login. (Note that some might already be stored.)

2. Open Network Utility and click through the tabs. If you'd like, use Whois to look up the domain name of your favorite Web site.

PART IV

Advanced System Configuration

Hour

Hour 15

Sharing Your System: Multiple Users

As you know from previous hours, Mac OS X is a true multiuser operating system because it incorporates some standard features of UNIX systems into the convenience of the Mac desktop interface. Longtime Mac users will be happy to learn that they can still run their computers much as they did before Mac OS X. But the multiuser aspects of Mac OS X do require special attention, in terms of both their benefits and problems. In this hour, you learn

- How to use system logins
- The different types of users
- The steps for creating, editing, and deleting users
- How to set up file permissions

Understanding Mac OS X User Accounts

In a multiuser system, everyone who works on the computer can have a separate account in which to store personal files. In practice, that means when one user saves a document to the desktop, it does not appear on the desktop that the other users see. Also, each person can set system preferences that show up only when he or she is logged in. Users can customize the Dock and the desktop appearance and expect them to remain that way.

An interesting feature of multiuser operating systems has to do with remote access. Because the operating system assigns a separate desktop to each account, multiple users can use files on a single computer at the same time. Although this requires connecting to the machine from another computer and enabling remote login, the OS is designed to cope with different simultaneous processes so that users can work as though they were alone on the system.

The home folders for user accounts are located in the Users folder of the Mac OS X hard drive, as shown in Figure 15.1. A house icon is used in the Finder window toolbar to represent a user's home folder. Inside the home folder are several different folders, which were discussed briefly in Hour 2, "Using the Finder and Dock," when we talked about file structure.

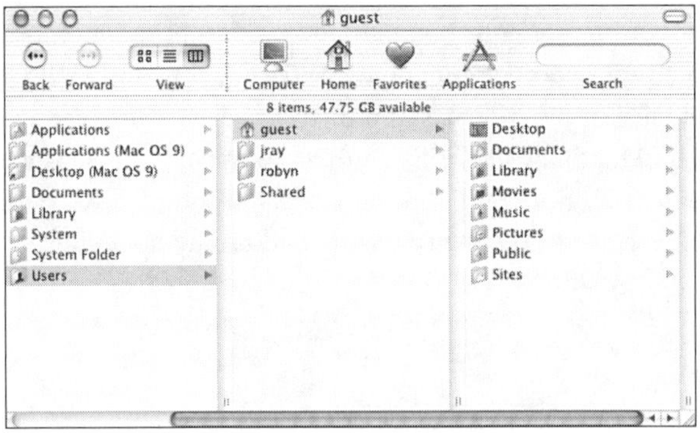

FIGURE 15.1

Every user has a home folder in which to store his or her files.

Although individual users can see the contents of most files on the hard drive, they might not be able to see each other's files. That's because users in a multiuser system can set permissions on their files that restrict access to keep their work private. They can specify whether a file can be read or altered by everyone, by a limited number of other people, or only from within the account in which the files were created.

For example, Figure 15.2 shows what the home folder of the user robyn looks like to another user. Most of the folders have an icon with a red circle containing a minus sign. That means these folders are not accessible by users who do not own them.

FIGURE 15.2

By default, other users are restricted from accessing all but the Public and Sites folders.

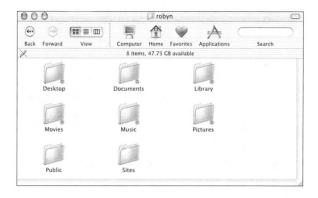

 As you learned in Hour 2, you can change the permissions on a file or folder that you own under the Users and Permissions section of the Get Info panel (Commmand+I). We discuss permissions further later in this chapter.

Logging In

One aspect of maintaining a multiuser system is controlling who can use the computer, which files they have access to, and where their work is stored. These objectives are met by requiring people to sign in before using the machine. This process of identifying your-self to the system, which involves presenting a username and password, is known as a *login*.

If you're logged in on a Mac that's used by other people with their own accounts, you must log off when finished. This allows the computer to return to a state that enables oth-ers to log in. If someone forgets to log off, that person's account and files could be accessed by anyone because the system does not know that the owning user is no longer at the controls.

By default, Mac OS X sets the system to login automatically to the account of the first-created user every time the computer starts up. In this mode, your computer won't require you to enter your username and password. If you don't see a need to force a login each time your computer turns on, you can keep this setting.

However, if other people have access to your computer, you might want to create separate accounts for them and require them to log in. Many people dislike the idea of requiring a login to use their computers, but it is a good idea to disable automatic login if your computer has more than one user. Why? Without required logins, your documents and system settings can be modified by whoever uses the machine. Besides, giving each user his or her own desktop can cut down on clutter, prevent accidental deletion of files, and enable everyone to customize his or her settings.

To change your system so that it requires each user to log in, go to the System section of the System Preferences panel, and click the Accounts button. In the Accounts panel, uncheck the box in front of Log In Automatically as [Username]. We look at the options for customizing the login screen in the next section.

Customizing the Login Window

The screen in which users supply their names and passwords is referred to as the *login screen*. An example is shown in Figure 15.3.

FIGURE 15.3
Mac OS X gives the option to choose an icon for each user.

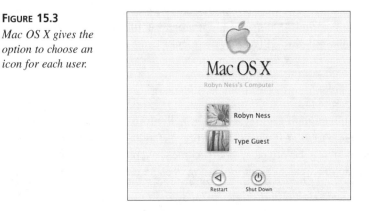

Although the login screen looks quite simple, several of its characteristics can be altered in the Login Options tab of the Accounts Preferences panel. You can indicate what you would like the login window to look like: either a list of usernames with an associated picture, as shown in Figure 15.3, or two blank fields for username and password. When a login picture format is used, clicking on a user reveals a space to type the user's password.

To disable the login screen from an administrator account, return to the Users tab of the Accounts Preferences panel and click the button for Set Auto Login. You are prompted for your password to authorize the change. Then, the next time you login, your computer automatically opens to the account of the first-created user.

15

Another option in the Login Options tab is whether to display the password hint onscreen after three tries. A *password hint* is a clue that users specify when creating their accounts. It serves to remind forgetful users of what they chose for their secret password. However, hints should be used with caution. Providing hints after several failed login attempts might help users, but it can also aid unauthorized users who are trying to guess passwords and gain access to your system.

You can also choose whether to allow users to access the Shut Down and Restart buttons on the login screen.

Adding Login Items

There's another benefit of having individuals log in, even if they are friends or family members. That is the option to have applications boot automatically on startup.

When you log in to your Mac OS X computer, you can choose to have it start applications for you automatically. However, if all users had their favorite applications start at once, regardless of who was using the machine, it would take a long time for the system to be ready. With separate accounts, only the applications of the logged-in user are started.

Figure 15.4 shows the Login Items Preferences panel where you can add applications to start automatically when you log in. To do this, just drag the application icon in the system Applications folder to the Login Items pane.

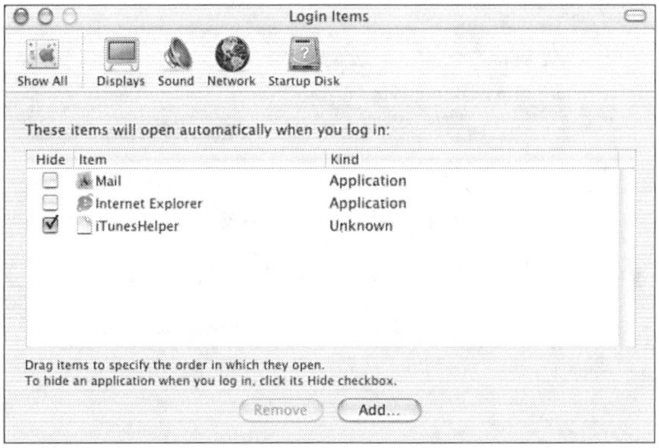

FIGURE 15.4

By using the Login Items pane, your favorite application can be ready and waiting every time you log in.

Hide	Item	Kind
☐	Mail	Application
☐	Internet Explorer	Application
☑	iTunesHelper	Unknown

Login Items

Show All Displays Sound Network Startup Disk

These items will open automatically when you log in:

Drag items to specify the order in which they open.
To hide an application when you log in, click its Hide checkbox.

Remove   Add...

Adding and Removing Users

When you first installed Mac OS X, an account was created using the name you supplied. The system uses the short name you gave as your account name, but you can use either your full or short name to log in to the system at the console. Because this account can access system settings and install new software, it's referred to as an *administrator account*.

When logged in with an administrator account, you're granted the privilege of adding other users and you can choose to give them administrative privileges as well. Remember, that means other people can add new accounts and modify the system, so you should be cautious about creating other administrative accounts. Be sure that you trust your users not to delete important files or disrupt the system in other ways before you give them administrator privileges.

New user accounts are added from the Users pane of the Accounts Preferences panel, shown in Figure 15.5.

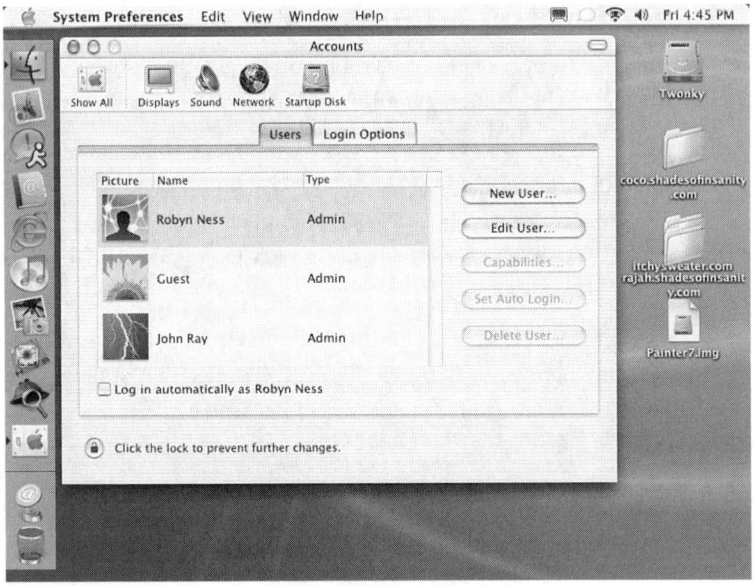

FIGURE 15.5

The Users pane of the Accounts Preferences panel lists current users and enables you to edit them or add new ones.

To create a new user account, follow these steps:

1. Click the New User button to open the sheet shown in Figure 15.6.

FIGURE 15.6

Enter a username and password and select an image for the new user.

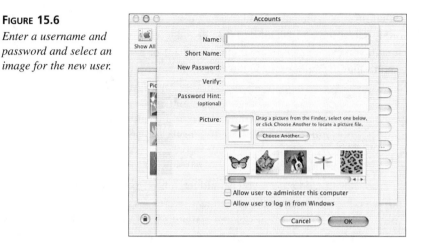

2. Type the name of the person using the account as well as a short name to be displayed for logging in.

3. Type the password once, and then type it again to verify it. The Password Hint box is for a short description or question to remind the user of his password when he forgets it.

4. Choose the picture that shows up next to the user's name in the login screen.

5. If you want your new user to have administrative powers, as discussed previously, check the box labeled Allow User to Administer This Computer.

6. If you want Windows users to be able to connect to the new user's home folder, check the box for Allow User to Log In from Windows.

7. When you're done, click OK.

The Users Preferences panel now lists your new user, who has a folder in the Users folder.

If you want to further control the access of users who aren't allowed to administer the computer, you can click the Capabilities button to choose which applications are visible to them, whether they can access System Preferences, and burn CDs or DVDs. You can also enable a setting called Simple Finder, which simplifies system navigation by opening all Finder elements in a single window.

Through a similar process, you can edit an existing user account, including changing the password. Simply select the user account to be edited and click the Edit User button. Note that although you can change many things about a user account, you can't alter the short name used to log in. Choose wisely the first time.

 To alter the settings for the currently active administrative account, you must enter your current password to provide authorization.

Now that you know how to add a user, you should learn how to remove a user. This again requires you to open the Users tab of the Accounts Preferences panel. To delete a user account, simply select the account to be deleted and click the Delete User button. In this way, you can delete any user account *except* the original administrator account. A sheet appears to confirm your choice and to inform you that the deleted user's files are stored as a disk image (.dmg file) in the Deleted Users folders. If you don't want the contents of the deleted account, you can open that folder and delete the .dmg file.

 When an account is deleted for the first time, the Deleted Users folder is created. Even though you can delete the .dmg files inside it, there is *no* way to delete the folder itself from within the Mac OS X interface. If you attempt this, you will be denied permission.

Controlling File Permissions

In addition to letting you decide who can log in to your computer, Mac OS X enables you to control who can interact with your files. If you create a file while you're logged in to your account, you own that file. Without your password, other users can be prevented from accessing your folders and files in any way; they can neither read nor alter your files and folders. For example, the folders in the home folder created for each user have some of these restrictions set by default.

Changing privileges in a file or folder is done though the Info panel of the Finder. These are the steps to use this panel:

1. Highlight the icon of the file or folder whose access you want to change. Users who are administrators can change the permissions on almost any file, but those who are normal users can change the permissions only on files they themselves own.

2. To open the Info panel, choose Get Info from the File menu. Alternately, you can use the key command Command+I.

3. Open the Ownership & Permissions section of the panel. If the lock button shows a closed lock, click it to unlock the settings.

4. Access can now be set so that different users have different privileges. The main options for levels of access are Read & Write, Read Only, and None. For folders, there is also the Write Only option, which enables a drop-box feature so that users can copy files into the folder, but only the owner can view it.

5. When you've set the permissions you need, close the panel.

 When changing access options for a folder, you also have the Apply to Enclosed Items button to apply the access rights you've selected to all files and folders within the original folder. Remember, just because a folder doesn't have read permissions doesn't mean that the files inside it can't be read or modified.

Understanding Groups

You might have noticed that the Ownership & Permissions section of the Info panel enables you to specify permissions for the owner of the file, the group to which that user belongs, and others. But what is a group? Let's look at that concept briefly now.

In UNIX systems, users can be classified into many different groups so that they can access, or be excluded from accessing, certain information. In other words, some files are needed by more than one person, but shouldn't be accessed by everyone. To facilitate appropriate file sharing, groups are defined to identify who can have access to which system features.

There are many possible groups to choose from in the Owner and Group pop-up menus of the Ownership & Permissions section. Among them are the names for each of the user accounts on your computer, which are used to assign a file to those users. Other than those, the only groups you should be concerned with are admin and staff, which grant access to only administrative users and everyone with an account on the computer, respectively. The other options are specialized groups that you won't need unless you plan to treat Mac OS X as a UNIX system.

The Root Account

During the discussion on Mac OS X's file structure in Hour 2, you learned that the folders at the top level of the hard drive can't be modified, which has been done to preserve system order and stability. The technical reason that even administrative users can't make these changes is that those folders are owned by another account called the root, or superuser, account. This account exists on a completely different level, one that most users of Mac OS X never need to see. Although the administrator account works for most Mac OS X system administration, the root account is much more powerful.

Let's talk about that power. The root account is an addition to the Mac OS that comes from the UNIX operating system. Traditionally, the root account has been reserved for the people who control the invisible workings of networks and are responsible for providing stable and usable systems for many users. From the root account, you can change any file or use the identity of another user without having to know his or her password. Basically, the root account can do whatever it chooses.

Although this power might seem appealing, it comes with great risk. If you aren't careful about what you type, you could *very easily* erase important files that are necessary for the system to even start up. For this reason, Apple has tried to ensure that only users who understand its power will use the root account. Although most UNIX systems assign root privileges to the first administrative account, Mac OS X comes with the root account shut off. As an added protection, even when the root account is activated, logging in as root requires extra effort. Hour 20, "UNIX Command Line Tour," details enabling and accessing the root account.

Summary

Multiuser systems are new territory for most Mac users, but the basics aren't difficult to understand. This hour introduced you to this concept as it relates to Mac OS X and explained different types of users, user groups, and file privileges and how to work with them. You also explored some of the settings you need to create, delete, and edit user accounts and to change read/write file permissions.

Q&A

Q **I have automatic login enabled. When I choose Log Out instead of Shut Down from the Apple menu, my computer requires me to log in the next time I use it. Doesn't this produce the same effect as turning off automatic login from the Accounts preference panel?**

A Not quite. After choosing Log Out, the computer returns to the login screen, but the next time someone chooses Shut Down, the computer opens to the account of the original user. If you're certain that no one can log in through any of the user accounts, this is an easy way to keep people out of your files on a short-term basis without changing the settings for automatic login. However, if people can log in to another account, they could easily restart the computer and reach your account, too.

Q When I went in to change privileges on my files, I noticed that I could make it so that even *I* can't read or write to my files. Why is that option available?

A If you've ever accidentally deleted an important file, you can see why this is an option. Sometimes it's best to impose a few rules on yourself to avoid bigger problems. Remember, though, that file owners can always change the permissions, even after they've turned off read or write access for themselves.

Workshop

The workshop contains quiz questions and activities to help you solidify your understanding of the material covered. Try to answer all questions before looking at the "Answers" section that follows.

Quiz

1. How do you activate automatic login?

2. What's the only aspect of a user account that you can't alter in the Users Preferences panel?

3. How do you access the Info panel?

Answers

1. Open the Accounts Preferences panel, and click the Set Auto Login button. The next time the computer boots, it automatically opens into the account of the first-created user.

2. The short name.

3. Choose Get Info from the Finder's File menu.

Activities

1. Go to the Login Items tab of the Login Preferences panel and add your favorite application so that it opens when you log in.

2. If you have any documents saved on the hard drive, use the Info panel to change their privileges to suit your needs.

Setting Up Printers and Fonts

The Macintosh has always been good at creating works of art, but to share your creations, you might want to print them. This hour looks at both font and printer management—two important factors in producing quality output from your system. Over the next hour, you learn

- How to configure printers for your system
- Basic printing settings and options
- Supported fonts and how to install them
- How to use the Mac OS X Fonts panel

Using Print Center

In Mac OS X, the Print Center application (path: /Applications/Utilities/Print Center) maintains and manages everything printer related.

When you start the Print Center application, it opens a small window listing all the available printers that have been configured on your system. For example, in Figure 16.1, one printer is configured for my computer.

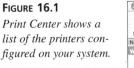

If a printer is set as the default printer, its name appears in bold type. You can make a different printer the default by choosing its name in the list, and then selecting Make Default (Command+D) from the Printers menu.

Setting Up Printers

Obviously, switching between printers isn't of much use until you set up a printer or two on your system. To do this, first click the Add button at the top of the Printer List window. A printer selection sheet appears, similar to the one in Figure 16.2.

At the top of the dialog box is a pop-up menu that offers several different ways in which you can find and connect to your printer:

- **AppleTalk**—Shown in Figure 16.2, AppleTalk is the choice to make if you're connecting to a local network Mac printer.
- **Directory Services**—If you're connected to a Mac OS X server computer or another directory service, there's a chance it's sharing printer information with

your system. Choosing Directory Services displays the printers available to your computer through a network directory server.

- **IP Printing**—LPR is used for many types of printers that allow access over TCP/IP. If you need to access a printer that isn't on your local network, this is probably the choice you want to make.

- **USB**—USB printers are the personal printers that plug into the USB ports on your computer. Canon, Epson, and HP printers typically connect via USB.

Below the four main ways of connecting are any manufacturer-specific drivers that have been installed on the system, such as Epson and Lexmark. If you're using one of these printers, you should select the corresponding option here.

If you choose AppleTalk or USB, Print Center attempts to locate potential printers that your machine can access and automatically displays them. To finish adding a printer, select it from the list of detected devices. Mac OS X then attempts to automatically detect the type of printer you've chosen and select the appropriate driver. Sometimes, however, you must use the Printer Model pop-up menu at the bottom of the dialog box to manually pick a printer type. Finally, click Add to add the selected printer to the Print Center listing.

IP printers are configured a bit differently. If you choose IP printers in the pop-up menu, you're asked for information on where the printer is located and how to connect, as shown in Figure 16.3.

FIGURE 16.3

IP printers require additional configuration.

Talk to the printer's administrator to determine the IP address and queue name for the remote device. Many times you can choose to use the default queue and simply enter an IP address. Because of the nature of IP connections, you *must* manually choose a printer model. Click Add to finish adding the printer.

For any of the printer connection types, if Mac OS X can't automatically find your printer model, you might need to contact the manufacturer and download additional drivers for the system.

Managing Your Printer Queue

After you start using your printers, you might occasionally want to cancel a print job that you've created or see what other print jobs are slowing yours down. You can easily do this by accessing the printer's *queue*—a list of the print jobs it is currently working on. To examine the queue, simply double-click the printer name in the Print Center printer listing. Figure 16.4 displays a printer queue.

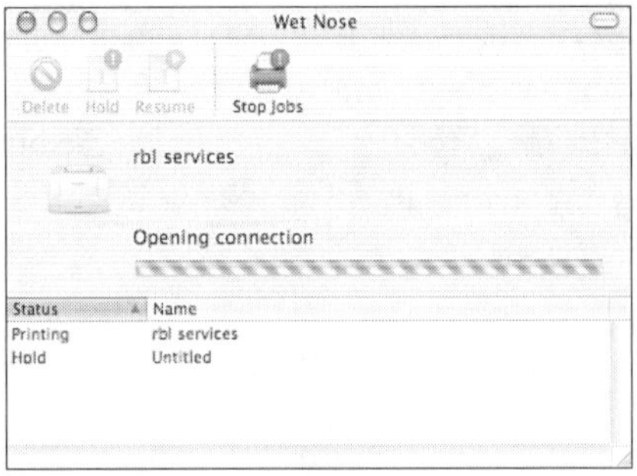

FIGURE 16.4
Double-click a printer's name to display its queue; this queue shows a print job on hold.

When viewing a printer queue, you can drag an individual print job up and down in the listing to adjust its priorities. You can also select a job and use the Delete button to remove it from the print queue entirely.

To completely stop the printer, click the Hold button. This prevents any further jobs from being processed. To resume printing, click the Resume button.

Common Printer Settings

Before anything shows up in the print queue, it must first be submitted to the printer. There are two menu commands shared by most applications that you use when printing:

- **Print** (Command+P)—Print the active document and configure settings for your chosen printer
- **Page Setup** (Shift+Command+P)—Choose how the document is laid out when printing

Let's start with the standard Page Setup dialog box, shown in Figure 16.5.

FIGURE 16.5

*Choose the basic lay-
out settings for your
print job.*

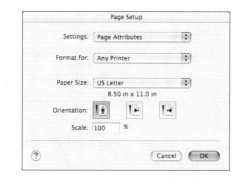

In the Page Setup dialog box, you can use the Settings pop-up menu to choose Page
Attributes, Custom Paper Size, or Summary to see a description of how the page will be
printed, including margin and size information.

The Format For pop-up menu enables you to choose which printer the page is being laid
out for. Because different printers support different page sizes and margins, it's important
to format a document for the appropriate printer before starting the print process. Use the
Paper Size settings to select from standard paper sizes that your device supports.

Finally, you can use the Orientation buttons to choose from normal, landscape, and
reverse landscape layouts and to set the Scale value to enlarge or shrink the output.

After making your Page Setup settings, it's time to use the Print dialog box shown in
Figure 16.6 to finish configuring your printer and start the print job. Choose Print from
the File menu or use the keyboard shortcut Command+P to open the Print dialog box.

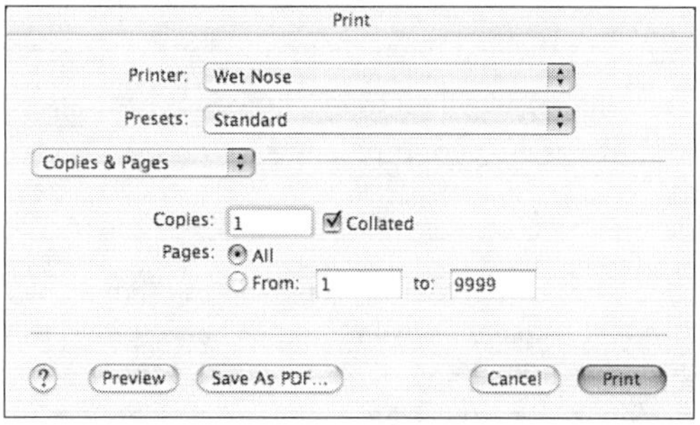

FIGURE 16.6

*The Print settings are
used to configure the
printer and start the
print job.*

If you've used a printer before, you probably recognize most of these settings. You can
enter your page print range, the number of copies, and so on, and then click Print to start
printing the document.

One extremely interesting feature that relies on the Mac OS X Quartz technology is the Preview function, which displays content from another program in a PDF format. If a Mac OS X application can print, it can generate a PDF. Clicking the Save As PDF button opens a Save As dialog box from which you can save any file as a PDF.

The default information displayed when you open the Print dialog box is the Copies & Pages settings. Using the pop-up menu near the top of the dialog box, you can select other common setting panes for your printer. These are a few that you may see:

- **Layout**—Have your printer print multiple document pages per printer page. This setting is useful if you want to print a long document for review.

- **Duplex**—Toggles printing to both sides of a piece of paper, if available.

- **Output Options**—If you want to output directly to a PDF file, you can set this option in the Output Options pane.

- **Error Handling**—You can choose how the system responds to errors that occur during printing. The options are No Special Reporting and Print Detailed Report.

- **Paper Feed**—Many printers have multiple paper trays. The Paper Feed settings enable you to choose which feed is active for a given print job.

- **Printer Features**—The Printer Features pane contains any special features offered by the connected printer.

- **Summary**—The Summary settings displays the status of all the preceding settings in one convenient location.

If you change several settings and want to save them for use from time to time, choose Save As under the Presets pop-up menu. Your custom settings will show up under Presets at the top of the Print dialog box for any later work.

A nifty extra of the Mac OS X printing system is the Print Center icon. When printing, it displays an animation of pages going through your printer and a count of the remaining pages to print. If there is an error, it displays a red page containing an exclamation mark to get your attention.

Adding Fonts

To create effective output, you need professional images and text. Mac OS X comes with a larger collection of fonts than any other version of the Mac operating system and supports more font formats than ever before including

- .dfont suitcases
- .ttf TrueType fonts
- .ttc TrueType font collections
- .otf OpenType fonts
- PostScript Type 1 fonts
- All previous Macintosh font suitcases

In short, if you have a font, chances are that you can install it on Mac OS X and it will work

Font files are stored in the system /Library/Fonts folder or in the Library/Fonts folder inside your home directory. If you have a font you want to install, just copy it to one of these locations and it becomes available immediately. You must restart any running applications that need access to the fonts, but you don't need to restart your computer.

Using the Mac OS X Fonts Panel

Applications that enable you to choose fonts often use the built-in font picker shown in Figure 16.7. This element of the Macintosh operating system is designed to make finding fonts easier and more among different pieces of software. To see the Fonts panel for yourself, open the TextEdit application (path: /Applications/TextEdit), and then choose Format, Font, Show Fonts from the menu.

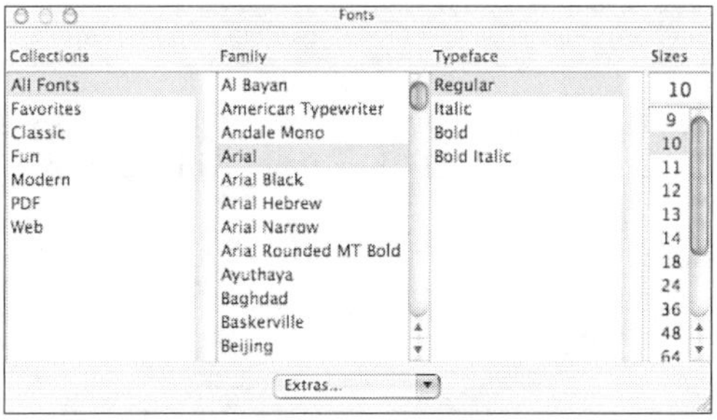

FIGURE 16.7

The Fonts panel is a systemwide object for choosing fonts.

In its expanded form (as shown in Figure 16.7), the Fonts panel lists four columns: Collections, Family, Typeface, and Sizes. Use these columns much as you use the Column view of the Finder—working from left to right. Click a collection name (or All Fonts to see everything), and then click the font family, typeface, and, finally, the size.

> If you prefer a more simplified view of the panel, use the window resize control in the lower-right corner of the panel to shrink the Fonts panel to a few simple pop-up menus.

Near the bottom of the expanded Fonts panel is the Extras pop-up menu, from which you can select several special features of the new font system:

- **Add to Favorites**—Add the current font choice to the Favorites font collection.
- **Edit Collections**—Create and edit new collections of fonts.
- **Edit Sizes**—Choose the list of sizes that appear as choices in the Fonts panel, or use a slider to control the size.
- **Show Preview**—Show a that preview of the selected font.
- **Show Characters**—Shows the that : Character palette displaying each of the characters for a selected font.

> Instant access to the Character palette from any application can be added in the Input Menu tab of the International System Preferences panel. Simply check the box in front of Character Palette and an icon appears in the menu bar of any active application. To remove the icon, simply return to the Input Menu tab and uncheck the box.

- **Color**—Pick a color for the font.
- **Get Fonts**—This selection launches your Web browser and takes you to a :special Apple page from which you can buy fonts. This service is not yet in operation, but it appears to be coming soon.

One final note about fonts: Not all applications use the system Fonts panel. When it's not supported, you're likely to see pull-down menus listing every installed font.

Summary

In Mac OS X, printers are managed entirely through the Print Center application and share a common look and feel throughout each of their settings panels.

The font system is equally easy to use. The addition of a systemwide Fonts panel makes it simple to build font collections and find your way through hundreds of available typefaces.

16

Q&A

Q What printers does Mac OS X support?

A Out of the box, Mac OS X 10.2 supports hundreds of PostScript printers and the most popular inkjet printers. I recommend contacting the printer manufacturer to make sure that drivers are available.

Q I don't see any printers listed in the AppleTalk printer connection list, but I know there should be some. Where are they?

A Make sure that you've enabled AppleTalk before trying to connect to AppleTalk printers. Hour 13, "Using Network Sharing," should help with this.

Q Why would I ever need Adobe Acrobat if Mac OS X can create PDFs?

A Although Mac OS X can create PDFs, it doesn't support all the PDF editing features of Acrobat. It's good in a pinch, but Acrobat is still a valuable product.

Q What is the best place to put font files?

A If you have a license for all users on your system to use the font, place them in /Library/Fonts; otherwise, place them in your personal Fonts folder.

Workshop

The workshop contains quiz questions and activities to help you solidify your understanding of the material covered. Try to answer all questions before looking at the "Answers" section that follows.

Quiz

1. How can you create PDFs from inside an application?

2. What types of fonts does Mac OS X support?

3. How can you create a more condensed view of the available system fonts?

Answers

1. You can click Save As PDF button in the Print dialog box to quickly generate a PDF of anything you're printing.

2. All TrueType, OpenType, and PostScript Type 1 fonts.

3. Resize the Fonts panel by using the control in the lower-right corner of the panel.

Activities

1. Install and test your printer settings. If you're using an AppleTalk-based printer, be sure to turn on AppleTalk in the Network Preferences panel.

2. Use the TextEdit application to explore the Fonts panel. Try making a collection of your favorite fonts.

Hour 17

Monitors and ColorSync

Your Macintosh is a fantastic tool for communicating visually. However, there are some tricks for keeping what you create on your screen looking the same no matter where it's viewed. Images look different when viewed on different monitors or when printed. To solve the problem of "what you see isn't quite what you get," Apple created ColorSync—a means of ensuring consistent color reproduction on different output devices. This chapter introduces ColorSync and walks you through the process of calibrating your system's monitor. You learn everything you need to know about color calibration and how to work with Mac OS X's monitor settings. In this hour, you

- Use and manage monitors
- Learn what ColorSync does and how it integrates with your system
- Create a ColorSync profile for your monitor
- Explore the additional Mac OS X tools for working with ColorSync

Configuring Displays

To change settings for your monitor, there's only one place to do it: the Displays System Preferences panel in the Hardware category. This panel is a bit unusual in that it can change drastically depending on what type of monitor is connected to your system. Users of Apple's CRTs see geometry information for adjusting image tilt, size, and so forth. The exact panel display depends on the monitor type. Those who have more than one monitor can arrange the monitors' location on the desktop and choose where the menu bar appears.

Resolution and Colors

To access your Display tab settings, open the Displays panel of System Preferences. Here you can see the basic settings for your monitor—color depth and resolution—as shown in Figure 17.1. What you see might vary slightly depending on the type of monitor you're using.

FIGURE 17.1

The Display tab of the Displays System Preferences panel controls monitor colors and resolution.

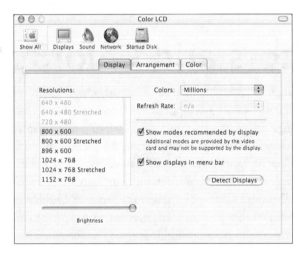

Available resolutions for your display are listed in the left column. Choosing a new resolution immediately updates your machine's display. At times, the panel might not show all the possible resolutions that your computer supports. In that case, you can uncheck the Show Modes Recommended by Display check box to see all the possible resolutions.

If you set the resolution or color depth on your monitor, it changes the system setting for everyone who uses that computer. The settings are not specific to your account.

Displays Menu Extra

If you find yourself switching colors or resolutions often, click the Show Displays in Menu Bar check box. This activates a Menu Extra, shown in Figure 17.2, that makes it simple to switch between different settings.

FIGURE 17.2

The Displays Menu Extra provides instant access to color and resolution settings.

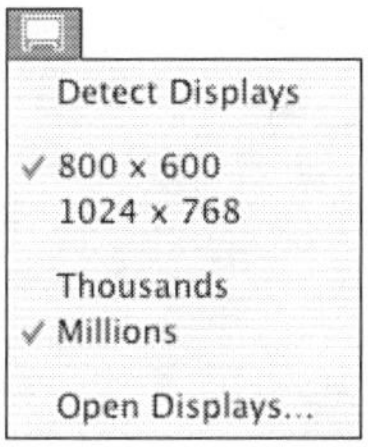

Detect Displays

✓ 800 x 600
1024 x 768

Thousands
✓ Millions

Open Displays...

Multiple Monitors

If you're lucky enough to have multiple monitors to connect to your system, Mac OS X enables you to use all of them simultaneously as a single large display. Note that you still need a video card for each monitor you're connecting or dual display support from a single video card. Users of iBooks and iMacs see a mirroring of their desktop on any added monitors rather than an addition of new desktop area.

Mac OS X automatically recognizes when multiple monitors are connected to the system and adjusts the Displays Preferences panel accordingly by adding an Arrangement tab. For example, Figure 17.3 shows the settings for a PowerBook G4 with an external VGA monitor connected.

There's no need to reboot to connect an external display. Just plug it in and start mousing!

In the Arrangement tab, you can control how the two monitors interact by dragging the corresponding rectangle. To move a monitor so that its portion of the desktop falls on the left or right of another monitor, just drag it to the left or right in the Arrangement tab. The menu bar can also be moved by clicking its representation in the Arrangement tab and dragging it to the monitor you want it displayed on. The changes you make to the arrangement take effect immediately; no need to reboot!

FIGURE 17.3

*The Displays System
Preferences pane
changes to handle mul-
tiple monitors.*

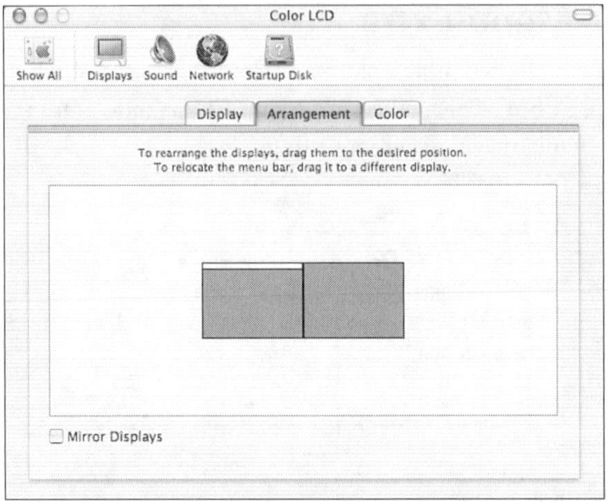

If you have multiple monitors connected, you'll also notice that each monitor has its own copy of the Displays System Preferences pane displayed in
the center of the screen. By using these separate panes, you can change the
color and resolution for each display independently.

Geometry

If you're using an Apple CRT display or a third-party CRT display that supports geometry settings through software, you might see an additional Geometry tab in the Displays
Preferences panel. This tab is used to fine-tune the image on your display through
actions such as rotating or resizing so that it has no obvious distortions. Read the opera-
tor manual that came with your monitor for more information.

Using these controls actually creates minuscule adjustments to the voltages that produce
images on your screen. LCD displays generate their pictures in an entirely different manner and don't require separate geometry settings.

Color

The final tab in the Displays System Preferences panel, Color, is where you can create
the ColorSync profile for your monitor or choose from one of the preset profiles that
come with the system. A Colorsync profile is a collection of parameters that define how
your device (in this case, your monitor) outputs color. Figure 17.4 shows the available
color settings.

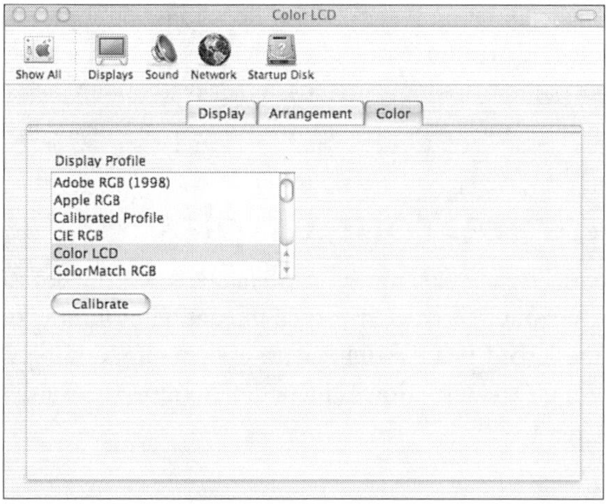

FIGURE 17.4

The Color settings are used to choose a ColorSync monitor profile or launch the calibration utility to make a new profile.

By default, Mac OS X tries to pick the profile it thinks is best for your system, but that doesn't mean it is necessarily in "sync" with your monitor. The color quality of both CRTs and flat panels varies over time, so you still might want to run a calibration even if there's already a setting for your monitor. To start the color calibration process, click the Calibrate button.

Even if you're not at all interested in graphics output and are absolutely convinced that there's no need to calibrate your system, you might still want to run the calibration utility. It gives you the ability to change how your screen looks in ways that the built-in brightness controls cannot.

For example, with a few clicks, you can create deeper, richer colors, or make whites warmer and more appealing. In short, you might have to be a graphics professional to understand the technical details of the calibration process, but the results speak for themselves.

Using the Display Calibrator Assistant

The Display Calibrator application is a simple assistant that walks you through the process of creating a profile for the monitors connected to your computer. If you didn't launch the calibrator through the Displays System Preferences panel, you can run it directly from /Applications/Utilities/Display Calibrator.

The steps in the calibration process differ depending on the type of monitor you're using. Adjustments to CRT (cathode ray tube) monitors follow these steps: set up, native gamma, target gamma, tristimuli values, target white point, and conclusion. For LCD monitors, the calibration process skips over several of the steps that aren't applicable.

Task: Calibrate Your Display

1. When the Display Calibrator Assistant starts, it provides a brief explanation of what it's about to do and gives you the option of turning on expert mode, as shown in Figure 17.5. Click the right arrow at the bottom of the window to begin. You can use the right and left arrows at any time to move forward and backward between the different steps.

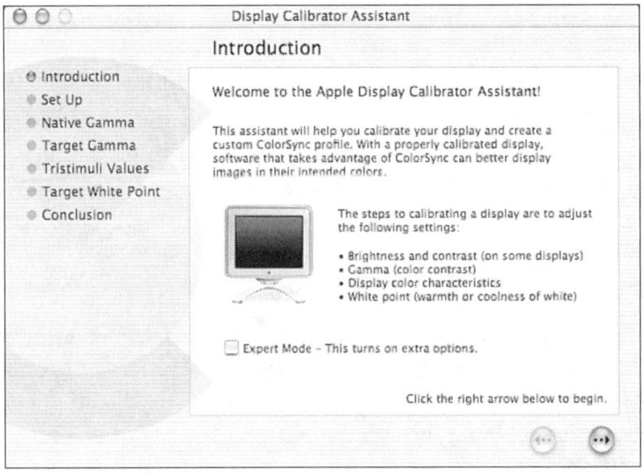

FIGURE 17.5

Turning on expert mode enables more precise adjustment; sticking with the normal mode limits your options to predefined settings.

2. The first step, Set Up: Display Adjustments, matters for CRT monitors only. It helps you adjust the brightness on your display to achieve the right black levels. To begin, turn the contrast control on your monitor up as high as it goes. Next, take a close look at the block in the middle right of the window. At first glance, the block, shown in Figure 17.6, might look completely black. In reality, the dark block is composed of two rectangles with an oval superimposed on them.

   Using your monitor's brightness control, adjust the image so that the two rectangles blend together and the oval is barely visible. It's best to sit back a little, away from your screen, to gauge the effect.

3. The next step, Determine Your Display's Current Gamma, also applies only to CRT monitors. Brightness does not increase linearly on computer displays. As the display increases a color's brightness on the screen, it isn't necessarily the same size

step each time. To correct this, a *gamma* value is applied to linearize increases in brightness. In the second step of the calibration process, you adjust the gamma settings for the different colors your computer can display. For more information about Gamma, visit `http://www.bberger.net/gamma.html`.

FIGURE 17.6

Adjust the brightness level on your display until the block blends together.

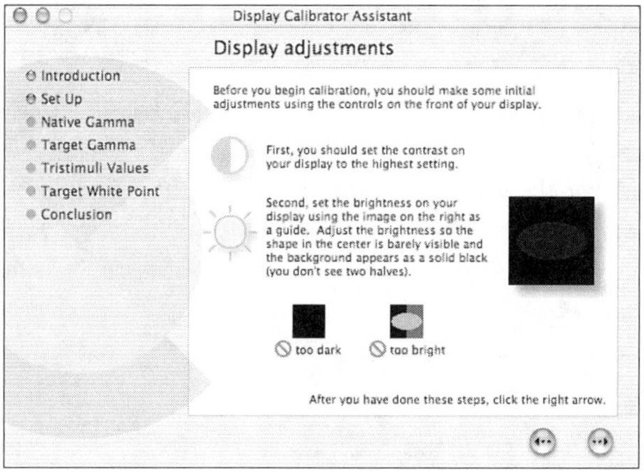

As shown in Figure 17.7, the current gamma calibration shows a block containing the Apple logo. Using the sliders below the block, adjust the logo's brightness so that it matches the background color as closely as possible. It's impossible to get a perfect match, so don't worry if you can still see the apple. It's best just to squint your eyes until you can't make out the text on your screen, and then perform the adjustments. (If you're in expert mode, you're prompted to adjust lightness and darkness for each of the primary colors of light [red, green, and blue].)

FIGURE 17.7

Match the apple color to the block background.

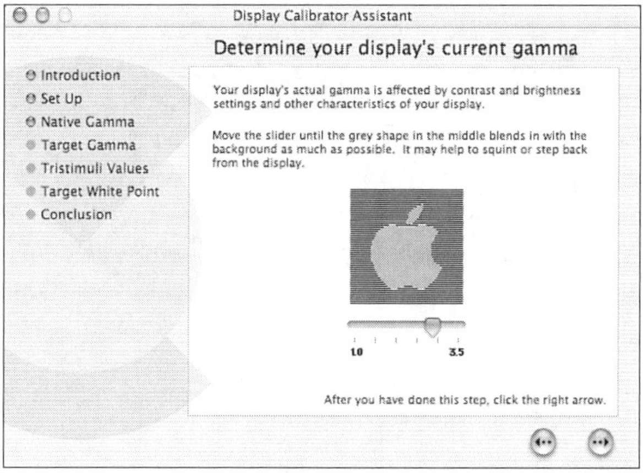

4. The next step, for both CRT and LCD monitors, is Select a Target Gamma. The target gamma for your display is useful for deciding what images on your monitor look like on other displays. PCs and televisions have varying gamma settings that don't match your Macintosh defaults. This makes it difficult to create graphics on your Mac that look right on a PC monitor. Using the target gamma settings shown in Figure 17.8, you can make your Mac's display look very much like that of a standard PC.

To adjust the gamma setting, select the radio button corresponding to your viewing needs. The picture in the upper-right corner of the window gives you an idea of what your choice does to your monitor's output. Choosing Uncorrected Gamma usually results in a very bright and washed-out image. (Those in expert mode use a slider to set the gamma, which offers more precise control.)

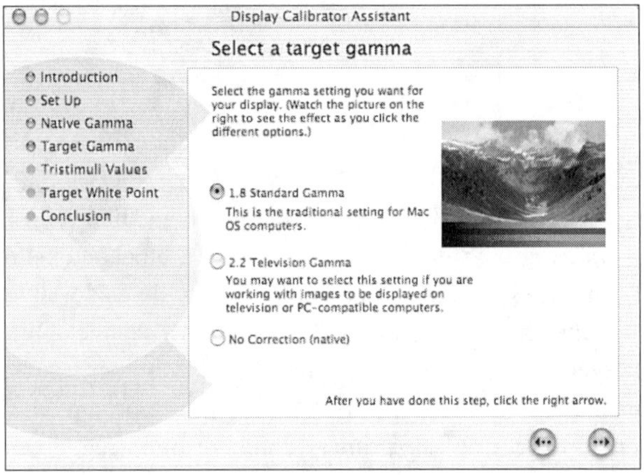

FIGURE 17.8

Choose the gamma setting to use on your monitor.

Gamers might have noticed that some titles appear too dark in places. To compensate for this, just decrease your monitor's gamma settings.

5. For those with CRT monitors, the next step is Tristimuli Values, which relates to the variation in chemical phosphors used in tube monitors. Here, the goal is to select the menu item that most closely matches your monitor.

6. The final calibration step for both CRT and LCD displays is Select a Target White Point. As you know, the *color* white is not a color, and is hardly ever truly *white*. When your computer displays a white image, it probably has tinges of blue, yellow, or even red. This variation is known as the *white point*. The white point settings are displayed in Figure 17.9.

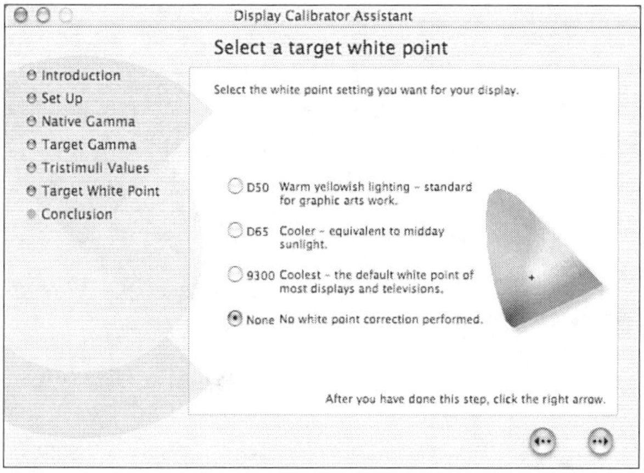

FIGURE 17.9

Choose the target white point setting to use on your monitor.

To set a white point, choose from the listed options by selecting the appropriate radio button. Once again, those in expert mode have a slider to set a more precise level. The higher the white point value, the cooler the display; the lower it is, the warmer the display. You might need to uncheck the No White Point Correction [Native] check box before you can make any modifications (in expert mode).

7. At the conclusion of the calibration process (see Figure 17.10), you're prompted to name your profile. Entering a descriptive name for your creation makes it simple to tell them apart. Save the profile by clicking the Create button. The new profile goes into effect immediately. Remember that you can switch between profiles in the Color tab of the Displays System Preferences panel.

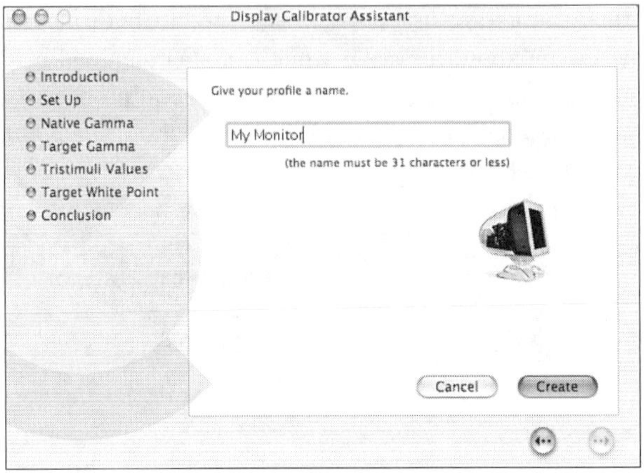

FIGURE **17.10**

Enter a name for your calibrated profile.

Introduction to ColorSync

As you work with color images and color output devices, you soon realize that there is no standard color monitor, printer, or scanner. A *color space* is a method for representing the possible output colors for a device by using a hypothetical one- to four-dimensional space. Each dimension in the space represents different intensities of the components that define a color. For example, a common space is RGB (red, green, blue). This three-dimensional color space is defined by using the three primary colors of light. Many other spaces exist that address other specific needs, such as printed color.

Although every monitor you buy is undoubtedly an RGB monitor, the RGB color space it supports varies depending on the quality of the monitor's components. Different phosphors produce slightly different shades of red, green, and blue. Cheap monitors might have a slight yellow or green tint to them, whereas LCD panels have vibrant hues but less consistency in gradations than professional CRT displays.

The same goes for printers and scanners. A scanner that costs more is likely to have a far broader and more consistent color space than its cheaper cousins. If you've ever seen a scan that looks dull and muddy, you're seeing a limitation of the scanner's supported color space.

ColorSync's challenge is to make sure that the colors you intend to print or display are what you end up getting. To do this, ColorSync uses a CMM, or color matching module, to translate between different color spaces. In addition, different devices (including your

monitor) can have ColorSync profiles that describe the range of color they can repro-
duce. Using Display Calibrator Assistant, as discussed in the previous section, you can
create a profile for your system's monitor. You'll find other profiles on the disks that
come with your peripheral devices. You can install profiles by dragging them to the
/Library/ColorSync/Profiles folder at the system level or in your home directory.

ColorSync System Preferences Panel

To make it simple for graphics professionals to switch between different groups of
ColorSync settings, or *workflows*, Apple included a ColorSync Preferences panel in Mac
OS X. Using this panel, you can set up a workflow for your input devices, display, output
devices, and proofing.

In addition, ColorSync Preferences enables you to set default profiles for each of the
ColorSync-supported color spaces (RGB, CMYK, and Gray) and choose a default color-
matching technology that maps from one Colorsync profile to another. Many of these
features aren't active unless you've installed additional software on your computer, however.

Figure 17.11 shows the main tab of the ColorSync Preferences panel: Default Profiles.

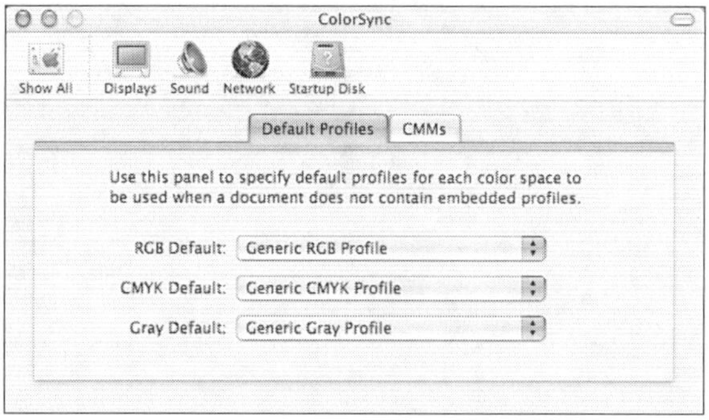

FIGURE 17.11

*The ColorSync
Preferences panel
enables you to set up
default collections of
profiles.*

Use the pop-up menus to choose from the installed Input, Display, Output, and Proof
profiles. This chooses the default profile to be used with a document when a document
doesn't specify a profile of its own. Don't be surprised if you don't see many options
under these menus. You might want to check the disks that came with your digital camera
or scanner to see whether they include color profiles.

The other tab, CMMs, functions similarly. The CMMs tab offers the option of selecting alternative color matching modules. The default Mac OS X installation includes only one CMM, so there's very little to see here.

ColorSync Utility

The final component of the ColorSync system is the ColorSync utility, located at /Applications/Utilities/ColorSync Utility. This program has a number of different functions, such as verifying and repairing ColorSync profiles, viewing the installed profiles, and listing ColorSync-compatible devices that are registered on your system.

When first launched, the ColorSync Utility defaults to the Profile First Aid function shown in Figure 17.12. Click the Verify or Repair button to check the installed profiles on the system.

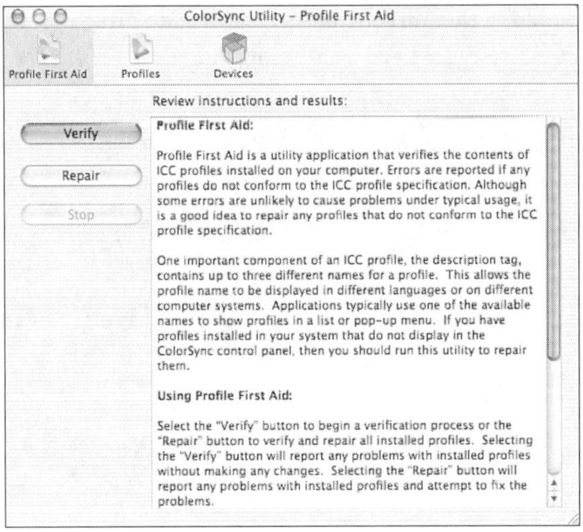

FIGURE 17.12

Verify and repair installed profiles.

To switch between the utility's different functions, click the icons at the top of the window. The second feature is the profile viewer, which is viewed by clicking the Profiles icon.

In this window, you can navigate through the installed ColorSync profiles on the system and display details for each one by selecting it from the list at the left of the display. Figure 17.13 shows the details for one of my profiles.

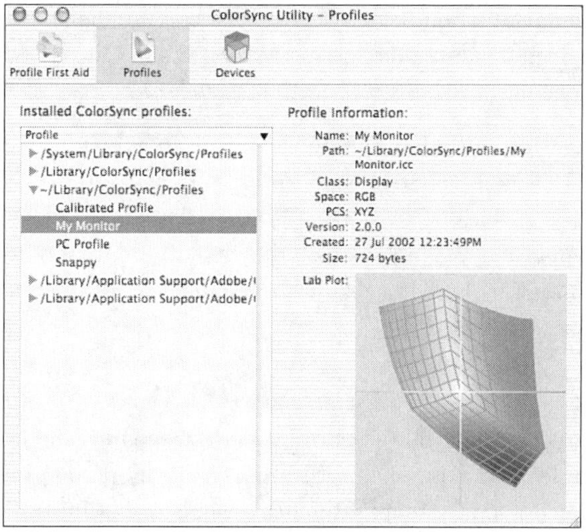

FIGURE 17.13
Easily navigate through all the installed profiles and display their details.

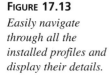

Click the Devices icon at the top of the window to view the utility's final feature. Each type of device is displayed as a category at the left of the window. Expanding a category shows the supported devices in that classification. For example, the Displays category features Color LCD and VGA Display devices, as shown in Figure 17.14.

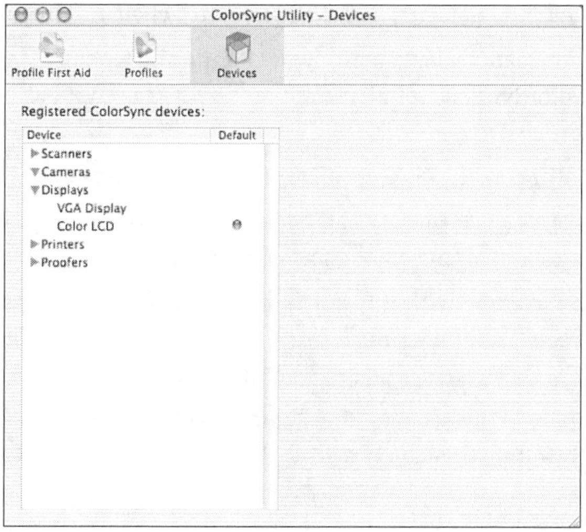

FIGURE 17.14
View the available ColorSync devices on your system.

When you find the device you want to configure, select it from the list. The right side of the window is updated to show information about the device, including its factory profile and any custom calibration profile you've created. Use the pop-up menu to choose a new profile for a given device, and click the Make Default Display button to set a device as the default to be used in a given ColorSync category.

Whew! I know this all sounds complicated, and, frankly, it is! Color calibration is an important part of the Macintosh operating system and part of what makes it widely revered among graphics professionals. If you fall within that group, it's good to know that these features are available. If not, they're still fun to play with because they can breathe new life into a monitor that has a less-than-perfect picture.

Summary

Apple gives you a great deal of control over your monitor and how it displays images. In this hour, you learned about monitor settings and calibration as well as the ColorSync system and the related System Preferences panels and utilities. Even if you don't use your Mac for precise graphic design and composition, you might find that creating custom ColorSync profiles for your system can benefit games, amateur photography, and anything else that involves the display of color on your monitor!

Q&A

Q I'm a graphic designer but I've never touched ColorSync. Should I?

A Some applications have their own color profile technology, but they can benefit from ColorSync as well. Even if you've never used it before, you should take a look now.

Q What other Mac OS X applications use ColorSync?

A The Image Capture utility can embed a ColorSync profile in an image file. This helps it retain its true colors no matter where it's viewed.

Q My device came with a ColorSync profile, but the output still doesn't match my screen. What's wrong?

A Be sure that you've disabled any internal color profiles or color enhancements for the device. Many printers offer built-in color correction, which could interfere with ColorSync functioning correctly.

Workshop

The workshop contains quiz questions and activities to help you solidify your understanding of the material covered. Try to answer all questions before looking at the "Answers" section that follows.

Quiz

1. Where can you adjust the position of individual monitors on a multiscreen desktop?

2. Why is color calibration necessary?

3. What's a color space?

4. Where can you view and manage installed profiles?

Answers

1. In the Arrange tab of the Displays Preferences panel.

2. Different monitors and devices generate their images with different inks, phosphors, and so on. Color calibration provides a means of determining how a given color can be generated on each device.

3. A color space is a theoretical multidimensional "space" defined by the mathematical values that make up a color. RGB color, for example, is a three-dimensional color space defined by the values of its three components: red, green, and blue.

4. The ColorSync utility is a "one-stop shop" for viewing, managing, and repairing the ColorSync profiles installed on your system.

Activity

Compare a photograph on the Macintosh to an identical photograph on a PC. You should notice a drastic difference in the image's brightness because of the PC's different gamma settings. You can compensate for this by using the Display Calibrator Assistant to adjust the gamma settings for your monitor.

17

HOUR 18

Accessibility Features and Additional System Preferences

System preferences are settings that control aspects beyond a single application and that might even affect the entire system. We've already covered many of Mac OS X's system preferences while addressing specific topics. However, some settings don't apply elsewhere. In this hour, we fill in the remaining gaps in system configuration and let you know where to find the system preferences discussed in other hours. We pay special attention to the accessibility features available in System Preferences.

Among the various and sundry System Preferences settings we consider are the following:

- Screen effects and energy use control
- Keyboard and mouse options
- Universal Access

As you've seen in previous hours, System Preferences items are categorized by jurisdiction into four groups, as shown in Figure 18.1. They are Personal, Hardware, Internet and Network, and System.

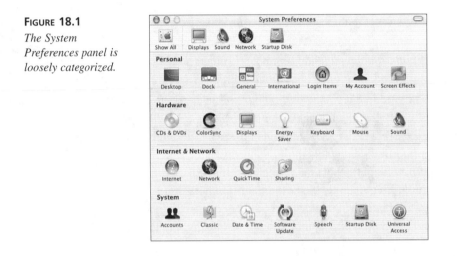

Within those sections, each button may have a large number of features (accessible after clicking it) and contain tabs or pop-up menus that organize its features into smaller units. This could mean that you have to click through several options before you locate the setting you want to change. Use the tab labels and explore pop-up menus to help guide you.

Personal System Preferences

The options in the Personal section of System Preferences affect your personal desktop. Each user can decide individual settings without interfering with the settings of others. These items include desktop backgrounds, Dock settings, and login items that we looked at in Hour 2, "Using the Finder and Dock," and Hour 15, "Sharing Your System: Multiple Users." In this section, we look at the remaining Personal Preferences panels: General, International, My Account, and Screen Effects.

General

The General Preferences panel enables you to choose between Blue and Graphite for a general color scheme for menus, buttons, and windows on your desktop. You can also pick the highlight color for selected items. Other settings are the placement of arrows in the scrollbars, the number of listings for recent applications and documents, and activation of font smoothing.

My Account

The settings under My Account enable users to change their own passwords, picture icon, and card in the Address Book application. (You might recall that users with administrator privileges can change the password and picture for any user from the Users tab of the Account panel.)

International

The International settings control the language displayed, as well as date, time, and number conventions. You can also choose keyboard layouts to support different languages.

Screen Effects

Under Screen Effects Preferences, mentioned briefly in our look at iPhoto in Hour 6 and .Mac in Hour 10, you can choose among several preinstalled screen savers. The preview window shown in Figure 18.2 enables you to view your selection before applying it.

FIGURE 18.2

Choose a screen saver and how it activates.

18

You can also choose how the screen saver activates by setting time until activation and whether to require a password to return to the desktop. The Hot Corners tab enables you to pick corners of the screen that activate or prevent activation of the screen saver when your mouse enters a given corner.

Hardware System Preferences

Hardware preferences, such as those for monitor, keyboard, and mouse, are found in the Hardware section of System Preferences. Displays and ColorSync were discussed in Hour 17, "Monitors and ColorSync." In this section, we look at the CDs & DVDs,

Energy Saver, Keyboard, Mouse, and Sound panes. For those with compatible graphics tablets, the Ink preferences also appear in this section, as discussed in Hour 3, "Basic Applications for Productivity and Recreation."

CDs & DVDs

The CDs & DVDs panel enables you to direct your computer what to do when CDs and DVDs are inserted in your drive. The default configuration, shown in Figure 18.3, launches the appropriate application included with Mac OS X when you insert a music CD, photo CD, or DVD. When you insert blank media, the Finder prompts you to choose an application to suit your purpose.

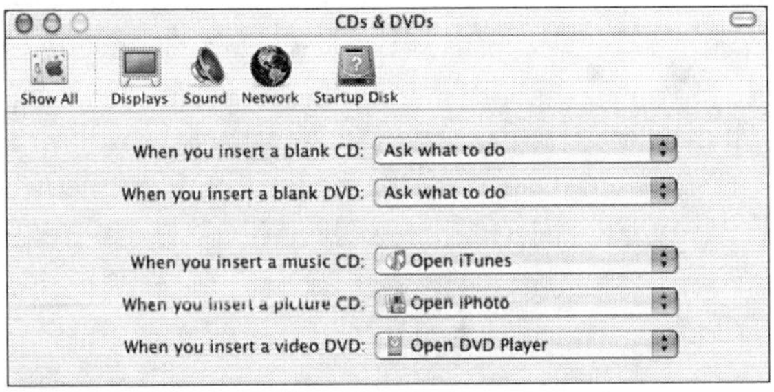

FIGURE 18.3

Choose which application is activated when you insert a CD or DVD.

Energy Saver

The Energy Saver pane, shown in Figure 18.4, enables you to set Sleep and Wake options for your machine. Laptop users also have the option to show the battery status in the menu bar. Notice that separate settings exist for the display and the hard disk.

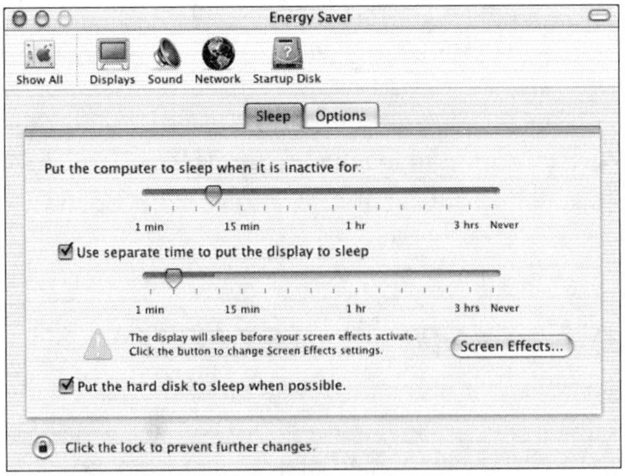

FIGURE 18.4

Energy Saver lets your system conserve power in response to monitor and hard drive in-activity.

After you've set Sleep options, use the Options tab of the Energy Saver pane to set Wake options.

> When performing functions that require lengthy periods of keyboard inactivity, such as CD burning or digital video rendering, it's best to set the Sleep option to Never to avoid disruption to the process that can result in skips in the output.

Keyboard

In the Keyboard pane, you can set the repeat rate of the keyboard and the delay before keys start to repeat when you hold them down. The Full Keyboard Access tab, shown in Figure 18.5, can be used to customize keyboard shortcut settings that enable users to control menus, windows, and other interface elements from the keyboard.

FIGURE 18.5

Use keyboard controls in addition to your mouse in changing system focus and navigation.

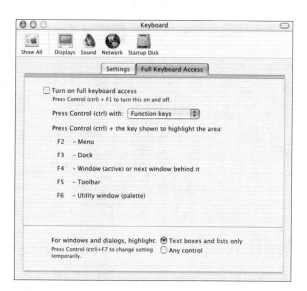

Mouse

Just as the Keyboard panel enables you to control keyboard sensitivity, the Mouse panel enables you to control tracking and double-click speeds. You might need to test the options a bit to find the most comfortable settings for your system. If you find yourself thinking that your desk space is too small for your mouse, you might just need to speed up your mouse tracking.

Laptop users will be delighted to find an Ignore Trackpad While Typing option. This disables the trackpad temporarily while the keyboard is being used. No more messed-up sentences because you accidentally hit the trackpad with your thumb while typing.

Sound

The Sound pane, shown in Figure 18.6, contains Sound Effects options and volume controls for alerts and the main system, as well as the option to choose your sound output and input devices. You can also change the overall volume levels from the keyboard sound controls.

If you have multiple sound input and output devices (such as an iSub) connected to you computer, you can choose between them here. In addition, you can use the Show Volume in Menu Bar check box to add a volume control Menu Extra to your menu bar.

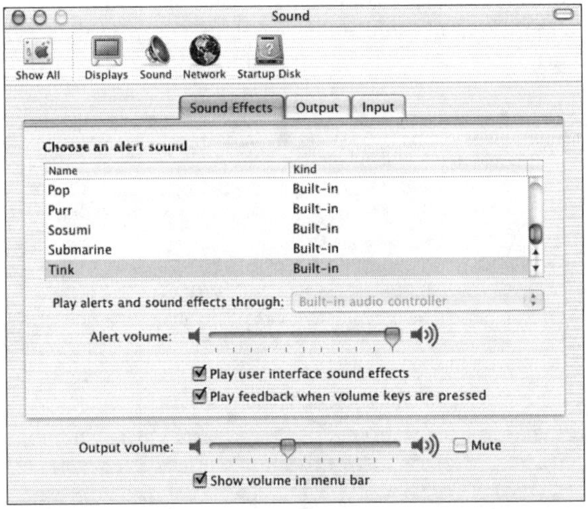

FIGURE 18.6

The Sound Preferences panel enables you to pick error alerts and select from which audio output they emanate.

Internet and Network System Preferences

The next grouping of preferences, Internet & Network, determines how your machine talks to other computers on the network and works with your Internet services, such as email and Web. We discussed the Internet preferences in Hour 10, "Web Browsing and .Mac," and the Network preferences in Hour 9, "Setting Up Mac OS X Networking." QuickTime, which is often used as a browser plug-in, was covered in Hour 7, "QuickTime and iMovie." Hour 13, "Using Network Sharing," explained the Sharing preferences.

System Preferences

The System section of System Preferences controls settings relating to use of Classic applications and choosing a startup disk, as discussed in Appendix B, "Running Classic Applications." It also contains the Accounts panel covered in Hour 15 and Software Update, which is explained in Hour 24, "Maintenance and Troubleshooting."

Date & Time, Speech, and Universal Access preferences will be examined in detail here.

Date & Time

Not surprisingly, you set the system date and time in the Date & Time tab of the Date & Time Preferences. But you can also set your time zone in the Time Zone tab. If your computer remains connected to the Internet, you can also choose a network time server under the Network Time tab to control your system clock. Finally, you can choose whether to show the date and time in the menu bar and choose what form it should take.

Speech

The Speech pane controls two separate, but related, elements: speech recognition and text-to-speech conversion.

Speech Recognition

In the Speech Recognition pane, shown in Figure 18.7, the primary option is to turn the Speakable Items feature on or off. As the name suggests, Speakable Items is a group of commands; when you speak one of these commands, your computer reacts to it. You can specify whether you would like this option enabled at login. You can also open a panel of helpful speech-recognition tips and choose a feedback sound to inform you when your commands have been recognized.

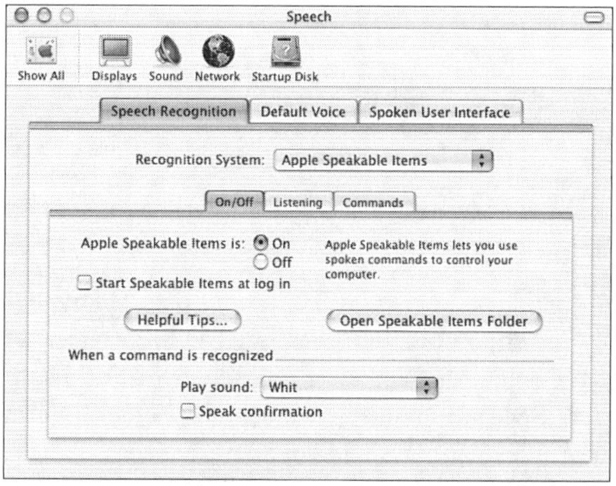

FIGURE 18.7
Use Apple's speech recognition application to perform elementary system functions.

The Speech Recognition Listening pane enables you to choose how you interact with the computer when speaking commands to it. The first option is whether you must press the Esc key before voicing your command or whether you can address the computer without using the listening key.

If you choose not to interact with the keyboard before your commands, you have the option to give the computer a name so that it knows when you're directing it, or you can simply hope that it recognizes the commands without warning by setting the Name Is pop-up box to Optional Before Commands.

> Keep in mind that addressing your computer by a name means it is always listening unless you manually toggle listening with the chosen key. No, this statement isn't meant to stir up paranoia. But it does mean that your computer has to determine which sounds are directed toward it and which ones are environmental or incidental. Depending on the circumstances, this might be very difficult, and your computer is simply unable to obey. To avoid undue frustration, we recommend using Speakable Items only while a key is pressed.

The final option on the Listening pane gives you information on which microphone, if more than one is available, is receiving your spoken input.

If you turn on speech recognition, the circular Speech Feedback windoid appears on your screen, as shown in Figure 18.8. You might recognize this window if you've played Chess, which we discussed in Hour 4.

FIGURE 18.8

The Speech Commands window shows a record of the functions carried out.

This unusual windoid shows the level of sounds detected by the microphone by filling in the lines in the lower portion of the window. The Speech pane of System Preferences and the Speech Commands window are accessible by clicking the arrow at the bottom of the window. The Speech Commands window shows the commands that you may speak to the computer. It also displays a log of all recognized commands and the system response enacted.

Default Speech

The Default Voice tab of the Speech pane lets you set the voice and rate of speech used by applications that speak. For example, this feature is used by the Finder to read alerts when they haven't been responded to after a reasonable amount of time has passed. To test each voice, just click the different voice names. Mac OS X automatically plays a short sentence using the selected voice.

Spoken User Interface

The Spoken User Interface tab is where you enable features in applications that speak. You can activate spoken alerts and choose an introductory phrase to announce them. You can also have your computer speak to get your attention or have your computer read the text under your cursor or selected text.

Now, let's look at the accessibility features built into Mac OS X under the Universal Access Preferences.

Universal Access

The Universal Access Preferences enable you to interact with your computer in alternative ways to provide greater accessibility for those with disabilities. The Seeing and Hearing tabs contains special settings for users with low vision or poor hearing. If you have difficulty using the keyboard and the mouse, Universal Access also enables you to customize their sensitivity.

> While you're in the Universal Access panel of System Preferences, your computer reads you the items under your cursor as if you've enabled the Text Under the Mouse option of the Spoken User Interface tab of the Speech panel.

Seeing

The options under the Seeing tab, shown in Figure 18.9, affect the size or contrast of the elements on screen.

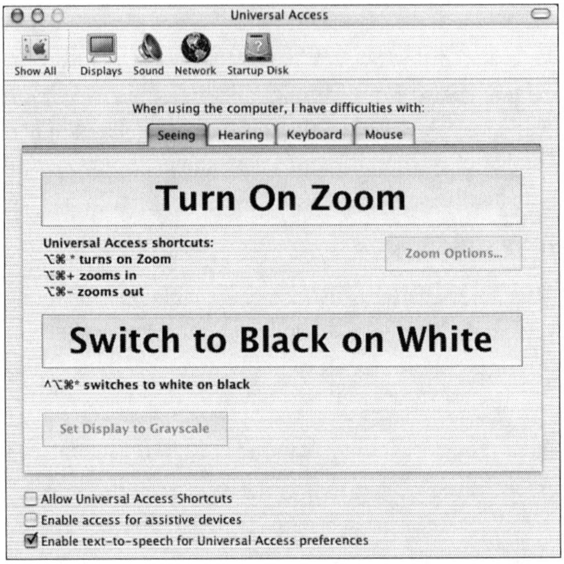

FIGURE 18.9

The Seeing tab controls zoom and contrast options.

Turn Zoom On activates a feature that enlarges the area of the display near the mouse cursor. Using key commands, you can zoom in (Command+Option++) several levels to examine text or detail in any application, and then zoom back out (Command+Option+-). In Zoom Options, features such as degree of magnification can be configured.

Switch to White on Black displays white detail on a dark background. You can also toggle the display between color and grayscale, which shows only white, black, and shades of gray.

Hearing

The Hearing tab enables you to have your computer notify you of alert sounds by flashing the screen. You can also open the Sounds Preferences panel to adjust volume.

Keyboard and Mouse

The Keyboard tab is shown in Figure 18.10. The Sticky Keys option helps with typing key combinations, such as Command+C, so you can press only one key at a time. After Sticky Keys is set, you can turn the feature on or off by pressing the Shift key five times in succession. You can also use the Set Key Repeat button to open the Keyboard pane settings minimize accidental multiple key presses.

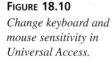

FIGURE 18.10

Change keyboard and mouse sensitivity in Universal Access.

For those who would rather use the numeric keypad than the mouse to direct the cursor, you can turn on Mouse Keys under the Mouse tab. Like Sticky Keys, Mouse Keys can be turned on or off by pressing the Option key (instead of Sticky Keys' Shift key) five times. The Mouse tab also contains settings to control mouse movement.

Summary

This hour gave a brief synopsis of System Preferences options that haven't been discussed elsewhere. These preferences adjust settings for system functions ranging from individual user's desktop settings to overall hardware configurations. They also include features that make Mac OS X accessible to a wide range of users with different physical abilities. To help you realize the range of their effect, Mac OS X has arranged them in four groups based on their spheres of influence. Also, preference panels with a larger number of settings have been broken into multiple tabs or sections accessible via pop-up menus.

Q&A

Q Why would you have your system clock set by a network time server?

A Network time servers are useful if you don't want to worry about setting the correct time on a computer that's connected to the Internet every time it's in use. However, if you choose this option, your computer might take longer to start up if it can't find the network time server.

Q   When I open some of the System Preferences panels, all the options are grayed out. Why?

A   Some panels—those with a lock button at the bottom—can be changed only by a user with administrator privileges. These tend to be preferences that affect the operation of the entire system (including Energy Saver, Network, and Accounts). To change them, you must click the lock button and enter the username and password of an administrator.

Workshop

The workshop contains quiz questions and activities to help you solidify your understanding of the material covered. Try to answer all questions before looking at the "Answers" section that follows.

Quiz

1. Where can you change your system language settings?
2. Which settings are specific to a single user?
3. When should you disable the Sleep mode?

Answers

1. In the International panel under Personal Preferences
2. The Personal System Preferences
3. If your system is performing a task that leads to long periods of keyboard inactivity, such as burning a CD

Activities

1. Open System Preferences and set the desktop background, date and time display, and volume levels to your liking.
2. Experiment with Speakable Items by calling forth the Finder and emptying the Trash. (Remember, you can open the Speech Commands window to tell you what phrases are recognized.)

PART V

Advanced Mac OS X Features

Hour

HOUR 19

Automating Tasks with AppleScript

Mac OS X provides dozens of ways to automate your system—most of which depend on writing programs in one of the many included UNIX programming languages. That's great if you're interested in learning the ins and outs of UNIX processes or are striving to become a UNIX administrator, but it isn't very helpful for the day-to-day tasks that the Macintosh is known to excel at. So, how can ordinary Macintosh users control their Mac without resorting to hardcore programming?

The answer is AppleScript—Apple's Mac OS X built-in scripting language. Using AppleScript, you can make your existing programs work together in ways that the original publishers never intended. It does take some work to get accustomed to the AppleScript language, but even nonprogrammers can quickly pick up on its English-like syntax. In this hour, you learn

- What makes AppleScript the ideal means of automating tasks on your Mac
- How the Script Editor can be used to record your onscreen actions into scripts
- The basics of the AppleScript language

What Is AppleScript?

AppleScript is, at its simplest, a way to record your actions when you use a program and then play them back later. By using the AppleScript editing utility, you can simply record actions as you perform them manually. Then, in the future, when you want to repeat your steps, you just play them back. Each set of actions is called an *AppleScript*—or a *script* for short.

Multiple applications can be used in a single script, making it possible for complex sequences to be carried out with little work. For example, the hypothetical script to play DVDs could also open up the e-mail application and send your friends a message that invited them to come and enjoy the movie.

The typical response that many people have when they learn about AppleScript is, "Ack! I'm not a programmer—I don't know where to begin!" If you find yourself feeling the same way, don't worry; Apple designed AppleScript to be simple and straightforward for all levels of users. For example, consider the following lines:

```
tell application "DVD Player"
    activate
    select window "Controller"
end tell
```

Believe it or not, this is a basic script to open the DVD Player and bring the Controller window to the front. The code, as you read through it, is virtually self-documenting in its simplicity! Although it's possible to write large scripts that are seemingly impenetrable, it's quite easy to get started with only a few commands and a basic understanding of the structure. You learn all about the AppleScript syntax in a little bit, but don't skip ahead just yet; there's more you need to know about how AppleScript works before you start.

You might not be aware of it, but AppleScript is hardly a new invention. Available in the Mac OS since the mid-1990s, AppleScript has made significant inroads in the publishing crowd for automating simple tasks.

Apple recently introduced an entirely new developer product called AppleScript Studio. AppleScript Studio is Apple's integration of the AppleScript programming language with Apple Developer Tools that

> enables programmers to create AppleScript programs that make use of the Aqua interface elements (such as dialog boxes) for a more seamless integration with other Mac OS X applications.

What makes AppleScript different from macro utilities (such as QuicKeys) you might have used is that each scriptable application understands how to accept and process requests for its services rather than simply replaying actions. Each application that can be controlled by a script contains what is called a *dictionary*. Much like a printed dictionary, this electronic version defines all the words and special functions that an application can recognize. For example, the iTunes application dictionary defines commands that can be used to open and play music files. It does not, however, define elements that aren't related to its core functions, such as creating folders or emptying the Trash—those features are part of the Finder's dictionary.

The choice of what goes into an application's dictionary is an arbitrary decision made by the developer. Usually the basic and most useful features of an application are made scriptable. Unfortunately, there's no rule that says a piece of software must be scriptable at all—and, as you'll find, many applications don't support AppleScript at all. The situation is improving, however, and a willingness to learn AppleScript now will almost certainly pay off in the very near future!

Using the Script Editor

To start creating your own AppleScripts, launch the Script Editor (path:/Applications/AppleScript/Script Editor). The basic Script Editor window, shown in Figure 19.1, is your control center for recording, editing, and running scripts.

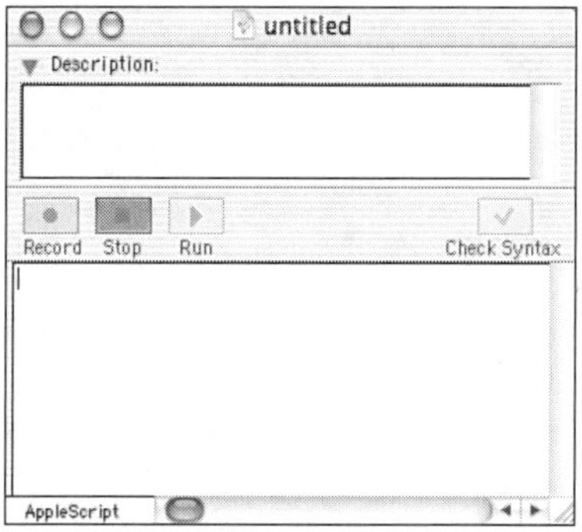

19

FIGURE 19.1

The Script Editor is used for recording, editing, and debugging AppleScripts.

The Script Editor window is composed of script recording and editing controls, which include

- **Description**—This area is used to advertise the purpose and usage instructions of an AppleScript.

- **Record/Stop/Run**—Similar to a tape deck, these buttons are used to control recording and playback of an AppleScript. Click the Record button (Command+D) to start monitoring your system for Apple events (mouse clicks, keyboard input, and so on) in scriptable applications. These events are then stored in a script. The Stop button (Command+.) is used to stop recording, and the Run button (Command+R) carries out the actions.

- **Check Syntax**—This item is used to review the syntax of the current script for errors and to automatically reformat the script if needed.

- **Content**—The content area is used to compose and edit script content. It functions like any Mac OS X text editor, but has the benefit of auto-formatting code when syntax is checked or the script is run.

Task: Recording a Script

Let's try recording a script using the Editor. Just follow these steps and you'll have your very own scripts in no time:

1. Open the Script Editor application.

2. Click the Record button.

3. Open another application, such as QuickTime Player, and click a few buttons.

4. As you work with the application, a script builds in the content area of the Editor. Click Stop to end the recording. Figure 19.2 displays a script that has just finished generating.

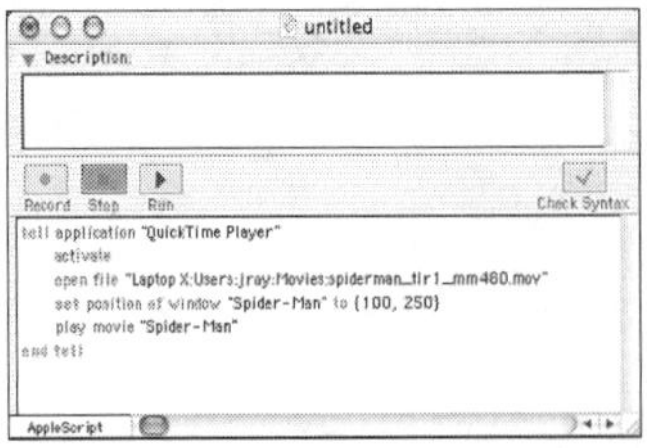

FIGURE 19.2

Use the Record and Stop buttons to record your AppleScripts.

AppleScript recording is still *barely* functional in Mac OS X 10.2. You might find that some programs record correctly—sometimes.

After the script is recorded, you can edit it in the Script Editor's content area as you would edit any text file. The Script Editor does what it can to automatically format the script to be easy to read. As you edit the text manually, it's likely to lose some of the formatting. You can force it to be reformatted by clicking the Check Syntax button. This also tells you if you've made any syntax errors in your script.

To use a script that you've written or recorded, just click the Run button; the recorded steps are played back from the beginning.

Saving a Script

Obviously, an AppleScript wouldn't be of much use if it had to be rewritten each time you wanted to use it. Thankfully, you can save it to be run whenever you want. Choose Save As or Save As Run-Only from the File menu. The Run-Only option should be used to protect the script from being edited in the future. Figure 19.3 displays the Save dialog box.

FIGURE 19.3

Scripts can be saved as script files or double-clickable applications.

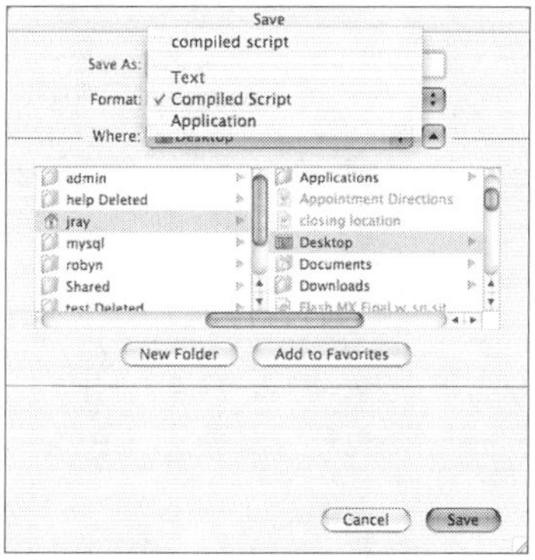

There are three possible file formats for scripts:

- **Text**—Save the contents of the script in a plain-text file.
- **Compiled Script**—Save the script as a compiled binary file, which speeds up run-time on subsequent executions.
- **Application**—Save the script for double-click execution under Mac OS X.

19

The best choice for saving most of your scripts is as an application. This creates a file that looks identical to the other applications on your system—just double-click and go. When saving, you might notice two additional options. Select the Stay Open check box to have a script remain open after running, or the Never Show Startup Screen check box to remove the AppleScript splash screen when the program runs.

Using the Scripting Dictionaries

Obviously, AppleScript's biggest draw is its capability to create scripts from scratch. Recording is a good way to get a quick start, but can't be used to add logic or decision-making to a program. The basic AppleScript syntax is covered later in this hour in the "Scripting Syntax" section. Even this, however, is useless without knowledge of which commands an application can accept. To solve that problem, you can view a scripting dictionary that shows the functions and properties offered by a given piece of software.

To access a scripting dictionary for any application, choose Open Dictionary from the File menu. A list of the available scriptable applications is displayed, as shown in Figure 19.4.

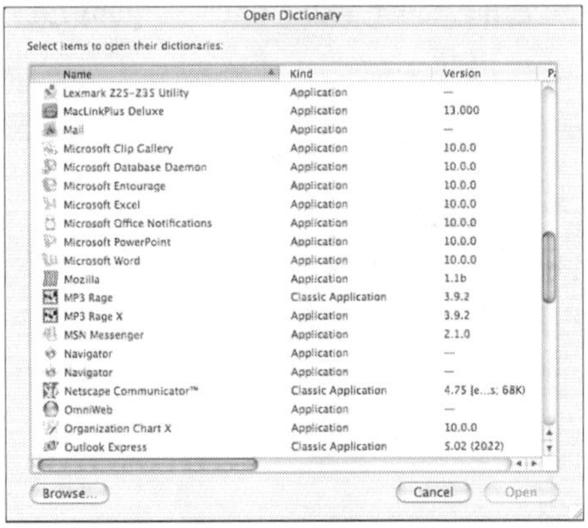

FIGURE 19.4

Choose from the available scriptable applications.

Don't be surprised if the list isn't complete—some applications might not be shown. The Browse button at the bottom of the window opens a standard File Open dialog box for choosing an application that isn't listed. After you choose an application, a dictionary window should appear, as seen in Figure 19.5.

Along the left side of the dictionary window is a list of the provided AppleScript functions. The functions are divided into categories, depending on their purpose. These categories are called *suites*. To display the syntax for a given item, click its name in the list. Highlighting a suite name displays a description of the functions in that group and a complete view of the syntax for each function.

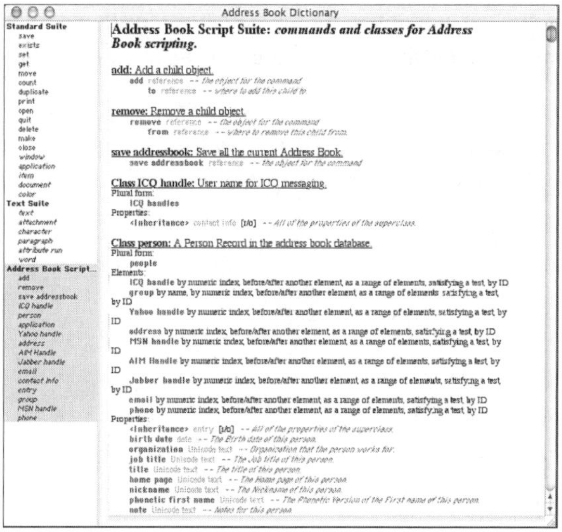

FIGURE 19.5

The dictionary documents the available AppleScript functions.

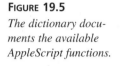

Hold down Shift and click each of the suite headings to create a master list of the available scripting functions. Use Print (Command+P) from the File menu to print a hard-copy reference guide for AppleScripting your favorite applications.

Scripting Syntax

19

As much as I wish it were possible to teach everyone the basics of programming in a single hour, it just isn't feasible. This section, therefore, is of most interest to those who know a little about using programming languages—and even then, there's much more information available about AppleScript than can be covered in this hour.

Describing the AppleScript syntax to a programmer familiar with languages such as REALbasic or C isn't as straightforward as you might think. AppleScript uses an entirely different programming model based on an English-like structure that, after a few minutes of use, leaves the programmer feeling as though he is having a deep, intellectual conversation with his computer. I highly recommend that you look through the scripts that Apple includes in the /Library/Scripts directory and use them as a basis for building your own creations.

The `tell` Statement

The basic building block of an AppleScript is the `tell` statement. `tell` is used to address an object and give it instructions to perform. Objects are usually applications or parts of an application, such as windows. As the name of the statement suggests, a programmer uses `tell` to instruct an object to carry out a task, such as opening a file or closing a window.

A `tell` line is written in one of two common forms: a block or a single statement. The block format enables the programmer to send multiple commands to an application without stating its name each time.

Single:

```
tell <object> <object name> to <action>
```

Block:

```
tell <object> <object name>
      <action>
      <action>
      <action>
      ...
end tell
```

For example, the following two statements are identical, but are structured with the single and block forms of `tell`:

```
tell application "Finder" to empty trash
```

and

```
tell application "Finder"
      empty trash
end tell
```

Both of these short scripts cause the Finder to empty the Trash. Although the second form might seem like more to type, it's likely to be the form you most often see when looking through existing scripts. Most scripts interact with objects to perform complex compound operations rather than simple commands. In addition, the second version of the AppleScript is easier to read and view the functional components. Maintaining readable code is a good idea no matter what programming platform you're using.

Variables: `set/get`

Variables store information that is used in a program. In AppleScript, variables are automatically created when they're set. A variable name can be any combination of alphanumeric characters, as long as the first character is a letter. No special prefixes are required to denote a variable in the code.

The `set` command stores information in a variable. Usually, AppleScript does its best to figure out what kind of information you're storing (numbers, text, and so forth), but, if need be, you can force data to take a particular form, as shown in the following line:

```
set <variable/property> to <value> [as <object type>]
```

For example, both of the following lines set variables (`theValue` and `theValue2`) to 5, but the second line forces the variable to be a string (text):

```
set theValue to 5
set theValue2 to 5 as string
```

Variables can take on simple values, such as numbers or strings, or more complex values in the form of lists. Lists are equivalent to arrays in traditional programming languages. A list is represented by a comma-separated group of values, enclosed in curly brackets ({ }). For example, the following line sets a variable, `theposition`, to a list containing two values:

```
set thePosition to {50, 75}
```

This format is often used to set coordinate pairs for manipulating onscreen objects, but can be made up of any object. In fact, lists can even contain lists of lists, as shown in this line:

```
set theListOfPositions to {{50, 75}, {65, 45}, {25, 90}}
```

Here, a variable called `theListOfPositions` is set to a list of lists. Item 1 of the list is {50,75}, item 2 is {65,45}, and so on.

To retrieve values from variables or properties from objects, you use the `get` command. Used by itself, `get` retrieves the value of an object or variable and stores it in a special automatically created variable called `result`:

```
get the <property/variable> [of <object>]
```

For example, earlier we set the contents of `thevalue` to 5. To retrieve and display this information, you could write

```
get thevalue
display dialog result
```

Traditional programmers might feel uncomfortable with retrieving results into a temporary variable (`result`). In that case, they can combine the `get` and `set` commands to immediately store the results of a `get` command in another variable or object property:

```
set <variable/property> [of <object>] to get the <property/variable>
➥[of <object>]
```

19

For example:

```
set myMessage to "Hello"
```

This sets a variable called myMessage to the string Hello.

When dealing with list values, you can reference individual items in a list by referring to them as just that: items. For example, assume that you've run the following command:

```
set thePosition to {50, 75}
```

To retrieve the value of the first item in the list, you can use this line:

```
get item 1 of thePosition
```

When dealing with lists within lists, just embed item statements within one another. Assume that this list has been entered:

```
set theListOfPositions to {{50, 75}, {65, 45}, {25, 90}}
```

To retrieve the value of the second item of the second list within a list, you could write the following:

```
get item 2 of item 2 of theListOfPositions
```

This line retrieves the value 45. Don't let this stuff scare you! AppleScript takes time to get used to, but it's not insurmountable. Our goal is to show you the sorts of script elements you might see so that you understand how scripts you encounter on your system work.

The if Statement

The power of programming comes from being able to create code that can check for certain conditions and adapt to them. The most common way to do this is through the if-then-else statement, which is used to check the value of an item and react appropriately. This is the syntax for a basic if statement:

```
If <condition> then
       <action>
end if
```

For example, the following code asks the user to enter a value, checks whether the value equals 5, and outputs an appropriate message if it does:

```
1: display dialog "Enter a number:" default answer ""
2: set theValue to (text returned of the result) as integer
3: if theValue = 5 then
4:     display dialog "Five is my magic number."
5: end if
```

Line 1 displays a prompt for a user to enter a value. Line 2 sets the variable theValue to the text returned from the dialog, and forces it to be evaluated as an integer. Line 3 checks theValue; if it's equal to the number 5, line 4 is executed. Line 4 displays an onscreen message, and line 5 ends the If statement.

The if statement can be expanded to include an else clause that's executed if the original condition is not met:

```
1: display dialog "Enter a number:" default answer ""
2: set theValue to (text returned of the result) as integer
3: if theValue = 5 then
4:     display dialog "Five is my magic number."
5: else
6:     display dialog "That is NOT my magic number."
7: end if
```

In this modified version of the code, line 6 contains an alternative message that's displayed if the condition in line 3 is not met.

Finally, the else clause can be expanded to check alternative conditions by using else if. This enables multiple possibilities to be evaluated within a single statement:

```
1: display dialog "Enter a number:" default answer ""
2: set theValue to (text returned of the result) as integer
3: if theValue = 5 then
4:     display dialog "Five is my magic number."
5: else if theValue = 3 then
6:     display dialog "Three is a decent number too."
7: else
8:     display dialog "I don't like that number."
9: end if
```

The latest version of the script includes an else if in line 5. If the initial comparison in line 3 fails, line 5 is evaluated. Finally, if line 5 fails, the else in line 8 is executed.

The repeat Statement

Another common programming technique is *looping*, which enables programs to repeat a series of actions over and over. AppleScript uses a single loop type to handle a variety of looping needs. The repeat statement has several different forms that cover while, until, and other types of traditional loops.

There are many different forms of the repeat statement. A few of the most common are shown here:

- **Repeat Indefinitely**—This loop repeats a group of statements indefinitely or until the exit command is called:

19

```
repeat
    <statements>
end repeat
```

- **Repeat #**—Using this second loop format, you can choose the number of times a loop repeats:

```
repeat <integer> times
    <statements>
end repeat
```

- **Repeat While**—Loop indefinitely while the given condition evaluates to true:

```
repeat while <condition>
    <statements>
end repeat
```

- **Repeat Until**—Loop indefinitely until the given condition evaluates to true. This is the inverse of the repeat while loop.

```
repeat until <condition>
    <statements>
end repeat
```

- **Repeat With**—Called a for/next loop in traditional languages, this form of the repeat loop counts up or down from a starting number to an ending number. Each time the program goes through a loop, it updates a variable with the latest loop value.

```
repeat with <variable> in <list>
    <statements>
end repeat
```

Subroutines

Hang in there—we're almost done! The final building block that we cover in AppleScript is the subroutine. *Subroutines* help make scripts easier to maintain by breaking them into smaller, more manageable segments. Each of these segments processes information, and then, if necessary, returns a result that is available to the rest of the script.

A subroutine is usually written in a format like this:

```
on <subroutine name> ([<variable 1>,<variable 2>,<variable n>,...])
    <statements>
    [return <result value>]
end <subroutine name>
```

Most subroutines receive their input from the main program through parameters. *Parameters* are variables, or pieces of information, that are passed to a subroutine when it is called. For example, the following BeAnnoying subroutine takes a text string and a number as parameters, and displays a dialog box with the text string (theMessage). The display is repeated until it matches the number given (howAnnoying).

```
1: on beAnnoying(theMessage, howAnnoying)
2:     repeat howAnnoying times
3:         display dialog theMessage
4:     end repeat
5: end BeAnnoying
```

Line 1 declares the subroutine beAnnoying and its two parameters: theMessage and howAnnoying. Line 2 starts a loop that repeats for the number of times set in the howAnnoying variable. Line 3 displays a dialog box with the contents theMessage. Line 4 ends the loop, and line 5 ends the subroutine.

If you enter this code into the AppleScript editor and run it, you'll find that it does absolutely nothing. Because it's a subroutine, it requires that another piece of code must call it. To call this particular routine, you could use a line such as

```
beAnnoying("Am I annoying yet?",3)
```

This line causes the subroutine to activate and display the message Am I annoying yet? three times.

A more useful subroutine is one that performs a calculation and returns a result. For example, the following example accepts, as input, a number containing a person's age in years. It returns a result containing the given age in days.

```
1: on yearsToDays(theYears)
2:     return theYears * 365
3: end yearsToDays
```

Because this subroutine returns a value, it can be called from within a set statement to store the result directly into a variable:

```
set dayAge to yearsToDays(90)
```

When working in subroutines, you must explicitly define variables that are used only in the subroutine, as opposed to those that can be accessed from anywhere in the AppleScript application. A variable that's visible to all portions of a script is called a *global variable* and is defined by using the global keyword. Similarly, the local keyword can be used with a variable so that it's accessible only within a subroutine. For example, try running the following AppleScript:

```
1: set theValue to 10
2: reset()
3: display dialog theValue
4:
5: on reset()
```

19

```
6:      local theValue
7:      set theValue to 0
8: end reset
```

In line 1, a variable called theValue is set to 10. In line 2, the reset subroutine is called. It appears to set the contents of theValue to 0, yet when the result is displayed in line 3, the original value remains.

The reason for this strange behavior is found in line 6. Line 6 defines theValue as a local variable in the reset() subroutine. That means any changes to that variable don't affect it outside the subroutine.

To see the behavior you expect (the contents of theValue are set to zero everywhere), swap the local keyword with the word global:

```
1: set theValue to 10
2: reset()
3: display dialog theValue
4:
5: on reset()
6:      global theValue
7:      set theValue to 0
8: end reset
```

This tiny modification tells the reset() subroutine that it should use the global representation of the variable theValue. When theValue is set to 0 in line 7, it replaces the initial value set in line 1.

Other Sources of Information

AppleScript is a capable scripting language that offers many advanced features that are impossible to cover in the space this hour allows. What's provided here should be an ample start to creating scripts of your own and editing the scripts included with Mac OS X. If you're interested in more information on the AppleScript syntax, I strongly suggest that you check the following resources:

- **AppleScript Language Guide**—
  http://developer.apple.com/techpubs/macosx/Carbon/interapplication-comm/AppleScript/AppleScriptLangGuide/index.html

- **AppleScript Guide Book**—
  http://www.apple.com/applescript/begin/pgs/begin_00.html

- **AppleScript in Mac OS X**—http://www.apple.com/applescript/macosx/

Script Menu

The Script Menu (path: `/Applications/AppleScript/Script Menu.menu`) adds an Extra to your menu bar that can be used to quickly launch AppleScripts located in the /Library/Scripts folder or ~/Library/Scripts. To launch the Script menu, double-click its icon.

The Script Menu Extra is shown in Figure 19.6.

FIGURE 19.6

The Script Menu Extra adds a menu bar launch point for all your scripts.

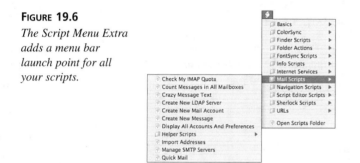

Any compiled scripts placed in either of the `Scripts` locations become accessible from the menu. To create submenus for categorizing scripts, just create multiple folders within the Scripts folders. As with everything in Mac OS X, items stored in /Library/Scripts are accessible by all users, whereas those in your personal ~/Library/Scripts folders can be used only by you.

Summary

AppleScript carries on its tradition of being one of the best secret Apple technologies. If you've programmed before, you might be surprised by how English-like the syntax can be. The Script Editor is the centerpiece of script development and offers novice users the ability to record their interactions directly to an AppleScript. Although very few applications can currently be recorded with AppleScript, this situation is bound to change as more mainstream applications are released. In the meantime, you can practice learning the AppleScript syntax and building your own scripts and applications.

19

Q&A

Q Does AppleScript replace macro products like QuicKeys?

A The QuicKeys macro tool is actually a great complement to AppleScript. It enables you to control applications that aren't normally scriptable—filling a niche.

Q If a command isn't included in an application's dictionary, what do I do?

A Contact the developer. Unfortunately, you have access only to what the programmer wants you to have and nothing more.

Q What is a good approach to learning AppleScript syntax?

A Look through the sample scripts in /Library/Scripts and try editing them by using the rules you learned in this hour. I've found that the best way to understand AppleScript is to see it in action and to play with it.

Workshop

The workshop contains quiz questions and activities to help you solidify your understanding of the material covered. Try to answer all questions before looking at the "Answers" section that follows.

Quiz

1. Where can you find the commands an application understands?

2. How can a user generate an AppleScript with no hands-on programming?

3. What are the AppleScript commands to assign and retrieve information from variables?

Answers

1. The scripting dictionary defines all the keywords and commands that a given application accepts. Access the dictionary through the Script Editor.

2. Recording how you interact with a scriptable application can create basic scripts.

3. The set command stores a value in a variable, and get retrieves the stored information.

Activities

1. Start the Script Editor recording, and then click through your system to find out which applications are recordable by watching as script lines appear in the Editor window.

2. Try writing a script or two by hand. Don't be discouraged if things don't work as planned right away. The sample scripts included with Mac OS 10.2 provide a great starting place for seeing how scripts can be used to create complex interactions with applications.

19

HOUR **20**

UNIX Command Line Tour

In the past five or so years, an open source operating system known as Linux (a UNIX-like operating system) has sprung from obscurity to the front page of every IT publication in the world. Three camps have formed: the Mac users, the UNIX/Linux users, and "those Windows people." Mac OS X merges the Macintosh with a powerful UNIX subsystem and brings us, in essence, the ultimate non-Windows platform. In fact, by the end of 2002, Apple will be the largest producer of UNIX-based operating systems on the planet!

During this hour, you learn how to access the UNIX system beneath Mac OS X, including such aspects as

- Working with files and directories
- Managing processes
- Common command-line tools

Terminal: The Window to the Underworld

If you've been using Mac OS X for a while now, you might be wondering what all this command-line talk is about—after all, you certainly haven't needed to type a command on your system, nor have any of your applications required you to access a command prompt. That's precisely what Apple intended when creating Mac OS X.

Beneath the veneer of Aqua lies the powerful BSD (Berkley Software Distribution) version of the UNIX platform. This layer sits behind many of the tasks you perform on your machine and coordinates the actions that make using your Macintosh possible. At the same time, it provides a wealth of opportunities of its own, such as the capability to write scripts and access thousands of existing command-line tools that, despite their lack of a GUI interface, can prove to be very productive members of your Mac OS X software library.

The Terminal application (/Applications/Utilities/Terminal) provides your point of access to the BSD subsystem of Mac OS X. It's not, as its name might suggest, a program for connecting to remote computers through the phone line. It's similar in use to the Windows cmd.exe application and UNIX's xterm software. Opening Terminal creates a new window with a beckoning command prompt, just waiting for some input, as shown in Figure 20.1.

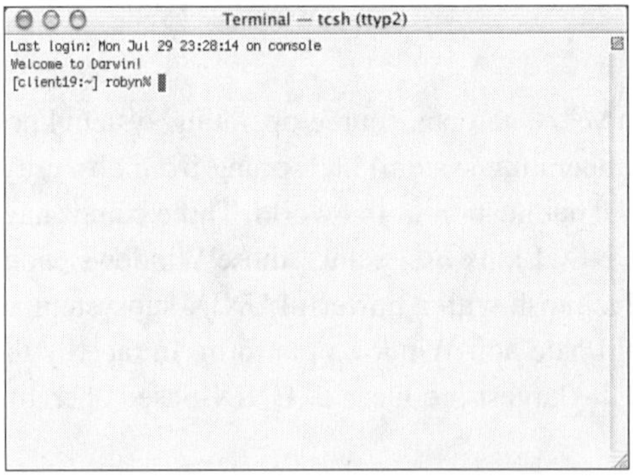

FIGURE 20.1

Terminal opens a window into the UNIX layer of Mac OS X.

You can customize the appearance of the Terminal application in a number of ways, such as changing the font, resizing the window, and setting a title in the Window Settings, found in the application menu. One of the most important changes you can make, however, is setting an unlimited scrollback buffer.

As you use the Terminal program and begin to explore UNIX, you might want to scroll back to check on the output of commands that you've entered. By default, the Terminal remembers 10,000 lines. This might seem like a lot, but you'll quickly see that it isn't. To change to an unlimited scrollback buffer, follow these steps:

1. Open the Terminal Application Window Settings, found in the application menu.

2. Click the Buffer option in the pop-up menu at the top of the window.

3. Select the Unlimited Scrollback radio button, shown in Figure 20.2.

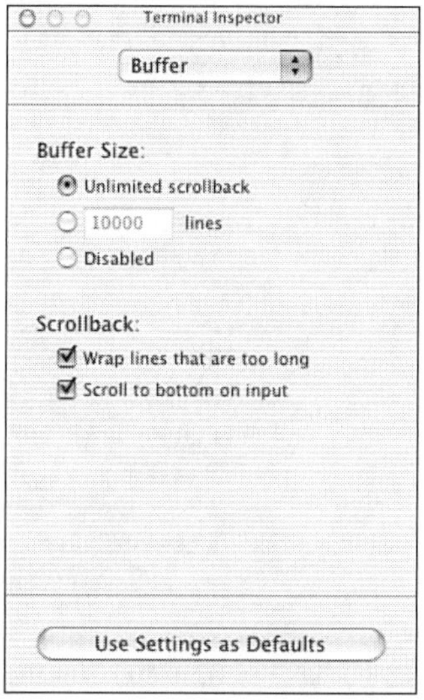

FIGURE 20.2

An unlimited scroll-back buffer helps you keep track of the things you've done.

4. Close the settings by closing the window or click Use Settings as Defaults.

5. Open a new Terminal window by choosing New from the Shell menu (Command+N).

6. The new window is ready for use with an unlimited scrollback buffer.

Now that you've found the command prompt, let's see what you can do with it. Whenever possible, I'll try to relate the command-line tools to their graphical Mac OS X alternatives.

20

Working with Files: Basic Commands

As you work with the Mac OS X Finder, you get to know a sequence of mouse commands for working with the files and folders on your system. These same actions can be carried out from the command line very easily. In some cases, you might find that the command line is actually faster for some tasks than the Finder.

Basic Commands

Let's start with some of the basic commands for listing, moving, and copying files. Obviously, you can't do much with your files unless you can see them, so we start with the ls (or list) function.

ls

Typing **ls** at the command prompt displays all the available files in the current directory (folder). Because the Terminal opens to your home directory and you haven't learned how to change directories, you probably see a list of the files inside your home that's similar to the list that follows:

```
[client18:~john] john% ls
4032other                              Pictures
4032other.zip                          Public
Active Projects                        QLOG
Applications                           Shared
Appointment Directions.pdf             Sites
Desktop                                TheVolumeSettingsFolder
Documents                              X10transceiver.pdf
Downloads                              aliases.db
Library                                closing location.pdf
Movies                                 itchysweater.pdf
Music                                  unixad.jpg
Network Trash Folder
```

As you know, your Mac OS X files also have permissions on them. To view the listing with permissions showing, use ls -l and you see a list similar to the following:

```
[client18:~john] john% ls -l
total 94296
drwxr-xr-x   6 john   staff      204 Apr 30 00:07 4032other
-rw-r--r--   1 john   staff    36196 Apr 28 21:13 4032other.zip
drwxr-xr-x   8 john   staff      272 Apr 17 20:50 Active Projects
drwxr-xr-x   2 john   staff       68 May 17 00:45 Applications
-rw-r--r--   1 john   staff   609581 Jun 12 19:18 Appointment Directions.pdf
drwx------   9 john   staff      306 Jul 25 01:11 Desktop
drwx------  49 john   staff     1666 Jul 10 23:55 Documents
drwxr-xr-x   6 john   staff      204 Jun  5 00:22 Downloads
drwx------  41 john   staff     1394 May 30 18:58 Library
drwx------   6 john   staff      204 Mar 30 02:40 Movies
drwx------   3 john   staff      102 Mar 30 02:40 Music
drwx---rwx   3 john   nobody     102 Dec 23  2001 Network Trash Folder
drwx------   6 john   staff      204 Jul 10 23:55 Pictures
drwxr-xr-x   6 john   staff      204 Mar 30 02:40 Public
-rw-r--r--   1 john   staff     6352 Jul 16 18:26 QLOG
drwxr-xr-x   2 john   staff       68 May  7 23:46 Shared
drwxr-xr-x  16 john   staff      544 Jul 10 23:55 Sites
drwxrwxrwx   2 john   nobody      68 Dec 23  2001 TheVolumeSettingsFolder
```

```
-rw-r--r--  1 john  staff    146969 Jul 19 01:24 X10transceiver.pdf
-rw-r--r--  1 root  staff     16384 May 15 21:20 aliases.db
-rw-r--r--  1 john  staff    313617 Jun 26 22:31 closing location.pdf
-rw-r--r--  1 john  staff    225340 Jun  1 01:55 itchysweater.pdf
-rw-r--r--  1 john  staff    382527 Apr 15 02:02 unixad.jpg
```

For the most part, the listing is self-explanatory. The second column is a count of the number of files in a directory. The third and fourth columns are the owner and group, respectively. The fifth column contains the file size, whereas the sixth and seventh columns are the modification date and filename.

The first column, however, is filled with strange letters, such as drwx (repeated several times). The first character of this sequence of letters indicates what kind of file it is. In the listing example, the first characters are all the letter d—for directories. The rest of the nine letters represent read, write, and execute permissions for the user, group, and everyone, respectively.

> The Mac OS X GUI doesn't provide a control over the execute permission of a file. This attribute, as its name suggests, controls whether the file can be executed or, in Mac terms, *run*.

For example, assume that you see a column with drwxr-xr--. Following the pattern we set up, the first letter, d, indicates that this is a directory, and the next three letters, rwx, tell us that the owner has read, write, and execute permissions. The middle three positions, r-x, show read and execute permission for everyone within the file's group, and the last three, r--, tell us that everyone else has read permission for the file.

When looking through file listings, you might notice a few special directories in the listing:

- .—A single period represents the current directory.
- ..—Two periods represent the parent directory of the current directory.

You can use this directory notation with the other commands we look at in this section.

20

cp

The next command we look at is the cp, or copy, command. Copy, as its name suggests, is used to copy files or directories of files. The syntax for cp is simply

```
cp <source file path> <destination file path>
```

For example, to copy the file `test.txt` to `testcopy.txt`, you would type

cp test.txt testcopy.txt

This does nothing more than create an exact duplicate of the file `test.txt` named `test-copy.txt` in the same directory. To copy a file to another directory, just include the full pathname of the file.

In the case of copying a directory, you must perform a *recursive* copy, which copies the contents of the folder and the contents of any folders within the source. Do this by supplying the `-R` option to `cp`. For example, if I want to copy the directory /Users/jray/testfiles and all of its contents to the folder /Users/robyn/otherfiles, I use the following command:

```
cp -R /Users/jray/testfiles /Users/robyn/otherfiles
```

Simple enough, isn't it? You might recognize this as the equivalent of Option-dragging a file within the Finder, or using the Copy contextual menu command.

> If you play with `cp`, you might notice that it cannot copy Macintosh-specific files (applications, files with custom icons, and so on.). To get around this, you can use the `ditto` command, which copies one directory to another, complete with all the information that makes a Macintosh file special.

mv

"Moving" right along, the `mv` command can move a file or directory from one place to another or rename it. It uses the same syntax as `cp`:

```
mv <source file path> <destination file path>
```

This is the same as clicking and dragging an icon from one place to another within the Finder.

For example:

```
mv myfile.txt myoldfile.txt
```

This moves the file `myfile.txt` to `myoldfile.txt`, effectively renaming the file. Like copy (`cp`), you could move the file to another directory by using its full pathname.

For example:

```
mv myfile.txt /Users/robyn/robynsfilenow.txt
```

Here the file `myfile.txt` is moved to /Users/robyn and stored with the new name: `robynsfilenow.txt`.

rm

Now that you can list, move, and copy files, you should probably also learn how to delete them. The `rm` (remove) command erases a file from your system. It's extremely important that you pay attention to what you're doing with `rm` because no Undo command or Trash exists from which to remove a deleted file.

When using `rm`, I recommend using the `-i` option along with it. This forces the system to ask you before removing a file. The basic syntax for `rm` is

```
rm -i <filename>
```

If you want to remove an entire directory, you must also add the `-r` option to the mix to force `rm` to go through the directory and remove all the files within it. For example, suppose that you want to remove a directory called `myjunkfiles`, including all the files inside it. To do that, type the following:

```
rm -ri myjunkfiles
```

The `rm` command steps through each file in the directory and prompts you to confirm that the file should be deleted.

Wildcards

When working with files, you can use a few special symbols in place of characters in the filename. Specifically, the following sequences are available:

- `*`—Matches any number of characters in a filename
- `?`—Matches a single unknown character
- `[0-9]`—Matches a range of characters

For example, if I want to list only the files in a directory that contain the letters `memo` anywhere in their names, I would type

```
ls *memo*
```

If, on the other hand, I want to be a bit more specific, such as listing all files that start with `memo` and end with exactly two characters that I don't know, I could use

```
ls memo??
```

Finally, to be even more exact, I could match a range of characters using the format `[<start>-<end>]`. Assume that I have a group of files, all named `memo`, followed by two

20

extra characters—some of which are numbers. To list all the memo files that are followed by the numbers, I could enter

```
ls memo[0-9][0-9]
```

Wildcards make it easy to work with groups of files and directories without having to list each name separately.

Editing Files with pico

Creating and editing files is another important part of mastering the Mac OS X command line. This is a definite necessity for performing remote administration of the system, enabling you to make changes to your system's configuration from almost any terminal connected to the Internet.

A number of text editors are available that you can use from the Mac OS X command line:

- **emacs**—The emacs editor is an extremely powerful editor that can be used for programming, basic editing tasks, and can even be programmed using the Lisp language.

- **vi**—vi is the choice editor for diehard UNIX fans. It's fast and omnipresent—it's available on just about any UNIX machine that exists.

- **pico**—The pico editor is a modern editor for beginners. Like vi, it's extremely fast, but it's much simpler to use and is the focus of our attention here.

To use pico, start it from the command line with the name of the file you want to edit or from a new file that you want to create:

```
pico <filename>
```

The pico editor is shown running in Figure 20.3.

FIGURE 20.3

Pico is an easy-to-use command-line editor.

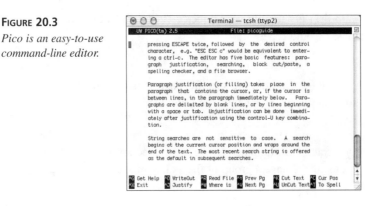

To operate `pico`, use the arrow keys on your keyboard to move the cursor around the screen. Typing enters new text, whereas pressing Delete removes existing characters. You can also use a number of control characters during editing:

- **Control+G**—Opens a help screen with basic usage instructions
- **Control+O**—Writes (save) the file
- **Control+R**—Reads a new file into the editor
- **Control+Y**—Jumps to the previous page
- **Control+V**—Jumps to the next page
- **Control+W**—Searches the file for a given sequence of characters
- **Control+X**—Exits `pico`

You can use Mac OS X text editors such as Pepper, BBEdit, and TextEdit to edit the files on your system, but a command-line editor can come in very handy if you're using SSH to access the system remotely, see Hour 13, "Using Network Sharing," for details.

> You can certainly use `pico` to read files as well as edit them, but if you just want to quickly scroll through a file, use `more <filename>` to move through the file a page at a time.

File Permissions

The final file operations that we look at are how to modify permissions. You've already discovered how you can tell what the permissions of a file are (using `ls`)—now let's see how you can change them.

chown

By default, you own every file that you create. That's fine, but you might want to change the owner of a file so that you can give it to someone else. The `chown` command (change ownership) performs this task with ease. Although you can also do this in the Finder, you can use the command-line `chown` command with filename wildcards to handle multiple files simultaneously.

To use `chown`, all you need is the name of the file you want to change and the username of the person you want to assign ownership to:

```
chown <username> <filename>
```

To change the ownership of a file called `test.txt` to the user robyn, you would type

```
chown jray test.txt
```

20

You might need to prefix the line with the sudo command, which you learn about a bit later in this hour.

chmod

The chmod command (change mode) modifies file permissions—the read, write, and execute attributes that you saw earlier when learning about the ls function.

The chmod command takes as its parameters a filename and the permissions that you want to assign to it. The permissions are given using a symbolic representation based on the letters u, g, o, and r, w, and x. The u, g, and o are user, group, and other, respectively. The letters r, w, and x represent the read, write, and execute permissions.

Combining these letters with + and -, you can add or subtract any permission from any type of access level:

```
chmod <permission> <filename>
```

For example, to remove write permission for the owner of a file named nowrite.txt, you would enter

```
chmod u-w nowrite.txt
```

Likewise, to add read permission for other users (the rest of the world), use this syntax:

```
chmod o+r nowrite.txt
```

As you can see, the UNIX commands give you a much greater level of control than using the equivalent Get Info feature in the Finder.

Managing files in UNIX is the same as managing files in Mac OS X's Finder, but instead of mouse actions, typed commands are used to tell your computer what to do. Before moving on, try editing a few files and using the basic mv and cp commands to move them around. When you feel comfortable with the process, move on to the next section, "Process Management." There you learn how the UNIX side of your computer views running applications.

Process Management

As you use your Mac OS X computer, you create dozens of processes and support processes that you probably never realized existed. In Hour 22, "System Utilities and Monitors," you learn about some of the GUI tools that enable you to manage these processes in a point-and-click manner. In this section, however, you see the commands that can provide you with the raw data of what is happening on your system.

Viewing Processes

To view the active processes on your computer, you can use one of two commands. The first command, ps, creates a process listing of whatever's running in the foreground (or, modified, everything that's running). The second command, top, shows a list of the applications that are using up the most resources on your computer.

ps

To use the ps command, all you need to do is type **ps** at the command prompt. This generates a list of the foreground processes that you control on the computer. For example:

```
[localhost:~] jray% ps
  PID  TT  STAT      TIME COMMAND
  707 std  Ss     0:00.25 -tcsh (tcsh)
```

Here, the foreground process is my command-line shell (tcsh), which isn't very interesting. To list everything that's running on a Mac OS X computer, add the argument -ax to the command, like this:

```
[localhost:~] jray% ps -ax
  PID  TT  STAT      TIME COMMAND
    1  ??  SLs    0:00.05 /sbin/init
    2  ??  SL     0:02.75 /sbin/mach_init
   41  ??  Ss     0:01.94 kextd
   68  ??  Ss     0:22.85 /System/Library/Frameworks/ApplicationServices.framew
   70  ??  Ss    40:38.78 /System/Library/CoreServices/WindowServer
   72  ??  Ss     0:07.96 update
   75  ??  Ss     0:00.01 dynamic_pager -H 40000000 -L 160000000 -S 80000000 -F
  103  ??  Ss     0:00.61 /sbin/autodiskmount -va
  127  ??  Ss     0:03.28 configd
  185  ??  Ss     0:00.38 syslogd
  218  ??  Ss     0:00.02 /usr/libexec/CrashReporter
  240  ??  Ss     0:01.37 netinfod -s local
  247  ??  Ss     0:04.32 lookupd
  257  ??  S<s    0:05.72 ntpd -f /var/run/ntp.drift -p /var/run/ntpd.pid
  270  ??  Ss     0:01.38 /System/Library/CoreServices/coreservicesd
  277  ??  Ss     0:00.00 inetd
  288  ??  S      0:00.00 nfsiod -n 4
  289  ??  S      0:00.00 nfsiod -n 4
  290  ??  S      0:00.00 nfsiod -n 4
  291  ??  S      0:00.00 nfsiod -n 4
  298  ??  S      0:00.27 DirectoryService
...and so on.
```

For each process, you'll notice a PID number in the listing. This is the process ID, and it uniquely identifies the program running on your computer. There's also a TIME field, which contains how much cumulative processor time the software has used on your machine.

20

You might also notice the TT and STAT columns in the listing. These display the controlling terminal of a given process and its status. Unfortunately, these topics are beyond the scope of this book and are best addressed by an advanced book, such as *Mac OS X Unleashed* from Sams Publishing.

Keep track of the PID values—you need them in a few minutes.

top

If you want a more interactive means of monitoring what's running on your system, try using the top command. The utility, shown in Figure 20.4, shows a listing of the most active and processor-intensive applications running on your machine. It can provide a very good means of uncovering unusual activity on your computer and answering why your system is sluggish at a given point in time.

FIGURE 20.4

Use top to get an interactive view of the processes on your computer.

```
                    Terminal — ttyp3
Processes: 40 total, 2 running, 38 sleeping... 87 threads      23:41:08
Load Avg: 0.08, 0.01, 0.00     CPU usage: 1.0% user, 5.8% sys, 93.3% idle
SharedLibs: num =   7, resident = 2.21M code, 160K data, 560K LinkEdit
MemRegions: num = 2520, resident = 31.4M + 6.02M private, 92.8M shared
PhysMem: 32.5M wired, 109M active, 106M inactive, 248M used, 8.12M free
VM: 1.62G + 3.61M   9132(0) pageins, 397(0) pageouts

PID COMMAND      %CPU  TIME    #TH #PRTS #MREGS RPRVT RSHRD RSIZE VSIZE
595 screencapt   0.0%  0:00.05  1   22    25   212K  708K  828K  30.5M
593 top          3.8%  0:01.01  1   14    17   196K  336K  488K  13.6M
575 tcsh         0.0%  0:00.02  1   10    15   344K  592K  780K  5.73M
574 login        0.0%  0:00.64  1   12    33   244K  388K  568K  13.7M
567 Terminal     0.9%  0:07.44  3   64   128  1.37M  8.25M 7.12M 51.4M
562 System Pre   0.0%  0:02.56  1   81   212  2.86M  8.00M 8.27M 52.1M
561 Microsoft    0.0%  0:00.77  2   68    94  1.75M  8.21M 4.26M 49.1M
560 Microsoft    0.0%  0:53.39  1   62   242  11.0M  51.5M 25.5M  293M
558 Finder       0.0%  0:13.82  2   80   123  3.46M  16.3M 11.8M 63.4M
557 SystemUISe   0.0%  0:01.27  1  142   125  1.26M  5.39M 4.19M 47.6M
554 Dock         0.0%  0:01.39  2   91   106   784K  7.67M 5.08M 46.6M
551 pbs          0.0%  0:00.47  2   27    27   408K  884K  1.23M 14.4M
546 loginwindo   0.0%  0:01.63  4  150   149  1.89M  8.87M 7.68M 53.9M
545 Window Man   0.9%  0:23.18  2  164   395  5.45M  26.5M 24.0M 87.9M
385 DirectoryS   0.0%  0:01.15  3   58   115   672K  2.44M 2.64M 19.6M
```

When running top, the most active processes are shown at the top of the listing. Usually the Mac OS X components ranks very highly in the list (such as the Finder). Watching the CPU (percentage of CPU being used), TIME (total amount of CPU time the application has consumed), and RSIZE (amount of memory the application is using) columns gives you the most useful information about what your computer is doing. If you see an unusual piece of software that you didn't install (perhaps your coworker's copy of Seti@Home) in the listing, you can write down its PID, and then force it to quit.

From the command line, you can use UNIX to force any application to quit. Although powerful, this can also pose a danger to the system: Users can easily force important parts of the operating system to quit!

Killing Processes

As violent as it sounds, the action of forcing a running UNIX process to quit is called *killing* it. Appropriately enough, this action uses a command called `kill`.

The `kill` command's actions don't need to be as drastic as forcing an application to quit. In reality, the `kill` command simply sends a signal to a process that can be interpreted in a number of ways. Some signals simply cause the software to reload its configuration, whereas others do indeed force it to exit.

The two most common signals you'll encounter are `HUP` (to force a reload) and `KILL` (to truly kill a process). Along with a signal, the `kill` command also requires a process ID (the numbers supplied in the `PID` column of the `ps` or `top` commands).

Armed with this information, you can kill a process using this syntax:

```
kill -<signal> <process id>
```

For example, to force a process with the ID of 1992 to quit, I would type

```
kill -KILL 1992
```

> Killing a process with the `KILL` signal does not save any data that the application is processing. Use this as a last resort for gaining control of a piece of software.
>
> Also be aware that indiscriminately killing processes on your system could make Mac OS X unstable or even crash the operating system.

The `kill` command can be used remotely to control what's running on your machine and shut down processes that shouldn't be active. In the next section, you learn how to gain complete control over the command line.

Server Administration

20

Although everything that you've learned so far this hour is valid, it isn't necessarily completely functional. For example, you can't change the owner of a file you don't own. In most cases, that's fine, but for complete control over the machine, you should be able to do whatever you want.

The command that makes this possible is `sudo`. When `sudo` is placed in front of any other command, it enables you to execute the command as the root user. Root has complete control over everything on your system, so be careful when using the command; you could end up removing all the files from your computer.

For example, to kill a process that you didn't create, you could use the following:

```
sudo kill <signal> <process ID>
```

sudo starts, asks you for your user password, and then executes the given command with root's permissions.

The commands themselves stay the same but gain a whole new level of capability. Using this technique, you can easily remove, copy, or rename files belonging to other users.

> Don't let the power go to your head! Users on your system should have a right to privacy, unless you explicitly tell them otherwise. Reading files you don't own is unethical and, depending on the circumstances, often illegal.

Getting Help with Manpages

Almost every function and utility that exists on your system includes a built-in help file called a *manpage* (manual page). The man command returns all the information you need to understand the arguments a given utility takes, how it works, and the results you should expect. Consider the more command, for example. Although this has been mentioned only briefly, you can quickly learn more information about it by typing

man more

For example:

```
[localhost:/etc] john% man more
man: Formatting manual page...

MORE(1)                                                         MORE(1)

NAME
        more, page—file perusal filter for crt viewing

SYNOPSIS
        more  [  -cdflsu  ] [ -n ] [ +linenumber ] [ +/pattern ] [
        name ...  ]

        page more options

DESCRIPTION
        More is a filter which allows examination of a  continuous
        text  one screenful at a time on a soft-copy terminal.  It
        normally pauses after each screenful, printing the current
        file name at the bottom of the screen or --More-- if input
        is from a pipe.  If the user then types a carriage return,
```

```
one  more  line  is  displayed.  If the user hits a space,
another screenful is displayed.  Other  possibilities  are
enumerated later.
```
...and so on...

This is only a tiny portion of the total manpage for the more command. There are more than five pages of information for this function alone!

> If you don't know exactly what command you're looking for, use apropos *<keyword>* to search through the man page information for a given word or phrase.

Other Useful Commands

Thousands of other commands and utilities on Mac OS X could potentially be covered in a UNIX chapter. Rather than trying to do the impossible and document them all in 15 to 20 pages, we close out the hour by listing a few interesting functions that you can explore (remember to use man!) if you choose to do so.

- **curl**—Retrieves information from a given URL. Useful for downloading files from the command line.
- **ncftp**—A simple, yet surprisingly user-friendly FTP client.
- **cat**—Displays the contents of a file.
- **file**—Shows the type of a file (what it contains).
- **locate**—Quickly finds a file based on the text in its name.
- **find**—Locates files based on their size, modification dates, and so on. This is the UNIX equivalent of Sherlock.
- **grep**—Searches through a text file for a given string.
- **shutdown**—Shuts down a Mac OS X computer.
- **reboot**—Reboots a Mac OS X computer.
- **date**—Displays the current date and time.
- **uptime**—Shows the amount of time your computer has been online and what the current system load is.
- **passwd**—Changes your Mac OS X password.
- **df**—Shows the amount of free and used space on all available partitions.
- **du**—Displays disk usage information on a directory-by-directory basis.

20

- `tar`—Archives and dearchives files in the UNIX tar format.
- `gzip`/`gunzip`—Compresses and decompresses files.

Again, I want to stress that this should serve as a starting place for exploring the UNIX subsystem. You will find commands that aren't listed here. However, with the documentation provided in this hour, you're prepared for how they work and understand how to get more information about them.

Summary

In this hour, you learned some of the basics of the UNIX command line. You should now be capable of performing many of the standard Finder functions from a command prompt. Although many gaps exist in what was covered, UNIX is a very broad topic and one that takes years to master. Hopefully you're on your way to becoming a future UNIX guru!

Q&A

Q What about aliases; how can I make aliases from the command line?

A Aliases are known as *links* in UNIX and are created with the `ln` command, much like using `cp` or `mv`.

Q Why can't I use some of the commands as documented?

A You're probably trying to operate on files that don't belong to you. Try using `sudo` to run the command as root.

Q What's the difference between a shell and a command prompt?

A The command prompt is generated by a shell. The default shell on Mac OS X is called `tcsh`. For the sake of keeping this hour as straightforward as possible, *shell* and *command prompt* were used interchangeably.

Q How can using the command line be dangerous?

A The command line is dangerous only because it's new and isn't nearly as friendly as the Finder. For instance, when you delete a file in the Finder, it goes to the Trash, where you can later remove it. When you delete a file at the command line, it's gone for good.

Workshop

The workshop contains quiz questions and activities to help you solidify your understanding of the material covered. Try to answer all questions before looking at the "Answers" section that follows.

Quiz

1. What command changes the owner of a file?

2. How can you generate a listing of all running processes on your system?

3. What's the easiest way to find additional information for the commands on your computer?

4. Does this hour cover all available UNIX utilities?

Answers

1. The `chown` function is used to set a new owner for a given file.

2. Type **ps -ax** at a command prompt to show a list of everything that's active on your computer.

3. Much of the UNIX software included on Mac OS X has its own man page with extensive usage documentation. You can display this information by typing `man <command name>`.

4. Not by a long shot! Thousands of files, utilities, and applications are located on your system. This hour gave you the tools to find and work with them.

Activities

Much like the beginning hours of this book recommended that you play around with Mac OS X, I recommend that you now do the same for the command line from a non-administrative account. Read through the manpages of the commands you learned, and then try out the commands. There's much to discover!

20

HOUR **21**

UNIX Advantages: The Power of UNIX

In the previous hour, you learned about the underlying UNIX portion of Mac OS X. It can be a bit overwhelming to say the least. To counter the overload, this hour focuses on some real-world advantages that the UNIX system offers. This hour serves as a starting point for finding UNIX technologies that you want to use, including

- Taking control of your computer with scripting languages
- Using the X Window System to expand your software reach
- Advanced server features of Mac OS X

Scripting Languages

In Hour 19, "Automating Tasks with AppleScript," you learned about the AppleScript programming language. AppleScript is a native Macintosh technology that provides powerful control over user-level processes.

Administrators typically use scripting languages to help automate mundane system tasks. Surprisingly, you can create some pretty complex applications in a very short period of time with nothing more than Mac OS X and your choice of a GUI or command-line text editor.

Your computer also contains a variety of other scripting tools and languages that can work with the UNIX command line, such as shell scripts and Perl. Shell scripts have relatively limited functionality because they use the same interpreter that processes your command-line input. Perl, on the other hand, provides a very robust language that can do just about anything, so it is our focus here.

Introduction to Perl

Perl (Practical Extraction and Reporting Language) has grown from having a cult following in the early 1990s to being a massive hit today. Originally designed to make working with text data simple, Perl has been expanded by developers to handle tasks such as image manipulation and client/server activities. Because of its ease of use and capability to work with ambiguous user input, Perl is an extremely popular Web development language.

For example, assume that you want to extract a phone number from an input string. A user might enter 555-5654, 5552231, 421-5552313, and so on. It's up to the application to find the area code, local exchange, and identifier numbers. Try entering the following Perl program into your computer using a text editor. Save it as `phone.pl` within any directory on the system.

```perl
#!/usr/bin/perl
print "Please enter a phone number:";
$phone=<STDIN>;
$phone=~s/[^\d]//g;
$phone=~s/^1//;
if (length($phone)==7) {
    $phone=~/(\d{3,3})(\d{4,4})/;
    $area="???"; $prefix=$1; $number=$2;
} elsif (length($phone)==10) {
    $phone=~/(\d{3,3})(\d{3,3})(\d{4,4})/;
    $area=$1; $prefix=$2; $number=$3;
} else { print "Invalid number!"; exit; }
print "($area) $prefix-$number\n";
```

After entering and saving the code, you need to make it executable from the command line. Do this by typing **chmod +x phone.pl** within the Terminal. Then execute the simple script by typing **./phone.pl** at your command prompt. The following appears on your screen:

```
[www:~] jray% chmod +x phone.pl
[www:~] jray% ./phone.pl
Please enter a phone number:614 xfg555 lkef1234 z
(614) 555-1234
```

This program accepts a phone number as input, strips any unusual characters from it, removes a leading 1 (if included), and formats the result in an attractive manner. If there's any chance of finding a valid U.S. phone number in a sequence of letters and numbers, phone.pl can do it!

Perl can also interact directly with the Mac OS X system by calling utilities that alter the operating system. Many users have asked, for example, for a way to add accounts without going to the Users System Preferences panel. I use the following script to do just that on my Web server:

```perl
#!/usr/bin/perl

$lastid=`nidump passwd . | cut -f3 -d ":" | sort -n | tail -1l`;
chomp($lastid);
$uid=$lastid+1;
$dir="/Users";
$gid="20";
$shell="/bin/tcsh";

print "Adding UID $uid.\n";
print "Username : ";
$username=<STDIN>; chomp($username);
print "Real Name: ";
$realname=<STDIN>; chomp($realname);

`niutil -create . "/users/$username"`;
`niutil -createprop . "/users/$username" realname "$realname"`;
`niutil -createprop . "/users/$username" uid "$uid"`;
`niutil -createprop . "/users/$username" gid "$gid"`;
`niutil -createprop . "/users/$username" home "$dir/$username"`;
`niutil -createprop . "/users/$username" shell "$shell"`;
`mkdir "$dir/$username"`;
`mkdir "$dir/$username/Sites"`;
`echo "Your website starts here." > "$dir/$username/Sites/index.html"`;
`chown -R $username:staff "$dir/$username"`;
`chmod -R 755 "$dir/$username"`;

exec "passwd $username";
```

Remember that any script you use on your Mac OS X computer must first be made executable with the command chmod +x <script name>.

21

As you can see, scripting languages can be extremely powerful tools on your computer. If you're developing scripts on your computer, keep in mind that the script runs with the same capabilities of your user account—even as an administrator. If you're developing a script that potentially could be dangerous, I recommend running it under a basic user account that doesn't have administrative permissions until you're positive that it does not cause any harm.

Other Resources

For more information about creating shell and Perl scripts, I recommend exploring resources beyond this simple introduction. You can always use the UNIX `man` command to view help information about a given command or function, or use the `perldoc` utility to view Perl documentation.

You might also want to check out some of the following publications and Web sites:

- **Perl.com**—`http://www.perl.com`. A fine collection of articles, tutorials, and information about the Perl programming language.
- **SHELLdorado**—`http://www.shelldorado.com`. A collection of resources and links for UNIX shell scripting.
- *Sams Teach Yourself Perl in 21 Days*—ISBN: 0672313057. A step-by-step guide to learning the Perl scripting languages.

X Window System

Much as Perl can expand your capability to control your computer from the command prompt, the X Window System can open your computer to running new graphical applications or even accessing applications on remote servers (such as Linux) that don't run natively on Mac OS X.

Many people find it hard to understand what exactly the X Window System is and does, so let's try to sort through some of the common myths that surround the software.

First, the X Window System is not an operating system like Microsoft Windows. It's a set of standard procedures that allows applications to draw images and text on your computer screen. In fact, the sole purpose of the X Window System is to provide a basic set of windowing services to computers. Doing so enables developers to create full GUI applications that can be compiled on a number of different operating systems and still offer the same features under each.

Second, the X Window System applications are not ugly or underpowered. Many people are under the impression that X Window System applications do not take advantage of the power user interfaces or deliver solid products. This simply isn't true. The X Window System does not define a look and feel on its own. That's the job of an additional piece of software called a *window manager* that determines how windows look when drawn onscreen. Some of the most advanced user interfaces (aside from Aqua, of course) are currently showing up on X Window System–based systems.

Finally, the X Window System is not used only for running applications from other machines. The X Window System made *network computing* popular before that became a common phrase. The X Window System software that you install on your computer is a server; it knows how to accept commands from applications, whether they're installed on your computer or elsewhere on the network, and draws on the screen accordingly. For example, Figure 21.1 shows Netscape 4.7 running from a remote Linux server directly on the Mac OS X desktop. The X Window System server, however, can certainly process requests from local applications. In fact, an entire world of X Window System applications is just waiting to be downloaded and compiled on your computer.

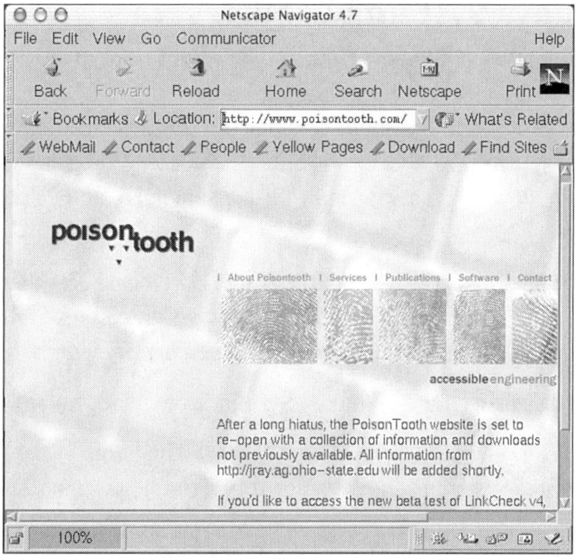

FIGURE 21.1
The X Window System can run remote applications directly on your computer.

X Window System Distributions

If you want to install the X Window System on your computer, you have a variety of choices—from free to commercial offerings. Each has its advantages, so I urge you to check the home page for each distribution to find the particulars.

21

- **XDarwin**—http://www.mrcla.com/XonX/. A completely free X Window System distribution based on the popular XFree86 used on Linux. In addition, you can install the XDarwin Oroboros window manager (http://oroborosx.sourceforge.net/download.html) and have X Window System applications take on the Mac OS X Aqua appearance.

- **Xtools** —http://www.tenon.com/products/xtools/. The Tenon Xtools product is an excellent implementation of the X Window System based on Apple's Cocoa environment. It allows X Window System applications to seamlessly blend into the Mac OS X environment and uses the Aqua appearance as the window manager for applications.

- **eXodus** —http://www.powerlan-usa.com/exodus/. Like Xtools, Powerlan's eXodus X Window System server is a powerful commercial solution. The eXodus package has been available on the Macintosh for many years and is a time-tested and extremely Mac-friendly piece of software.

X Window System Resources

After installing the X Window System, you might want to try downloading some software to use with it. An excellent program to try is the GNU Image Manipulation Program (GIMP). A few prebuilt versions of the software are available through the VersionTracker (http://www.versiontracker.com) Web site. Make sure that the application you're downloading was built for the same version of the X Window System you installed.

I personally recommend installing the Apple developer tools that came with Mac OS X and compiling the software yourself. This, however, can take time and patience and requires additional study of the command-line environment

Check out these sites for X Window System source code and information:

- **XFree86** —http://www.xfree86.org/. The home of the free, popular, and powerful XFree system is a great place for learning about the X Window System.

- **X.org** —http://www.x.org/. The official home page for the X Window System specification and host to a large library of contributed software.

- **Comp.windows.x.apps** —http://www.ee.ryerson.ca:8080/~elf/xapps/. A FAQ page for the comp.windows.x.apps newsgroup. This is a great place to look for beginner information and download links.

Server Applications and Tools

Underneath the Mac OS are a number of powerful server processes that can handle enterprise-level business. Apple did a great job of hiding these processes behind the beautiful Aqua interface. At the same time, however, Apple also covered up a great deal of the functionality that the servers can offer on your system.

In this section, we take a look at how the power of Mac OS X can be uncovered from behind the user interface.

Apache

Apache is an extremely popular piece of server software that can be used for just about anything you would ever want to do on a Web site. For example, one of the most interesting things you can do is develop interactive applications, such as Common Gateway Interface (CGI) programs for use on Apache. This can be used to turn static Web sites into dynamic masterpieces.

Installing CGI Web Applications

By default, Mac OS X can run systemwide CGI applications that are stored in the /Library/WebServer/CGI-Executables directory on your server. For example, enter the following Perl code into a file named images.cgi within the CGI-Executables directory:

```perl
#!/usr/bin/perl
print "Content-type: text/html\n\n";

$columns=3;

@imagelist=glob("/Library/Webserver/Documents/imagefolder/*jpg");

print "<TABLE BGCOLOR=\"#FFFFFF\" BORDER=\"1\" BORDERCOLOR=\"#000000\">";
while ($x<@imagelist) {
    print "<TR>";
    for ($y=0;$y";
            $imagename=~s/.*Documents\///;
            print "<IMG SRC=\"\/$imagename\" width=\"120\" height=\"90\"><br>";
            $imagename=~s/.*imagefolder\///;
            print "<FONT TYPE=\"Arial\">$imagename</FONT>";
            print "</TD>";

    }
    print "</TR>";
}
print "</TABLE>";
```

21

After storing the file, make it executable by typing **chmod +x images.cgi** at the Terminal prompt. Next, create a directory named imagefolder inside the /Library/Webserver/Documents folder and copy a handful of JPEG images to the folder.

Now, make sure that Apache is turned on using the Sharing System Preferences panel. With a bit of luck, you've successfully installed a CGI that automatically displays thumbnails of all the files contained in the imagefolder directory that have the filename extension .jpg, as demonstrated in Figure 21.2. You can access this CGI by typing the URL **http://localhost/cgi-bin/images.cgi** in your browser.

FIGURE 21.2

This sample CGI generates a contact sheet of images within a folder.

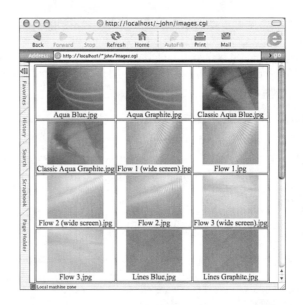

In case you're wondering, the CGI-Executables directory is aliased (by Apache) to the URL /cgi-bin. Anything you place in the CGI-Executables folder is accessible through the cgi-bin URL.

Adding PHP Support

Mac OS X includes a very popular programming language called PHP that can be used to create dynamic Web applications. PHP includes advanced database access, graphics, and network features that would cost hundreds of dollars to add to other similar languages, such as Microsoft's Active Server Pages.

Even though this software is installed, it isn't active on your computer by default. To make it useable, you must open and edit the /etc/http/httpd.conf file and make some changes:

Look for the lines that read

```
#LoadModule php4_module          libexec/httpd/libphp4.so
#AddModule mod_php4.c
#AddType application/x-httpd-php .php
#AddType application/x-httpd-php-source .phps
```

As you can see, a pound symbol (#) begins these lines. You must remove this symbol for Apache to recognize PHP files.

After making the changes, save the configuration file, and restart Apache with the command sudo /usr/sbin/apachectl restart or simply reboot your computer.

You should now be able to add PHP files with the suffix .php to any of the Web sites (personal or systemwide) and have them execute correctly. For example, try creating a file called info.php with the following line in it:

```
<?php phpinfo(); ?>
```

You should now be able to load info.php into your browser and see a status display much like the one in Figure 21.3 for the PHP programming language.

FIGURE 21.3

A single-line PHP script should tell you whether things are working.

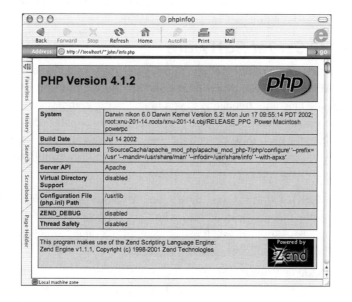

21

Unlike CGIs and other executables, PHP files don't need to be made executable to run. Just write them and they're ready to go!

Web Programming Resources

You're not going to turn into a Web programmer overnight, and if you've never seen a CGI or Web language before, much of this is completely foreign to you. The important thing to understand is that these features are available on Mac OS X when you need them. To learn more about configuring Apache for advanced services and developing Web applications, check out these resources:

- **Apache**—http://www.apache.org. The home of the Apache Web server. This site provides a reference for the hundreds of configuration directives that are used to set up and control the world's most popular Web servers.
- **CPAN** —http://www.cpan.org/. The Comprehensive Perl Archive Network. Although not directly CGI related, CPAN contains prewritten modules that can speed up creation of advanced software applications.
- **PHP** —http://www.php.net/. The home of PHP includes an excellent annotated reference to every PHP function (there are thousands!) and examples of its use. If you have any programming experience, the PHP site is probably all you need to get up and running.

Other Server Software

In addition to the installed applications, you can download and install many other powerful free servers on your Mac OS X computer. As you probably guessed, you'll see the command line quite frequently if you intend to run complex server applications. Mac developers are working to create GUI front ends to popular open source software. So, over time, the need to work with the command line will decrease. For now, however, there's still much to be done and much to be gained from applications such as the following:

- **MySQL**—http://www.mysql.com. MySQL is a powerful relational database server that can be combined with Perl, PHP, and other languages to create dynamic database applications. It offers many of the same features as Oracle or MS-SQL, but at a significantly reduced price: $0.
- **Jakarta Tomcat**—http://jakarta.apache.org/tomcat/index.html. A full implementation of JavaServer Pages (JSP) for Mac OS X. Tomcat can work with popular JSP authoring applications such as Macromedia's UltraDev to build complex online systems through a point-and-click environment.

- **Mod_dav**—`http://www.webdav.org/mod_dav/`. The WebDAV module for Apache enables you to create your own Web-based file shares, similar to Apple's iDisk. Because WebDAV shares are cross-platform, you can access them from anywhere, even through firewalls, because they're based on HTTP.
- **Samba**—`http://www.samba.org/`. Samba provides a complete Windows NT/2000 file server replacement. If you need to turn your Mac into a power Windows server, this free product happily does just that.

Many UNIX applications are available as precompiled binary packages that you can double-click to install, others require downloading source code files and compiling (building) the software. If you don't want to deal with the nitty-gritty details of compiling software on your system, check out the VersionTracker Web site for links to these packages and more.

As you can see, Mac OS X is a very powerful platform for whatever you do. This is the first time that a powerful desktop environment has been successfully married with the strength of UNIX. Learn to work with both faces of your computer, and you'll find an entirely new world of software and capabilities never before realized on the Macintosh platform.

Summary

This hour looked at a few of the powerful technologies that Mac OS X makes available to its users. Without installing or purchasing any additional software, you can immediately start writing scripts, programming Web applications, and running GUI applications that might never have been planned for the Mac platform. By further exploiting some of the strengths of the UNIX side of Mac OS X, you can create a powerful Internet server presence based on some of the most popular server packages on the Internet. It's amazing how far we've come, isn't it?

Q&A

Q Why do I have to type `./` in front of a command-line program to run it?

A When running programs from the command line, the system has a few preset places to look for them. This is called the *system path*. Because of security concerns, the current directory is not one of them. Therefore, to run a program located in the directory you're currently using, you prefix it with `./`, which tells the system that the file is located in the same place that you are.

21

Q Can I download PPC Linux X Window System applications and use them on Mac OS X?

A No. To use an X Window System application, it must be compiled for Mac OS X and for the X Window System distribution you're using.

Q What's the advantage to using Apache or other UNIX server software, such as MySQL, over applications such as WebSTAR or FileMaker?

A Use what works for you! Much of the UNIX-based software is free and extremely flexible—which is appealing to those with a limited budget and a love of the command line. However, something can be said for desktop applications that take full advantage of the Mac OS X user interface.

Workshop

The workshop contains quiz questions and activities to help you solidify your understanding of the material covered. Try to answer all questions before looking at the "Answers" section that follows.

Quiz

1. What must you do before executing a just-written Perl script or CGI?
2. Where's the systemwide CGI directory located?
3. Where can you download the X Window System operating system?

Answers

1. Before running a script, you must make it executable using the chmod +x command.
2. The default CGI directory on Mac OS X is located at /Library/WebServer/CGI-Executables.
3. The X Window System isn't an operating system; it's a server that can draw primitive windowing objects on your screen. Three distributions of the X Window System were covered in this hour, along with their download locations.

Activities

1. Test the examples given in this hour by typing them into a text editor, saving them, and running them. It's one thing to read about the capabilities of Mac OS X in a book, but it's another to see them in practice.

2. Download and install an X Window System distribution. If you have other UNIX machines on your network, talk to your system administrator about how you can use your Mac OS X computer to access the applications on these servers remotely.

21

Hour **22**

System Utilities and Monitors

Apple has included an eclectic sampling of utilities in Mac OS X that, at some point in time, you might find useful. Everything from CD image burning, RAID software, and CPU monitors is buried in your system's Utilities folder. This hour explores the Mac OS X 10.2 system utilities, how they work, and what they can do to improve your user experience. In this hour, you learn

- How Disk Utility can be used for repairing and partitioning your disks
- Why Disk Copy is so much more than a way to mount disk images
- What software can be used to monitor your system's CPU usage
- How to find out what programs are hogging your machine's resources

Disk Utility

There's a great deal of information to cover in this hour, so we move quickly. The first application we'll look at is Disk Utility, located at

/Applications/Utilities/Disk Utility. Disk Utility is a piece of software for everything disk related—from repairs to partitioning and formatting.

You can't use Disk Utility on the drive you're currently booted from to repair disk errors. If you intend to work only with a secondary disk or partition, launch Disk Utility from the Finder. To use Disk Utility to work on your primary disk, follow these steps:

1. Insert your Mac OS X Install CD into your computer.
2. Start (or restart) your Macintosh while holding down the C key.
3. Wait for the Installer to boot.
4. Choose Open Disk Utility from the Installer application menu.

Whichever method you use to launch it, the application opens to the first of five different panels: Information, First Aid, Erase, Partition, and RAID. Each panel performs a different function in the application—as you might guess from its name.

Along the left side of the window are the available storage devices on the system, including mounted disk images. If a device has a disclosure triangle to the left of its icon, it can be expanded to display available partitions.

Choose the disk or partition that you want to work with, and then click the tab to move to the appropriate panel. We start with the Information panel.

Information

Shown in Figure 22.1, the Information panel displays data about the currently selected resource, but doesn't perform any operations on the device.

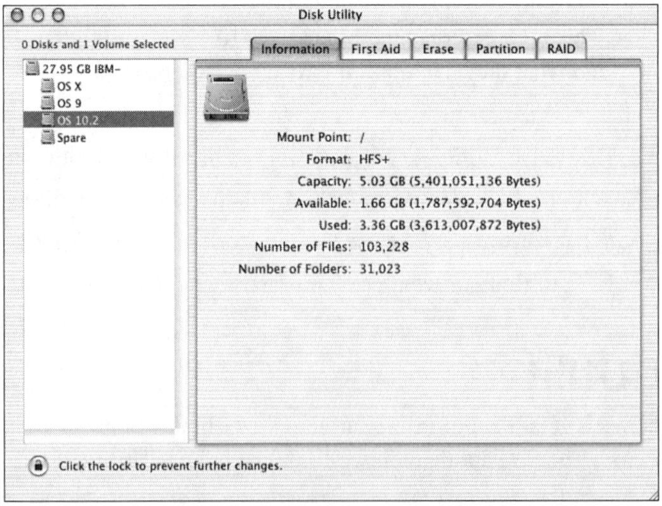

FIGURE 22.1

The Information panel shows the specs of the device you've selected.

When you select a storage device, the Information tab's display reflects the hardware's physical statistics—such as manufacturer, capacity, and how it is connected (ATA, SCSI, FireWire, and so on).

> The figures depicting Disk Utility in this hour show four hard drive volumes. That's because I partitioned my hard drive into four sections when I first set up my system in order to test early versions of Mac OS X 10.2 without disrupting my other work. Partitioning, even into separate volumes for Mac OS X and Mac OS 9, has the added benefit of enabling you to boot into one volume in the unlikely event that another fails. If the drive has a mechanical failure it, unfortunately, affects all partitions. You can find out more about partitioning your drive in Appendix A, "Installing Mac OS X."

Choosing a partition within a storage device reveals even more data, including the mount point (usually /Volumes/<*partition name*>), format, capacity, available space, used space, and the total number of files and folders.

First Aid

You use the First Aid tab, shown in Figure 22.2, to perform basic repair operations on a drive. Disk First Aid functions on UFS, HFS+, *and* HFS volumes—meaning that you can repair both types of Mac OS X partitions and both types of Mac OS 8/9 partitions. Unfortunately, Disk First Aid is not capable of repairing some types of disk damage, so third-party utilities such as Micromat's Drive 10 and TechTool Pro (http://www.micromat.com/) are still an important part of every software library. Note that disk utilities can fix only corrupted data on the drives, not mechanical drive problems. More is said about those tools in Hour 24, "Maintenance and Troubleshooting."

To check or verify a disk, select the disk and partition from the volume list at the left of the window. Next, click the appropriate action button:

- **Verify Permissions**—Displays any oddities in the file permissions on your system, but doesn't attempt to repair them. This function operates only on system directories, not the files in your home directory.

- **Repair Permissions**—Performs the same tests as Verify Permissions, but automatically resets the permissions to their original state.

- **Verify Disk**—Displays any errors found in your disk, but doesn't attempt to repair them.

- **Repair Disk**—Performs the same tests as Verify, but automatically fixes any errors it might find.
- **Stop**—Halts the current action (Verify or Repair).

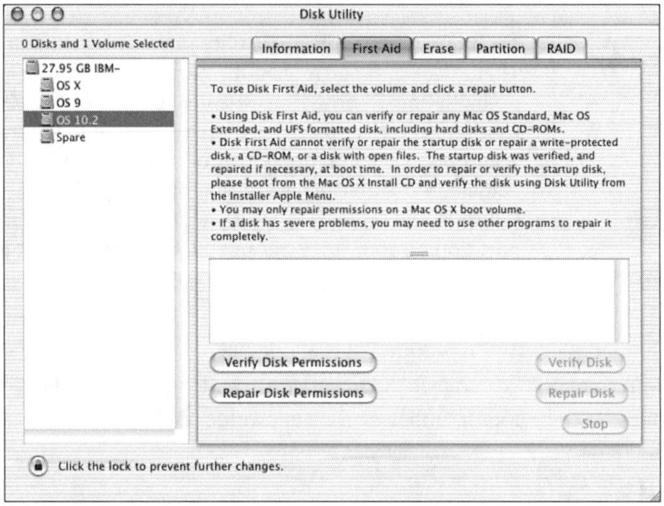

FIGURE 22.2

Repair minor damage to your drives.

Verify Permissions and Repair Permissions come in handy if you find that you can't open or write to the usual folders, which can happen through strange software interactions or user error.

Verify Disk and Repair Disk check for several errors, including

- **Extents Overflow File**—The Extents file keeps track of file information that couldn't be placed contiguously on a disk. As files become fragmented, the locations of the fragments are stored here.
- **Multi-Linked Files**—Files that are incorrectly linked to the same allocation blocks on the disk. (In other words, two or more files think they're in the same spot on the disk.)
- **Catalog**—Contains the information that forms the structure (files and folders) of the disk.
- **Bitmap**—A binary picture of the disk that records which blocks are allocated to files and which are free space.

If disk errors cannot be repaired, Disk Utility warns you that it's incapable of fixing your system. If this happens, try rerunning the repair—Disk First Aid often requires two passes to work correctly. If the repair *doesn't* work, Apple's suggested course of action is to back up the drive, erase it, and then restore your files. I recommend trying another disk repair tool before resorting to such desperate measures.

 You can batch-repair multiple volumes by selecting several disks from the volume list. Just press Command and click the icons to add to the selected list.

Erase

The next tab, Erase, does exactly what you think it should: It erases drives and partitions. It's essentially a quick-and-dirty partitioning and initialization tool. It creates a single empty partition on the selected device by erasing anything that was previously there. The Erase tab is shown in Figure 22.3.

FIGURE 22.3

You'll never guess what the Erase tab does!

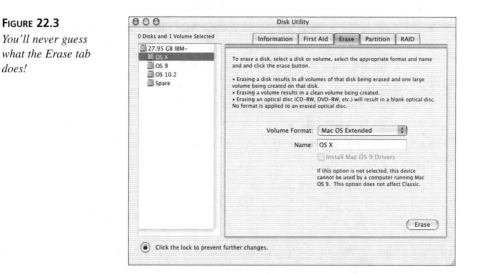

Use the Volume Format pop-up menu to choose between HFS+ (Mac OS Extended) and HFS (Mac OS Standard) partition types. If you intend to use the volume in Mac OS X, you should use the Mac OS Extended format.

Next, enter a name for the new volume, which appears as your disk label on the desktop. If the drive is to be used with Mac OS 9 directly (not through the Classic environment), you can install Mac OS 9 drivers by clicking the Install Mac OS 9 Drivers check box.

Finally, click Erase to remove all existing information from the device and install the selected file system.

Partition

To create a more complex drive layout, use the Partition tab. This is the control center for working with your drive. You can find more information about partitions and what they are in Appendix A. Be warned that changes here erase any information on the target drive!

The Volume Scheme section of the Partition panel contains a visual representation of the partitions on the system. Each box is a partition, and the highlighted box is the active partition. You can change a partition's size by dragging the dividers between the partitions up and down to shrink or increase the available space. As you drag the bar, the Size field in the Volume Information section on the right changes to show the current settings.

In addition to working with the partition's visual view, you can use the various pop-up menus, fields, and buttons to set other parameters:

- **Name**—Sets the name of the highlighted partition.
- **Format**—Sets the highlighted partition to be Mac OS Standard (HFS), Mac OS Extended (HFS+), UNIX File System (UFS), or free space.
- **Size**—Manually enter a new size for the selected partition.
- **Locked for Editing**—When checked, this setting freezes the current partition's settings. You can continue to work with other partitions, but not one that's locked. Clicking the lock icon in the partition's visual view also toggles the lock.
- **Split**—Splits the current partition into two equally sized partitions.
- **Delete**—Removes the active partition.
- **Revert**—Returns the partition map to its original state.
- **Partition**—Commits the partition table design to the drive. This destroys all current data on the device.

Clicking the Partition button is the final step to designing your volume's layout. After you click the Partition button, you're prompted with a final confirmation, and the changes are written to the disk.

RAID

RAID, or *redundant array of independent disks*, is a collection of multiple drives that function together as a single drive. By using drives performing in parallel, the computer can write and read information from the RAID set at a much higher rate than a single drive. By including RAID support directly in the Mac OS X system, Apple sets a high standard for server and user operating systems.

Two common types of RAID are available in Mac OS X:

- **Level 0**—Disk striping, which increases I/O speed by reading and writing to multiple drives simultaneously. It offers no ability to recover from error, but is useful when working with very large files, including digital video.
- **Level 1**—Disk mirroring, which creates a fault-tolerant system by creating an exact mirror of one drive onto another as data is written. If an error occurs on one drive, the other can take over without skipping a beat.

The Mac OS X RAID capabilities are easy to configure if you have multiple drives in a machine. However, you can't use RAID on the startup disk.

To set up a RAID set, drag the icons of the drives you're adding to a set from the volume list to the RAID tab's Disk section. Using the RAID Scheme pop-up menu, choose what type of RAID support to enable for the disks, and supply a name in the RAID Set Name field for the resulting virtual drive that represents the combination of devices.

Finally, choose a volume format for the RAID set in the Volume Format pop-up menu (this is identical to choosing a format for any volume), and click the Create button to generate the RAID set. The new volume is mounted on the desktop.

Disk Copy

The next application we examine is Disk Copy (path: /Applications/Utilities/Disk Copy). In recent years, Disk Copy has become a common and convenient way to distribute software. Instead of creating an archived folder, developers write their applications to a virtual disk that's loaded into memory when used. This disk image file appears to the computer as a *real* disk and can be manipulated like any other disk. For the end user, it's a simple way to work with new applications, as you saw in Hour 4, "Installing New Applications."

A single disk image file can contain applications, support files, and any other data that a program might need—and it never needs to be decompressed. In fact, many applications can actually run directly from disk images, without needing to be copied to your hard drive. Disk Copy even has built-in CD-burning capabilities to make turning a disk image into a real CD a matter of a few clicks.

To launch the Disk Copy application, double-click a disk image file (usually named with a .dmg extension), or double-click its application icon. The icon for Disk Copy appears in the Dock, but no windows open.

If you launched Disk Copy by double-clicking an image file, the image is automatically mounted. The application checks the image's validity and the image appears as a white drive icon on your desktop or at the Computer level of the Finder.

To mount an image if you've opened Disk Copy manually, either select Mount Image from the File menu or drag a disk image into the Disk Copy icon in the Dock.

From this point, you can copy files from the disk to wherever you want, or use them directly from the mounted image.

Task: Creating Disk Images

Disk Copy can create images as well as mount them. This is useful for creating an exact duplicate of software you don't want to lose or for making a master image to distribute software over a network. For each image you create, you must have enough free space on your hard drive. For example, to create a CD image, you need approximately 650MB free. Currently shipping Apple computers come with at least 10GB drives, so this really shouldn't be an issue.

1. There are two ways to generate an image: by copying an existing item, or by creating an empty image file, mounting it, and then copying files to it. To create an empty image file, choose Blank Image (Command+N) from the File menu's New submenu. The dialog box shown in Figure 22.4 appears.

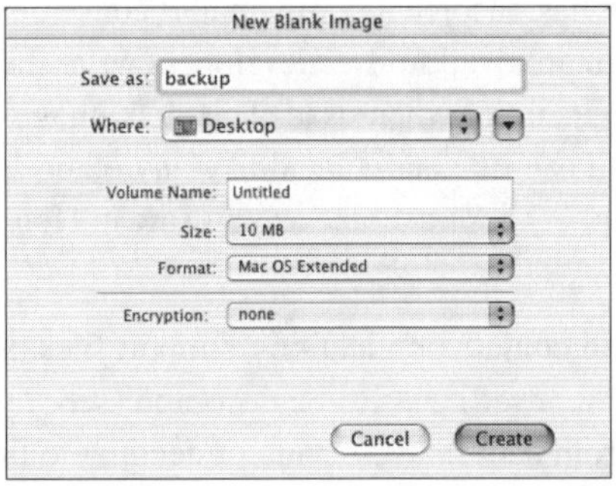

FIGURE 22.4

Make a new image, and then copy to it.

2. Fill in the Save As field as you normally would—this is the name of the image file, not the volume that's going to be created. Set the name of the volume in the Volume Name field. Choose a size for the image from the Size pop-up menu. There are a variety of preset sizes for common media, such as Zip disks, CDs, DVDs, and a Custom setting for arbitrary sizes.

3. Next, choose a volume format in the Format pop-up menu. In addition to the Mac OS Standard (HFS), Mac OS Extended (HFS+), and UNIX File System (UFS) options supported as native Mac OS X file systems, you can also choose MS-DOS File System to create a Windows-compatible image.

4. Finally, if you want to encrypt the disk image, choose AES-128 in the Encryption pop-up menu and click Create. The new disk image is created and can be used immediately.

Creating an image from an existing folder or drive is even easier and is a great way to make quick backups that retain all the file permissions and attributes of the originals.

1. Choose Image from Folder or Volume (Command+I), or Image from Device (Option+Command+I [to work with the entire hard drive]) from the New submenu of the File menu. Disk Copy opens the standard Open File window from which you can surf to the item you want to make an image of.

   If you choose New Image from Device, Disk Copy displays a list of all active devices. Click the disclosure triangle in front of each device to display the individual partitions.

2. Select the item to image, and then click the Image button. You are prompted for the location to save the image. Using the Format pop-up menu, choose the type of image to create: read-only, read-write, compressed, or CD/DVD master. Apply encryption to the image file by choosing AES-128 in the Encryption pop-up menu.

3. Finally, click Save to copy an image to your hard drive.

Task: Burning CDs

In Hour 2, "Using the Finder and Dock," you learned how to create CDs in the Finder. You can also use Disk Copy to author CD-ROMs. Although I still recommend Roxio's Toast (http://www.roxio.com/) for advanced burning features, Disk Copy can be used for almost everything.

> To burn a CD from within Disk Copy with an external burner, you must have your CD writer connected and powered on. Check Apple's Web site for supported writers.

1. Place a blank CD-R or CD-RW in your CD writer.

2. Select Burn Image from the File menu, and choose a disk image file when prompted. If the image is suitable for CD burning, Disk Copy prepares to burn a CD-R or CD-RW.

3. Expand the Burn Disk dialog box by clicking the disclosure button. You see settings for the speed you want to use during the burn process, along with whether you want to verify and eject the disk after it finishes. (A check box for Allow Additional Burns also appears because some burners enable you to continue adding data to a CD containing data until the disk is full.)

4. When you're satisfied with your settings, click the Burn button, and Disk Copy begins writing the CD.

> You might be surprised to find that you can burn any standard format CD by using this method—even CDs that aren't for the Macintosh. I've used it numerous times to burn images of the latest Red Hat Linux disk images from its Web site.

System Profiler

Next up is the Apple System Profiler, located at /Applications/Utilities/Apple System Profiler. System Profiler is a great utility to use if you ever need to call for technical support and are asked the exact system configuration of your computer. System Profiler's sole purpose is to collect data on your computer, peripherals, and software and prepare a report on the results.

When System Profiler launches, it might take several seconds to collect information. The initial window is a summary of your system configuration, as shown in Figure 22.5.

FIGURE 22.5
System Profiler displays your system's hardware and software configuration.

		Apple System Profiler
	System Profile	Devices and Volumes	Frameworks	Extensions	Applications	Logs

▼ Software Overview

System version	Mac OS X 10.2 (6C106)
Boot volume	OS 10.2
Kernel version	Darwin Kernel Version 6.0: Sat Jul 20 19:50:10 PDT 2002; root:xnu/xnu-340.obj~1/RELEASE_P
User name	Robyn Ness (robyn)

▼ Hardware Overview

Machine speed	700 MHz
Bus speed	100 MHz
Number of processors	1
L2 cache size	512K
Machine model	iBook (version = 1.2)
Boot ROM info	4.3.6f3
Customer serial number	UV2220N0-LQ6-ff10
Sales order number	Not available

▼ Memory Overview

Location	Type	Size
DIMM0/BUILT-IN	SDRAM	128 MB
DIMM1/J12	SDRAM	128 MB

▼ Network Overview
  ▼ Built-in

Flags	0x8863<Up,Broadcast,b6,Running,Simplex,Multicast>
Ethernet address	00.03.93.98.59.3E

  ▼ Airport

Each of the topics can be expanded or collapsed by clicking the disclosure triangle in front of the topic. Disclosure triangles are used extensively throughout the application, so be sure to click around—you'll be surprised at the total amount of available information.

A total of five information topics are available: System Profile, Devices and Volumes, Frameworks, Extensions, and Applications. Click the appropriately labeled tab to move among the topics. Let's look at the categories now.

System Profile

The System Profile tab, which you saw in Figure 22.5, contains a summary of the base computer and operating system configuration. By expanding each of the topics, you can find everything from the amount of built-in memory and your current network configuration to the serial and sales order number that was assigned when your machine was first built.

Devices and Volumes

To see the devices that are connected to your computer (including the internal disks and storage devices), click the Devices and Volumes tab.

The Devices and Volumes display is unique. Instead of a linear view of the connected devices, it presents the data as multiple trees, with each of your system buses at the base:

- **USB**—Universal Serial Bus is a slow (12Mbps) bus used for connecting external peripherals, such as low-speed storage, scanners, printers, cameras, mice, and keyboards.

- **FireWire**—An Apple-developed bus technology that supports speeds of 400Mbps and hot-swappable devices, such as high-speed storage and digital video cameras. The FireWire bus is also known by its IEEE name, 1394, and the Sony name, iLINK.

- **PCI**—The Peripheral Component Interconnect bus was developed by Intel (yes, that Intel), and is the standard for connecting internal video cards, sound cards, and so on.

- **EIDE**—The Enhanced Integrated Drive Electronics standard was developed by Western Digital and is used for internal CD-ROM and disk storage.

- **SCSI**—The Small Computer System Interface is an extremely fast bus for high-speed storage devices, typically used on server-class computers.

By following the tree from the base, you can examine the devices that are connected, the manufacturer of the device, and the drivers that are installed.

Frameworks

Selecting the Frameworks tab displays a list of libraries that are installed on your computer, along with the version and whether the framework is an Apple creation.

There are dozens of frameworks in the base installation of Mac OS X, ranging from AppleShare to Speech Recognition. Similar to the other tabs, you can click the disclosure triangle in front of a framework to show the name of the library, general information, copyright, and version. Again, this data is really only useful for debugging purposes. If a framework is accidentally replaced with an older version, it's likely to cause problems with the system. The Frameworks tab can be used to quickly view the version numbers for comparison.

Extensions

Extensions, like frameworks, provide functionality to the operating system. Unlike frameworks, they work directly with the hardware to enable the operating system to access devices such as network cards, sound cards, and other components. Mac users are familiar with extensions. In Mac OS 8 and 9, extensions had similar capabilities, but often made the operating system unstable. In Mac OS X, the traditional extension is replaced by a file with the extension .kext (kernel extension). These plug-ins for the Mach kernel cannot be installed by users without admin privileges and are no longer appropriate or useful for creating cool (but crash-causing) additions to the system.

The layout of the Extensions tab is identical to that of the Frameworks tab. Each extension is displayed, along with its version and an identifier to determine whether it's Apple software.

Applications

The Applications tab scans your drive to display all the installed applications (the BSD subsystem utilities aren't taken into account). Like the Extensions and Frameworks tabs, you can use the basic list to determine an application's version and location.

Logs

Finally, the Logs tab stores information about system events, such as application crashes, that can be used to diagnose problems.

Chances are you won't find much use for Apple System Profiler in day-to-day life, but if you need to diagnose problems on a computer that isn't your own, it's a great way to become familiar with the system.

Process Viewer

In Hour 1, "A Tour of Mac OS X," you learned about force quitting an application from the Apple menu. The Process Viewer application is similar to the list of applications shown in the Force Quit dialog box, but it contains information on *all* the system's processes, including any command-line UNIX software that's running. Figure 22.6 shows the Process Viewer display with the disclosure button at the bottom clicked.

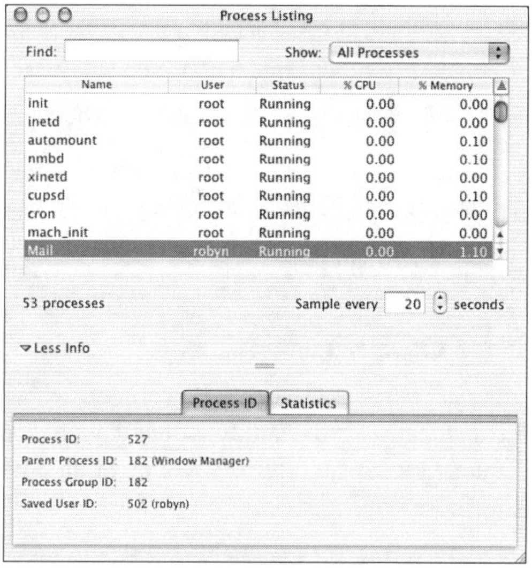

FIGURE 22.6

The Process Viewer can show you everything that is running on your computer.

The Find and Show features at the top of the window help to limit the amount of data in the Process Listing window. Typing into the Find field filters processes that match the given string. For example, typing **Internet** would limit the displayed processes to those with the word *Internet* in their names, such as Internet Explorer. The Show pop-up menu filters processes based on the owner. You can change the setting to show only processes owned by your account (User Processes), the system (Administrator Processes), or NetBoot. (NetBoot processes are not likely to be of value on most Mac OS X non-server installations.)

The Process Listing is not, as you might first think, an instant view of what is happening on your computer. The information is dynamic and, therefore, always changing. To avoid overwhelming you with a list that jumps all over the place, the process list is updated only every few seconds. Using the Sample Every *X* Seconds option just below the list, you can change the rate at which the list is refreshed. The larger the number, the longer you must wait for updates.

Processes are listed based on five columns: Name, User, Status, %CPU, and %Memory. Each column can be sorted by clicking on the column heading. Click the small triangle in the upper-right corner of the process list to reverse the sorting order. Using the basic listing, you can glean the following information about a process:

- **Name**—The name of the process or application.
- **User**—The user account that launched the process.
- **Status**—The status of the process. Most should be running, although users who access the command line can also suspend processes.
- **%CPU**—The percentage of available CPU time being used by the process.
- **%Memory**—The percentage of available memory being used by the process.

If you want even more information about a process, you can click it in the listing, and use the More Info disclosure triangle in the lower right of the window to reveal the Process ID and Statistics tabs, as shown earlier in Figure 22.6.

Force Quit a Process

Everything you need to access is in the single Process Viewer window. One of the most useful features of the application is the ability to quit any process you own. If you've enabled the root account, you can quit *any* running program on the machine! To force a process to quit, follow these steps:

1. Find the process in the Process Viewer.
2. Highlight the process and choose Quit Process (Option+Command+Q) from the Processes menu.
3. You are prompted to Quit or Force Quit the application. Choosing Quit attempts to shut down the program safely, but the Force Quit option stops the program immediately.
4. Click the Quit button if you want, or Cancel to not do anything.

Be careful when using the Process Viewer to stop running programs—you might quit something your system needs to run! If all you're looking for is a way to monitor your overall system performance and activity, Process Viewer might be too much for you. The final application in this hour, CPU Monitor, is good for keeping an eye on your system without completely boggling your mind.

If you've started using the Mac OS X command line, you might recognize that this application is similar to the top function.

CPU Monitor

With the multitasking capabilities of Mac OS X, users might want to check just how much of their computer's processor time is being used. In Mac OS X, each program has a small slice of time it can use to complete its task. As more and more programs use the system, there are fewer slices to give out.

CPU Monitor, found at /Applications/Utilities/CPU Monitor, can illustrate how busy your system is on a simple graph, showing a range from 0% to 100%. If you have multiple processors, a graph is displayed for each CPU in your machine. Three types of graphs can be displayed in a number of different ways (configurable through the Preferences panel and Processes menu). Figure 22.7 shows several available graph styles.

FIGURE 22.7
The CPU Monitor has a number of ways to display how busy your computer is.

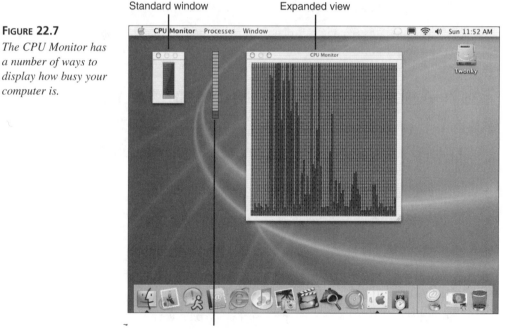

Most users are comfortable with the Standard view. In this mode, the CPU monitor displays a window with a vertical graph of the CPU activity. If you prefer to keep the monitor visible at all times, choose the Floating Window view, which creates just the graph itself as a floating image that can be positioned anywhere on the screen—including the menu bar. An alternative to the Floating Window view is the Icon view of either the standard or expanded view, which can be set in the application Preferences panel. These views take advantage of the Dock's ability to display dynamic information in its icons. The CPU activity is graphed within CPU Monitor's Dock icon instead of taking up additional screen space.

The Standard and Floating Window views show an average of all the activity on your computer. The Expanded Window view differentiates between three types of processes:

- **System**—Processor usage by the system functions, such as drawing windows and making the beautiful Aqua interface.
- **User**—CPU time used by your (and other users') processes and applications.
- **Nice**—CPU time used by processes running with an altered scheduling priority. These processes have been changed at the command line by using the `nice` or `renice` commands, so it's unlikely you'll see anything here.

You can control the windows displayed, their orientation, and their appearance through a combination of Preferences settings and the use of the Processes menu.

Task: Adding the CPU Monitor to Your Menu Bar

I prefer putting a horizontal processor graph in my menu bar. To configure your system similarly, follow these steps:

1. Open the CPU Monitor application.
2. Choose Toggle Floating Window (Command+F) from the Processes menu to display the floating CPU usage window.
3. Open the application Preferences panel, and click the Floating View tab.
4. In the Display the View section, click the Horizontally radio button.
5. Close the Preferences panel.
6. Click and drag the floating processor graph onto your menu bar.

You can set the CPU Monitor to launch automatically upon login using the Login Items Preferences panel to set the CPU Monitor application to automatically launch when you log in.

By using the CPU Monitor Preferences panel, you can change the CPU graph's colors, its level of transparency, its position, and whether it's displayed as part of the Dock icon. The monitor helps keep track of your system's resources, and if you're using it as a server or to run software in the background, it lets you know whether you should consider upgrading your system's capacity.

Summary

In this hour, you learned about the utilities and applications that help you work with your system and analyze its performance. The Disk Utility enables you to control the storage devices connected to your machine, partition and erase volumes, and create RAID arrays. Disk Copy can create and work with disk images and even burn CDs. The other applications, System Profiler, Process Viewer, and CPU Monitor, provide feedback on the software installed on your computer, who is running it, and how much of your system resources are being consumed. If you find that you rarely need these utilities, that's great, but when you do, you'll be glad they're there!

Q&A

Q How is the CD-burning capability of Disk Copy different from the Finder?

A Disk Copy makes it simple to burn pre-existing images to a CD. The Finder is best for creating new disks from scratch.

Q How is the Process Viewer better than using the UNIX utility discussed earlier?

A It isn't—it simply offers a pretty user interface to the user commands ps, top, and kill. You're welcome to use whatever works best for you.

Workshop

The workshop contains quiz questions and activities to help you solidify your understanding of the material covered. Try to answer all questions before looking at the "Answers" section that follows.

Quiz

1. How do you run Disk Utility's First Aid on the disk you are currently logged in to?
2. Where are Disk Copy images mounted?
3. How can you force quit any process in Process Viewer?
4. What does the CPU monitor standard graph display?

Answers

1. You must boot from a CD when repairing your boot disk with Disk Utility. Insert your Mac OS X install CD into your CD drive and restart your Macintosh while holding down the C key.

2. Disk Copy mounts images in exactly the same place as other system volumes (/Volumes), and can be accessed from the Computer level of the Finder or, in most cases, your Desktop.

3. Only the root user can force quit any process that's currently running. If you're logged in to the system as root, you have the power; otherwise, you can control only your own processes.

4. The standard graph is a display of the average of the different types of system activity. It shows you how busy your system is at any given time.

Activities

1. Verify (and repair, if necessary) the storage devices connected to your computer.

2. Use System Profiler, Process Viewer, and CPU Monitor to explore your Mac OS X environment and processes. Get to know what normal is on your machine—it's the only way you'll ever know if your machine is behaving abnormally!

HOUR **23**

Security Considerations

Mac OS X is a powerful operating system, and with that power comes a new set of security risks. If you're connecting your computer to the Internet, it's necessary that you closely monitor your system as well as take preventive measures to guard against attack. My personal computer, which is connected to the world via cable modem, is attacked dozens of times a day. Keeping intruders out is the focus of this chapter. During this hour, you learn

- Steps to take to prevent local attacks on your machine
- How to examine your computer for unneeded network processes that might be running
- Ways to prevent network attacks from taking place

Mac OS X Security

Mac OS X presents a friendly and familiar face to the user, but as you discovered in Hour 20, "UNIX Command Line Tour," there's much going on behind the scenes. These hidden processes present the greatest risk to Mac

OS X security by creating potential openings for network attacks. To compound the issue, third-party software can install additional components that cannot be disabled through a convenient interface such as Mac OS 9's Extension Manager.

There are two steps to network security: figuring out what your machine is doing and disabling those things that you'd rather it *not* do. Neither of these tasks is as easy as it sounds because you must check a number of places before you can be sure that your machine is secure. The end result, however, is a Mac OS X computer that you can leave online without worrying about the consequences.

Network Services

Your Mac OS X computer has several built-in methods of sharing information over the Web, through network shares, FTP, and more. Each of these features relies on a special Mac OS X background application called a server daemon, or simply a *service*. As its name implies, a *service* provides additional functionality to the system. With network services, this functionality can be accessed remotely over a network connection. Therein lies the potential for a cracker to access and modify your computer, and is the primary source of our concern.

Each network service that runs on your computer requires a *port* that can be used to accept incoming connections. Think of network ports as power receptacles with multiple outlets. Connections to your computer are "plugged" in to the outlet, and then communications can begin. Mac OS X has the capability to accept a large number of incoming connections via many different ports.

To view the network services that are running on your computer, use the Network Utility's Port Scan function (located in /Applications/Utilities/Network Utility).

 You should *never* run a port scan on a computer that isn't yours or isn't on your network. This could be considered a network attack in and of itself.

1. Open the Network Utility application.

2. Click the Port Scan tab.

3. Enter the IP address of the computer to examine. For the computer that you're sitting in front of, type in `127.0.0.1`.

4. To scan for *all* open ports, make sure the Only Test Ports Between # and # check box is unchecked.

5. Click Scan to begin. The port scan will probably take a minute or two.

After the scan is finished, each port that's listed represents a network service on your machine. Figure 23.1 displays a completed scan.

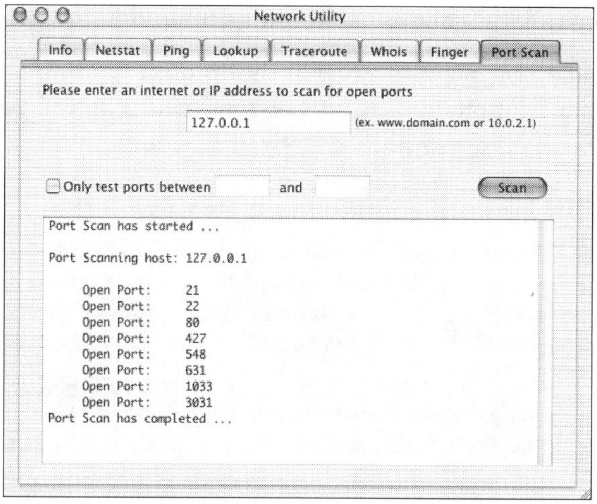

FIGURE 23.1

Network Utility's Port Scan function can reveal what services are running on your computer.

The biggest risk of having several network services active is that there could be a bug or backdoor. The Mac OS X architecture uses extremely complex open source applications to provide its network services. Improperly setting up one of these services, or failing to keep your system updated, could result in a user account being compromised and files being modified or deleted. Even worse, an intruder could take over your machine and use it to launch attacks on even more computers!

The traditional Mac OS used entirely proprietary software for providing its limited network services, effectively limiting the number of people capable of finding serious flaws in security. Although bugs were occasionally found, the effect of compromising a service was usually a system crash or maybe a changed file. The transition to a multiuser system puts far more control and tools in the hands of a potential attacker, and makes network security something that everyone should be concerned about.

Local Security

In addition to the added ability to compromise network services and gain control of the host machine, there are further implications of having a computer with BSD UNIX at its core.

Mac OS X is a true multiuser operating system. In Mac OS X, you have complete control over who can do what, but you must realize that exercising that control is essential if you intend to have a publicly accessed computer that doesn't self-destruct after one or two adventurous users decide to play around.

Depending on how you use your system, managing local security can be as simple as clicking a button or as complex as defining rules for what each user can run. Hour 20 provides an introduction to BSD file ownership and permissions. It's highly suggested reading for anyone wanting to implement local system security.

Attacks from within might not seem likely, but an unmanaged public computer can easily be turned into a powerful tool of attack—sometimes unintentionally.

Knowing Enough to Do Damage

When it comes to public computers, it's best to assume that your users know just enough to cause damage, both to themselves and to your computers. Limiting access to tools that can cause trouble is critical if you can't monitor your Mac OS X system 24 hours a day, 7 days a week.

For example, consider an event that occurred several years ago. As you read along, be aware that the computer being used had exactly the same tools as Mac OS X. A similar situation could easily occur on your Macintosh.

Two college students were engaged in an ongoing battle to outdo each other in filling each other's campus email boxes with pointless messages. One of the students worked at a large research firm that had powerful UNIX workstations on each desktop. Realizing the potential of the UNIX operating system for automating tasks, that student decided to create a simple shell script that would repeatedly send an email to the other student.

However, the student wasn't aware of the speed at which this script would be executed. He left it running for a few minutes, and then shut it off and left for home.

Unfortunately, those few minutes that the script ran were enough to queue up hundreds of thousands of messages on the company's email servers. The messages quickly ate up disk space and caused so many outgoing mail processes to be started that no other software could be started on the company servers.

At the same time, the university's computers were swamped with all the incoming mail. Within 30 minutes, all available disk space on the mail server was filled, and messages started to bounce. These bouncing messages were returned to the originating company's servers, adding to their already overloaded state.

Within half an hour, two extremely large mail servers were rendered useless, and a company with more than 900 employees was brought to a standstill.

Both students faced disciplinary action for the trouble they caused, and, as you might guess, the company whose computers were used in the prank was less than forgiving.

Although this incident happened almost 10 years ago, all the software required to replicate it is included in the basic version of Mac OS X. Given the increases in processing speed and network bandwidth made during that time, the danger that a single Mac OS X computer could cause even more damage is real.

Implementing Local System Security

23

Much of local system security is common sense coupled with a reasonable amount of watchfulness. Because implementing a local security policy is easier than maintaining network security, that's where we start.

Your first decision is what type of computer you're setting up.

If the machine is destined to be in a public library and serve as both a UNIX and a Macintosh workstation, your security considerations are far more complicated than if it sits at your desk and has only you as a user.

Let's take a look at a series of steps you can take to minimize the risks to your system. Some obviously don't apply to your particular circumstances, but they're worth noting regardless.

Create Only "Normal" Users

Many people aren't clear on what happens when you create a user in Mac OS X. Two types of user accounts can be created in the User Control panel: normal users and admin users. The only difference when setting up accounts is the presence of check box that reads Allow User to Administer This Computer.

Many systems that I've visited have had all the users set to be administrators. When asked why, the owners replied that they wanted everyone to be able to use the computer to its fullest. An understandable sentiment, but the implications of using this setting are enormous. A user who has this check box set can

- Add or delete users and their files
- Remove software installed in the systemwide Applications folder
- Change or completely remove network settings
- Activate or disable the Web service, FTP service, or SSH (secure shell)

Although it's unlikely that administrators could completely destroy the system (they aren't able to delete the System folder and files), they can make life difficult for others even if they don't mean to.

To add or remove administrative access from an existing user, follow these steps:

1. Open the System Preferences panel.

2. Click the Accounts item under the System section.

3. Double-click the name of the user to edit, or select the name and click Edit User.

4. A sheet showing the administrative check box you're looking for appears. It's shown in Figure 23.2.

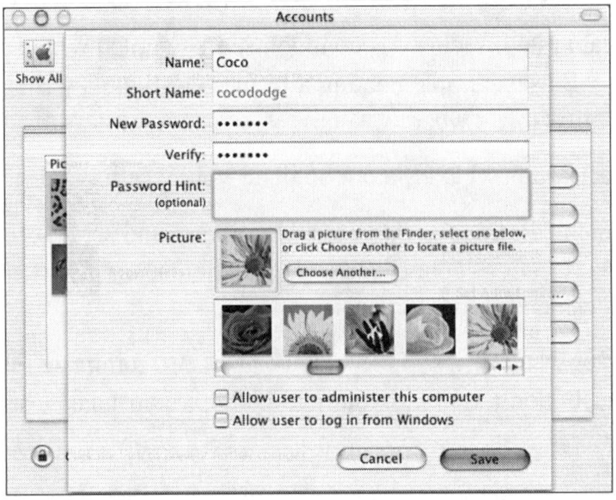

FIGURE 23.2

Create as few administrative users as possible.

5. Uncheck Allow User to Administer This Computer to remove administrative access.

6. Click Save to save to apply the changes.

If your computer has only a few accounts for people you know, this security precaution is probably the only one you need. However, if you want your system to be a bit more impenetrable, keep reading.

Removing BSD Support

Underneath all the shine of Aqua is the Berkeley Software Distribution (BSD) subsystem, which you learned about in Hour 20. It has several tools for users that could potentially be used to launch attacks or write scripts that eat up system resources behind the scenes.

If you're setting up the system to work only as a Macintosh workstation, there's no need to have the BSD subsystem active because most common applications don't require it. Although you can't remove the subsystem after the operating system has been installed, you can prevent it from being added when you install Mac OS X.

Removing the BSD subsystem won't disable common Mac applications such
as Microsoft Word or Adobe Illustrator. It affects only software based on the
UNIX system.

To remove BSD support from the system, click the Customize button when installing
Mac OS X, uncheck the BSD Subsystem check box, and then click Install to continue.
Learn more about the installation procedure in Appendix A, "Installing Mac OS X."

It is true that most applications, such as Microsoft Office or Appleworks,
don't require the BSD subsystem, but a few hybrid applications might need
the added functionality.

As developers start to embrace the many faces of Mac OS X, they might
develop applications that rely on the BSD subsystem in addition to the more
traditional Macintosh toolbox routines. Keep this in mind when deciding
whether to remove BSD.

Disabling Shell Access

Removing the ability to access a shell for all users except the administrative users is a
good way to keep the power of UNIX available for yourself while securing your system's
"innards" from less experienced users.

To access your system's command line, you must run the Terminal application. In turn,
the Terminal application launches one of the available shells on the system, which
processes commands. The easiest way to prohibit users from accessing the command line
through the Terminal application or a remote ssh-login session is to change the permissions of the Mac OS X shells so that they can be run only by administrative users.

If you've logged in as an administrative user, follow these steps:

1. Open a Terminal window.

2. At the prompt, type **cd /bin** and press Return to change to the bin directory, which
   contains all the shells.

3. Type **sudo chmod o-x *sh** and press Return. Enter your password when
   prompted.

4. Close the Terminal window.

The effect of this command is to remove execute permissions for all but administrators
from the shell files in the /bin directory.

To test the change, try logging into a nonadministrative account, and then attempt to open the Terminal application. The application starts, but immediately stops upon trying to display a command prompt. Your window should look similar to Figure 23.3.

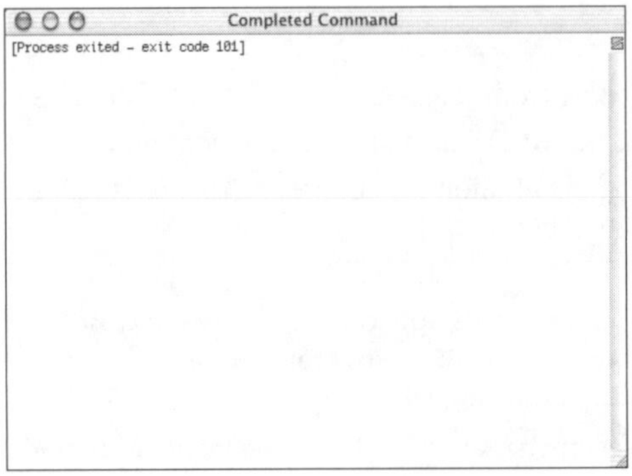

FIGURE 23.3

Removing access to the system shells is a good way to prevent mischief.

Similarly, attempting to log in to the system via SSH immediately closes the connection and displays the following:

```
[localhost:/bin] jray% slogin -ltest macosx.mytestmachine.com
test@localhost's password:
Welcome to Darwin!
Connection to localhost closed.
```

Finally, let's take a look at a few other settings you'll want to make on a publicly accessible system.

Disable Hints and Names

It's obvious that Apple wanted to create a system that would be friendly and accessible for any level of user. In doing so, it also set a few defaults that make it easy for a public system to be "cracked" by a persistent attacker with direct access to the machine.

There are two options to consider if you plan to place your computer in a public area without strict monitoring:

- **Password Hints**—By default, Mac OS X displays a hint for a password if the user fails to correctly enter it three times in a row. It's easy enough to just not enter password hints, but it's safer to disable the feature globally.

- **Login Window Names**—Another default setting—the capability to display icons for each user account on the machine and require only a click to start the login process—is nice, but it also gives away part of the system's security. Attackers usually need both a username *and* a password to log in to a machine. If the usernames are prominently displayed, attackers are already halfway to their goal.

Both of these risky features are disabled from the Login Preferences panel. To shut off both features, follow these steps:

1. Open System Preferences.

2. Click the Accounts button in the System section.

3. Choose the Login Options tab.

4. Click the Display Login Window as Name and Password radio button to select it.

5. Uncheck the Show Password Hint After 3 Attempts to Enter a Password check box.

6. When you're finished, the Login Options panel should resemble Figure 23.4. Close the panel to save the settings.

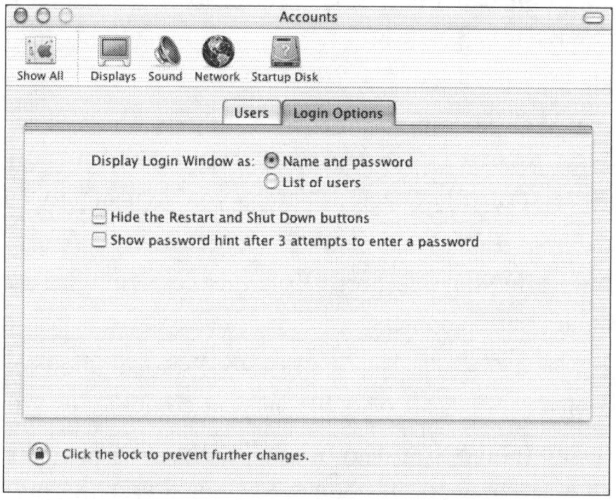

FIGURE 23.4
Disable password hints and change to a simple username/password login window.

Maintaining Security Online

When your computer is connected to the Internet via a direct connection to a cable modem or DSL line, it can be a direct target for attack from outside. The more network services that are running, the greater the chance that a potential intruder can discover and compromise your system.

You must also consider that Mac OS X makes it easy for a user to accidentally install new network services without even knowing they're running. Earlier in the hour, you saw how to use the Port Scan feature of Network Utility to find out what services are running on a computer. Now let's find out what network services are and what you should do about them.

Network Sharing Services

Your first concern should be the network services that Apple included with your system. Although it's tempting to go through your system and activate every feature, doing so isn't always a good idea. If you turn on *everything* in the Sharing Preferences panel (see Hour 13, "Using Network Sharing"), a port scan of your system would show the following services active:

- **FTP Access** (port 20 or 21)—FTP is a quick and easy way to send and retrieve files from a computer. FTP Sharing starts an FTP server on your computer. Unfortunately, it provides no password encryption and is often targeted by attackers. If you don't have to use FTP, don't enable it.

- **Remote Login—ssh**(port 22)—The secure shell enables remote users to connect to your computer and control it from the command line. It's a useful tool for servers, but only presents a security risk to home users.

- **Personal Web Sharing** (port 80)—Your personal Web server is really an enterprise-class Apache server. Apache is a very stable program and should be considered the least of your concerns, unless you've manually customized its configuration files.

- **Windows File Sharing** (port 139)—Enables Windows users to access the shared folders on your computers.

- **svrloc** (port 427)—The Service Locator Protocol allows remote computers to detect what services areavailable on your computer over the Internet.

- **afpovertcp** (port 548)—The Apple File Protocol is used to share your disks and folders over a network. If you have Personal File Sharing turned on, be aware that potentially anyone on the Internet can connect to your computer.

- **Printer Sharing** (port 631)—Enables other users on the network to use printers connected to your computer.

- **ppc** (port 3031)—Program-to-program communication enables remote applications to connect to your computer and send it commands. It's unlikely that you would need this feature in day-to-day use. PPC is controlled by the Remote Apple Events setting in the Sharing Preferences panel.

If your list doesn't quite match up with this, there are two possibilities. If your list shows fewer ports active, that's great! You don't have everything turned on, and your system is more secure. If, however, you see additional ports open, it could mean that software you've installed has added its own network services.

To disable any of these built-in network services, follow these steps:

1. Open the System Preferences panel.

2. Click the Sharing item under the Internet & Network section.

3. In the Services tab, uncheck the boxes for the listed services to toggle them on and off, as shown in Figure 23.5.

FIGURE 23.5

The Sharing Preferences panel controls the built-in network services.

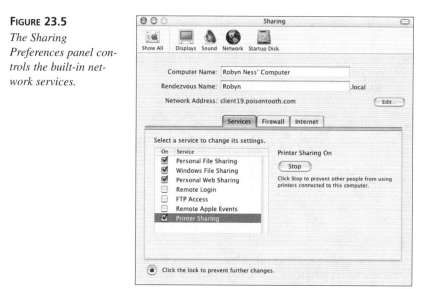

4. Close the Sharing Preferences panel to save your settings.

As you shut off these services, use Network Utility to run a port scan on your computer. With each service that you shut off in the Sharing Preferences panel, the corresponding service disappears from the port scan results.

Unfortunately, this procedure covers only the network services that are controlled in the System Preferences. So what do you do if you see other services that are running? Well, that's where things become complicated, and that problem is what we're going to address for the rest of the hour.

Finding and Shutting Down Installed Services

As you install software on your Mac OS X computer, you might notice new messages on your screen telling you about features that have been added to the system. Where do you look to find these additions in Mac OS X? Unfortunately, there's no one place to look!

The StartupItems Folder

The best place to start is the folder /Library/StartupItems. This is the location where Apple asks third-party developers to add new startup items. A folder containing several files that tell the machine how to use the new features represents each service that has been added to the system. To disable a service, just move the corresponding service folder out of the StartupItems folder.

For example, I installed a database server on my system called MySQL. In my StartupItems folder, there's a MySQL folder. All I have to do to disable the service is drag the MySQL folder somewhere else. I created a DisabledStartupItems folder in the Library folder to hold the services that I disabled.

 If you don't have any additional services on your computer, you might not even have a /Library/StartupItems folder. This isn't unusual, so don't worry!

To have your changes take effect, simply reboot your computer.

Inetd Services

Unfortunately, not all services are installed in the StartupItems folder. There is a special type of network service that's started only when it's needed, not when your machine boots. It's a special type of UNIX service called an inetd process.

The only default Mac OS X network service that is an inetd service is FTP, but again, software you install could add new services. It's important that you understand how to disable them. To see what services you have running and to get ready to disable them, follow these steps:

1. Open the TextEdit application.
2. Choose Open from the File menu, type **/etc/inetd.conf** in the Go To field, as shown in Figure 23.6, and then click the Open button.
3. A list of inetd processes is displayed.

The contents of this file might seem a bit confusing, but don't worry—you don't need to understand the format to shut down unneeded network features. For example, here is a portion of the inetd.conf file:

```
#
# Internet server configuration database
#
#    @(#)inetd.conf    5.4 (Berkeley) 6/30/90
#
```

```
# Items with double hashes in front (##) are not yet implemented in the OS.
#
#finger   stream   tcp   nowait   nobody   /usr/libe XEc/tcpd   fingerd -s
ftp        stream   tcp   nowait   root     /usr/libe XEc/tcpd   ftpd -1
#login    stream   tcp   nowait   root     /usr/libe XEc/tcpd   rlogind
#nntp     stream   tcp   nowait   usenet   /usr/libe XEc/tcpd   nntpd
#ntalk    dgram    udp   wait     root     /usr/libe XEc/tcpd   ntalkd
#shell    stream   tcp   nowait   root     /usr/libe XEc/tcpd   rshd
```

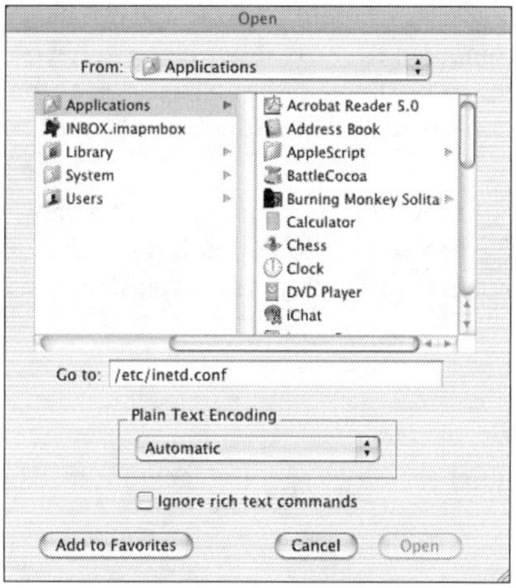

FIGURE 23.6

*Open the
/etc/inetd.conf file
to display your inetd
processes.*

Each line defines a network service that could potentially be running on your system.
The first word in the line is the name of the service. The lines that begin with a pound
sign (#) are disabled.

In this sample section of the file, the only available service is FTP. To disable it, all you
need to do is put a # in front of the line you want to disable, and then save the file. The
next time your computer reboots, the disabled service isn't available!

> If you pay attention to the software you install and what its intended pur-
> pose is, you won't need to search through your system to shut down security
> holes.
>
> If, however, you aren't the only administrative user of your system, or have
> inherited the computer from someone else, it's a good idea to poke around
> to make sure that everything's in order.

Firewalls

The "ultimate" solution to network security is the use of a *firewall*, a piece of hardware or software that sits between your computer and the Internet. As network traffic comes into the computer, the firewall looks at each piece of information, determines whether it's acceptable, and, if necessary, keeps the data from getting to your machine.

You might be asking yourself, "If a firewall can be a piece of software that runs on my computer, how can it both look at network traffic *and* keep it from reaching my machine?" After all, to look at the information and determine whether it's trouble, the data obviously must have reached my computer!

That's true, but firewall software operates at a very low level, intercepting network traffic before your computer has a chance to process it and make it available to components such as your Web server or FTP server.

Software Firewalls

A software firewall is the quickest way to get unwanted traffic blocked from your machine.

If you're adventurous, Mac OS X has built-in BSD firewall software that can be accessed from the command line. Although they offer more flexibility, firewalls run from the command line can be extremely complicated, and, if improperly used, can seriously damage your operating system. For more information on creating UNIX firewalls by hand, I suggest reading *Mac OS X Unleashed*.

Mac OS X 10.2 includes a built-in personal firewall, accessible from the Firewall tab of the System Preferences Sharing panel shown in Figure 23.7.

To activate the firewall, click the Start button. Checked boxes appear next to those services/ports that you've turned on under the Services pane of the Sharing Preferences panel.

Other than starting or stopping your personal firewall, there are no other settings to configure in the Firewall panel. Because disabling a port disables its service and unenabled ports require no securing, you must go to the Services panel to change the status of the services in the Firewall panel.

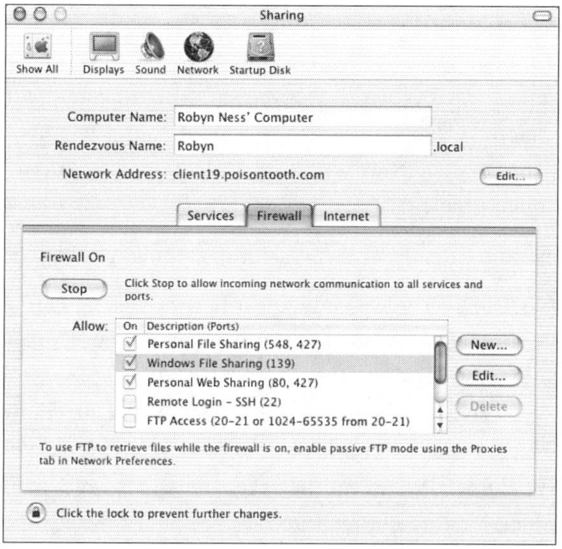

FIGURE 23.7
The Mac OS X personal firewall can be enabled to secure the services/port you don't want to operate.

23

If you need more flexibility, there are several other firewall builder packages that make it easy to point-and-click your way through setting up a firewall on your computer. Most of these programs simply ask you a series of questions, and then set up the firewall rules for you. Here are a few to consider:

- **Symantec Norton Personal Firewall**
  (`http://www.symantec.com/consumer_products/home-mac.html`)—Created as a consumer product, the Norton Personal Firewall is very user-friendly, easy to use, and recommended for those who aren't interested in controlling every aspect of their network security.

- **BrickHouse** (`http://personalpages.tds.net/~brian_hill/`)—BrickHouse is an excellent piece of shareware developed by Brian Hill for Mac OS X. Its easy-to-use wizard can help novices get up and running quickly, yet it offers advanced configuration features for those who need it.

- **Firewalk X** (`http://www.pliris-soft.com/products/firewalkx/index.html`)—Another shareware utility, Firewalk X is a very comprehensive solution, but is best handled by those with networking experience.

These software packages use the same firewall tool, ipfw, which is used to configure firewalls from the command line, so you're essentially choosing the best interface for your needs.

Hardware Firewalls

A growing number of network hardware appliances can virtually eliminate the threat of attack by making your computer unreachable from the Internet. Costing roughly $100–$200, these devices are well worth considering if you plan to be online frequently. Although slightly more expensive than a software-only solution, they provide a worry-free answer to the problem of network security!

Here are a few Mac-friendly firewall solutions you might be interested in checking out:

- **Apple AirPort**—The Apple wireless network server can make an effective firewall when configured with the option to Share a Single IP Address Using DHCP (Dynamic Host Configuration Protocol) and NAT (Network Address Translation). Although more expensive than other options, it's an extremely Mac-friendly solution and a great way to gain security and go wireless at the same time.

- **LinkSys Cable/DSL Routers** (`http://www.linksys.com`)—Largely responsible for creating the first mass-produced personal firewall, LinkSys has a variety of different options available for home users. LinkSys offers both traditional wired and wireless products. I use a LinkSys with my home systems and couldn't be happier.

- **D-Link Broadband Routers** (`http://www.dlink.com`)—Much like the LinkSys routers, the D-Link offerings are available in wired and wireless configurations and feature easy Web configuration and an attractive price point.

> As you shop for a hardware firewall, you might notice that many of the devices you see are advertised as routers. A *router* is simply a generic term for a network device that moves network information from one place to another. For your personal system, it routes information from your computer to the Internet and vice versa.
>
> It's during the process of routing data that the device also performs its firewall activity.

The biggest drawback to using a personal hardware firewall is that if you run a Web server (or other processes that enables people to connect to your machine over the Internet), you must specially configure the firewall to let requests pass through to your computer. This isn't usually difficult, but it requires more than simply plugging it in and having it work.

Summary

Mac OS X security presents several challenges for Mac users. Its underlying BSD UNIX subsystem makes it an extremely attractive target for network crackers as well as any unscrupulous person who might have access to the system. In this hour, you learned several ways to help protect your system from both local and network attacks by limiting access to critical features and shutting off network services that you might not need. The topic of security is extremely broad, so this hour should be considered a start to implementing a secure computer—not an end-all guide.

As we finish our 24 hours together in Hour 24, "Maintenance and Troubleshooting," you'll learn how to prepare for the worst and recover with grace.

23

Q&A

Q Do I really need to worry about local security with my family computer?

A With Mac OS X, yes! The UNIX system, although a wonderful tool, is very unforgiving. Typing `rm -r *` from the wrong place can quickly erase your entire system without any warning. Even experienced UNIX users occasionally slip up and type something they shouldn't. Although I encourage you to get your family interested in the system, be sure everyone understands the consequences of the command line!

Q How can I check for attack attempts?

A Many of the network firewall packages mentioned in this hour can log attempts to attack your system. In addition, you can keep an eye on the `/var/log/system.log` and `/var/log/secure.log` files to see whether there are any login attempts that have failed. To reach them, select Go To File from the Finder's Go menu and type `/var/log/`.

Workshop

The workshop contains quiz questions and activities to help you solidify your understanding of the material covered. Try to answer all questions before looking at the "Answers" section that follows.

Quiz

1. Why is showing a list of usernames at login dangerous?
2. How are password hints disabled?

3. What's a network service? What's a port?

4. What are the two common places to check for added network services that might be on your system?

Answers

1. It gives potential crackers half the information they need to log into the system. Most UNIX computers (like Mac OS X) require a username and password to log in. With a list of users displayed, crackers need to guess only one piece of information.

2. Disable password hints in the Login Options tab of the Accounts Preferences panel.

3. A network service listens at a port on your computer for requests for information. A Web server, for example, listens for requests for Web pages on port 80.

4. Services that activate when your machine boots are added to /Library/StartupItems, but on-demand services are activated through the /etc/inetd.conf configuration file.

Activities

1. Configure your system's local and network security. If you've enabled network features you don't need, disable them now. If you're using a computer you didn't originally set up, check it to verify what services are running.

2. Run the Network Utility Port Scan feature to check the active services on your computer; shut off those you don't need. Note: You should *never* run a port scan on a computer that isn't yours or isn't on your network. This could be considered a network attack in and of itself.

Hour **24**

Maintenance and Troubleshooting

In the final hour of this book, you learn some maintenance and troubleshooting tips that will help keep your computer running smoothly. As a Macintosh system administrator, I've seen many users who work for years without ever updating their computers. With Mac OS X, this might not be possible. Apple frequently releases critical security updates and patches that should be installed quickly. In this hour, you learn a variety of maintenance and preventive procedures, including

- Using the automated Apple system updates
- How to boot into verbose or single-user modes
- What to do if you forget a system password
- Where you can find state-of-the-art Macintosh virus scanning utilities

Automating Software Updates

To keep your system secure and functioning at its best, you should make frequent use of Apple's automatic software updates. This utility automatically connects to Apple's site, and then downloads and installs fixes and enhancements to your computer. With Mac OS X, it's important to maintain the most up-to-date system; the updates could (and have) include critical security fixes for the OS.

Mac OS X automates the process of upgrading software through the Software Update Preferences panel, shown in Figure 24.1.

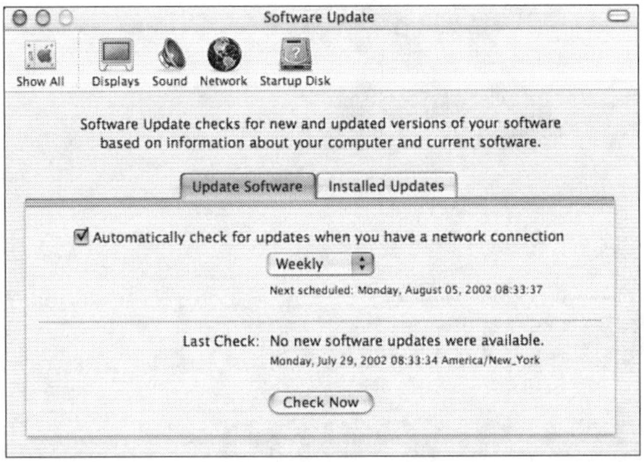

FIGURE 24.1

The Software Update Preferences panel controls automatic system updates.

Software Update

Show All   Displays   Sound   Network   Startup Disk

Software Update checks for new and updated versions of your software based on information about your computer and current software.

Update Software | Installed Updates

☑ Automatically check for updates when you have a network connection

Weekly ⬍

Next scheduled: Monday, August 05, 2002 08:33:37

Last Check: No new software updates were available.
Monday, July 29, 2002 08:33:34 America/New_York

(Check Now)

Click the Update Software tab, then use the radio buttons to choose whether to run the Software Update application automatically or start it manually. I highly recommend setting an automatic schedule so that you don't have to remember to upgrade your machine. To automate updates, follow these steps:

1. Click the Automatically Check for Updates When You Have a Network Connection check box.

2. Use the pop-up menu to choose daily, weekly, or monthly updates. The Weekly option should be sufficient for most users. Server operators might want to choose Daily just to stay on top of any critical patches.

3. Close the Software Update Preferences panel, or click the Check Now button to force your first update to take place.

An automatic update doesn't install the software it finds without asking you. It prompts you to verify the installation before it proceeds.

When an update takes place, your Mac OS X computer contacts Apple, detects available software packages, and displays a list of the different components that need to be updated. Click the check box in front of each package that you want to download, and then click Install to start the process. You're prompted for an administrator password before continuing.

> Sometimes the list of updates includes features you don't need or want, such as printer drivers for foreign languages. Although not checking the box for those items prevents them from being installed, they continue to show up in your Software Updates window unless you choose Make Inactive from the Update menu. If you ever change your mind, you can choose Show Inactive Updates and Make Active from the Update menu to allow the system to perform the update.

During the download, the system displays a status bar in the same window that you used to choose the package to update. Depending on the software package, you might see a license agreement at some point during the installation. In addition, the install process is likely to pause for a *very* long time while it optimizes your installed packages. This is completely normal, albeit slightly annoying.

When the update is finished, the Software Update application might prompt you to restart your system.

Backing Up Your Data

Although keeping a secure and updated operating system is important, it's perhaps less so than maintaining an archive of your important applications and data. Several manufacturers offer software to assist with backing up data. For extremely critical data of limited size, however, I recommend using the Mac OS X CD-burning capabilities discussed in Hour 2, "Using the Finder and Dock."

> The UNIX users out there are probably scratching their heads, asking, "What about utilities such as tar?" Although tar is a perfectly good solution for Mac OS X installations based on the UNIX File System (UFS), or UNIX and Cocoa applications based on HFS+, it's *not* suitable for Classic or Carbon applications. Their dependency on the HFS+ resource fork severely limits what software can be used to back them up.

Many Mac OS files are really made up of two files: the resource fork and the data fork. The resource fork contains images, window layouts, and so on, whereas the data fork contains the "meat" of the file. Unfortunately, these two forks are inseparable, and both must be present for the file to work properly. Most UNIX utilities see only the data fork, and if it's used to work with these types of Mac files, it creates corrupt versions of the files.

Let's take a look at some of the backup software that's available for Mac OS X.

Retrospect

Retrospect is by far the most powerful backup solution for Mac OS X. It features the capability to back up and restore to Windows and Macintosh systems over a network using a small Retrospect client application, store backups on FTP servers, and more. Figure 24.2 displays Retrospect Backup 5.0 for Mac OS X.

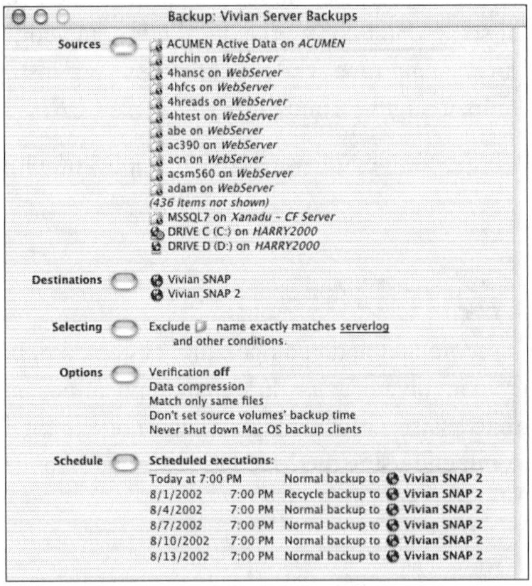

FIGURE 24.2

Retrospect for Mac OS X is the best full-service backup solution available.

Retrospect Backup clients can be installed on any Mac OS X computer and accessed via Retrospect 5.0 Server, running on your main Mac OS X system.

From a master Retrospect server, the system administrator can locate the Mac OS X client, select the files to back up, and store them on a variety of media, including CD-RW, digital audio tape (DAT), and Internet storage sites. Backups can be scripted for automatic execution or can be run at any time with the click of a mouse. Restoring files from a backup is a simple point-and-click operation that automatically copies files from the source media back to the client.

Administrators of mixed-platform networks will be happy to find that Retrospect clients are available for older Mac systems as well as Windows. You can find out more about Retrospect Backup and buy/download the Retrospect Mac OS X client from www.dantz.com/.

Other Backup/Sync Tools

Here are some other recommended synchronization and backup utilities

- **Backup**, from Apple, is available to .Mac members to back document files up to an iDisk or to help burn them to CD or DVD (http://www.mac.com/1/iTour/tour_backup.html).
- **Carbon Copy Cloner**, from Bombich Software, uses the power of AppleScript to back up any file on the system (http://www.bombich.com/software/ccc.html).

Diagnostics

With a complex operating system such as Mac OS X, things can sometimes go wrong, and you're left with little recourse for solving the problem. Operations such as repairing damaged Mac OS X installations, resetting the root password, and fixing damaged disks can all be performed even if your machine isn't booting into the operating system properly.

Safe Boot

Mac OS X 10.2 .introduces Safe Boot mode in Mac OS X (or, rather, brings back a feature from Mac OS 8 and 9). By holding down the Shift key while starting up your Mac, you bypass loading any additional software other than what's absolutely necessary to get your system running. This is an excellent way to start a computer that isn't functioning properly and remove software that might be conflicting with the operating system.

Verbose Boot

When Mac OS X starts, dozens of support processes and drivers are loaded at the same time. If something fails, it's left to the user's imagination to guess exactly what has gone wrong. In many cases, users might not even be aware that there are problems with the system configuration because the boot process hides behind a very simple GUI startup screen.

To view *exactly* what's happening as the Mac OS X system boots, you can hold down Command+V at powerup to force a verbose startup. A verbose boot displays all status and error messages while the computer starts. This can be a bit startling to many Mac users because instead of the usual blue or gray background seen during startup, the screen is black and filled with text. Windows and Linux users will feel right at home.

The startup messages can be seen after booting by typing **dmesg**, and then viewing the /var/log/system.log file:

```
Jun 29 17:30:30 localhost mach_kernel: .Display_RADEON: i2cPower 1
Jun 29 17:30:30 localhost mach_kernel: .Display_RADEON:
➥user ranges num:1 start:9c008000 size:640080
Jun 29 17:30:30 localhost mach_kernel: .Display_RADEON:
➥using (1600x1024@0Hz,32 bpp)
Jun 29 17:30:30 localhost mach_kernel: AirPortDriver:
➥Ethernet address 00:30:65:11:37:15
Jun 29 17:30:30 localhost mach_kernel: ether_ifattach called for en
Jun 29 17:30:30 localhost mach_kernel: kmod_create:
➥com.apple.nke.ppp (id 58), 6 pages loaded at 0xc27a000, header size 0x1000
Jun 29 17:30:30 localhost mach_kernel: kmod_create:
➥ com.apple.nke.SharedIP (id 59), 5 pages loaded at 0xc28d000, header size
0x1000
Jun 29 17:30:30 localhost mach_kernel: kmod_create:
➥IPFirewall (id 60), 5 pages loaded at 0xc292000, header size 0x1000
Jun 29 17:30:30 localhost mach_kernel: ipfw_load
Jun 29 17:30:30 localhost mach_kernel:
➥IP packet filtering initialized, divert enabled, rule-based forwarding
➥enabled, default to accept, logging disabled
Jun 29 17:30:31 localhost sharity[161]: [0] Sharity daemon version 2.4 started
Jun 29 17:30:39 localhost ntpdate[204]:
➥ntpdate 4.0.95 Sat Feb 17 02:38:39 PST 2001 (1)
Jun 29 17:30:43 localhost ntpdate[204]:
➥no server suitable for synchronization found
Jun 29 17:30:43 localhost ntpd[206]:
➥ntpd 4.0.95 Thu Apr 26 13:40:11 PDT 2001 (1)
Jun 29 17:30:43 localhost ntpd[206]: precision = 7 usec
Jun 29 17:30:43 localhost ntpd[206]:
➥frequency initialized 0.000 from /var/run/ntp.drift
Jun 29 17:30:43 localhost ntpd[206]: server 128.146.1.7 minpoll 12 maxpoll 17
```

This small sample of the verbose output shows the Apple Radeon driver loading, followed by the AirPort software, Classic SharedIP driver, firewall, Sharity, and NTP (network time protocol) software.

Interestingly enough, in capturing this example, I ascertained what I had suspected for several weeks: The ntpdate utility, which is responsible for automatically contacting a remote time server for synchronization, has been failing:

```
Jun 29 17:30:39 localhost ntpdate[204]:
➥ntpdate 4.0.95 Sat Feb 17 02:38:39 PST 2001 (1)
Jun 29 17:30:43 localhost ntpdate[204]:
➥no server suitable for synchronization found
```

Similar .feedback is provided for almost all the services on the computer. If your computer hangs during boot, you can use the verbose startup mode to determine exactly where the sequence has gone amiss.

Single-User Mode

Another interesting modification to the startup process is booting into single-user mode. Holding down Command+S starts Mac OS X in single-user mode, enabling an administrator to directly access the system through a command-line interface. This is a last-resort method of booting your computer that should be used only if absolutely necessary.

Single-user mode boots in a text-only fashion, just like verbose startup mode. The process finishes by dropping the user into a shell:

```
Singleuser boot -- fsck not done
Root device is mounted read-only
If you want to make modifications to files,
run '/sbin/fsck -y' first and them '/sbin/mount -uw /'
localhost#
```

Be aware that the single-user mode command prompt carries with it full root access. This is not a place for playing games or learning UNIX.

The `fsck` Command

Using the `fsck` command, you can repair local file systems from the command line. To fix a damaged file system, type **`fsck -y`** at the single-user prompt. This is equivalent to running the First Aid Disk utility:

```
localhost# fsck -y
** /dev/rdisk0s9
** Root file system
** Checking HFS Plus volume
** Checking Extents Overflow file.
** Checking Catalog file.
** Checking multi-linked files.
** Checking Catalog heirarchy.
** Checking volume bitmap.
** Checking volume information.
** The volume Rmac OS XS appears to be OK.
```

24

If an error occurs during this process, you might have to tell the system that it's okay to perform repairs by following the command-line prompts.

If you find yourself in this situation, I highly recommend that you boot from the installer CD and launch Disk Utility as discussed in Hour 22, "System Utilities and Monitors," or use a third-party application to try to repair your drive.

> When booted into single-user mode, the Mac OS X file system is mounted read-only as a precaution. If you've installed a new daemon or script that's stalling the system at startup, it would be useful to be able to edit files in single-user mode. To mount the file system with write permissions, use `/sbin/mount -uw /`.

Commercial Repair Tools

At the time of this writing, two disk repair utilities are available under Mac OS X: Norton Utilities 7 from Symantec and Drive 10 from Micromat. However, because Mac OS X uses the same default file system as Mac OS 9, you can also use utilities such as TechTool Pro that were written for Mac OS 9.

- **Norton Utilities** by Symantec, Inc. (`www.symantec.com/product/home-mac.html`) is the oldest and best-known Macintosh repair software available. NU focuses entirely on drive repair, optimization, and data loss prevention.

- **Drive 10** by Micromat Inc. (`www.micromat.com/drive10.html`) offers extensive disk diagnostic utilities, ranging from power supply tests to buffer validation. Unfortunately, it's lacking several of the more useful features—such as more generalized system diagnostics—of its big brother, TechTool Pro.

- **TechTool Pro** by Micromat Inc. (`www.micromat.com/techTool_Pro3`) is the undisputed king of systemwide diagnostics. Although this application hasn't yet been made available to run under Mac OS X, it can be run under the Classic environment. TechTool Pro can locate problems with almost any hardware component, from memory to CPU failures. It also includes extensive drive repair and optimization facilities.

It's been my experience that TechTool Pro and Norton Utilities can be used with one another to successfully diagnose and solve problems that neither can handle alone. Drive 10, although effective as a complete disk drive diagnostic tool, doesn't offer as complete a package as the non-native TechTool Pro.

Reinstall

Most Windows users are familiar with the word *reinstall*. I've listened in on many support calls, only to hear the technician give up and tell the end user to reinstall. Unfortunately, Mac OS X users might find themselves doing the same thing. The difference, however, is that reinstalling Mac OS X *does not* replace your system accounts, information, or configuration.

I've found on numerous occasions that rerunning the Mac OS X installer is the fastest and easiest way to return to a viable system. There are, however, a few drawbacks—most notably, the system updates are replaced by the original version of the operating system. After running the Mac OS X Installer to recover a damaged system, you must force an update on your computer by going to Software Update and clicking the Check Now button.

Another anomaly is that if you've moved or removed any of the system-installed applications, they're restored during the install process.

Restoring the Administrator Password

If the Mac OS X administrator password is forgotten or misplaced, Apple provides a facility for restoring a password. Boot your computer from the Mac OS X install CD (hold down the C key while turning your computer on with the CD in the CD-ROM drive). When the Installer application starts, choose Reset Password from the Installer application menu. Figure 24.3 shows the interface to the Password Reset facility.

FIGURE 24.3

Use the boot CD and Password Reset application to ease your forgetful head.

Detected Mac OS X volumes are listed along the top of the window. To reset a password, follow these steps:

1. Click the main boot drive to load the password database for that volume.

2. Next, use the pop-up menu to choose the user account that you want to reset.

3. Fill in the new password in both of the password fields.

4. Finally, click Save to store the new password.

After rebooting your system, you can immediately log in with the new password.

Viruses

Few, if any, viruses affect Mac OS X. Unfortunately, this doesn't mean that viruses that affect it can't, or won't, be created—it's better to be safe than sorry.

There are two popular consumer virus scanners that you might want to check out: Symantec Norton AntiVirus and NAI's Virex scanner (marketed by McAfee). The Symantec offering caters to the traditional Macintosh user; it's easy to use and simple to update. Find out more at `http://www.symantec.com/nav/nav_mac/`.

Virex (`http://www.mcafeeb2b.com/products/virex/default.asp`), although not quite as easy to use as Norton AntiVirus, has several advanced features that make it attractive. Virex enables you to update the virus definitions whenever a threat appears by using the standard `.dat` virus definition files used on other UNIX and Windows systems. This means that even the most recent Word macro viruses can be stopped using Virex, just as they can on other platforms. Virex receives the added endorsement of Apple offering it for download to paying members of its .Mac web service (refer to Hour 10, "Web Browsing and .Mac," for more information). The Virex scanner GUI is shown in Figure 24.4.

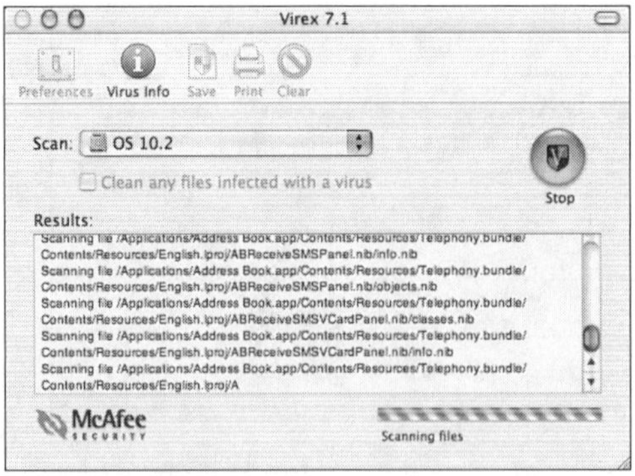

FIGURE 24.4

The Virex scanner features an easy to use GUI.

Regardless of which product you choose, I highly recommend that you *do* purchase a virus-scanning utility for Mac OS X. There has never been an operating system that brings so much desktop and command-line power to the user, and you can bet that nefarious individuals are just waiting to take advantage of it!

Summary

Mac OS X gives you a great deal of flexibility, but it also requires more responsibility to run. To successfully keep your computer running smoothly and safely, you must stay current with system patches, create backups, and be prepared to diagnose potential problems by using techniques you've never had to use in earlier versions of the OS. Throughout the book, we've tried to give you the tips and techniques necessary to best use the computer. If you have any comments, questions, or suggestions, don't hesitate to email us at

johnray@mac.com

robynness@mac.com

Thanks for reading!

Q&A

Q Why can't I just drag the Mac OS X folders to another drive to copy the system?

A Dragging the visible folders and files to another volume wouldn't copy many of the critical hidden files necessary to operate your computer.

Q Is single-user mode the same as opening a Terminal window?

A Not exactly. Although it does give you access to the command line, it also gives you root access to the command line. Therefore, it's potentially far more dangerous than just opening a Terminal prompt.

Q Is it really necessary to purchase a third-party disk utility?

A Yes, Apple's built-in utilities cannot (and won't) fix all drive problems. I highly recommend Micromat's Drive 10 utility as a comprehensive disk solution.

Workshop

The workshop contains quiz questions and activities to help you solidify your understanding of the material covered. Try to answer all questions before looking at the "Answers" section that follows.

24

Quiz

1. How often should you schedule automatic updates?

2. Can a forgotten password be restored?

3. What are the advantages of the Virex virus-scanning software?

Answers

1. There is no right answer. I recommend the Weekly option for ordinary users and Daily for server operators.

2. Yes, by using the Reset Password utility on your Mac OS X installer CD.

3. Virex features command-line tools and can use industry-standard .dat files to gain access to the most recent virus definitions.

Activities

1. Configure your system's software update schedule and force a manual update. Install any recommended updates that might appear.

2. If possible, invest in a good backup solution and a virus scanner. Be sure to read the product information for each of the programs before buying. This hour contained my personal recommendations, but you might find that alternative packages better suit your needs.

3. Enjoy using Mac OS X.

PART VI
Appendices

Appendix

APPENDIX **A**

Installing Mac OS X

Mac OS X System Requirements

This appendix guides you through the basics of installing Mac OS X as well as a version of Mac OS 9.

Wait a minute! Why would you install Mac OS 9 after buying this book on Mac OS X? To put it simply, your computer can have *both* operating systems. Because Apple realized that the software its longtime users have come to know and love might not be available immediately in Mac OS X–compatible versions, Mac OS X was specially designed to cooperate with the "classic" Mac OS, versions 9.1 and up. More about running Classic applications is available in Appendix B, "Running Classic Applications."

The first thing you must do is make sure that your system can handle Mac OS X.

The system requirements for Mac OS X are higher than previous versions of the Mac OS. According to Apple, Mac OS X runs on all original G4 computers, all iBooks and iMacs (including the Bondi 233), all PowerBooks (except the original Powerbook G3), and all beige desktop G3s.

Although Mac OS X can run on a wide range of processors, the minimum requirement for decent performance is considered by many to be at least a 350MHz G3. If you're using an older or slower Macintosh, it might exhibit extreme sluggishness with Mac OS X. Users of original iMacs and iBooks might want to stick with an earlier version of the Mac OS.

In addition to the processor requirement, Mac OS X needs 128MB of RAM and 1.5GB of available storage. If you meet these requirements, you're ready to begin!

> Along with its serious system requirements, there might be other reasons to postpone your upgrade to Mac OS X. Some peripheral devices, such as printers and scanners that worked under previous Mac operating systems, might not work under Mac OS X. (This condition is likely to be temporary as software/driver updates become available for many popular models.) If you have concerns, check with your device's hardware manufacturer about whether it functions under Mac OS X.

Preparing Your Hard Drive for Mac OS X

You have several choices about how to configure your system. The best configuration depends entirely on your needs.

The simplest path to Mac OS X is to upgrade to the latest version of Mac OS 9, and then to install Mac OS X. Apple recommends this approach only if you have existing data and cannot start from scratch. If you choose this path, your system is ready for Mac OS X installation after you install Mac OS 9.

Another configuration option is a *clean install*, which means you want to disable your current system folder and install a new one. Why choose this option? Although installing on top of an existing Mac OS 9 system is acceptable, it might not lead to the best possible performance. You avoid some types of system problems if you clear out your system and start from scratch. However, you must move your system preferences from the folder labeled Previous System to your new system folder so that your application settings aren't lost.

Even though a clean install won't delete your existing data, backing up your documents is still a recommended practice. System updates often update the drivers for your hard disks, which, although unlikely to cause problems, is a serious enough action to take the cautious route.

An additional decision to make before you install Mac OS X is whether to partition your hard drive. *Partitioning* means dividing your computer's hard disk into separate parts, each of which can be formatted for a different file system. In this case, drive partitioning allows Mac OS 9 and Mac OS X to have their own spaces, making it easier for each to work without interfering with the other. One benefit to users of this setup is that if either Mac OS 9 or Mac OS X fails, the other system is likely to be unaffected.

 Partitioning or formatting erases all the data on your drive.

If you decide to go with a clean install, you might want to think about partitioning your existing drive into separate volumes for Mac OS 9 and Mac OS X. (If you want to install Mac OS X in the same partition as Mac OS 9, skip to the "Installing Mac OS 9" section later in this appendix.)

A

Partitioning Your Drive

If you choose to do a clean installation and like the idea of keeping Mac OS 9 and Mac OS X separate on your hard drive, here are the steps you need to follow for partitioning:

1. Boot your Macintosh from the Mac OS 9 CD-ROM that came in your Mac OS X package. To do this, start the computer with the CD-ROM in the drive while holding down the C key.

 It's important that you use the Apple-supplied Mac OS 9 CD-ROM rather than an earlier version of the operating system because some versions contain elements that could be incompatible.

2. After your Macintosh boots, start the Drive Setup application in the Utilities folder. There will probably be two entries: one for the CD-ROM that booted the system and one for the hard drive.

3. To begin partitioning, choose the disk in the list that matches the drive you want to use for your Mac OS X installation, and then click the Initialize button. If Initialize is grayed out, you've probably accidentally chosen your CD-ROM instead of the hard disk.

4. Drive Setup warns you that all the data on your drive is about to be deleted. Click the Custom Setup button to create a new partition scheme.

5. In the Custom Setup dialog box, choose the number of partitions that you want to use in the Partitioning Scheme pop-up menu at the top. By default, the partitions use the Mac OS Extended file system (HFS+), which is the option you'll most likely need.

> If you're using an older iMac or G3, the first partition (located at the top of the volume layout) must fall within the first 8GB of drive space.

6. After choosing the partition layout using the Partitioning Scheme pop-up menu, click the OK button.

7. If you're sure that there's nothing you want on the disk, click Initialize.

In less than a minute, the newly created drive partitions will be mounted on your Mac OS 9 desktop. You should take this opportunity to name them. The first partition is typically the Mac OS X partition and the other is for Mac OS 9. You might want to name these partitions based on what you plan to install on them. You can change the names by selecting the icons in the Finder and then pressing the Enter key to edit the labels.

You're now ready to continue with the installation. (In case you're wondering, partitioning the hard drive from within Mac OS X is covered in Hour 22, "System Utilities and Monitors.")

Installing Mac OS 9

The procedure for installing Mac OS 9 should be quite simple, and is discussed here only briefly. If you already have Mac OS 9 installed, jump ahead to the "Installing Mac OS X" section later in this appendix.

If you just partitioned your drive, you're probably already booted from the Mac OS 9 CD-ROM. If not, boot from the CD-ROM by holding down the C key while turning on your computer with the CD-ROM inserted. Then double-click the Mac OS Install application.

A Mac OS 9 installation is like most script-driven installations—you mostly click Continue. Click the Continue button in the Welcome screen. Next, the Select Destination screen prompts you for the drive that will contain Mac OS 9. If you're going with a multi-partition setup, you should have named the drive that will store Mac OS 9; select it in the Destination Disk list box. If you're on a single-partition setup, only one choice is available. Click Select to continue.

Next, the installation software displays several information screens, including the software license agreement and some reminders, such as to plug in laptops before continuing. It's a good idea to read through this information so that you don't miss important announcements.

After you're past those screens, you're ready to start the actual installation. In the Install Software screen, click Start. When the installation finishes, you're prompted to reboot your machine.

> Even if you're an experienced Mac user, it's best not to use any of the customization options that are available during the installation procedure. Mac OS X makes modifications to the Mac OS 9 installation so that the two systems can work together. Certain components must be present for it to work correctly.

When Mac OS 9 boots for the first time, you're taken through a series of assistants to configure your system. Because you'll be installing Mac OS X next, you might not need to go through with this process. When Mac OS X updates the Mac OS 9 installation, it builds in additional software so that Mac OS 9 will inherit your settings from the Mac OS X environment. You can save yourself the effort of setting up twice by choosing Quit from the File menu to close the assistant.

> Because the shared settings are stored under Mac OS X, opting out of this setup could lead to difficulties if you plan to boot directly into Mac OS 9 without going into Mac OS X first. If you want the option to boot straight to Mac OS 9, you should go through the setup process for both Mac OS 9 and Mac OS X.

After Mac OS 9 is installed, you're ready for Mac OS X!

Installing Mac OS X

Installing Mac OS X is much like installing Mac OS 9—installation wizards do most of the work. Follow these steps to start installing Mac OS X:

1. If you're running Mac OS 9 and have inserted the Mac OS X CD-ROM, double-click the Install Mac OS X icon. Your computer will display a welcome message, restart after a few moments, and begin to boot from the CD-ROM. If you're starting the installation from a power-off state, make sure that the CD-ROM is in your drive, and start the computer while holding down the C key.

   While the installer boots, you'll see a Mac OS X loading screen. It's normal for this screen to stay visible for a few minutes. The installation procedure begins immediately after the operating system is loaded.

2. The next several screens are similar to those in the Mac OS 9 installation. You're asked to choose the language in which you'd like the entire operating system to be displayed. You must click Accept for the licensing agreement.

3. Next, you must choose the drive that will contain Mac OS X. Click the icon of the drive that corresponds to the volume you've prepared for Mac OS X. A circle and arrow form over the selected drive. Click Continue to move on to the final step.

4. Click the Install button to copy all the standard Mac OS X components to your computer. If this is the first time you've used Mac OS X, this is the best course of action to take. Advanced users might want to click the Customize button to display the individual components that can be added and removed from the system.

APPENDIX B

Running Classic Applications

As briefly discussed in Hour 1, "A Tour of Mac OS X," the Classic environment is a way for Mac OS 9 to function under Mac OS X. Using Classic, almost any application that's functional in Mac OS 9 can run inside Mac OS X as long as a recent version of Mac OS 9 is also installed. (If you need help installing Mac OS 9, refer to Appendix A, "Installing Mac OS X," which also discusses installation of Mac OS 9.)

> You *must* have at least 128MB of memory to use Classic. Also, a 400MHz G3 (or faster) computer is recommended. *Why?* Classic is a process running *under* Mac OS X. When it's in use, your computer is supporting two operating systems simultaneously. As you can imagine, this is quite resource intensive.

Launching Classic

The Classic environment needs to be launched only once during a Mac OS X login session, and it can be launched manually or automatically. After it's running, Classic remains active until you log out or manually force it to shut down.

How can you find out whether a piece of software on your hard drive is indeed a Classic application? You can always ask the Finder. Simply select the icon for the program in question and choose Get Info (or press Command+I) from the Finder's File menu. A Kind of Classic Application indicates that the software requires Classic to operate.

There are two ways to launch the Classic environment: through the Classic panel in System Preferences and by double-clicking a Classic application.

First, let's start Classic from the System Preferences panel. Here's what to do:

1. Locate the System Preferences icon in the Dock and double-click it (the icon looks like a wall-mounted light switch) or choose System Preferences from the Apple menu.

2. In System Preferences, click the Classic icon to open its Preferences panel.

3. Click the Start/Stop tab of the Classic Preferences panel. Here you see several options, including a Stop or Start button for manually turning Classic off or on, Restart for when you want to reboot Classic, and Force Quit for when the Classic system is unresponsive after a crash.

4. In the Start/Stop tab, click the Start button to launch Classic. Mac OS 9 takes a few minutes to boot, and then you're ready to run your older applications.

Let's try the second way to launch Classic:

1. Locate an older, non–Mac OS X application in your Mac OS 9 Applications folder, and double-click it.

Yes, there's only one step. If Classic isn't already running, it boots automatically before the application you've chosen is launched. Remember that, after it's started, Classic remains in the background until you log out of Mac OS X or manually stop Classic. Even when you log out of all Classic applications, Classic itself is still running.

The Classic System Preferences panel shows the status of the Classic environment—that is, whether or not it's running. Because Classic does not appear as an active task in the Dock, this is one way to check its status.

Although it's true that in most cases Classic will run until you log out or manually stop the process, it's still (like Mac OS 9 itself) susceptible to crashes. If Classic crashes, so do any applications running within it. You must restart the Classic process to continue working.

The Boot Process

To boot into Classic, Mac OS X requires that the installed version of Mac OS 9 be 9.1 or later. If you're running an earlier version, you must upgrade it first. The first time that Mac OS X boots the Classic environment, it must add some software to your computer to be able to operate. This software acts as a bridge between the Mac OS X process monitors and I/O systems. If you choose not to add these components when prompted, Classic cannot operate and quits.

If you have a Mac OS X–compatible version of Mac OS 9 that isn't the most current release, Mac OS X might give you a warning with instructions on how to update the earlier operating system.

Although at press time Mac OS 9.2 is the preferred Classic OS for Mac OS X 10.2, users with 9.1 can boot into Classic.

B

As Classic boots, it loads all the extensions and control panels that you had previously installed on your Mac OS 9 installation. If you installed Mac OS X from scratch, you should be in good shape. If you upgraded from an older system, you might find that some extensions cause Classic to crash. You can use the Advanced tab of the Classic System Preferences panel to shut off extensions while booting Classic. Try removing extensions that work with external peripherals—hardware access has largely been removed from the Classic environment.

Running Classic Applications

The first time you open a Classic application, you'll notice that several interesting things happen.

Be careful not to alter settings in a Mac OS 9 control panel! When running Classic, the Mac OS X menu bar is replaced by the Mac OS 9 menu bar. Using the Mac OS 9 Apple menu, you can access all the earlier system's control panels and associated functionality. Settings in control panels such as Appearance and Sound are harmless enough, but it's possible to accidentally disrupt your network connections by working with the TCP/IP and AppleTalk control panels. It's best to avoid the Mac OS 9 control panels altogether.

Visually, Classic applications look just as they would under Mac OS 8 and 9. The Aqua appearance does not carry over to the windows, buttons, and other interface elements, but the Mac OS X Dock and Process Manager do recognize Classic applications.

If you use the Process Manager to force quit a Classic application, you should follow up immediately by saving other open documents running in Classic and then restarting the environment. This is another area in which Classic hasn't benefited from the advanced features of Mac OS X.

After it starts, Classic is easy to use without extra detail about how it interacts with Mac OS X. You simply operate programs as you would under System 9. However, there are a few exceptions that might be confusing for you:

- **Copy and paste/drag and drop**—Two of the most common means of moving data in the Mac OS suffer when working between native and Classic applications. It can take several seconds before data copied from one environment is available for pasting into another. Dragging and dropping text and images between native and Classic applications fails altogether.

- **Favorites**—Although Favorites are available in the Mac OS 9 environment, they do not transfer between Classic and Mac OS X.

- **Mac OS 9 desktop**—A Mac OS 9 Desktop folder alias is one of the default icons on the Mac OS X desktop. Double-clicking the alias displays the contents of the Mac OS 9 desktop. This alias is specific to Mac OS 9 when it's booted directly. It does *not* apply to the Classic environment. When using Classic, items that are saved to the desktop appear, as expected, on the Mac OS X desktop.

- **Open and Save dialog boxes**—Mac OS X applications are aware of the special folders and files used by the system and take care to hide them. The same cannot be said for Classic applications. The Open and Save dialog boxes clearly show the invisible items. Although normal, these invisible files could be alarming to users unused to seeing them.

> Note that when using the Classic environment, the Mac OS 9 accesses all hardware through Mac OS X, so software trying to access hardware directly will fail for devices not compatible with Mac OS X. However, you can boot directly into Mac OS 9 to run such devices, as explained later in this appendix.

Users expecting a completely seamless work environment might be disappointed by these shortcomings, but they're relatively minor quirks in a very convenient arrangement.

Classic Options

Classic functions best when it is used as a means of accessing legacy applications and data. You might want to shut off any extraneous features of Mac OS 9, such as the Finder sound track (in the Appearance control panel) and talking alerts. These features slow down system performance and can cause hiccups in Mac OS X.

Apple has kindly included two features in Mac OS X that help fix a common Classic problem and speed up overall system functions: putting Classic to sleep and rebuilding the desktop. They're located in the Advanced tab of the Classic System Preferences panel.

Let's see how to use these advanced features to gain greater control of Classic:

- **Put Classic to Sleep When It Is Inactive for**—When Classic is running, it's using your system resources. The Classic environment continues to use CPU time even if you aren't running a Classic application. This is because Mac OS 9 must keep up the basic system maintenance and monitor processes that happen behind the scenes. If you choose to put Classic to sleep, it'll stop using these resources after the length of time you specify.

B

Putting Classic to sleep works well—most of the time. The drawback is that it takes longer for Classic applications to launch and wake up the pseudo-sleeping computer. In addition, waking up *does* fail from time to time, forcing you to restart Classic. Make sure that you're using the latest version of Mac OS X for the best possible Classic support.

- **Rebuild Desktop**—Rebuilding the Mac OS 9 desktop can help solve "generic icon" problems (as illustrated in Figure B.1) as well as the problem of documents that can't find the appropriate Classic application to open them. If your Classic environment starts to act unusual, rebuilding the desktop is a good place to start.

FIGURE B.1

Generic icons appearing where custom icons once existed, such as the one for RealPlayer 7 Basic, are a good indicator of a desktop that needs rebuilding.

Direct Booting to Mac OS 9 and Back to Mac OS X

As easy as it is to run applications inside Mac OS X with the Classic mode, you might want to return to Mac OS 9 sometimes. This might be necessary when you're operating software that accesses hardware directly, such as some video cards and CD writers (refer to the note in the "Running Classic Applications" section). At times, using Mac OS 9 can also save you from the headaches of dealing with the inconsistencies and incompatibilities of Classic and offer greater speed and ease of use.

To boot directly into Mac OS 9, you must first start your computer in Mac OS X, and then do the following:

1. Click the System Preferences icon in the Dock or choose System Preferences from the Apple menu.

2. Click the Startup Disk icon under the System heading in the System Preferences panel to open the Startup Disk panel.

3. Each of the accessible system folders appears as an icon in the Startup Disk panel. (This can take a few seconds while the system locates your options.) Click the icon for Mac OS 9; a status message appears at the bottom of the panel to verify your choice.

4. When you've made your selection, quit the Startup Disk panel or click the Restart button to boot into Mac OS 9 immediately.

5. When your computer reboots, it boots into Mac OS 9 and shows no trace of the Mac OS X desktop.

After you've chosen Mac OS 9 as your startup disk, you must again change your startup disk to get back into Mac OS X. This process is similar to switching from Mac OS X to Mac OS 9, but you're working in the Mac OS 9 environment. Here's what you need to do:

1. From the Apple menu, choose Control Panels, and then select the Startup Disk control panel.

2. Each mounted disk is displayed on a line in the control panel. To boot into Mac OS X, highlight the Mac OS X disk in the list, and then click the Restart button in the lower-right corner. If you have multiple systems on a single disk, you might need to click the disclosure triangle to show the individual system folders and select the appropriate one. If you don't want to restart immediately, close the control panel. The next time the system restarts, it will boot into Mac OS X.

B

APPENDIX C

Working with Files, Folders, and Applications

In addition to helping you locate your files, the Finder handles all common tasks such as creating, deleting, moving, and copying files and folders. This appendix is a quick reference to the standard file and application operations of the Finder.

Moving Files and Folders

Moving a file changes its location, but doesn't alter the contents of the file or its creation and modification dates. To move a file, drag its icon to the folder or location where you want it to reside. Folders in Mac OS X 10.2 are spring-loaded. If you would like to move a file to a subfolder, drag the file icon on top of the parent folder until it opens.

If you move a file from one device (such as a disk) to another, the file is *copied* instead of moved. The original file stays in its current location, and a new version is created on the other storage media. You must delete the original copy of the file if you don't want to keep multiple versions of it.

Renaming Files

To rename a file in the Finder, click once to select the file, and click a second time on the file's name. The filename will become editable in a few seconds. Alternatively, you can use the Show Info option in the Finder File menu (Command+I) to edit the name in a larger field.

Copying Files and Folders

Copying a file creates an exact duplicate of an original file. The new file contents and creation/modification dates are identical to those of the original. There are a number of ways to create a copy in Mac OS X:

- **Drag a file to a different disk**—Dragging a file to a disk other than the one it is currently stored on creates a copy with the same name as the original.

- **Drag a file while holding down the Option key**—If you drag a file to a folder on the same disk it is currently located in while holding down the Option key, a duplicate of that file is created in the new location. The copy has the same name as the original.

- **Choose Duplicate from the contextual or Finder menu**—If you want to create an exact duplicate of a file within the same folder, highlight the file to copy, and then choose Duplicate from the Finder's File menu (Command+D), or Ctrl-click the icon and choose Duplicate from the pop-up contextual menu. A new file is created with the word *copy* appended to the name.

As the file is copied, the Finder displays an alert box in which you can see the progress of the copy operation. If multiple copies are taking place at the same time, the statuses of the operations are shown stacked on one another in the Copy alert box.

If you attempt to copy over existing files, the Finder prompts you and asks whether you want to replace the files. Also, if you attempt to replace existing files to which you don't have access, the copy operation fails.

Deleting Files and Folders

Deleting files and folders permanently removes them from your system. Like copying a file, there are a number of ways to delete one:

- **Drag to Dock Trash**—Dragging an icon from a Finder window into the Dock's Trash is one of the most obvious and easy ways to get rid of a file.

- **Finder toolbar**—A Delete shortcut can be added to the Finder's toolbar (refer to Hour 2, "Using the Finder and the Dock," for details). Any items selected can be quickly moved to the Trash by clicking the Delete shortcut. Delete is *not* one of the default toolbar icons.

Moving an item to the Trash does not delete it permanently. Instead, it places the item inside a special folder. The Trash icon in the Dock fills with crumpled paper when it contains items waiting to be deleted. To completely remove a file from your system, choose Empty Trash from the Finder's Application menu or press Shift+Command+Delete.

If you want to rescue a file you've accidentally sent to the Trash, you can click the Trash icon and drag the file's icon out of the window.

Creating Aliases

An *alias* is a representation of a file that for all intents and purposes appears to be the file. Windows users will recognize an alias as similar to a desktop shortcut.

Instead of duplicating a file and maintaining two copies, you can create an alias of the original file and place it wherever you'd like. Although the icon for an alias behaves similarly to the icon for an original files, you can tell an alias from the original by the arrow in the icon's lower-left corner.

There are two ways to create an alias:

- **Drag a file while holding down Option+Command**—If you drag a file to a folder while holding down the Option and Command keys, an alias of that file is created in the new location.

- **Choose Make Alias from the contextual or Finder's File menu**—If you want to create an alias of a file within the same folder, highlight the file to alias, and then choose Make Alias from the Finder's File menu (Command+L) or Ctrl-click the icon and choose Make Alias from the pop-up contextual menu. A new file is created with the word *alias* appended to the name.

Although an alias can be used to represent an original file, throwing away an alias *doesn't* delete the original file. Also, deleting the original file doesn't delete the alias, but the alias does become broken.

To locate the file to which an alias points, select the alias and choose Show Original (Command+R) from the Finder's File menu. The original file is highlighted in the Finder.

C

Opening Unrecognized Files

If you attempt to double-click a document that the system does not recognize, Mac OS X warns you that there is "no application available to open the document." If you're sure that a program on your system is capable of viewing the file, select the Choose Application option. You are prompted to choose the application that can open the file.

By default, the system tries to guess the best application for the job—but sometimes it fails. If the system doesn't allow you to pick the appropriate application, change the selection in the Show pop-up menu to read All Applications rather than Recommended Applications.

Force Quitting Applications with the Process Manager

Another feature that's sometimes necessary when using applications is Force Quit, which exits a program that has stopped responding. In Mac OS X, the Option+Command+Esc keystroke brings up a process manager that contains a list of running applications. Applications that the system deems to have stopped responding are marked in red. To force an application to close, choose it in the list and click the Force Quit button.

 Forcing an application to quit does not save any open documents. Be sure that the application is truly stalled, not just busy, before you use this feature.

You can also access the Force Quit feature from the Apple menu, or by opening the pop-up Dock menu for a running application and pressing the Option key to toggle the standard Quit selection to Force Quit. If the system deems that an application has stopped responding, a Force Quit option appears in the Dock pop-up menu.

If the Finder seems to be misbehaving, you can choose it from the application list. The Force Quit button becomes the Relaunch button, enabling you to quit and restart the Finder without logging out.

INDEX

How can we make this index more useful? Email us at indexes@samspublishing.com